Christians
in Society

Christians in Society

Luther, the Bible, and Social Ethics

William H. Lazareth

Fortress Press
Minneapolis

CHRISTIANS IN SOCIETY
Luther, the Bible, and Social Ethics

Book design: Beth Wright

Library of Congress Cataloging-in-Publication Data

Lazareth, William Henry, date–
   Christians in society : Luther, the Bible, and social ethics / William H. Lazareth.
     p. cm.
   Includes bibliographical references and index.
   ISBN 0-8006-3292-3 (alk. paper)
    1. Christian ethics. 2. Sociology, Christian (Lutheran) 3. Social ethics. I. Title

BJ 1253 .L395 2001
241'.0441—dc21

2001033634

The paper used in this publication meets the minimum requirements of American National Standard for Information Sciences — Permanence of Paper for Printed Library Materials, ANSI Z329.48-1984.

Manufactured in the U.S.A.

AF1-3292

05   04   03   02   01   1   2   3   4   5   6   7   8   9   10

Contents

Preface

T HIS BOOK FOCUSES ON THE BIBLICAL NORMS of Martin Luther's theological ethics. It demonstrates why Luther's theological ethic, by providing scriptural support for the church's continually adapted programs of Christian social ethics, rightly endures as a classical authority.

In the sixteenth century, it was Luther's biblically grounded conviction that character governs conduct and that the character of Christians is transformed and nurtured by those gifts of the Holy Spirit that organically accompany faith in the gospel of Jesus Christ. In other words, the sanctified renewal of redeemed sinners is always an essential part of the total human response to the good news of God that is uniquely revealed in the Holy Scriptures and then historically traditioned in the councils, creeds, confessions, and catechisms of the Christian church. Moreover, Luther coupled his evangelical zeal for righteous character with a twin regard for life in community. This takes place through our active participation within the God-mandated structures of society and by our responsible membership in the holy catholic church. Christians guided by the Holy Spirit through the Holy Scriptures are called to shun both privatized autonomy and societal quietism.

Today's situation is far different. In a secularized society characterized by a pluralism of coexisting human cultures, ethical proposals for human moral conduct most frequently seek their validation from the conflicting anthropologies and ideologies of current philosophies and the social sciences. When absolutized, the impact of these corrosive forces has become so powerful that even many Christian ethicists now substitute instant relevance for eternal reverence in their public endorsement of social ethical projects that are no longer governed by theological ethics defined by the Word of God in Holy Scripture. Without faithful conformity to God's holy image in Christ (*conformitas Christi*) under God's universal command of love (Rom. 8:29), the prevailing analytical categories of benefits and costs are totally confused with good and bad, to say nothing of right and wrong, in the church's understanding and advocacy of a blessed life in community under God.

We may therefore welcome a major sign of ecumenical hope in the recent achievement of major theological and ethical agreement between the Roman Catholic Church and the 125 member churches of the Lutheran World Federation. After decades of biblical and doctrinal study, Roman Catholics and Lutherans have agreed on "a consensus in basic truths on the doctrine of justification. . . . Together we confess: By grace alone, in faith in Christ's saving work and not because of any merit on our part, we are accepted by God and receive the Holy Spirit, who renews our hearts while equipping and calling us to good works" (*Joint Declaration*, 15).

Consequently, all authorized signatories of this international *Joint Declaration on the Doctrine of Justification* (1997) have officially declared in 1999 that the mutual condemnations (anathemas) issued in the sixteenth century on the doctrine of justification were henceforth no longer applicable to their respective ecclesial counterparts today. Both Roman Catholics and Lutherans may now publicly profess and practice with others of similar convictions that faithful and loving Christians are called to be God's coworkers in society.

In 1997, the Evangelical Lutheran Church in America had also affirmed a relation of "full communion" with three churches of the Reformed tradition: the Presbyterian Church (USA), the Reformed Church in America, and the United Church of Christ. Over the years, the participants in this Lutheran–Reformed Dialogue discovered that "efforts to guard against possible distortions of truth have resulted in varying emphases in related doctrines which are not in themselves contradictory and in fact are complementary" (cf. Paul C. Empie and James I. McCord, eds., *Marburg Revisited: A Reexamination of Lutheran and Reformed Traditions* [Minneapolis: Augsburg, 1966], ii). Thereby complementarity of "mutual affirmation and admonition" has become the accepted joint responsibility of new ecumenical partners in coordinating Christian life and mission.

In coauthoring this ecumenical group's original "Summary Statement" on theological ethics, the present writer already then contended:

> We are agreed that there is a common evangelical basis for Christian ethics in the theology of the Reformers. Both the Lutheran and Reformed traditions have emphasized the new obedience of Christians through faith active in love and the inseparability of justification and sanctification.
>
> While there remains a difference among us as to the importance we attached to the need for the instruction of God's law in the Christian life, we do not regard this as a [church] divisive issue. We affirm together that Christians are free from the bondage of the law in order to live in love under the direction of God's Word and Spirit to the end of good order and eternal life. (p. 177)

In that continued conviction, our present research here seeks to demonstrate a construal of Luther's biblically grounded theological ethics that might further reconcile historical differences and facilitate more common societal witness among these major Christian communions. We do so by wholly disavowing nineteenth-century German Lutheran dualistic quietism or societal indifference (*apolitie*) and by championing instead Luther's original dynamic interaction of God's twofold rule within the world's two kingdoms through the ecclesially complementary forces of love and law (Lutheran-Reformed) along with justification and sanctification (Lutheran-Roman Catholic). Augustine, Luther, and Calvin are surely not identical in their witnesses to the gospel of Jesus Christ, but there is also far more that unites them than divides them, especially in theological ethics.

Our study is devoted to the necessary ecclesial reception of these unprecedented ecumenical developments, to which was also later added a "full communion" agreement between the Evangelical Lutheran Church in America and the Episcopal Church USA (*Called to Common Mission,* 1998), with similar social-ethical implications. We seek here to contribute to the healing of those open wounds in the broken Body of Christ that have resulted from centuries of post-Reformation mutual misunderstanding and acrimonious strife.

This book is written to serve as a basic text or reference work for those American seminaries or universities that still offer course work in the history and theology of Christian ethics. It offers to guide interested theological students (along with pastors, priests, and lay persons) through the rather formidable primary and secondary sources involved in the comprehension of a central theme in serious Luther research today.

The text also tends to be user-friendly. For example, English translations are provided for all foreign technical terms. An extensive survey of recent foreign research on Luther's public theology is first classified and then limited to the first chapter. For future reference, all the remaining chapters let Luther speak for himself. They are largely composed of close analyses of those pertinent biblical and theological texts that are now helpfully organized into the most commonly cited and comprehensive collection in English, the American Edition of *Luther's Works* (Concordia Publishing House and Fortress Press). It was within this set that the present author was also privileged to prepare the general introduction for those of Luther's texts related to the major theme of "The Christian in Society" (vols. 44–47). Finally, our cross-referenced construals are extensively documented with chronologically dated quotations in order to prevent the common misuse elsewhere of Luther citations taken out of their original theological or chronological context. Moreover, while Luther's sixteenth-century, gender-exclusive language has not been altered, it has also nowhere been used by the present author. Finally, all citations from the Lutheran Confessions (1580) are taken from the latest definitive English translation of *The Book of*

Concord, edited by Robert Kolb and Timothy J. Wengert (Minneapolis: Fortress, 2000).

For the sake of scriptural fidelity and doctrinal coherence, the interrelated but distinguishable elements of Luther's theological ethics are also intentionally structured sequentially and cumulatively within the successive chapters of this study (see diagram on the next page). Part One presents two background chapters, the first devoted primarily to twentieth-century Protestant misinterpreters of Luther's theological ethics in terms of nineteenth-century quietistic German Lutheranism, and the second concentrating hermeneutically on Luther's evangelical catholic principles of biblical interpretation for governing the church's life and mission.

Part Two eschatologically contrasts the world's dualistic and antagonistic two kingdoms (*duo regna*). Chapter 3 depicts the inauguration of God's kingdom of grace in the Garden of Eden, and chapter 4 traces the rise of Satan's opposing kingdom of sin in the fall of Adam and Eve. It is on this perennial spiritual battlefield, uniquely revealed in Holy Scripture, that God graciously elects to act for and through us within human history.

Part Three then portrays the dramatic and dialectical twofold rule (*zweierlei regimente*) of the one Triune God against Satan through Caesar and Christ in preserving creation and renewing redemption by the intersecting functions of the law and gospel for Christian salvation and service. Righteous but sinful Christians are centered in the crossfire. Chapters 5 and 6 develop consecutively the law's judging function before God (*coram Deo*) and its corollary preserving function within society (*coram hominibus*). This "strange work" of God (*opus alienum;* responsive to human sin) is likewise complemented by the interpenetrating two functions of the gospel in carrying out the Lord's "proper work" (*opus proprium;* reflective of divine grace) by way of effecting Christ's justification of sinners before God (chapter 7) and the Holy Spirit's accompanying sanctification of believers within society (chapter 8). The Afterword reflects again briefly on the potential contribution of this research for overcoming past divisions and uniting the reconciled churches' ethical service in society to the glory of God.

The essential features of Luther's theological ethic were determined by his Christocentric reading of the Old and New Testaments. While composed of central doctrines of the church, his ethic is itself less a doctrine than a pastoral and hermeneutical "paradigm," that is, a characteristically comprehensive viewpoint that enables biblically guided Christians to interpret the totality of human life, and especially their new life in Christ, in organic relation to the adoration of God and beliefs of the Christian faith. It aims to describe the fullness of right living (*orthopraxia*) based on right believing and right worshiping (*orthodoxia*).

God's Twofold Rule of the World's Two Kingdoms
(Luther's Theological Ethic)

1. Survey: Post-Nazi Recovery

2. Ethics and Scripture

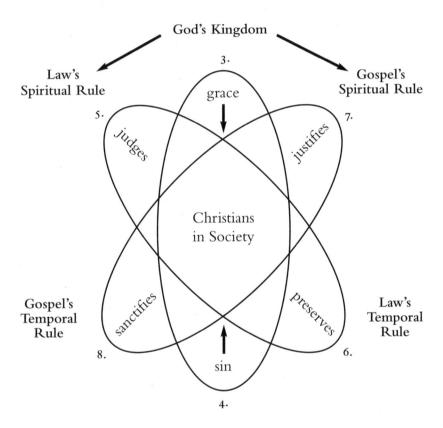

Afterword

It is my pleasant duty to conclude with a sincere word of thanks for the many benefits I have received from two major forces of theological renewal in the United States today. The first is the editorial staff of Fortress Press, especially Dr. Harold W. Rast, who patiently encouraged me to update and summarize a lifetime of Luther research that continues to provide Christocentric guidance for the church's life and mission. The second is the collegial team of Princeton's Center of Theological Inquiry, especially Dr. Wallace M. Alston Jr., who generously provided me with both the time and the logistical services necessary to complete this challenging and gratifying project. Finally, I dedicate this book to my wife, Jacqueline, with loving gratitude for our enduring partnership in marriage and ministry together.

Part One

Ethical Strife and Biblical Norms

Chapter 1

Survey: The Post-Nazi Recovery of Lutheran Public Responsibility

T HE CLAIM OF LUTHERAN CHRISTIANITY is that the evangelical theology of the Reformation recovered the biblical "narrow gate" between the church's perennial societal temptations of secularism and clericalism.[1] In formulating a theology of society that was organically related to a theology of salvation, Luther tried to obey Christ and render what was due both to God and to Caesar (Luke 20:25). He rejected the totalitarian pretensions of both church and state in the name of the biblical Lord of history who rules all persons everywhere by the power of the Word of God.

In view of our public plight today, it is no surprise that Luther's thought enjoys new and avid attention. In fact, so many scholars of the twentieth century researched his theology and ethics that it is now quite common to speak of a "Luther Renaissance." So great has been its depth and breadth that we could not begin to do justice to any complete review of all this scholarship here. Our aim is simply to focus attention for English-language readers on some of the most important trends in the primarily foreign research devoted to Luther's theological ethics. Such a survey provides us with an illuminating case study in the interplay of public conduct and theological ethics in the oldest and largest of the Protestant churches.

Roland H. Bainton, distinguished Society of Friends historian of the Western church, has given us a penetrating summary of the ambiguous interaction that has taken place between the ethical and political forces released by the Reformation. Our survey in this chapter serves to document his contention that diversity of circumstances, especially in Germany, is largely responsible for differences in international Lutheran theory and practice.

> When a comparison is made between the political consequences of Lutheranism and Calvinism, the common generalization is that Lutheranism made for totalitarianism and Calvinism for democracy. There can be no question that in Germany, and notably in Prussia,

2

Lutheranism became a state church. The Bismarckian policy had the support of the Lutherans, whereas Catholics in Germany, and only in Germany in the nineteenth century, were allied with political liberalism. A further step is taken by some interpreters who say that Lutheranism paved the way for National Socialism by teaching implicit obedience to the commands of the state.

On the other hand, Calvinism in France, Scotland, and New England was associated with revolution and even tyrannicide. The indisputable facts in this picture are that Lutheranism was the established church in Germany at the time of the rise of National Socialism and that Calvinism in various lands has been the party of revolution. At the same time one must not forget that the state church in Germany in the twentieth century was a combination of the Lutheran and the Reformed; nor can one overlook the fact that the Confessional Church, which opposed Hitler, was also Lutheran and that in the Scandinavian lands Lutheranism has not issued in totalitarianism. On the score of Calvinism, one must bear in mind that in France, whenever the monarchy was favorable to the Huguenots, Calvinist political thinking veered to royalism.

All this suggests that in these instances, *circumstances had more effect than religion upon the political theories of religious bodies.* Rather one might say that for all Protestants religion transcended politics and the chief concern was to give free course to the Word of God. Just as the Catholic church will make a concordat with any regime which allows freedom to administer the sacraments, freedom to propagate the faith, freedom to hold property, and freedom for the monastic orders, so Protestantism has been willing to tolerate any form of government which accords religious liberty to Protestantism.[2]

Deplorably, it took the horrors and suffering of a major economic depression and two World Wars to tear most of Lutheranism, especially post-Nazi German Lutheranism, out of its ecclesiastical ghetto into the full exercise of its public responsibility. During this same period, moreover, it also took four rather devastating theological attacks to awaken the slumbering bear of twentieth-century German Lutheranism to the need for reexamining its societal teaching and conduct in the light of Luther's original biblical teachings. If modern Christian theology has been greatly enriched by a renaissance of Luther studies, a good part of the reason is due to the vigorous attacks upon the Reformer's theological ethics by Ernst Troeltsch ("Conservatism"), Karl Barth ("Quietism"), Johannes Heckel ("Dualism"), and Reinhold Niebuhr ("Defeatism"), along with their many academic followers.

Ernst Troeltsch versus Luther's "Social Conservatism"
Luther's teaching on theological ethics was the major concern of the stimulating pre-Nazi criticism of Ernst Troeltsch (1865–1923). In his monumental

work, *The Social Teaching of the Christian Churches* (2 vols., trans. 1931), Troeltsch laid the guilt squarely at Luther's feet for the "social conservatism" of the Lutheran church in Germany.

As a religious liberal with little firsthand knowledge of Luther's theology, Troeltsch was able to provide but a few quotations from Luther's writings for his sweeping generalizations. Documented or not, however, his analysis was telling enough in cultural and sociological insight to prod, encourage, and shame scores of Lutheran theologians into attempting to find the documentation necessary to refute or substantiate his charges. Ernst Troeltsch is still a force to be reckoned with, and rightly so. Even many of those who have shown him to be completely mistaken about Luther's ethics have had to admit that he was often absolutely right about the reactionary ethics of nineteenth-century German Lutheranism. Indeed, his inability or unwillingness to make this crucial distinction between Luther's ethics and nineteenth-century German Lutheran ethics may well have been his basic error.

We can provide only the roughest outline of Troeltsch's position here. Basically, it is this: sociologically, Christianity has expressed itself in three classical patterns in relation to society. The first is the "church type," which stresses the divinely appointed institution as entrusted with the objective means of grace for human salvation, at the cost of emphasizing the subjective holiness of the members who are baptized, nurtured, and buried in its custody. In its unchallenged monopoly position, the church type can afford to be world-affirming, adaptable, and compromising, even to the point of absorbing non-Christian moral elements into the territorial inclusiveness of its ethos. The "sect type," on the other hand, stresses the voluntary, gathered fellowship of reborn Christians who feel called out of the world to live together with other true believers in an exclusive Christian community of love in expectation of the coming kingdom of God. Its sectarian spirit is church dividing and culture denying, seeing in both the worldly contaminations of sin and evil. Finally, there is the "mystic type," which seeks to transcend the limitations of the finite and the historical in personal religious experiences that aim at the spiritual union of the creature with one's Creator. This has been the path taken largely by unusual individuals, rather than larger groups, in the history of Christianity.

Within the bounds of these three basic types, Troeltsch proceeds to categorize Luther's theological ethics. Despite early elements in the Reformer's thought, which point clearly toward the sect type (freedom of faith, universal priesthood of believers, true community of the faithful, gospel ethic of pure love), Luther, almost despite himself, eventually reaffirmed the classical church-type pattern of Roman Catholicism in order to insure the Reformation's institutional survival under the protection of friendly territorial rulers. Troeltsch insists that this basic decision necessarily prompted a fourfold world-indifference in Luther's theology:

1. Culturally, Luther remained essentially within the medieval socio-religious synthesis of the *corpus Christianum* (Christendom), demanding uniformity of beliefs from all those living within a Lutheran territory;

2. Biblically, Luther made the Sermon on the Mount of the New Testament subservient to the Decalogue of the Old Testament as the religious basis for evangelical social ethics;

3. Ethically, Luther sanctioned a double-standard morality for Christians in his teaching on the two kingdoms (*Zwei Reiche*), which commanded that *private* morality be governed by the "absolute" natural law of love, while allowing *public* morality to be guided merely by the "relative" natural law of justice;

4. Socially and politically, Luther limited the power of Christian faith and love to the realm of inner, personal experience and disposition (*Innerlichkeit*), thereby leaving society-at-large free to act as an autonomous law unto itself (*Eigengesetzlichkeit*). This proved to be historically disastrous when combined with Luther's refusal to sanction the personal right of Christians to engage in political revolution;

5. "Thus, down to the present time, the Lutheran church has never advanced farther than the renewed ideal of charity; it has never made any effort to initiate a real social transformation at all. Most Lutherans simply repeat the old doctrine of the inwardness of the church and of the duty of leaving all external matters of legislation and social welfare to the state."[3]

Troeltsch illustrated this comprehensive thesis, on the one hand, with those nineteenth-century proponents of Lutheran "patriarchal conservatism" who never moved beyond remedial institutional charity to preventive social reform. Notable examples include the "altar and throne" philosophy of Friedrich Stahl, the Inner Mission work of Johann Wichern, the Lutheran deaconess program of Theodore Fliedner, and the Bethel "colony of mercy" approach of Friedrich von Bodelschwingh.

On the other hand, Troeltsch decried the ethical conservatism inherent in the influential Luther interpretations of Adolf Harless and especially Christoph Ernst Luthardt in his *Ethik Luthers in ihren Grundzuegen* (Luther's Ethic in Outline, 1875) and *Geschichte der Christlichen Ethik* (History of Christian Ethics, 1888–93), which stress the Reformer's alleged theory of "the inwardness of Christianity in contrast with external life in the world" (*Ethik Luthers*). The result in Luthardt is a dualistic chasm between personal life and public affairs: "the gospel has absolutely nothing to do with outward cultural existence, but only with eternal life." Troeltsch was not surprised at the ultimate secularization of the religious social ethical attempts

(National Social Association) of Friedrich Naumann. And had he lived long enough, he would not have been surprised when some Lutheran theologians like Wilhelm Walther in *Deutschlands Schwert durch Luther geweiht* (German's Sword Consecrated by Luther, 1914) and Hermann Jordan in *Luthers Staatsauffasung* (Luther's View of the State, 1917) blessed the German aggression of World War I on the basis of the state's alleged moral autonomy (*Eigengesetzlichkeit*).

Troeltsch's frontal attack on the Lutheran church's seeming inability to meet the new social crisis in German at the end of the nineteenth century met with wide success. An immediate ally was found in the brilliant religion-sociologist, Max Weber, who wrote a great deal on the relation of the "intramundane asceticism" of the Protestant church to society. He stressed Calvinist activism as a necessary alternative to Lutheran quietism in *The Protestant Ethic and the Spirit of Capitalism,* published in English (1930) independent of his *Gesammelte Aufsaetze zur Religionssoziologie* (Collected Essays on the Sociology of Religion, 3 vols., 1920–21). Other Germans influenced by Troeltsch were Karl Eger, Karl Mueller, and George Wuensch.

Following the First World War, however, the challenges of the Troeltsch school were taken up boldly by arguably the outstanding Luther interpreter of the last century, Karl Holl. If any one scholar epitomized the richness and vitality of the Luther Renaissance, it was he. Blending the best of both historical and theological research, Holl was strongest where Troeltsch was weakest—in the original writings of Luther himself, newly made available to scholars in the Weimar critical edition of Luther's multivolumed works.

Holl contended that Troeltsch had never seen the true sixteenth-century Luther because he always viewed him through the distorted spectacles of nineteenth-century Lutheranism (for example, via the dualistic misinterpretation of Luthardt). He insisted that the theology of Luther must be distinguished from the later doctrinal formulations of Scholastic Lutheranism, which owed much to the mediating views of Philip Melanchthon. Holl capitalized on new text discoveries (for example, Luther's original glosses and *scholia* in the *Lectures on Romans,* 1515–16), to reinvestigate the "young Luther." Hence, he concentrated chiefly upon the early evangelical prophet (versus Rome) rather than on the later church Reformer. Holl clearly exhibited the interrelated wholeness of Luther's theology and ethics. Holl believed that Luther's original contribution to Christian thought and social ethical life lay in his demonstration of the interrelation of conscience and community in the Christian life, wherein faithful fellowship with God results in just and loving fellowship with one's fellow humans.

Moreover, Holl saw that Luther's contributions were vital to the justifiable breakup of the Roman Catholic medieval synthesis. He contended, first, that Luther was far more biblical than medieval in rejecting the ethical alliance of the law of Christ with the Aristotelian metaphysical law of nature that obtained in Roman Catholic moral theology. Second, he taught that Luther was far more modern than medieval in rejecting the clerical domination of the European states by the Roman church. On both counts, Holl believed Troeltsch to be wrong concerning Luther's alleged medieval ethical conservatism.

Holl worked out these views in a series of richly documented essays in *Gesammelte Aufsaetze zur Kirchengeschichte* (Collected Essays in Church History, vol. 1, *Luther,* 2nd ed., 1923), among which the most influential remain "Was verstand Luther unter Religion?" ("What Did Luther Understand by Religion?" trans. 1977); "Der Neubau der Sittlichkeit" ("The Reconstruction of Morality," trans. 1979); and "Die Kulturbedeutung der Reformation" ("The Cultural Significance of the Reformation," trans. 1959). These Holl studies provide the student with a broad panorama of Luther's entire theological system in both theology and ethics. The uncritical acceptance of Troeltsch's views on Luther in the United States may be traced in no small measure to the historical fact that Troeltsch's work was translated into English during the early crucial decades of the rise of the Anglo-Saxon Social Gospel activist movement, and Holl's work was not.

In the years between the two World Wars, Luther and Reformation research flourished at unprecedented heights. Under Holl's impetus and guidance, hardly any major dimension of Luther's theology remained unexamined and untreated. However, a fatal blindspot became increasingly evident in many of the adherents of Holl's conscience-centered interpretation of Luther and the Reformation. It was the Achilles' heel of long-frustrated German nationalism and its romantic glorification of the German state, accompanied by its belated entry into foreign colonialism. Influenced strongly by theological anti-Romanism and philosophical Idealism—for example, God's judgment in justification as analytical rather than synthetic, at the expense of God's imputing to faith Christ's "alien righteousness" (*iustitia aliena*)—the whole of late-nineteenth-century neo-Lutheranism was unduly impressed with the heroic figure of Luther as the national liberator of the German *Volk* ("People").

All of these modern developments paved the way for the most shameful tragedy in early twentieth-century German Lutheran history: the duped seduction, prudent complicity, and even active religious support of the neo-pagan, racist ideology of the totalitarian National Socialist German Workers' Party (Nazism) by a number of prominent Lutheran theologians in the 1930s. Horrendous anti-Semitic persecution and atrocities were often either ignored or rationalized by the antibiblical alliance of Aryan mythology and Germanic natural theology: the *Blut und Boden* ("blood and soil") mystical idolatry of a Teutonic master race (popularized by Alfred Rosenberg), reinforced by autonomous *Schoepfungsordnungen* ("orders of creation"), such as the idealized state, that were considered morally subject neither to God's will in creation nor Christ's gospel in redemption.

Among the theological works that were often used (though sometimes also blatantly exploited) in the government's abortive propaganda attempts to baptize Nazism in the name of Luther's social ethics were Paul Althaus, *Grundriss der Ethik* (Outline of Ethics, 1931), *Die Deutsche Stunde der Kirche* (The German Hour of the Church, 1933), *Theologie der Ordnungen* (Theology of the Orders, 1935), and *Politischer Christentum* (Political Christianity, 1935); Franz Xavier Arnold, *Zur Frage des Naturrechts bei Martin Luther* (Natural Law in Martin Luther, 1937); Werner Bethge, *Luthers Sozialethik* (Luther's Social Ethics, 1934); Arno Deutelmoser, *Luther, Staat und Glaube* (Luther, State and Faith, 1937); Friedrich Gogarten, *Politische Ethik* (Political Ethic, 1932), *Einheit von Evangelium und Volkstum* (Unity of the Gospel and the People, 1933), *Ist Volksgesetz Gottesgesetz?* (Is the Law of the People the Law of God? 1934), and *Die Lehre von den Zwei Reichen und das Natuerliche Gesetz* (The Doctrine of the Two Kingdoms and Natural Law, 1935); Emanuel Hirsch, *Die Gegenwaertige Geistige Lage im Spiegel Philosophischer und Theologischer Besinnung* (The Present Spiritual Situation Mirrored in Philosophical and Theological Reflection, 1933), and *Deutscher Volkstum und Evangelischer Glaube* (The German People and Evangelical Faith, 1934); Hans Mueller, *Der Verleugnung Luther im heutigen Protestantismus* (The Disavowal of Luther in Current Protestantism, 1936); and Wilhelm Stapel, *Christliche Staatsman* (The Christian Statesman, 1932).

Symbolic of the widespread German Lutheran attraction to Nazism was the notorious *Ansbacher Ratschlag* (*Ansbach Counsel*) of June 1934. Composed by some Franconian theologians led by Hans Sommerer, Paul Althaus, and Werner Elert, the Council went beyond the coauthors' earlier support for the government's racist Aryan Paragraph (1933) in addressing "primarily our brethren in the National Socialist Evangelical Union of Pastors." As the self-proclaimed "voice of genuine Lutheranism," the Nazified Counsel shamelessly declared:

> The will of God binds us to a particular moment in the history of the family, nation, and race; i.e., to a particular moment in history. . . . In this knowledge, we as believing Christians thank the Lord God that in its hour of need he has given our people the *Fuehrer* as a "good and faithful sovereign," and that in the National Socialist State, God is endeavoring to provide us with disciplined and honorable "good government." Therefore we acknowledge our responsibility before God to assist the work of the *Fuehrer* in our vocations and callings.[4]

On the other hand, surveys of courageous German Lutheran opposition to Nazism and the pro-Nazi German Christian movement (*Deutsche Chris-*

ten) may be found in Leopold Klotz, ed., *Die Kirche und Das Dritte Reich: Frage und Forderungen Deutscher Theologen* (The Church and the Third Reich: Questions and Demands of German Theologians, 3 vols., 1930–32); Hermann Sasse, *Kirchliches Jahrbuch* (Church Yearbook, 1932); Kurt Dietrich Schmidt, ed., *Die Bekenntnisse und Grundsaetzlichen Aeusserungen zur Kirchenfrage des Jahres 1933* (The Confessions and Basic Declarations on the Church Question of 1933 [1934]); Heinrich Hermelink, ed., *Kirche im Kampf* (Church in Struggle, 1950); Franz Lau, "*Aeusserlich Ordnung*" und "*Weltlich Ding*" in Luther's Theologie ("External Order" and "Temporal Affairs" in Luther's Theology, 1933); Edmund Schlink, *Der Ertrag des Kirchenkampfes* (The Harvest of the Church Struggle, 1947); and Walther Kuenneth, *Der Grosse Abfall* (The Great Apostasy, 1947). Also valuable for further historical documentation in English are Arthur C. Cochrane, *The Church's Confession Under Hitler*, 1962; Robert P. Ericksen, *Theologians under Hitler: Gerhard Kittel, Paul Althaus and Emanuel Hirsch*, 1985; and Robert P. Ericksen and Susannah Heschel, ed., *Betrayal: German Churches and the Holocaust* (Fortress Press, 1999).

These works on the Church Struggle (*Kirchenkampf*) include many of the illegal pronouncements of the 1933 Pastors' Emergency League (*Pfarrernotbund*), a loose network of voluntary associations of clergy led by Pastor Martin Niemoeller. Totaling some 6,000 of the 14,000 Protestant-ordained pastors in Germany, this early form of the courageous Confessing Church (*Bekennende Kirche*) worked together with the intact regional Lutheran churches of Bavaria, Hannover, and Wuerttemberg, constituting a diversified array of ecumenical Protestant resistance to the Nazi state. Some of the leaders of the Confessing Church became victims in concentration camps and prisons (for example, Dietrich Bonhoeffer, Hanns Lilje, Martin Niemoeller, and Heinrich Grueber) because they chose "to obey God rather than any human authority" (Acts 5:29).

However small the number of Lutheran theologians who actually espoused the Nazi Party line, it is perhaps only natural in wartime that many non-Germans still felt that the Lutheran worldview was somehow instrumental in the rise of National Socialism and, consequently, partly to blame for World War II. On a political ideological level, anti–Luther wartime propaganda in England was included in some speeches by Anglican Archbishop William Temple and Dean William Inge. Even the earlier debunked slanders of such Roman Catholics as Janssen, Denifle, and Grisar were reheated by a nondescript Peter Wiener in a "Win the Peace" booklet titled *Martin Luther: Hitler's Spiritual Ancestor* (1944). That an able and uncontestable rejoinder was soon forthcoming from the English soil itself was very fortunate; that it should have been necessary at all was extremely regrettable. The answer was given decisively in Gordon Rupp's *Martin Luther: Hitler's Cause or Cure?* (1945).

Yet this did not deter another book from appearing two years later by William Montgomery McGovern called *From Luther to Hitler: The History of Fascist-Nazi Political Philosophy* (1947). Similar charges (confusing Luther's sixteenth-century theological anti-Judaism with twentieth-century racist anti-Semitism) were repeated over a decade later in William Shirer's *The Rise and Fall of the German Reich: A History of Nazi Germany* (1960), and once again repudiated as decisively afterwards in Uwe Siemon-Netto's *The Fabricated Luther: The Rise and Fall of the Shirer Myth* (1993).

Karl Barth versus Luther's "Law-Gospel Quietism"

Of far greater significance today, however, is the second major school of criticism directed against Luther's social and political ethics, which was also born amid the anguish of World War II: the attack of the great Swiss Reformed theologian Karl Barth. It is more telling than Troeltsch's charges because Barth's primary concern is neither political nor sociological, but essentially theological. He is thereby able to meet Luther on his own ground of Holy Scripture. Yet while traveling this entirely different route from Troeltsch, he arrives at much the same political conclusion.

Barth claims that Luther's "law-gospel quietism" separates law from gospel, creation from redemption, society from church. This results politically in an ethically impotent "bourgeois ghetto," which is helpless to check the autonomous whims of a demonic Nazi dictatorship as it flouts God's universal law from Rotterdam to Lidice and from Dachau to Buchenwald. German Lutherans too often passively withdraw from the struggles of society into the inner sanctum of faith, while submitting without protest to the world's violence and injustice. Barth's works, published after 1935 while he was in Swiss exile, were carefully heeded internationally in his many prophetic, however polemical, opinions on this subject.

It dare never be forgotten that it was Barth's unequivocal witness to the universal lordship of Jesus Christ that provided the clearest theological rejection of Nazism in the Confessing Church's *Barmen Declaration* (1934). The 139 Lutheran, Reformed, and United Church delegates to the ecumenical Confessing Synod met in Barmen to "speak with one voice" in organized opposition to the convictions and activities of the collaborating movement of the Nazified German Christians (*Deutsche Christen*). Under Barth's theological leadership, they dared—in spite of other denominational differences—to "speak a common word" and to "confess the evangelical truths" set forth in six theses. The first two theses declare:

> Jesus Christ, as he is attested for us in the Holy Scripture, is the one Word of God which we have to hear, and which we have to trust and obey in life and in death. We reject the false doctrine as though the church could and would have to acknowledge as a source of its

proclamation, apart from and besides this one Word of God, still other events and powers, figures and truths as God's revelation.

As Jesus Christ is God's assurance of the forgiveness of all our sins, so in the same way, and with the same seriousness, he is also God's mighty claim upon our whole life. . . . We reject the false doctrine as though there were areas of life in which we would not belong to Jesus Christ, but to other Lords, areas in which we would not need justification and sanctification through him.[5]

After this Synod, however, this Protestant common front against the Nazified Brown Church of Reichsbishop Hans Mueller was seriously weakened when repeated conflicts broke out on the proper interpretation of these theses. The Reformed and the Lutherans had together opposed a common foe. Nevertheless, the Reformed generally followed Barth's "Christocratic" rejection of all "general revelation"—especially as blindly idolized in the Nazi's "Blood and Soil" racist ideology (*Blut und Boden*). However, many confessional Lutherans feared that Luther's law-gospel key to the twofold Word of God and its theological ethical corollary in God's twofold rule as Creator and Redeemer was being placed by Barmen's revisions of the original Frankfurt draft text ("One Word of God") in theological jeopardy.

Barth responded with a whole series of articles and tracts in criticism of the public ethics of Luther in general and of German Lutheranism in particular. These included: "Evangelium und Gesetz" ("Gospel and Law"), *Theologische Existenz Heute,* 32:1935; "Rechtfertigung und Recht" ("Justification and Justice"), *Theologische Studien,* 1:1938; *This Christian Cause* (trans. 1941); *Die Deutschen und Wir* ("The Germans and Us," 1945); "Christengemeinde und Buergergemeinde" ("Christian Community and Civil Community"), *Theologische Studien,* 20:1946; and *Eine Schweitzer Stimme* ("A Swiss Voice," trans. 1948), some of which are also translated in *Against the Stream* (1954) and *Community, State and Church* (1960). See also Hermann Diem, *Karl Barth's Kritik am deutschen Luthertum* (Karl Barth's Criticism of German Lutheranism, 1947).

Barth charged in a notorious 1939 open letter to the French Christians: "The German people suffer from the heritage of the greatest German Christian, from the error of Martin Luther with respect to the relationship of law and gospel, of worldly and spiritual order and power, by which its natural paganism has not been so much limited and restricted, as rather ideologically transfigured, confirmed, and strengthened." In the following year, he went even further in another wartime letter to the Dutch Christians: "To a certain extent, Lutheranism has provided a breathing space for German paganism, and has allotted it—with its separation of creation and law from the Gospel—something like a sacral precinct. It is possible for the

German pagan to use the Lutheran doctrine of the authority of the state as a Christian justification for National Socialism, and it is possible for the German Christian to feel himself invited by the same doctrine to a recognition of National Socialism. Both have in fact occurred."[6]

Barth's counterproposal is based upon a repudiation of Luther's dialectical opposition between law and gospel, the kingdom of the world and the kingdom of God. He contends that "the law is nothing other than the necessary form of the gospel, the content of which is grace" ("Gospel and Law," 30). Once this anti-Pauline union is effected, Barth moves on to a Christomonistic synthesis of the spiritual and civil spheres of life under the inclusive banner of the universal "lordship of Christ." He maintains that Christians who live in the power of the resurrected Lord must proclaim and implement his lordship over the whole of life and not limit it merely to the community of the faithful in the church. While not completely advocating the theocratic ideal of Calvinist Geneva, Barth does believe that in dealing with the state, dedicated Christians can work out "some of the parables, types, and analogies of that which is believed and preached in the Christian community concerning the Kingdom of God in the sphere of the external, relative, provisional question of the life of the civil community" ("Christian Community and Civil Community," 169).

Barth provocatively suggests here that by such an "analogy of relation" we might, for instance, derive civil justice from Christian righteousness, political liberties from Christian freedom, civil responsibility from Christian discipleship, cultural pluralism from the Christian diversity of gifts, or an international outlook from the catholicity of the church. On this universal christological basis, Barth believes that the church can manifest Christ's lordship over the whole of creation, thereby leaving none of it to God's law in secular autonomy from God's will. Barth can go so far in this work as to assert that his Christocentric ethic will help in the moulding of the state into the likeness of the kingdom of God.

In much the same way as Troeltsch, Barth's views generated a great deal of controversy. Some theologians agreed with both his diagnosis and his proposed cure; others were in sympathy with his analysis but could not accept his alternative as biblically sound in a Lutheran theology of the cross; still others contended that he was as mistaken as Troeltsch was about Luther—despite abnormal developments originating in nineteenth-century German Lutheranism and flourishing through two subsequent World Wars. Reflecting a strong Barthian influence in their criticism of Luther were the political ethics of Alfred de Quervain, Jacques Ellul, Gottfried Forck, Helmut Gollwitzer, Ernst Wolf, and William W. A. Visser't Hooft.

Postwar German Lutheranism began its social ethical self-examination with repentance. In October of 1945, church leaders of the Protestant Passive Resistance movement (*Die Bekennende Kirche*) met foreign ecumenical representatives for the first time since the war. In true Christian fashion, these earlier imprisoned spokespersons, who were politically least guilty of all, made a public confession of corporate guilt on behalf of their people. The signatures of Theophil Wurm, Otto Dibelius, Martin Niemoeller, and Hanns Lilje joined others of like martyr-caliber in the *Stuttgart Declaration*.

> We are all the more grateful for this visit as we know ourselves to be one with our people in a great company of suffering and in a great solidarity of guilt. With great pain do we say: through us endless suffering has been brought to many peoples and countries. What we have often borne witness to before our congregations, that we now declare in the name of the whole church. True, we have struggled for many years in the name of Jesus Christ against a spirit which found its terrible expression in the National Socialist regime of violence, but we accuse ourselves for not witnessing more courageously, for not praying more faithfully, for not believing more joyously and for not loving more ardently. . . . Now a new beginning is to be made in our churches.[7]

That such a new beginning was made is the general testimony of all who witnessed the German Lutheran church rise out of its ashes of ruins and repentance, including a new understanding of the public responsibility included in its divine commission to proclaim God's whole Word (law and gospel) to God's whole world (society and church). In the typical reaction of one observer:

> A singular phenomenon in post-war Germany has been the extremely important role played by the churches in the shaping of a new political outlook. . . . Behind this statement lies the difficult awakening of responsible Protestant leaders to the realization of the tragic depths to which their quietism in political affairs had allowed their country to sink. Behind it lies also the realization that the modern state in the Christian West does not automatically bear the attributes of a just government, such as Luther envisaged in his political views on obedience to ruling powers. Inherent in this rejection of quietism is a rediscovery of the need to apply the great principles behind the specific and time-bound views of Luther to the changing patterns of events in today's world.[8]

When the earlier Nazi-imprisoned president of the Lutheran World Federation, Bishop Hanns Lilje, wrote the inaugural editorial for a new church journal (*Lutheran World*), he struck this same resounding note with characteristic vigor and power.

> Christendom is committed to bear public witness to its Lord. . . . Our systematic theologians must show us how the theology of justification by faith is completed in the practical sphere by a theology of

stewardship. . . . It is not true that the Lutheran doctrine of the justification of the sinner must as a matter of principle result in a program
of other-worldliness. . . . [Yet] we can hardly deny that the Lutheran
Church is burdened with many a heavy historical mortgage.[9]

Implicit in all of these statements has been the humble realization that
the "historical mortgage" of periods of German Lutheran abuse has not
always been true to the usable theological heritage of Luther, reflecting the
legal maxim, "misuse does not destroy the substance, but confirms its existence" (*Abusus non tollit sed confirmat substantium*). This view was reinforced
by the opposing wartime experiences and studies of Lutheran and social
democratic Scandinavia. That the issues are far more societally complex
than either Troeltsch or Barth suggested was borne out by the unflinching
testimony of those like Norway's dauntless Bishop Eivind Berggrav who
answered Nazism and German "Lutheran servility" . . . with Luther!

> Luther became the liberator for the Norwegian Church. . . . I do not
> say that Luther was our only source of strength in our battle against
> Nazism and all that it implies. The most important source was the
> New Testament. But Luther's words were current, they showed us
> very clearly and powerfully what we should do. Above all, he was the
> very best remedy to expel all "Lutheran servility" to the state and sec-
> ular authorities.[10]

A multitude of fruitful Luther studies provided the theological background
for that kind of heroic witness. Here the chief Scandinavian leaders were
Gustaf Aulén, Anders Nygren, and Ragnar Bring, along with Lennart
Pinomma, Gustaf Toernvall, Arne Siirala, Lauri Haikola, Gustaf Wingren,
and Regin Prenter.

Luther's teaching on the "two kingdoms" and its effect upon socio-
political ethics and church-state relations understandably received major
attention. The first great advance came in the realization that the two kingdoms of God and Satan are to be understood eschatologically (in the sense
of the two aeons of the New Testament), rather than either sociologically
(Holl) or medievally (Troeltsch). Moreover, Luther's final intention was to
demonstrate God's twofold rule of the whole world by law and gospel and
not to separate it into two divorced realms of the sacred and the secular.
That was precisely the point of his sixteenth-century protest against the
Roman Catholic moral double-standard of New Testament "counsels of
perfection" (*consilia*) for the clergy and Old Testament "general precepts"
(*praecepta*) for the laity.

Corresponding to the Lord's twofold role as Creator-Preserver and
Redeemer-Sanctifier, God's Word rules Christians alone religiously by the
gospel but all people civilly by the law. Just as persons cannot be saved by

reason and the law, neither can society be ruled by faith and the gospel. However, as the curse of the law breaks through into the consciences of the redeemed, so, too, the fruits of the gospel break through reciprocally to nourish the life of society. In this way, civil and social life remain free of both state-rule (autonomy) and church-rule (heteronomy), but not from God-rule (theonomy). Moreover, it is precisely the church's public responsibility to proclaim and to demonstrate to Caesar that he is *not* autonomous, but morally accountable under the universal law of God.

This dialectical position of the mature Luther—so badly misunderstood by Troeltsch and Barth—has been summarized by Gustaf Toernvall in *Geistliches und Weltliches Regiment bei Luther* (Spiritual and Temporal Rule in Luther, trans. 1947). This dialectical and antidualistic approach has been championed especially by the entire Lundensian school of Luther research in Sweden. In the words of Anders Nygren:

> The question of the two kingdoms is one of the most pressing and delicate in contemporary religious and theological thought. No other aspect of Luther's theology has been so fiercely attacked as this doctrine.
>
> Are they right who hold that at this point Lutheranism should rid itself of the unfortunate heritage which crippled its activity in the past, and hence surrender Luther's doctrine of the two kingdoms? From the Lutheran side, our answer to this is a determined *No,* and this for two reasons. In the first place, the connection between the doctrine of the spiritual and worldly authorities and the secularization of society is so tenuous that, paradoxically, it is the only effective means of overcoming such secularization. Only if the distinction between spiritual and temporal authority is maintained can the church speak clearly on the realm of the world. In the second place, the conception of the two realms is not a specifically Lutheran doctrine to be retained or abandoned, but is based on the New Testament [two aeons] and expresses an essential Christian truth. It arises so immediately and logically out of the Gospel itself that to surrender it would entail a surrender of the Gospel.
>
> It should be noted that it is God himself who rules in both these realms. He never drops the reins. To speak of either is thus to speak of a kingdom which is God's, and it is with him that we deal in matters spiritual and temporal both. This realization is all-important. We are sometimes in danger of looking on the temporal as something profane, as if God were active only in the spiritual. The temporal is not foreign to God, and Luther does not regard it as such. To him there is nothing which is profane, and no sphere in which God is not at work.[11]

Here is a clear rejoinder to Holl's earlier (anti-Roman) claim that Luther employed no natural law in his social ethics. It shows that Luther's major theological concern was to eliminate the law, reason, free will, and good works before God (*coram Deo*) as means of earning salvation. Here one is saved by grace, for Christ's sake, through faith alone. Yet Luther never denied—but encouraged—that all of these gifts, preeminently under the natural law of God the Creator, be fully employed for the political good and ethical service of neighbors in society (*coram hominibus*). Luther kept religious receptivity and ethical activity in a dialectical union. It was only in later reactionary German Lutheranism that works-righteousness and social quietism were polemically set against each other as false alternatives.

The problem of relating civil righteousness (social justice) to Christian righteousness (personal love) in Luther was also creatively addressed. There is a legitimate distinction between the morality grounded in reason of which a non-Christian person is the subject, and the piety rooted in Christian faith of which the Holy Spirit is the coagent. Toernvall strongly maintained, however, that for Luther the goodness of *both* Christian *and* civil righteousness comes from God, and that both constitute actual righteousness, absolute and relative, within God's loving twofold rule of humanity. What has been verified clearly is that Luther's theology of a living Triune God who is constantly in creative activity behind the "masks" (*larvae*) of divine creation makes any sacred–secular dualism impossible and any metaphysical form of natural law unnecessary in Christian theological ethics. This has very important implications for the church's political responsibility. The dialectical key to the misunderstandings of both Troeltsch and Holl, therefore, is in Luther's insistence that while the temporal life of persons in society cannot be ruled by the gospel of God the Redeemer, it is nevertheless still subject to the just and loving law of God the Creator.

We should also note some significant studies that were made on Luther's doctrine of vocation or calling. Einar Billing wrote two of the first important works in the Swedish Luther research in this area: *Luthers laera om staten* (Luther's Doctrine of the State, 1900) and *Vaor kallelse* (Our Calling, trans. 1947). In the first study, Billing contended that for Luther *vocation* was viewed essentially under the law as a means for the mortification of the flesh. He criticized this view as a "medieval remnant" in Luther's thought. Billing's second work aimed at correcting what he considered to be a weakness in Luther's position by developing Christian calling under the gospel as a synthesis of faith in providence and the forgiveness of sins, which issues in loving service to the neighbor.

Gustaf Wingren's *Luther on Vocation* (trans. 1957) and *Creation and Law* (trans. 1961) reexamined the whole issue and challenged Billing's position. Complementing the Spirit's gifts of renewal for Christians, the societal structures in which they are to be employed for the benefit of needy neighbors remain under God's universal law of preservation. Luther did not succumb to secular romanticism regarding daily work in his rejection of monasticism. He viewed one's calling in connection with God's strategy for combating the persistence of sin in the life of the redeemed and unredeemed alike. Thereby all persons are forced under God's law into the vocational service of their neighbors, whether they are always willing or not.

Unlike Karl Holl, who interpreted the created stations and orders of life as statically neutral until Christians infused them with obedient love, Wingren (following Lau) contended that Luther's living God works as much *on* imperfect Christians as *through* them, by means of the mandated structures of creation that ultimately serve the divine will. From this viewpoint, Luther would himself call into serious question the traditional German Lutheran type of ethical individualism whose only hope for a better world was the "societal spillover" of more converted Christians. Recent Luther research would suggest that this approach owes more to the later ethos of Pietism than to the public theology of the classical Lutheran Reformation epitomized in Luther's alleged axiom: "Better a wise Turk than a foolish Christian for mayor."

Finally, a new school of Scandinavian Luther research emerged in Finland under the Helsinki leadership of Tuomo Mannermaa. The groundbreaking text was Mannermaa's *Der im Glauben gegewaertige Christus: Rechtfertigung und Vergottung* (The Christ Present in Faith: Justification and Deification, trans. 1989). The thematic title highlights Luther's literal teaching in his 1535 Galatians Lectures: *in ipsa fide Christus adest* ("in faith itself, Christ is really present").

Developed in the course of Finnish Lutheran–Russian Orthodox ecumenical dialogues, this research model centers on Luther's idea of Christ's real presence and unity in faith (*unio cum Christo*), as well as in the Word and sacraments. Amplifying Melanchthon's "outside us" (*extra nos*) view of justification as reckoned, forensic, and juridical before God, Luther also develops justification as "real-ontic" in the power of Christ's indwelling Spirit. It is thereby also inclusive of the Christian's sanctified growth and eschatological participation in God's divine nature. Christians in faith and hope are "deified," that is, they participate in union with the whole Christ (*unio fidei*) and thereby in the Triune God, whose divine Son communicates the gracious righteousness of God. This is Luther's biblical basis (from Paul) for asserting his acclaimed "joyful exchange" (*froehliche Wechsel*) that faith effects between the sinfulness of human beings and the righteousness of God in Christ.

The controversial Mannermaa school directly repudiates a century of German Lutheran theologians who glorified the anti-Roman "young Luther" on the basis of their own neo-Kantian metaphysical presuppositions (for example, from Albrecht Ritschl through Adolph von Harnack to

Gerhard Ebeling). It is charged that these antichurchly, liberal German theologians massively neglect the trinitarian, ecclesiological, and sacramental
dimensions of Luther's abiding traditional theology, and thereby all the
ontological and cognitive contents of the Christian faith are intentionally
reduced to overpowering acts of God in existential, personal experience.
Totally ignored in Christians thereby are the real presence and unity of
Christ in faith, adoption, mutual interpenetration (*perichoresis*), participation
in God, and proleptic deification without any mystical union that abolishes
the essential difference between the Creator and human creatures.

These new Finns, therefore, interpret Luther as overcoming the Philip-
pist formal bifurcation of forensic justification and effective sanctification,
between being declared righteous and being made righteous, with an exclusively external justification inviting its enemies' caricature of a "forensic fiction." Indeed, the Christian's faithful union with the real presence of Christ
in faith (*Christus in nobis*) insures that renewing sanctification is not merely
the future consummation but also the present foundation of the imputed
and imparted righteousness of regenerated saints of God. While avoiding all
nonbiblical notions of metaphysical ontology and mystical pantheism, the
"real-ontic" reading of Luther in recent Finnish scholarship aims to enrich
Christian ethics with a far more coherent and holistic doctrine of the recti-
fication and renovation of persons created in God's image.

This Mannermaa-reorientation pattern is systematically developed in
consistently interrelated works such as Risto Saarinen, *Gottes Wirken auf
uns: Die transzendentale Deutung des Gegenwart-Christi-Motivs in der Luther-
forschung* (God's Work on Us: The Transcendent Meaning of the Presence
of Christ Motif in Luther Research, trans. 1989) and "The Word of God
in Luther's Theology," *Lutheran Quarterly*, 1990; Simo Peura, *Mehr als ein
Mensch? Die Vergoettlichung als Thema der Theologie Luthers von 1513 bis 1519*
(More than a Human Person? Deification as a Theme of Luther's Theology from 1513 to 1519 [1994]), "Die Vergoettlichung des Menschen als Sein
in Gott" ("The Deification of Human Persons as Being in God," *Lutherjahrbuch* [Luther Yearbook, 1993]), and with Antti Raunio, eds., "Die Teil-
habe am Christus bei Luther" ("Participation in Christ in Luther's
Thought") in *Luther und Theosis* (Luther and Deification, 1990); and Antti
Raunio, *Summe des Christlichen Lebens: Die Goldene Regel als Gesetz der Liebe
in der Theologie Luther's von 1510 bis 1527* (Sum of the Christian Life: The
Golden Rule as the Law of Love in Luther's Theology from 1510 to 1527
[1993]). Finally, the Finns' group introduction in the English-speaking
world is presented and evaluated by scholars, including the present author,
in Carl E. Braaten and Robert W. Jenson, editors, *Union with Christ: The
New Finnish Interpretation of Luther*, 1998.

Johannes Heckel versus Luther's "Augustinian Dualism"

We may now continue our survey of important schools of recent research in the area of Luther's theological ethics by concentrating on some of the more significant studies from Germany following the close of World War II. Scores of books, pamphlets, brochures, exegetical studies, and sermons were published to fill the German postwar vacuum in theology of politics and society. The most helpful organization and interpretation of these scattered materials is to be found in three voluminous studies. The first is the broad historical survey by Walther Kuenneth, *Politik zwischen Daemon und Gott* (Politics between Demon and God, 1954). The second is the more specialized theological focus of Rudolf Ohlig in *Die Zwei-Reiche-Lehre Luthers in der Auslegung der deutschen lutherischen Theologie der Gegenwart seit 1945* (Luther's Doctrine of the Two Kingdoms in the Exposition of German Lutheran Theology since 1945 [1974]).

The third study is an impressive multivolume project that provides an array of documentary evidence, demonstrating how the theological ethics of the Reformation were dualistically distorted in nineteenth-century German Lutheranism both by its reactionary proponents (Friedrich Stahl, August Vilmar, Theodor Kliefoth, Adolf Harless, and especially Christian Luthardt) and also by its liberal critics (Adolf von Harnack, Wilhelm Herrmann, Rudolph Sohm, Friedrich Naumaun, Ernst Troeltsch, and Max Weber). See Ulrich Duchrow et al., eds., *Umdeutungen der Zweireichen Lehre Luthers in 29. Jahrhundert* (Novel Interpretations of Luther's Doctrine of the Two Kingdoms in the Nineteenth Century, 1975). The pre–World Wars' extension and subsequent repudiation of this dangerously quietistic legacy is then extensively documented in both Germany and the United States by Ulrich Duchrow et al., ed., *Die Ambivalenz der Zweireichelehre in Lutherischen Kirchen des 20. Jahrhundert* (The Ambivalence of the Doctrine of the Two Kingdoms in Lutheran Churches of the Twentieth Century, 1976), and further internationally expanded in scope in Ulrich Duchrow, ed., *Zwei Reiche und Regimente: Ideologie oder Evangelische Orientierung?* (Lutheran Churches: Salt or Mirror of Society? Case Studies on the Theory and Practice of the Two Kingdoms Doctrine, trans. 1977). The parallel volume of the project is geared to English readers and discerningly presents the "American Reformation of Lutheran Political Responsibility in the Twentieth Century" in Karl H. Hertz, ed., *Two Kingdoms and One World*, 1976.

Significantly, none of the major ethical works that appeared in the aftermath of World War II espoused the christological "analogy of relation" approach of Karl Barth as a political substitute for Luther's doctrine of the two kingdoms, whatever qualifications and modifications they might have had concerning the latter. These studies would include: Werner Elert, *Das*

Christliche Ethos (The Christian Ethos, trans. 1957), the revision of his older standard work, *Morphologie des Luthertums* (The Structure of Lutheranism, trans. 1961), and *Gesetz und Evangelium* (Law and Gospel, trans. 1967); Helmut Thielicke, *Theologische Ethik* (Theological Ethics, vol. 1., *Foundations,* trans. 1966; vol. 2., *Politics,* trans. 1969), The Ethics of Sex, trans. 1964, and *Kirche und Oeffentlichkeit* (Church and the Public, 1948); and especially the works of the Lutheran pastor-theologian Dietrich Bonhoeffer, who was executed for his participation in a plot to assassinate Adolf Hitler: *Letters and Papers from Prison* (trans. 1953), *Life Together* (trans. 1954), *Ethics* (trans. 1955), and *The Cost of Discipleship* (trans. 1959). The theological dangers that Barth's ahistorical christological monism posits to biblical faith, revelation, and the Christ-event are explicitly developed in Helmut Thielicke, "Zur Frage Gesetz und Evangelium" ("To the Question of Law and Gospel"), in *Auf dem Grunde der Apostel und Propheten* (On the Foundation of the Apostles and the Prophets, 1950).

Emil Brunner's *Divine Imperative* (trans. 1947) and *Justice and the Social Order* (trans. 1945) summarily describe Barth's christological political ethics as both "fantastic and very dangerous." His *Christian Doctrine of Creation and Redemption* (trans. 1952) contains an explicit repudiation of it on both biblical and theological grounds. Brunner maintains in the latter book that by so subjective and arbitrary a method as that of analogy of relation, one could as easily derive allegedly Christian justification for slavery, dictatorship, and a denial of political freedom and justice, as for their opposites, if one were so inclined beforehand. If, for example, the civil analogy for Christian liberty is allegedly democracy, what are the recommended political analogies for *slave of Christ* and the *omnipotence of God*? Why not one *Reich* under the *Fuehrer* as the secular analogy for one kingdom under Christ?

By way of climactic conclusion to these controversial developments in postwar German Lutheranism, pride of place must be given to the significant theological debates on Luther's theological ethics that issued between Johannes Heckel and Paul Althaus. It may be recalled that Barth's scholarship, however magisterial in Reformed doctrine, never purported to specialize in the source analysis of Luther's theological ethics as such. The politics of Nazified German Lutheranism was his primary target. Therefore, the most technical textual debate took place only in the critical response of Paul Althaus and his colleagues to a major, well-documented work on Luther's theology of society written by a historian of church law, Johannes Heckel. As with Barth himself, sides were again quickly drawn in both Germany and Scandinavia, since many of the wartime theological wounds had not yet completely healed.

Perhaps the best place to begin is to recall two earlier books that had stressed that Luther never treated what later came to be known as the "two kingdoms" dogmatically as a major doctrine (Luthardt's and Barth's distinctive formulation). Luther used this doctrine in his applied biblical teaching, preaching, and pastoral care. This more ecclesial approach was emphasized both in Harold Diem, *Luthers Lehre von den Zwei Reichen, untersucht von Seinem Verstaendnis der Bergpredigt aus* (Luther's Doctrine of the Two Kingdoms and his Understanding of the Sermon on the Mount, 1938); and Hermann Diem, *Luther's Predigt in den Zwei Reichen* (Luther's Preaching in the Two Kingdoms, 1947). Franz Lau then published a judicious analysis of the historically-conditioned character of Luther's *Lehre von den Beiden Reichen* (Doctrine of the Two Kingdoms, 1952). Edmund Schlink contrasted the different approaches of Roman Catholicism and the Lutheran Reformers to original sin and consequently to the sinful and finite limits of apprehending God's general revelation outside Jesus Christ in "Das Theologische Problem des Naturrechts" ("The Theological Problem of Natural Law") in *Festschrift fuer Hans Meiser* (Honorary Volume for Hans Meiser, 1951).

Following an earlier article on "Recht und Gesetz, Kirche und Obrigkeit in Luthers Lehre von dem Thesenanschlag von 1517" ("Justice and Law, Church and Authority in Luther's Doctrine before the Nailing of the Theses in 1517"), *Zeitschrift der Savigny-Stiftung fuer Rechtsgeschichte* (1937), Johannes Heckel presented his important magnum opus, *Lex Charitatis: Eine Juristische Untersuchung Ueber das Recht in der Theologie Martin Luthers* (Law of Love: A Juridical Inquiry on Justice in the Theology of Martin Luther, 1953). This programmatic work was reinforced in later essays such as "Luthers Lehre von den Zwei Regimenten" ("Luther's Doctrine of the Two Kingdoms"), *Zeitschrift fuer Evangelisches Kirchenrecht* (1955), and "Der Ansatz einer Evangelische Sozialethik bei M. Luther" ("The Beginnings of an Evangelical Social Ethic in Luther"), in Theo. Heckel, ed., *Die Evangelische Kirche in den modernen Gesellschaft* (The Evangelical Church in Modern Society, 1956). Heckel's scholarship promptly set off another chain reaction of critical responses led by Paul Althaus in "Die beiden Regimente bei Luther" ("The Two Governments in Luther"), *Theologische Literaturzeitung* (1956), as well as in the extensive theological survey essay, "Luthers Lehre von den beide Reichen im Feuer der Kritik" ("Luther's Doctrine of the Two Kingdoms in the Fire of Criticism"), *Lutherjahrbuch* (1957).

These works clearly reflected the major reversal in Althaus's own theological and political ethics during and since the mid-1930s. While never actually a committed Nazi, but a conservative monarchist opposed to Communism, Althaus had originally favored a tactical coalition of his own German Nationalist Party with the National Socialists against a common foe. By 1936, however, he came to realize the demonic nature of Nazism and joined in its public opposition. After the German nation's defeat and the churches' beginnings of renewal, Althaus's new and more progressive position was expressed in *Die Christenheit und die Politische Welt* (Christianity and the Political World, 1948), in *Gebot und Gesetz* (The Divine Command, introduced favorably by the present writer, trans. 1972), in a revised foreword to the second edition of his 1931 *Grundriss der Ethik* (Outline of Ethics, 1953), and finally as capped later in his standard work *Die Ethik Martin Luthers* (The Ethics of Martin Luther, trans. 1972).

In this same critical postwar decade, a large number of thematically related books and essays by other Lutheran theologians quickly followed. These included Gunnar Hillerdal, *Gehorsam gegen Gott und Menschen* (Obedience to God and Humans, trans. 1995) and "Kirche und Politik" ("Church and Politics"), *Lutherische Rundschau* (1955); Peter Brunner, "Christ in den Zwei Reichen" ("The Christian in the Two Kingdoms") in *Evangelisch-Lutherische Kirchenzeitung* (1949); Ragnar Bring, "Der Glaube und das Recht bei Luther" ("Faith and Justice in Luther"), Ernst Kinder, "Gottesreich und Weltreich bei Augustin und bei Luther" ("Kingdom of God and Kingdom of the World in Augustine and Luther"), and Franz Lau, "Die Prophetik Apokalyptik Thomas Muentzers und Luthers Absage und die Bauernrevolution" ("The Prophetic Apocalyptic of Thomas Muentzer's and Luther's Rejection and the Peasants' Rebellion") in *Gedenkschrift fuer Werner Elert* (Honorary Volume for Werner Elert, 1955); Helmut Gollwitzer, "Die Christliche Gemeinde in der Politischen Welt" ("The Christian Congregation in the Political World"), 1954, and Franz Lau, "Legis Charitatis: Drei Fragen an J. Heckel ("Law of Love: Three Questions for J. Heckel"), in *Kerygma and Dogma* (1956); Wilfried Joest's widely influential *Gesetz und Freiheit* (Law and Freedom, 1951); H. H. Schrey, "Luthers Lehre von den zwei Reichen und ihre Bedeutung fuer die Weltanschauungssituation der Gegenwart" ("Luther's Doctrine of the Two Kingdoms and Its Meaning for the Present Worldview Situation"), in *Theologische Literaturzeitung* (1956); Gustaf Toernvall, "Der Christ in den zwei Reichen" ("The Christian in the Two Kingdoms"), in *Evangelische Theologie* (1950); "Die Sozialtheologische Aufgabe der Regimentslehre" ("The Social Theological Responsibility of the Doctrine of Governance"), in *Evangelische Theologie* (1957); Heinz-Dietrich Wendland, "Die Weltherrschaft Christi und die Zwei Reiche" ("Christ's Lordship in the World and the Two Kingdoms"), in H. H. Schrey, ed., *The Kingdom of God and the World* (reprinted 1969); and Ernst Wolf, *Peregrinatio* (1954). A brief survey of the major issues raised by many of these authors may also be found in Heinrich Bornkamm's *Luther's Doctrine of the Two Kingdoms in the Context of His Theology* (trans. 1966).

In the wake of all these negative reactions, Johannes Heckel chose to respond "representatively" to the central charges of Paul Althaus in "Im Irregarten der Zwei-Reiche-Lehre" ("In the Labyrinth of the Two Kingdoms Doctrine"), *Theologische Existenz Heute* (1957). The importance of the Althaus-Heckel exchanges is perhaps best demonstrated by the major, parallel entries on the "Two Kingdoms" in the German standard reference work, *Evangelisches Kirchenlexikon* (Evangelical Church Lexicon, III, 1959). The editors, unwilling to decide between the conflicting interpretations of Luther by Althaus and Heckel, finally settled for an unusual theological standstill. They published lengthy presentations by both authors side-by-side without attempting a harmonization. (Incidentally, it is precisely our own aim in this book to try to reconcile elements of both. We shall be presenting and adapting the essentials of Luther's theological ethic for the twenty-first century by taking due account of his stages of theological ethical development, his paradoxical and contextually conditioned formulations, and his temporally mistaken apocalyptic eschatology.)

What is really at stake here? As signaled by its title, Heckel's major thesis in *Lex Charitatis* (The Law of Love) is that the Reformer's theology of justice and society was wholly consistent with his governing doctrine of justification by faith in Christ alone. However, that is not necessarily considered praiseworthy. It raises for Heckel, as a law philosopher, the related issue of "whether Martin Luther understood the central significance of the problem of justice for his theology, and ever overcame it." Significantly, Luther was speaking exclusively and theologically/pastorally about Christ to Christians, whether in the church or in a sixteenth-century Christian society that was still largely unaware of any modern ideological or constitutional separation of church and state. Therefore, the universal and public "lordship of Jesus Christ" is all-decisive for Heckel's presentation of Luther's basic outlook: "The Reformer's doctrines of kingdom and justice point in all their chief features to one center, the reign of Christ and the spiritual law (*lex spiritualis*) or law of Christ (*lex Christi*) that governs in him" ("Labyrinth of the Two Kingdoms Doctrine").

For Heckel, Luther's two kingdoms represent his own sixteenth-century adaptation of the cosmic dualism between God and Satan that the former Augustinian monk inherited from Augustine's "two cities" (heavenly and earthly) in *The City of God*. Humanity is divided spiritually between Christians and non-Christians who live in two kingdoms (*Reiche*) under two corresponding governments (*Regimente*), the former internally by the Word and the latter externally by the sword. Augustine (and Luther) was determined by the comprehensive conception of the mystical body of Christ (*corpus Christianum*) in an organically united Christendom (*res publica Christiana*). What alone distinguishes the two is their historically different political applications: (1) Augustine faced his "earthly city" in the form of an all-powerful pagan Roman state prior to the West's medieval synthesis, whereas (2) Luther confronted his "earthly city" in the form of a political ambitious Roman Catholic Church at the end of the medieval period.

In tones strangely reminiscent of both Troeltsch and Barth, Heckel's Luther is made to speak of "two kingdoms" and "two governments" substantially *interchangeably* in this worldview. Therefore Christians, though still sinful, are faithful citizens of only one reign, the kingdom of God. Nevertheless, imitating Christ's compassionate love, they are sent also by God to serve and suffer for neighbors with whom they daily coexist within the fallen kingdom of Satan. So in the world there are two kingdoms and correspondingly two governments, but Christians belong solely to God's kingdom under Christ's public lordship.

Althaus protests that Heckel's presentations of Luther wrongly combine the earlier errors of both Troeltsch and Barth. On the one hand, its revived dualism again fatefully divorces Luther's views on justification and justice, discipleship and citizenship. On the other hand, its Christocratic (rather than Christocentrically trinitarian) character effectively denies any human apprehension of God's limited general revelation through reason and the law outside the Christ-event.

Historically, Althaus charges that Heckel overstresses the early Luther's monastic dependence on remnants of Augustine (against Aquinas), at the expense of the mature Luther's exclusively biblical dependence on Paul against both the Neoplatonism of Augustine and the neo-Aristotelianism of Aquinas. Contrary to Augustine and in deference to Paul, the mature Luther later went beyond the world's conflicting two kingdoms (*Reiche*) to teach also the loving God's intersecting (not dualistically corresponding) two governments (*Regimente*) within human history.

Theologically, Heckel's predilection for the political lordship of Christ results in falsely reading into Luther a dualistic absorption of God's two governments within the world's two kingdoms, rather than depicting Luther's pitting of the lordship of the Triune God against the kingdom of Satan dialectically in a twofold rule of history through both Caesar (temporal law and justice) and Jesus Christ (eternal gospel and justification). Until the world's end, there is no public lordship of Christ over society in the Pauline New Testament (see 1 Cor. 15:24-25). Hence, Christians and the church are to witness to the hidden lordship of Christ outside the church in conformity with Luther's theology of the cross (*theologia crucis*).

Ethically, Althaus concludes that Heckel unilaterally favors the church at the expense of the state, and redemption at the expense of creation. This results practically in the Christian's severance from political participation and social responsibility within the public callings of society. In contrast, Althaus's Luther advocates the believer's dual participation as both citizen and saint under law and gospel in practicing civil and Christian righteousness. The Creator God's "left-hand rule" against injustice, corruption, and oppression governs Christians and non-Christians alike. As public citizens, therefore, Christians obeying Christ can and should also render to Caesar what belongs to Caesar without thereby also serving Satan.

In short, Heckel and Althaus represent the two alternatives currently set for God's twofold rule between Luther's alleged societal dualism or biblical realism: (1) an exclusively christological foundation for Christian justice in Heckel's Luther (Christ *or* Caesar), or (2) an inclusively trinitarian basis for secular justice supported by both Christocentric Christians along with humanistic non-Christians in Althaus's Luther (Christ *and* Caesar). The basic agreement: There is not enough of God's general revelation (*revelatio generalis*) outside Jesus Christ for eternal salvation. The persisting disagreement: whether or not there is still enough of God's general revelation in human reason, conscience, and natural law outside Jesus Christ, but still under the Creator God, for Christians' critical cooperation with non-Christians in common societal service.

Reinhold Niebuhr versus Luther's "Cultural Defeatism"

Unfortunately, contributors to the Luther Renaissance in the English-speaking world have been largely limited to European translations, adaptations, and popularizations. In like fashion, the christological ethic of Karl Barth has not received much attention in America, although the potential affinities between his position on the lordship of Christ in political affairs and the ever-latent desire of the American Social Gospel to attempt to establish the kingdom of God on earth may still be exploited by those vainly seeking a Christian basis for their moralistic activism. Although the idea may sound fantastic at first thought, stranger theological bedfellows have been known in the history of Christian thought.

We lamented earlier that the refutations of Troeltsch in the studies of Karl Holl never enjoyed the timely translation and wide dissemination of Troeltsch himself in the English-speaking world. Yet this is not the whole story. It is also probably fair to say that the Anglo-Saxon predisposition for (semi-Pelagian) moralistic liberalism as a basis for Christian social ethics helped to prepare the way for the determinative acceptance of Ernst Troeltsch's critical evaluation of Luther's ethics.

The civil religion we unofficially espouse in America is still fired by the lingering embers of hope that once inspired many of its dedicated colonial settlers. They had a theocratic dream of transforming a pagan forest into a "Wilderness Zion." When it came time to enshrine this modified Calvinism into the (non-Constitutional) language of eighteenth-century political America, Deists and Theists alike could mutually compromise and together subscribe to the political quest for "the separate and equal station to which the laws of Nature and of Nature's God entitle them," on the basis of the self-evident truths "that all men are created equal, that they are endowed by their Creator with certain unalienable Rights, that among these are Life, Liberty, and the pursuit of Happiness." The quasi-religious overtones to "the American dream" and "manifest destiny" go right back to these crypto-covenantal formulations of the Declaration of Independence, however publicly secularized by the antibiblical Enlightenment of John Locke and Thomas Jefferson.

Perhaps the most influential proponent of this relative natural-law outlook in the United States has been Reinhold Niebuhr. Although Niebuhr's theology was richly and deeply influenced by the spirit of Luther's Pauline theology, his Reformed activism strongly disavowed the alleged cultural defeatism inherent in Luther's theological ethics. Endorsing the translated charges of Troeltsch, Niebuhr asserts that Luther and Lutheranism were guilty of "a complete severance between the final experience of grace and all the proximate possibilities of liberty and justice which must be achieved in history."[12]

> In Luther's doctrine of the Two Realms, justice is consigned completely to the realm of the law. There "nothing is known of Christ" even as in the realm of the kingdom of heaven "nothing is known of law, conscience, or sword." The law, in such a *rigorous dualism,* does not even contain within it the desire to do justice. It is no more than a coercive arrangement which prevents mutual harm. Love, on the other hand, is only *Agape* in its purest and most unadulterated form, which means in a form in which it is known in human experience only in rare moments of evangelical fervor or crisis heroism. This is why the Lutheran formulation of the relation of love to law is so irrelevant to the broad area of common experience in which one must balance claims and counterclaims and make discriminate judgments about competing interests.[13]

It is indefensible that Niebuhr's politicized caricature (reflecting World War II) wrongly conflates Luther's dualistic separation of the two realms (*zwei Reiche*) with his dialectical interactions of God's two governments (*zweierlei Regimente*). Luther's "rigorous dualism" is always between God and Satan, or faith and sin (*coram Deo*), but never between Christ and Caesar or love and law (*coram hominibus*). Indeed, Luther teaches that it is precisely the civil function of God's law (*usus civilis*) to promote justice, peace, and freedom in society, as Spirit-empowered and love-motivated Christians are called civilly, in Niebuhr's own words, to "balance claims and counterclaims and make discriminate judgments about competing interests."

Yet Niebuhr unrelentingly castigates Luther's "curiously perverse social morality," whose "inevitable consequence is to encourage tyranny . . . and defeatism in the field of social politics" because "it relegates the 'natural law' to the background." This perhaps shapes the militarily conditioned

conclusion of Niebuhr's Gifford Lectures in Edinburgh (1939) at the out-
break of World War II: "Luther's inordinate fear of anarchy, prompted by his
pessimism, and his corresponding indifference to the injustice of tyranny, has
had a fateful consequence in the history of German civilization."[14]

In answer to the Troeltsch-Niebuhr interpretation of Luther (followed
also by John A. Hutchinson and George F. Thomas), there arose a host of
English and American advocates of the schools of Holl and Lund. The
research of Holl and his German school was impressively presented, among
others, by Franklin Sherman, Gordon Rupp, Philip Watson, Theodore Tap-
pert, and Jaroslav Pelikan. The overlapping Lundensian Luther research of
Scandinavia was also cogently represented by Edgar Carlson, Conrad
Bergendoff, George Forell, Eric Gritsch, and Martin Heinecken. George
Forell's groundbreaking research, *Faith Active in Love* (1954), is worthy of
special mention here. Indeed, the culturally transplanted German-American
"dean" of postwar Luther researchers, the Reformed scholar Wilhelm
Pauck, expressed the sharpest theological judgment of all. It serves to
reconfirm our own charges against the idiosyncratic character of the mistaken *dualistic* theological ethics of elements of German Lutheranism.

> Precisely because Niebuhr is widely regarded as one who is bringing
> "classical Protestantism" to life among us, it is very important to rec-
> ognize that he fails to understand the whole of the faith of the
> Reformers and particularly that of Luther. First of all, it is to be noted
> that his thinking appears to be conditioned by a strange animosity
> against Luther which is all the more surprising in view of the fact that
> he is more closely related to Luther's faith than to any other. He takes
> frequent occasions to suggest inadequacies in Luther's teachings, but
> these criticisms do not seem to be founded on a careful study of
> Luther's work. They also seem to rise from a disregard of modern
> Luther research.
>
> It seems that Niebuhr's interpretation of Luther is still primarily
> determined by that of Ernst Troeltsch, who made the mistake of see-
> ing the Reformation too much in the light of the spirit of modern
> (nineteenth-century) German Lutheranism. Thus it is understandable
> that he can attribute a "cultural defeatism" to Luther's Reformation as
> if it were true that Luther had failed to articulate the ethical, and par-
> ticularly the social-ethical, implications of his faith. . . . I say all this in
> full awareness of the fact that while this charge does not apply to
> Luther, it may justly be levelled against certain features of Lutheranism
> as they developed after the Reformation as a result of historical con-
> ditions and in disregard of what could have been learned from Luther
> himself.[15]

The most coherent and comprehensive American postwar study on
Luther's ethics and its contemporary public relevance may be found in the

three-volume work edited by Harold C. Letts titled *Christian Social Responsibility* (1957). Officially commissioned by the United Lutheran Church in America, this symposium endorsed a strong participatory Lutheran approach to Christian public witness in a modern secular and democratic society. Comprising fourteen critical essays, this multi-year, interdisciplinary study can well be considered the first indigenous Lutheran social ethic of major proportions to emerge on Anglo-Saxon soil. The first volume analyzed *Existence Today,* the second volume covered *The Lutheran Heritage,* and the final volume presented *Life in Community* as an evangelical ethical statement geared to meet the needs of our modern public life.

Most germane to our survey are three of the essays that address themselves to the historical explication and present-day application of Luther's theological ethics. Jerald C. Brauer's presentation on "Luther and the Reformation, 1500–1580" was focused on the thesis that while the Reformation wrought by Luther was basically a religious revolution, it also "had vast implications for the life of faith as lived in society. The very nature of Luther's faith drove him to a reconsideration of the bases of contemporary social and cultural life" (vol. 2, p. 3). After illustrating his thesis in the areas of family, economic life, political affairs, and the relation of the Reformation to modern secularism, Brauer concludes: (1) that the Troeltsch-Niebuhr charge of Luther's "cultural defeatism" is an erroneous one which "misunderstands the true direction of Luther's social ethic" (vol. 2, p. 32), and that (2) "It is time for those who lay claim to the Lutheran heritage to reexamine the social implications of their faith" (vol. 2, p. 34).

Addressing this task are the first two essays of the third volume written by Joseph Sittler and the present writer. In "The Structure of Christian Ethics," Sittler first emphasized the Christ-centered quality of such an ethic with the following words:

> The Christian life is here understood as a reenactment from below on the part of men of the shape of the revelatory drama of God's holy will in Jesus Christ. The dynamics of this life are not abstractly indicated nor their creative power psychologically explicated. Suffering, death, burial, resurrection, a new life—these are actualities which plot out the arc of God's self-giving deed in Christ's descent and death and ascension. Precisely this same "shape of grace," in its recapitulation within the life of the believer and the faithful community, is the nuclear matrix which unfolds as the Christian life. (vol. 3, p. 9)

My own following chapter on "Christian Faith and Culture" then integrates this Christocentric depth within the trinitarian breadth of the twofold rule of God over humanity. Its aim is spelled out in these terms: "Just as it has been shown previously how God's redemptive act in Christ provides the Christian life with its structure and style, it shall be demonstrated here how God's creative activity supplies its theater of operation and his renewing Spirit its guiding power" (vol. 3, p. 41). An extensive treatment of this position (with cross-references from Luther's works where appropriate) is concluded with the following summary:

> We have thus established three fundamental theses which can serve theologically to undergird the necessity and justification of Christian social responsibility. First, that there is no sphere of life which is a law unto itself, autonomous of the absolute sovereignty of God, however free it must remain from ecclesiastical domination. Secondly, that all persons, even apart from Christ, are capable of a high degree of social justice in the building of a peaceful and humane society in which the Christian offers his or her critical co-operation and responsible participation. Thirdly, that it is in and through the personal and corporate witness of his faithful followers in their civic vocations, as well as their church worship, that Christ's lordship—however hidden in its servant form—is made manifest in our communal life in contemporary society. (vol. 3, p. 74)

The intentional ecclesial implementation of this basic theological orientation later enabled the Lutheran Church in America, between 1964 and 1984, to endorse officially in national biennial assemblies some twenty social statements (and study booklets) for the public ethical guidance for its members and other parts of interested American society. Carefully disavowing both internal casuistry and external lobbying, this public theology closely integrated the normative, descriptive, and regulative dimensions of such critical current issues as marriage and family, race relations, poverty, economic justice, criminal justice, capital punishment, social welfare, ecology, human rights, death and dying, religious liberty, church and state, Vietnam, selective conscientious objection (for the first time by any American church!), and world community.[16]

Richard John Neuhaus made the critical judgment in 1977 that almost all of these Lutheran statements "clearly want to assert a more positive assessment of two-kingdoms thought, both as to what can be expected from the political process and, more emphatically, as to the Christian obligation to participate in that process," and also that "the 'revisionism' evident in more recent Lutheran statements point the necessary direction for rehabilitating Lutheran social ethics."[17] Likewise, in retrospective evaluation over a decade later, Christa R. Klein and Christian von Dehsen were able to conclude: "In its quarter century, the Lutheran Church in America developed an admirably coherent tradition in theological ethics. Taken as a body, the social statements exhibit an approach to social issues that is identifiable and that reflects Lutheranism's confessional heritage. This 'evangelical ethic,' as it was called, was present from the onset."[18]

Robert Benne, after completing his own ethics text in *Ordinary Saints: An Introduction to the Christian Life* (1988), likewise felt justified in 1995 to make the documented claim that "it would not be brash to conclude that the LCA produced the most important array of official Lutheran public theology up to this point in American history."[19]

We have only to compare this ecclesial stance, refined still further in this volume, with some typical quotations from the beginning of the twentieth century to see how far the Lutheran church has come in the crucial area of public responsibility. In the autumn of the Victorian Age, the German Lutheran theologian Heinrich Thiersch could typically write, "Even a tyrant must be regarded as government once he has come into the possession of power." In the same quietistic spirit, J. Oehmke's popular guide to Luther's Small Catechism taught obedient German children that Romans 13 demands the blind political submission of all loyal Christians. "Is it true, then, that cruel and despotic rulers, revolutionists, and wild conquerors come from God? Answer: Yes, indeed! Like sickness, hailstorms, wars, and other conflagrations, so also do all godless rulers come from God."

Prodded theologically by Troeltsch, Barth, Heckel, and Niebuhr, and crushed politically by the successive onslaughts of Nazism and Communism, repentant and faithful Lutherans by the end of the twentieth century were finally driven back to the biblical foundations of Luther's theological ethics. We therefore turn next to Luther's Christocentric approach to the Holy Scriptures. Through them we have learned the hard way that we no longer dare render to the emperor Caesar the things that are God's (Luke 20:25).

Chapter 2

Ethics: Captive to God's Word

> For some years now, I have read through the Bible twice a year. If you picture the Bible to be a mighty tree and every word a little branch, I have shaken every one of these branches because I wanted to know what it was and what it meant.
>
> —Luther, *Preface to the Prophets,* 1532

uther's ethics was based on the Word of God in the Holy Scripture. The major purpose of the present study is to document from the sources that Luther's ethics as his theology was indeed "wholly determined by Scripture."[1]

Nevertheless, then and now, Luther's biblical viewpoints have frequently sparked heated controversy among theological and ethical friends and foes alike. In his predominantly Pauline exposition of the Scriptures, Luther proved himself to be theologically complex: at once an evangelical Christian who rejected Protestant fundamentalism, a catholic Christian who reformed Roman traditionalism, and a churchly Christian who repudiated sectarian fanaticism. Following the turmoil that ensued, more has likely been written about Luther than any other living person except Jesus Christ. Perhaps that is because Luther's primary concern, however often polemical, was to glorify Jesus Christ, both in ethics and faith, as "the Lord, who is the King of Scripture."[2]

Whether as monk, professor, preacher, counselor, theologian, or church leader, Luther's own life and vocation (1483–1546) centered on proclaiming the biblical Word of God. Although Luther recalled that he had "not yet seen a Bible" until the age of twenty, nine years later he had earned the degree of Doctor of Holy Scripture (*Doctor in Biblia*) at Wittenberg University.[3] As professor of Bible, from his earliest lectures on the *Psalms* (1513), *Romans* (1515–16), and *Galatians* (1516–17) to his final lectures on *Genesis* (1535–45) completed just three months before his death, Luther's entire academic career was primarily devoted to the theological exposition of the

Bible, especially the Old Testament. From 1522 to 1545, he periodically prepared, revised, and published his translations of the whole German Bible from Hebrew and Greek and also provided distinctively Christ-centered prefaces for all the books of the Old Testament, Apocrypha, and New Testament. Just as Luther's personal piety was decisively inspired by Paul's powerful witness to the "righteousness of God" (*iustitia Dei*) in Romans and Galatians, so too his churchly reforms were publicly defended at the Imperial Diet of Worms (1521) by his unswerving appeal to biblical authority: "Unless I am convinced by the testimony of the Scriptures or by clear reason . . . my conscience is captive to the Word of God."[4]

Consequently, it will prove highly beneficial for our own presentation of Luther's theological ethic if we first review some of the major principles of Luther's exegetical work as an exposition of the church's Scriptures. This is important for two reasons. On the one hand, over four centuries of subsequent biblical scholarship now obviously make it impossible for current Christians to accept many of Luther's sixteenth-century exegetical methods and historical interpretations, whether as inherited or as advocated by him. To cite but one obvious example, "We know from Moses that the world was not in existence before 6,000 years ago."[5]

On the other hand, Luther was also blessed with profound insights into the central gospel of the Old and New Testaments, which in theological ethics are as addressable to our day as they were to his own. Hence, in distinguishing the oral and written forms of the Word of God, Luther also taught: "The gospel signifies nothing else than the preaching and report concerning the grace and mercy of God which Jesus Christ has earned and gained for us with his death. It is properly not something written down with letters of the alphabet; it is more an oral proclamation and a living word: a voice (*viva vox*) which resounds into the whole world and is proclaimed publicly, so that we may hear it everywhere."[6]

Clearly Luther taught both enthusiastically about Scripture and scripturally about life. It was therefore singularly appropriate that the recent American edition of Luther's major writings (1955–86) should structure its fifty-four translated volumes into two major divisions: (1) the first thirty volumes devoted to Luther's commentaries on many of the *biblical* books, and (2) the following twenty-four volumes concentrating on the Reformer's chief *theological* works.

However, as our own documentary selections from each part will amply demonstrate, the dynamic and contextual nature of Luther's works characteristically include both doctrinal and ethical current applications within his biblical commentaries, along with related scriptural foundations and exegetical interpretations within his theological treatises. Luther's professorial podium and pastoral pulpit were never kept far apart. Popes, princes, and peasants serve to illustrate satanic temptation in the Garden of Eden at the opening of his *Lectures on Genesis* (1535), while Moses, Noah, Jesus, and Paul are called on for ethical and military counsel in determining *Whether Soldiers, Too, Can be Saved* (1526).

It follows that critical hermeneutical rigor is imperative for the current student of Luther's theological ethic. After all, Luther was a pre-Enlightenment biblical theologian, not a postmodern, technical, exegetical specialist. Fortunately, therefore, a world-class historian of Christian doctrine, Jaroslav Pelikan, was commissioned to serve as the General Editor of the first thirty volumes on Scripture in the cited American Edition of *Luther's Works*. In that capacity, he supervised the preparation of the historical and theological introductions and edited the critical apparatus devoted to each of Luther's individual works.

Moreover, Pelikan also composed a companion volume, *Luther the Expositor* (1959), to introduce us to the Reformer's exegetical principles. This volume grew out of Pelikan's conviction that the history of theology is basically the record of how the churches have interpreted the Scriptures. Pelikan fully documents the thesis that "in his exegesis—as in his doctrine, piety, and ethic—the Reformer represented himself as a son of the church and as a witness to the Word of God revealed in Jesus Christ and documented in the Sacred Scriptures."[7]

Principles of Biblical Interpretation

We cannot do better at the outset than to highlight and amplify Pelikan's brilliant development of three of the basic principles that govern Luther's biblical interpretation: (1) the authority of the Word of God in the Bible, (2) the organic relation of Scripture to the church's dogmatic tradition, and (3) the Bible as the history of the people of God.

1. The first principle governing Luther's exegesis is the relation of the Scriptures to the Word of God.[8] In the biblical record, the Lord is revealed as the God who speaks (*Deus loquens*). He decrees: "Let there be" or "Your sins are forgiven." Thereby the one Triune God both creates with power and redeems by love. "God's works are his words . . . his doing is identical with his speaking." It follows for Luther that, "When God speaks, the thing expressed by the Word leaps into existence"—whether it be the old creation of the world or the new creation of a believer.[9]

There are three interrelated forms of the Word of God in Luther's theology. First, there is the *personal* Word of God, both in eternity and in history. In the cosmic sense, the Word of God is the second person of the Holy Trinity, the eternal Logos, the preexistent Son of God. In the historical sense, God's Word became personally incarnate in Jesus of Nazareth. "It is God incarnate who has been sent into the world for the very purpose of willing, speaking, doing, suffering, and offering to all men everything necessary for salvation.[10]

Since the Triune God is one, the God of the Old Testament is also the same God of the New Testament, and vice versa. Hence, there is both creation and redemption, indeed both judgment and grace, both law and gospel in both the Old and the New Testaments. The personal Word of God was the promised Christ in the former, and also the historical Christ in the latter. Jesus Christ is uniquely the personal embodiment of God's eternal Word in history, both in his teaching revelation of God's will, as well as in his messianic redemption of a sinful humankind through his cross and resurrection.

Second, Luther highlights the *proclaimed* Word of God. Functioning both as law and as gospel, that is, as demands with threats and as promises with exhortations, it is God's Word that creates and governs all people. This is essential for human preservation and salvation, as the community of faith, the church, remembers and heralds God's mighty acts in history that culminate in Jesus Christ. The oral announcement of the good news, the apostolic gospel, originally took place long before the books of the New Testament were written and later assembled by the church into the biblical canon. To bring unbelievers to faith in Christ is the chief reason for the Word of preaching in the life and mission of the church. Hence, "Christ did not write; nor did he command the apostles to write, but only to preach."[11] Or again, "the church is not a pen-house, but a mouth-house."[12] Or yet again, "the gospel should not only be written, but shouted."[13]

Third, in Luther's theology, there is also the Bible as the *written* Word of God. Always biblical but rarely biblicistic, Luther would usually neither equate nor separate the Word of God and Holy Scripture. The Bible is revered rather as the definitive documentary on both the incarnational and oral revelation of God's Word.

The Scriptures witness faithfully and authoritatively to God's historical self-disclosure in words and deeds of accusation and pardon, both to Israel and in Christ. This is because the Bible is the "sure rule of God's Word." Scripture is rightly called "holy" because it is "the sanctuary in which Christ dwells"; it is "the Holy Spirit's proclamation"; it is "the vehicle of the Holy Spirit" whose original autographs were "written and recorded by the Spirit."[14] The written testimony of the prophets and the apostles is inspired by the Holy Spirit (*divino spiritu infusus*). They both sustain the Word's oral proclamation and also preserve it from later error. By the power of the Spirit, the canonical Scriptures are dynamically incorporated into God's ongoing mission and serve to convey God's living Word for the saving benefit of all following generations.

In sum, it is as a servant of the proclaimed Word's announcement of the personal Word's saving presence that the written Word of the Scriptures also serves authoritatively as the church's chief source and norm of the

Christian faith. "The Scriptures are words of life, intended not for speculation and fancy, but for life and action."[15] Especially in his heated polemics
against Word-demeaning mystics, philosophers of religion, and canon
lawyers, Luther would frequently appeal to the biblical Word of God as the
trustworthy written record of God's redemptive self-revelation.

> If you can convince me through Scripture, do not doubt that I will
> submit. . . . It is not certain how much custom and long usage could
> count with God, to whom we are responsible for the keeping of his
> Word and not of human teaching or custom. For this reason I want
> Scripture. Scripture, Murner; Murner, Scripture! Or else seek another
> combatant; I have other things to do than to attend to your scripture-
> less chatter.[16]

2. The second principle guiding Luther the expositor is the inseparable
relation of Scripture to church tradition.[17] This hermeneutical complex
was provoked by Luther's threefold presentation of God's Word as incarnate (Christ), oral (sermon), and written (Bible), in that descending order
of redemptive authority. Consequently, Luther asserted from the Scriptures
that the church's authentic teaching tradition centered in receiving and
transmitting the gospel about Jesus Christ as uniquely found in the Scriptures (1 Cor. 15:1-2).

Luther's ecclesial approach to the Word of God incited a "two-front
war": first against Roman traditionalists (adding to the gospel) and then later
also against Protestant biblicists (subtracting from the gospel). It was therefore as an "obedient rebel" (Pelikan) that Luther challenged unilateral expo-
nents of Scripture and tradition alike with the church's sole criterion of
authentic apostolicity: "Does it urge Christ?"[18] Moreover, it was Luther's
conviction that this Christocentric principle of biblical interpretation is
not externally imposed on Scripture but rather internally derived from
Scripture itself: "All the genuine sacred books agree in this, that all of them
preach and inculcate Christ. And this is the true test by which to judge all
books when we see whether or not they inculcate Christ."[19]

Historically, the ancient church was enabled to overcome the chronic
threats of Judaism, paganism, and heresy only by developing its own periodically unstable system of triadic authority. It consisted of (1) the scriptural canon, (2) the conciliar creeds, and (3) a monarchical episcopate to
employ these governing texts to oversee the church's faith and life. By the
Middle Ages, however, papalists and conciliarists continually struggled with
one another within the Western church itself in order to test just who held
the final political power for determining the content and application of the
church's scriptural and creedal teaching authority (*magisterium*).

It was the ambiguity inherent in this tenuous heritage that prompted
Luther's protest against both aspects of ecclesiastical traditionalism. In

prioritizing church authority, he advocated that Rome's late medieval doctrinal innovations should bow to the ancient patristic tradition and that the ancient patristic tradition, in turn, should be judged by the apostolic Word of God in its faithful witness to Jesus Christ in the Scriptures.

On the one hand, as a traditional Catholic, Luther rebelled against the late medieval church's perversions in subordinating Scripture to tradition as a supplementary source of revelation. Here he pitted earlier tradition against later tradition. Luther praised the early church's great theologians, such as Cyril, Gregory, Ambrose, and especially Augustine, for their scriptural fidelity, notably in contrast to his own contemporary adversaries. He does not thereby rigidly oppose Scripture and tradition, but listens rather for God's living Word witnessed successively within both. Back to the Bible, to Augustine and the church fathers! "I cannot stand it that they slander and blaspheme Scripture and the holy fathers in this way. They accuse Scripture of being dark . . . and they give the fathers credit for being the light that illumines Scripture, although all the fathers confess their own darkness and illumine Scripture only with Scripture."[20]

On the other hand, as an evangelical Catholic, Luther could just as readily in other contexts turn against the early church fathers themselves when he believed that they erred and failed to understand the kingdom of grace in Jesus Christ. "Were they not equally blind? Did they not simply overlook Paul's clearest and most explicit statements?"[21] It was the Bible's message of the gospel (*kerygma*) that was alone essential. His constant plea: "Let us hear the Scriptures!" (*Audiamus Scripturam*). Finally, Luther measured even the church's early tradition against the supreme authority of the scriptural Word of God:[22] "I follow the example of St. Augustine, who was among other things, the first and almost only one who was determined to be subject to the Holy Scriptures alone, and independent of the books of all the fathers and the saints. . . . I will not listen to the church or the fathers or the apostles unless they bring and teach the true Word of God."[23]

Hence, when commanded by the imperial authorities without Scripture to recant his views at Worms, Luther flatly refused. He publicly confessed: "I do not trust either in the pope or in councils alone, since it is well-known that they have often erred and contradicted themselves." Moreover, the church fathers themselves "were great men, but nevertheless they were human beings who erred and who were subject to error. So we do not exalt them as do the monks, who worship their opinion as if they were infallible."[24]

Certainly Luther recognized the legitimacy, indeed the obligation, of the church catholic to expound (but not expand) the Scriptures in Scripture-governed tradition (*paradosis*), by meeting new threats with new formulations of doctrine that may be stated even in nonscriptural language.

However, this is permissible only so long as it does not compromise the normative biblical substance itself. For example:

> Thus Scripture cleverly proves that there are three persons and one God. For I would believe neither the writings of Augustine nor the teachers of the church unless the Old and New Testaments would clearly show this doctrine of the Trinity.
>
> But that one should not use more or other words than those contained in Scripture—this cannot be adhered to . . . [especially when it] became necessary to condense the meaning of Scripture, comprised of so many passages, into a short and comprehensive word, and to ask whether they [the Arian heretics] regarded Christ as *homoousius* [of "one substance" with the Father, as in the Nicene Creed].[25]

Luther's insistence on the preeminence of scriptural over traditional authority served only to support his opponents' charges that such an operation would ultimately destroy the church's official bulwark against heresy. Who, if not the church's teaching authority, would decisively arbitrate among the multitude of individual contradictory claims of correct scriptural interpretation? Luther only reinforced their fears of subjectivism whenever he frankly claimed his own exegetical prowess: "I know and am assured, by the grace of God, that I am more learned in the Scriptures than all the sophists and papists. But so far God has saved me from pride, and will preserve me."[26]

In one sense, this entire volume aims to document the evidence for this audacious claim by its review of the profundity of Luther's obedient exposition of the Word of God. It was his deep conviction, derived directly from the heart of the Pauline Scriptures, that trust (*fiducia*) in the grace of God rather than trust in the performance of one's own moral deeds was indeed the authentic tradition of the apostolic church regarding salvation. In the New Testament there is recognition of both true and false tradition, and it is truth, rather than age, that makes all the difference. When the Pharisees and scribes came to Jesus from Jerusalem and asked, "Why do your disciples break the tradition of the elders?" Jesus responded by challenging them, "and why do you break the commandment of God for the sake of your tradition?" (Matt. 15:1-3).

3. The third principle that directs Luther the expositor is his view of the Bible as the history of the church as the people of God.[27] This exegetical norm can be demonstrated by our formally introducing his *Lectures on Genesis* (1535–1545), whose theological contents will be analyzed at considerable length in subsequent chapters. Our main concern here is to show how Luther employed this Old Testament material to buttress his Christocentric claim that God's true church was "established by the Word of God" not really first at Pentecost but already in Paradise, "through Adam and Eve, who believed God's promise."[28]

We must be very careful not to confuse this evangelical exegesis of Luther with the allegorical interpretations that were commonplace in medieval times. The former was grounded firmly in the Christ-centered climax of the biblical history of salvation (*Heilsgeschichte*); the latter were not. Luther rejects "toying with ill-timed allegories, for Moses is relating history; it is not interpreting Scripture."[29] The allegorists engage in "mere juggling," "a merry chase," "monkey tricks," "crazy talk of pulling about Scripture like a nose of wax."[30]

Luther knew whereof he spoke because he was personally trained earlier as a monk in the traditional *Quadriga* method of biblical exegesis. In order to provide church scholars with maximal developmental potential, all scriptural passages could be creatively interpreted with four different meanings: (1) the literal (historical content), (2) the allegorical (spiritual beliefs), (3) the tropological (moral conduct), and (4) the anagogical (eschatological future). So, for example, "Jerusalem" might be depicted either as a Jewish city, the church, a human soul, and/or heaven.

Without fidelity to the doctrinal norms of the Christian faith (*regula fidei*), however, fanciful speculation could easily abound unchecked in all directions. Luther taught that persons could thereby be tempted away from the gospel's central message about God's love in Christ. They could be seduced by the wiles of "Madame Hilda," "that lovely whore," "the devil's prostitute," in the illegitimate substitution of reason for faith in matters of salvation. No, insisted Luther, everything "must be weighted according to the analogy of faith (*analogia fidei*) and the rule of Scripture. . . . Holy Scripture is its own interpreter (*sui ipsius interpres*) . . . one passage of Scripture must be clarified by other passages."[31] Tracing his own evangelical growth, Luther recalls:

> When I was a young man, my own attempts at allegory met with fair success. And anyone who was somewhat more skilled in contriving allegories was also regarded as a rather learned theologian. . . . But ever since I began to adhere to the historical meaning, I myself have always had a strong dislike for allegories and do not make use of them unless the text itself indicated them or the interpretations could be drawn from the New Testament.[32]

Luther progressively developed his distinctively Christocentric combination of Scripture's "historical" and "spiritual" dimensions (*literaliter spiritualiter*). He interpreted the Bible as historical documents that were at once in essential agreement (*concordat*) with the salvific inner testimony of the Holy Spirit (*testimonium internum Spiritus Sancti*).[33] In other words, its literal-historical sense witnessed externally to God's creation through Christ, while its interacting prophetic-spiritual sense was wholly coherent internally with God's redemption in Christ.

After studiously employing all of the best hermeneutical and philolog-ical resources currently available to him (for example, Faber Stapulensis, John Reuchlin, Desiderius Erasmus), Luther then also emulated Paul and Augustine in his continual insistence that "the entire Scripture deals only with Christ everywhere, if it is looked at inwardly. . . . Hence Paul also says 'Christ is the end of the law' (Rom. 10:4), as if to say that all Scripture finds its meaning in Christ."[34]

Yet, admittedly, Luther's own style of discerning the Bible's "spiritual meaning" was also not what most post-Enlightenment biblical scholars today would consider to be legitimate historical-critical exegesis, in terms of literal, factual, dateable historicity. Nevertheless, it was a very common approach to the Old Testament within the New Testament itself. Although technically not allegorical (that is, interpreting myths as literary embodi-ments of nonhistorical truths), Luther's Augustinian exegesis was more typological (that is, tracing God's plan of salvation in setting apart an elect and public people, the church).

Such typological interpretation depicts "latent types" (Augustine) of Christ and his body, the church (totus Christus) amid persons, events, and institutions of the Old Testament. They are prefigured as historical "pre-views of coming attractions" in anticipation of Messianic fulfillment. Faithful to its patristic origins, this method stresses that the true church of God's people, however hidden, was already typified in the Old Testament as a real, covenanted communion within world history. From the ancient traditions of the Old Israel through the eschatological fulfillment of the New, the Word of God and the people of God are deemed to be histori-cally inseparable.

However, it cannot be denied that Luther's strained efforts to find his-torical allusions to Christ, the church, and the gospel of justification by grace through faith in the most remote chapters of the Old Testament fre-quently strike the modern biblical student as overly contrived. Neverthe-less, Luther at his best consciously emulated the New Testament writers in restricting the use of allegories to a merely subsidiary and illustrative role.

> Hence the rule of Paul should be observed here, that allegories should be kept in second place and be applied for the strengthening, adorning and enriching of the doctrines of faith, or, as he says in 1 Cor. 3:11ff., they should not be the foundation, but be built on the foundation, not as hay, wood and stubble, but as gold, silver and gems. This is done when, according to the injunction of Rom. 12:6, prophecy is accord-ing to the analogy of faith, namely, that you first take up a definite statement set down somewhere in the Scriptures, explain it according to the literal sense, and then in the end, connect it to an allegorical meaning which says the same thing.[35]

In Paul's Epistle to the Romans, Luther finds a powerful evangelical basis for interpreting the Old Testament in this Christocentric manner. Here the apostle appeals to "the gospel of God, which he promised beforehand through the prophets in the Holy Scriptures" (Rom. 1:1-2). In opposition to all nonbiblical speculation, Luther revels in a Pauline-based marginal gloss that introduces his *Lectures on Romans* (1516): "There is opened up here a broad approach to the understanding of Holy Scripture: we must understand it in its entirety with respect to Christ, especially where it is prophetic. Now it is in fact prophetic throughout, though not according to the superficial literal meaning of the text (Gal. 5:9ff)."[36]

Encouraged by the typological teaching of both Jesus (Luke 4:18-19) and Paul (Rom. 5:12-21), Luther also freely "unveiled" the Old Testament in the light of its New Testament fulfillment. So, when later turning to Genesis, he rejected allegorists in deference to the stance of his evangelical mentors: "When they hear the reading of the old covenant, that same veil is still there, since only in Christ is it set aside" (2 Cor. 3:14).

Of course, Luther knew that he was dealing on the surface historically with the ancient Hebrew Scriptures. At the same time, he confessed, theologically, that this was also the inseparable foundation of the church's revealed faith. God's gracious Word was addressed to the one faithful people of God, whether in God's Old Testament with Abraham, Isaac, and Jacob or in God's New Testament as centered in the cross of Christ (1 Cor. 1:23). In promises and curses, as well as in prefigurative incidents and declarations, Gentile Christians could rightly read the inaugurated gospel of Genesis through the realized gospel of Romans and conclude that "we are the people of God and the true church," as the spiritual (even though not physical) descendants of Abraham, who trust in Jesus as God's long-promised Messiah.[37]

In his struggles with the late medieval church, Luther therefore frequently interpreted the current meaning of the Scriptures by illuminating parallels and analogies. In the first place, there was perennial strife between the true church ("in suffering and cross") and the false church ("in name only").[38] As the clashes between Cain and Abel foreshadowed those between late medieval Rome and the Reformers, so the temptation of Adam and the fall of Eve prefigured heresy in the church and the rejection of God's Word. Luther found this biblical witness to human weakness and sin to be perennially and helpfully realistic. There had always been opposition between "two churches": Cain and Abel, Ishmael and Isaac, Esau and Jacob, the church of God and that of the devil.[39]

Moreover, Luther found comfort in the assurance of Genesis that God was always graciously on the side of those who were unjustly oppressed, the true church represented by Abel, Abraham, Isaac, and Jacob. Conversely, Genesis provided Luther with a warning for late medieval Rome: It was the "church of Cain," and on the Day of Judgment, "God will announce his approval of that suffering and hungering church, and also his condemnation of the hypocritical and bloodthirsty one."[40]

In the second place, Genesis illustrated the biblical truth that the presence of the true church was guaranteed only by the grace and mercy of God. "Thus the foremost article of our faith and our highest wisdom are confirmed—that the children of God are those who believe the promise; for it is by this promise alone that God wants to save those who believe in Christ."[41] Size, age, wealth, and political power were never essential for the people of God. Abraham forsook the religion of his homeland; Noah was alone; Isaac and Jacob were not the firstborn; Joseph was plunged into exile; Noah was mocked in ways with which Luther could personally empathize: "There is, therefore, no doubt that the perverse generation hated him intensely and harassed him in various ways while exposing him to ridicule; 'Is it you alone who is wise? Is it you alone who pleases God? Are all the rest of us in error?' . . . The wretched papists assail us today with this one argument."[42]

In the third place, Luther also found support in Genesis for the necessity of external forms in the church. He learned from the Hebrew Scriptures to oppose all human attempts to sever the spiritual from the material, the sacred from the secular. All authentic spirituality was grounded in the Holy Spirit's work in personally embodied creatures of God. Luther's incarnational and sacramental realism led him to assert that "the church cannot exist without the constant use of the Word, and the church has always had its sacraments, or tokens of grace, and its ceremonies."[43]

Ritual with external forms was essential, but ceremonialism as an end to itself was pagan superstition. The Ishmael story taught Luther that "the main and spiritual worship of God does not consist in building temples and proliferating ceremonies; for these things are childish amusements."[44] Maintaining the dialectical tension was often resented both by Roman monastics and by pseudo-Protestant iconoclasts (dubbed as "sacramentarians," "enthusiasts," and "fanatics" by Luther).[45] Nevertheless, the conservative Reformation at its best combined Luther's priestly stress on the need for externals with a prophetic warning against the spurious veneer of ceremonialism.

The decisive factor was the authority of the Word of God in sermon and sacrament within the people of God. From the very outset in Genesis, it was God's Word that distinguished the true church from the false church. Sermons and sacraments, mediated by a divinely set-apart ministry, were always constitutive of the church from the most ancient times: "the church is the daughter, born from the Word; she is not the mother of the Word."[46]

To illustrate: Going back to the Garden of Eden, the church's presence before the Fall was validated by the Lord's own preached Word to Adam.[47] Likewise, Noah demonstrated God's punishment for disobedience to the

Word; Abraham needed a new Word of God for a new church; Jacob's altar at Shechem "was not erected for pomp or show, nor for the sacrifice of the Mass, but for the preaching of the Word."[48]

Coupled with this continuous witness to God's commands and promises were also external signs providing the means of assurance that God was present and blessing the faithful in their true worship (for example, the tree of the knowledge of good and evil, clothes for Adam and Eve, the rainbow, circumcision). While interpreting the differing sacrifices of Cain and Abel, Luther insisted that there was no authentic sacrifice "without the preaching of the Word. God is not worshiped with a mute work; there must be the sound of a word." But God also "always establishes some outward and visible sign of his grace alongside the Word . . . an outward sign and work or sacrament. . . . Thus the church has never been without outward signs."[49] Genesis convinced Luther that God called the church of the patriarchs into being through promises and signs that prefigured the apostolic church's Word in oral sermons and visible sacraments.

Finally, this emphasis on the proclamation of promises accompanied by external signs led Luther naturally into consideration of the church's public ministry. As God's spoken Word sometimes came through angels, so it was also mediated through patriarchal leaders such as Adam, Methuselah, Shem, Abraham, Isaac, Jacob, and Joseph. If it was against Rome that Luther stressed the church's oral Word, then it was against the self-claimed private revelations of the Protestant "fanatics" (*Schwaermer*) that Luther emphasized the biblical witness to the Spirit's true work in the publicly gathered church. Therefore God set apart the church's public ministry to lead public reception of public means of grace that were publicly dispersed at the altar, the font, and the pulpit of the community of faith. "Direct your step to the place where the Word resounds and the sacraments are administered, and there write the title, 'the gate of God.'"[50]

In his diligent development of all these exegetical principles and ecclesiastical practices, Luther highlighted the biblical history of the church as the people of God gathered around the Word of God. While engaged viscerally in life-and-death controversy, Luther's kind of Christocentric extrapolation of Old Testament beginnings from New Testament endings was never intended merely to meet our present-day secular standards of a chronological record of events. Only the eyes of faith discern the eternal revealed under the historical. Of course, we now know that we cannot, with Luther, interpret some Old Testament prophesies as pointing literalistically to the historical person of Jesus as the promised Christ. Nevertheless, we may still claim with Luther that they do point in the direction of the messianic office later fulfilled by the historical Jesus; that is, they can operate Christocentrically even when not christologically.

So Luther's theological interpretation of Genesis proved to be historic, although not always historical. He rejected the late medieval penchant for allegorical flights of individualistic fancy in favor of providing theological expositions of pre-Christian Scriptures that were retroactively both coherent with and normed by their truly redemptive fulfillment in the Christ-event.

Indeed, it is highly likely that Luther's biblical commentaries have such a strong homiletical tone precisely because he was also an actively functioning pastor himself. When he regularly addresses himself to "the godly reader," his ultimate goal is to strengthen discipleship. So also when he completes his commentary on the first eleven chapters of Genesis, he stops to marvel at the "uninterrupted transmission of the promise concerning Christ through the ministries of those holy rulers of the first church, Adam, Seth, Noah and Shem." He finds confirmation that "the article of our creed is true when we believe one, holy, catholic church in all ages, from the beginning of the world to the end of the world." Therefore Christianity may be confident that "where the Word is, there the church is, where the Spirit is, there Christ is." In the power of the Holy Spirit, the church "has always been divinely preserved in the world through him who crushed the head of the serpent (Gen. 3:15)."[51]

This is the big picture of Genesis for Luther, and Christians are admonished not to get all tangled up with many unanswerable and inconsequential details along the way, such as "How is it that Arpachsad is begotten two years after the Flood, although he is Shem's third son, as Moses asserts in the previous chapter (Gen. 10:22)?" Luther the perplexed exegete is quickly reassured by Luther the confident pastor: "Our faith is not endangered if we should lack knowledge about these matters. This much is sure: Scripture does not lie. Therefore answers that are given in support of the trustworthiness of Scripture serve a purpose, even though they may not be altogether reliable."[52]

Christ Proclaimed in the New Testament

The previous section outlined the basic thrust of Luther's interpretation of Scripture. It is the written record of the living and loving Word of God, which authoritatively norms the doctrinal faith and ethical life of the people of God, both then and now. In our review, we have frequently alluded to the dynamic and paradoxical style of Luther's biblical expositions, with the eyes of faith perceiving what is often contrary to historical appearances (*sub contrario*). This was due primarily to his evangelical conviction that the historical Scriptures were uniquely inspired and powerfully illumined by the indwelling Holy Spirit to enable Christians to carry out God's mission through the church in a fallen world. When we start to judge Scripture,

Scripture ends by judging and forgiving and renewing us. "These are written so that you may come to believe that Jesus is the Messiah, the Son of God, and that through believing you may have life in his name" (John 20:31).

Highlighting this Christocentric gospel was the hallmark of Luther's intra-trinitarian approach to the record of God's self-revelation in the Bible. Decade after decade, Luther concentrated on the Father's sending of the Son in the Spirit for human salvation and service. Preaching and teaching the Scriptures as a faithful Christian, Luther interpreted the Old Testament in light of the New, creation in light of redemption, the law in light of the gospel, Moses in the light of Christ. It was the Christ of the Scriptures who saved the many dialectical distinctions in Luther's theology and ethics from degenerating into dualistic separations. "Therefore, if the adversaries press Scripture against Christ, we urge Christ against the Scriptures" wherever there is lack of clarity about the gospel. For Luther, against Marcion, Jesus Christ was the Bible's unifying Alpha and Omega, whether anticipated as "the Christ who was to come" in the written Scriptures of the Old Testament, or when proclaimed as "the Christ who has come" in the oral gospel of the New.[53]

Luther's hermeneutical approach is most explicitly articulated in editorial comments related to his masterful translation of the ancient books of the Bible, with appended prefaces, into German. We will now summarize this material sequentially, analyzing first the New Testament in this section and then the Old Testament in the next, intentionally in this historically reversed order. It is the gospel of the "hidden" (*absconditus*) lordship of Jesus Christ that paradoxically unites the Bible, alongside the radical distinction—not separation—of the gospel's interrelated parts of fulfillment and foretaste. For Luther, as the Old Testament provides the New with its historical foundations, so the New Testament illumines the Old with its theological significance.

It will serve us well to introduce Luther's biblical work alongside his ongoing homiletical activities as pastor of the parish church in Wittenberg. Shortly after the Imperial Diet of Worms, the first project Luther undertook during his protective custody at the Wartburg was the preparation of what eventually became the *Wartburg Postil* (1521), a series of sermons based on the epistles and Gospels for the church year. With the publication of the initial sermons that he rapidly prepared, Luther added a simple preface, *Brief Instruction on What to Look for and Expect in the Gospels* (1521).

Reflecting on his painfully Scripture-less experience at Worms, Luther deplores two "erroneous notions" that currently prevailed in the church. The first was to limit the New Testament gospel to the opening four Gospels at the expense of the following epistles. The second was to regard both the Gospels and the epistles as "law books in which is supposed to be taught what we are to do and in which the works of Christ are pictured to us as nothing but examples." Legalism and moralism thereby destroy the biblical gospel as a "joyful, good, and comforting message about Christ" in the church's public proclamation.[54]

Actually, there is "only one gospel," whether it is proclaimed in the Gospels or the epistles, and "yes, even in the teaching of the prophets, in those places where they speak of Christ." It is not the source, but the content, that is determinative for the gospel, which is essentially "a story about Christ, God's and David's son, who died and was raised and is established as Lord. This is the gospel in a nutshell." If one does not grasp "this understanding of the gospel, he will never be able to be illuminated in the Scripture nor will he receive the right foundation."[55]

We dare not make Christ into a new Moses, that is, a human teacher who merely provided laws and examples of human morality. To be sure, the Christ incarnate in Palestine was demonstrably that too, but immeasurably more.

> Therefore you should grasp Christ, his words, works and sufferings, in a twofold manner. First, as an example that is presented to you, which you should follow and imitate. . . . However this is the smallest part of the gospel, on the basis of which it cannot yet be called gospel.
>
> The chief article and foundation of the gospel is that before you take Christ as an example, you recognize and accept him as a gift, as a present that God has given you and that is your own. . . . This is the great fire of the love of God for us, whereby the heart and conscience become happy, secure and content. This is what preaching the Christian faith means.[56]

In strict order, as one's being precedes one's doing, so Christ as "gift" first nourishes your faith and makes you a Christian. Then second, Christ as "example" also exercises your loving service to your neighbor. These works "do not make you a Christian. Actually they come forth from you because you have already been made a Christian." Whereas a Christian's faith "possesses nothing of its own" (only the deeds and life of Christ), works of love do "have something of your own in them" (yet they should belong solely to the neighbor).[57]

Luther concludes that the gospel is therefore "not a book of laws and commandments which requires deeds of us, but a book of divine promises in which God promises, and gives us all his possessions and benefits in Christ."[58] To be sure, Christ and the apostles also secondarily "explain the laws," but even there the primary salvific gift of Christ transforms the subsequent ethical example of Christ.

> We see too that unlike Moses in his book, and contrary to the nature of a punitive demand Christ does not horribly force and drive us. Rather

> he teaches us in a loving and honorable way. . . . He teaches so gently
> that he entices rather than commands. He begins by saying, 'Blessed are
> the poor, Blessed are the meek,' and so on (Matt. 5:3,5). And the apos-
> tles commonly use the expression, 'I admonish, I request, I beseech,'
> and so on. But Moses says, 'I command, I forbid,' threatening and
> frightening everyone with horrible punishments and penalties.[59]

We will take ample time below to discuss the decisive difference in principle introduced here by Luther between the earlier law-oriented Mosaic
demands and the later grace-oriented dominical and apostolic admonitions
(chapter 3). Yet we must already underscore that Luther does not thereby
exclusively identify the relation of Moses and Christ with the relation
between the Old and New Testaments. The Old Testament is not all law
and the New Testament is not all gospel. As there are both the gospel of
Christ and the law of Moses in the New Testament, so there are also the
law of Moses and the gospel of Christ in the Old Testament. Holy Scripture points both forwards and backwards to its salvific center in Christ.

> Now the Gospels and epistles of the apostles . . . want themselves to
> be our guides, to direct us to the writings of the prophets and Moses
> in the Old Testament so that we might there read and see for ourselves
> how Christ is wrapped in swaddling cloths and laid in a manger (Luke
> 2:7); that is, how he is comprehended in the writings of the prophets.
>   It is there that people like us should read and study, drill ourselves,
> and see what Christ is, for what purpose he has been given, how he
> has promised, and how all Scripture tends toward him. For he himself
> says in John 5:46, "If you believe Moses, you would also believe me,
> for he wrote of me." Again, John 5:39, "Search and look up the
> Scriptures, for it is they that bear witness to me."[60]

Luther further illustrates the New Testament's fulfillment of the Old
with such passages as Isaiah 40 and 53, Luke 24, Acts 4 and 17, Romans 1,
and 1 Peter 1. So we are cautioned not to make the gospel into a law book
nor to change Christ into a Moses ("simply an instructor"). Rather, we are
encouraged to acknowledge "that the gospel itself is our guide and instructor in the Scriptures," no matter where it is to be found therein. Moreover,
the Scriptures are meant for our life-transforming proclamation. As the
gospel was originally a spoken "living word" (*viva vox*) that brought forth
the written Scriptures, so God's Word should now also be proclaimed with
joy, "for the preaching of the gospel is nothing else than Christ coming to
us, or we being brought to him."[61]

Luther went on to reinforce these Christocentric views more specifically in his *Prefaces to the New Testament*. These were begun in 1522 and then
periodically supplemented and revised until the final 1546 edition of his
complete German Bible. Once again, everything is centered in the gospel
of God, the "good message, good tidings, good news" about the crucified

and risen Christ, "who strove with sin, death, and the devil, and overcame them, and thereby rescued all those who were captive in sin, afflicted with death, and overpowered by the devil."[62]

Indeed, by employing this normative standard of the apostolic gospel, Luther was enabled to make his characteristically bold value judgments about which were "the true and noblest books of the New Testament." He did this on the explicit basis of preferring the preaching to the works in Christ's earthly ministry (to the relative detriment of the witness of the first three Gospels). Luther also especially commends an inner circle within the total biblical canon for its apostolic fidelity to the climactic gospel about Christ crucified and raised for us.

> In a word, St. John's Gospel and his first epistle, St. Paul's epistles, especially Romans, Galatians, and St. Peter's first epistle, are the books that show you Christ and teach you all that is necessary and salvatory for you to know, even if you were never to see or hear any other book or doctrine. Therefore St. James's epistle is really an epistle of straw, compared to these others, for it has nothing of the nature of the gospel about it.[63]

Following this lead, we shall introduce the most significant of the New Testament prefaces prepared by Luther, namely, his *Preface to the Epistle to the Romans* (1522). It is especially notable for setting forth the basic themes in Paul's theology of God's law and grace. Luther did so on the basis of his earlier *Lectures on Romans* (1515–16), along with his close colleague Philip Melanchthon's more recently published *Commonplaces* (*Loci communes theologici*, 1521), also notable as the first edition of the earliest systematic theology of the Lutheran church.

Luther begins with a dramatic claim: "This epistle is really the chief part of the New Testament, and is truly the purest gospel."[64] Moreover, he insists that this side of Easter we learn here "what Paul means by the words: 'law,' 'sin,' 'grace,' 'faith,' 'righteousness,' 'flesh,' 'spirit,' and the like." This is essential because "without such a grasp of these words you will never understand this letter of St. Paul, nor any other book of the Holy Scripture."[65]

We shall therefore briefly introduce these basic biblical categories here, even though their fuller development will have to await Luther's upcoming analysis of Paul's theology in both his *Lectures on Romans* (1515–16) and *Lectures on Galatians* (1535–36). Noteworthy is the closely integrated center of theological gravity. The "purest gospel" of Romans is outlined in terms of Christocentric salvation and service—how judged sinners are saved and how forgiven sinners are empowered to serve.

> 1. *Law.* The little word "law" you must not take in human fashion as a teaching about what works are to be done or not done. . . . But God judges according to what is in the depths of the heart. For this reason,

his law too makes its demands on the inmost heart, it cannot be satisfied with works, but rather punishes as hypocrisy and lies the works not done from the bottom of the heart. . . . Accustom yourself, then, to this language, that doing the works of the law and fulfilling the law are two very different things.[66]

2. *Sin.* Sin, in the Scripture, means not only the outward works of the body but also all the activities that move men to do these works, namely, the inmost heart, with all its powers. . . . And the Scriptures look especially into the heart and single out the root and source of all sin, which is unbelief in the inmost heart. . . . For this reason too, before good or bad works take place, as the good or bad fruits, there must first be in the heart faith or unbelief. Unbelief is the root, the sap, and the chief power of all sin.[67]

3. *Grace and Gifts.* This is the difference. Grace actually means God's favor, or the good will which in himself he bears towards us, by which he is disposed to give us Christ and to pour into us the Holy Spirit with his gifts.

The gifts and the Spirit increase in us every day, but they are not yet perfect since there remain in us the evil desires and sins that war against the Spirit. . . . His grace is not divided or parceled out, as are the gifts, but take us completely into favor for the sake of Christ our Intercessor and Mediator. And because of this, the gifts are begun in us.[68]

4. *Faith.* Faith is a divine work in us which changes us and makes us to be born anew of God (John 1:12-13). It kills the Old Adam and makes us altogether different men, in heart and spirit and mind and powers; and it brings with it the Holy Spirit. O, it is a living, busy, active, mighty thing, this faith. It is impossible for it not to be doing good works incessantly.

Faith is a living, daring confidence in God's grace, so sure and certain that a believer would stake his life on it a thousand times. This knowledge of and confidence in God's grace makes men glad and bold and happy in dealing with God and with all creatures.

And this is the work which the Holy Spirit performs in faith. Because of it, without compulsion, a person is ready and glad to do good to everyone, to serve everyone, to suffer everything, out of love and praise to God who has shown him this grace. Thus it is impossible to separate works from faith, quite as impossible as to separate heat and light from fire.[69]

5. *Righteousness.* Righteousness, then, is such a faith. It is called "the righteousness of God" because God gives it, and counts it as righteousness for the sake of Christ our Mediator, and makes a man to fulfill his obligation to everybody. For through faith a man becomes free from sin and comes to take pleasure in God's commandments. Thereby he gives God the honor due him. . . . Likewise he serves his fellowmen willingly, by whatever means he can.[70]

6. *Flesh and Spirit.* Flesh and spirit you must not understand as though flesh is only that which has to do with unchastity and spirit is only that which has to do what is inwardly in the heart. . . . "The flesh" is a man who lives and works, inwardly and outwardly, in the service of the flesh again and of this temporal life. "The spirit" is the man who lives and works, inwardly and outwardly, in the service of the Spirit and of the future life.[71]

By way of providing a theological bridge from Luther's New Testament to his Old Testament prefaces, we cannot do better than to quote Luther's own concluding words in this text. Whatever may be the outcome of the current ongoing debate among biblical specialists about the basic purpose of Paul's Epistle to the Romans (cf. chapter 5), Luther makes a strong case for the reciprocal interaction of both Testaments to exalt the Christ proclaimed in the New Testament: "It appears that St. Paul wanted in this one epistle to sum up briefly the whole Christian and evangelical doctrine, and to prepare an introduction to the entire Old Testament. For, without doubt, whoever has this epistle well in his heart has with him the light and power of the Old Testament."[72]

Christ Promised in the Old Testament

In his *Prefaces to the Old Testament* (1523), Luther proposes suggestions "for seeking Christ and the gospel in the Old Testament."[73] He does so in obedience to Christ (John 5:39), St. Paul (Rom. 1:2; 1 Tim. 4:13), St. Peter and St. Luke (Acts 17:11), who all themselves "base the New Testament" on communally interpreting Scriptures of the Old Testament. Indeed, Luther challenges, "what is the New Testament but a public preaching and proclamation of Christ, set forth through the sayings of the Old Testament and fulfilled through Christ?"[74]

While Luther discerns both God's law and God's grace in both Testaments, the law does predominate in the Old Testament and grace in the New. The Old Testament is chiefly a "book of laws" that teaches what we are to do and not do, whereas the New Testament chiefly teaches "where one is to get the power to fulfill the law." However, along with teaching grace, the New Testament also teaches laws and commandments "since in this life the Spirit is not perfected and grace alone cannot rule." Similarly, beside the laws, the Old Testament teaches "certain promises and words of grace, by which the holy fathers and prophets under the law were kept, like us, in the faith of Christ."[75]

After briefly sketching the contents of the first five books of the Old Testament (*Torah*), Luther highlights three features of "the books and office of Moses." Beyond the text of the books, the office (*Amt*) of Moses witnesses to its divinely ordained distinctive contribution to the biblical plan of salvation. "In the first place, Moses provides so exactly for the organization of the people under laws as to leave human reason no room to choose a single work of its own or to invent its own form of worship."[76]

Together with teaching fear, love, and trust toward God, Moses also prescribes specific ways of conducting public worship and carrying out daily life. After all, God has chosen this people and willed to be their Lord; Israel is called to be obedient. However, Moses goes so far as to prescribe rules "that are to be regarded as foolish and useless." Why? "In the second place, it should be noted that the laws are of three kinds. Some speak of temporal things. . . . There are some, however, that teach about the external worship of God. . . . Over and above these two are the laws about faith and love. All other laws must and ought to be measured by faith and love."[77]

External and formal obedience to laws does not truly meet God's primary requirements of faith and love. As a lawgiver, Moses fulfills his office as "Ruler-of-laws" by making people recognize their dislike for God's law and need for God's grace: "In the third place, the true intention of Moses is through the law to reveal sin and put to shame all presumption as to human ability."[78]

Luther comes to this radical and far-reaching conclusion in direct and explicit dependence on the apostle's consistent teachings in four of his epistles in the New Testament:

> St. Paul, in Gal. 2:17, calls Moses "an agent of sin," and his office a "dispensation of death," 2 Cor. 3:7. In Rom. 3:20 and 7:7, he says, "Through the law comes nothing more than knowledge of sin," and "By works of the law no one becomes righteous before God." . . . St. Paul calls sin "the sting of death" (1 Cor. 15:56), because it is by sin that death has all its right and power over us. . . . Rightly, then does St. Paul call the office of Moses a dispensation of sin and death (2 Cor. 3:7), for by his lawgiving he brings upon us nothing but sin and death.[79]

Nevertheless, Moses' office of bringing sin and death is still deemed by Luther to be "good and very necessary," because the law of God helps us both to "recognize sin" and to lead "an outwardly respectable life." In order to perform his office to shame human nature, Moses "not only gives [moral] laws like the Ten Commandments that speak of natural and true sins," but he also prescribes ceremonial laws that make sins of things that are in their nature not really sins.[80] Through this accusatory function of the good law of God, human nature can be brought to feel its sinfulness and long for the divine grace of God's New Testament or gospel in Christ. In the biblical history of salvation, only then can the "office of Christ" end by fulfilling the "office of Moses."

> When Christ comes the law ceases, especially the Levitical law which makes sins of things that in their nature are not sins. The Ten Com-

mandments also cease, not in the sense that they are no longer to be kept or fulfilled, but in the sense that the office (*Amt*) of Moses in them ceases; it no longer increases sin (Rom. 5:20) by the Ten Commandments, and sin is no longer the sting of death (1 Cor. 15:56). For through Christ sin is forgiven, God is reconciled, and man's heart has begun to feel kindly toward the law.[81]

In struggling with the profundity of Paul's dialectical stance regarding the law's proper use for ethics and improper abuse for salvation, Luther here introduces the categories of the "offices" of Moses and Christ to illumine the radical contrast between the Old and New Testaments within the one Bible of the Christian church. As Christ is no new Moses, so Moses is no old Christ. It is one and the same "Christ" (the Greek translation of the Hebrew "Messiah") who both fulfills the faithful hopes of Israel for a coming Messiah, but also radically corrects any replacement or supplementation of grace with law as the way of salvation revealed by the Messiah who is also our crucified and resurrected Lord and Savior. The "Christ fulfilled" in the New Testament qualitatively exceeded and revised the hope of the "Christ anticipated" in the Old Testament. "For this reason also, St. Paul calls the law of Moses 'the old testament' (2 Cor. 3:14), and Christ does the same thing when he institutes 'the new testament' (1 Cor. 11:25). It is confirmed by the death and blood of an eternal Person and an eternal land is promised and given."[82]

Following this Christocentric interpretation of the Mosaic law ("set Christ before you, for he is the man to whom it all applies, every bit of it"), we may turn next to Luther's parallel *Preface to the Prophets* (1532). In remarkable doctrinal congruity, the kingdom of Christ and apostasy from God are again afforded major twofold attention: "In the first place, the prophets proclaim and bear witness to the kingdom of Christ in which we now live, and in which all believers in Christ have heretofore lived, and will live until the end of the world."[83]

Luther derives strong comfort from the ancient prophetic witness to the one, true God, in opposition to false heresies and sects. The prophets are especially helpful in assisting us to become certain of the glory of Christ's kingdom and to realize that its coming is always preceded in this sinful world by crosses, shame, and suffering for the sake of Christ. "In the second place, the prophets show us many examples and experiences which illustrate the first commandments. For after they have prophesied of Christ's kingdom, all the rest is nothing but examples of how God has so strictly and severely confirmed his first commandment."[84]

Reading the prophets is to learn how God threatens the godless as "an angry Judge" (Exod. 20:5) and also comforts those who fear and trust their Lord as "a gracious Father" (Exod. 29:6). If there are more threats than promises in the prophets, it is because the godless always outnumber the righteous. The Old Testament prophets denounced especially the idolatry that replaced the true worship of God that was instituted in Jerusalem with other new forms and persons and times of worship. Hence, the prophets faithfully carried on what Moses had begun:

> They are nothing else than what Moses is. For they all propagate the office of Moses; they guard against the false prophets, that they may not lead the people to works, but allow them to remain in the true office of Moses, the knowledge of the law. They hold fast to this purpose of keeping the people conscious of their own impotence through a right understanding of the law, and thus driving them to Christ, as Moses does.[85]

A rapid bird's-eye view of the prophets documents their post-Mosaic role in witnessing to God's threats and promises. Isaiah "preaches a good deal to his people and rebukes their many sins," and also "prepares and supposes them to expect the coming kingdom of Christ, of which he prophesies more clearly and in more ways than any other prophet."[86] The early part of Jeremiah is "almost entirely rebuke and complaint of the wickedness of the Jews," but later he also "clearly prophesies of the person of Christ, of his kingdom, of the New Testament, and the end of the old Testament."[87]

When Ezekiel declares that Israel is to return home from its captivity in exile, he promises "the new covenant of the new Israel . . . the establishment upon earth of the new, spiritual, everlasting rule and kingdom of Christ" under and within "the old, worldly, temporal government."[88] Hosea "preached vigorously against the idolatry of his time and bravely rebuked the people," while he also "prophesied powerfully and most comfortingly about Christ and his kingdom."[89] Joel is "highly praised in the New Testament," and his citation (by St. Peter in Acts 2) shows that Joel "had to provide the first sermon ever preached in the Christian church, the one on Pentecost at Jerusalem when the Holy Spirit was given."[90]

Amos "denounces the people of Israel throughout almost the entire book until the end of the last chapter, when he prophesies of Christ and his kingdom."[91] Obadiah "at the end prophesies of Christ's kingdom, that it shall not be at Jerusalem only, but everywhere."[92] Micah constantly "refers to the coming of Christ and to his kingdom. . . . Unique among the prophets, he points with certainty to Bethlehem, naming it as the town where Christ was to be born."[93]

Though Nahum "can be understood to refer to the time of Hezekiah, after Sennacherib, nevertheless, this is a general prophecy referring also to Christ."[94] Finally Haggai "prophesies also about Christ in chapter 2, that he shall come as a 'comfort of all nations,' by which he indicates in a mystery that the kingdoms and the laws of the Jews shall have an end, and the kingdoms of all the world shall be destroyed and become subject to Christ. This has already taken place, and continues to take place until the Last Day when it will all be fulfilled."[95]

These final citations demonstrate clearly that Luther's Christocentric hermeneutic interprets the Old Testament sometimes both historically and spiritually ("time of Hezekiah . . . referring also to Christ") and, at other times, both as prophesied history and as fulfilled history ("this has already taken place"). In both cases, we have already amply documented that Luther's doctrinal commitment to a law-free gospel about Christ could never later have supported the later twentieth-century Nazi program of an Old Testament–excised Bible for its ideologically corrupted sect of "German Christians" (cf. chapter 1).

Christocentric Biblical Translation

It is against this comprehensive background that we may now turn finally to Luther's intentionally evangelical translation of the Holy Scriptures into German. Of course, it is a grammatical truism that all translation is an art rather than a science. Human language is always creatively nuanced, and every good translation is at once an interpretation. However, we have now seen that this is theologically as well as grammatically true of Luther in a special sense: He always interpreted the Old Testament promises in light of their New Testament fulfillment.

It is therefore a historical irony that some of the very opponents whom Luther charged with biblical liberalism (for example, Jerome Emser) quickly retaliated by accusing him of abandoning biblical literalism. Yet Luther admitted candidly that literalism as such was never his chief concern. What was determinative was what the author *meant* by what he said; indeed, this called for a far more demanding theological art. Luther called this the "first rule" for translating the Scriptures: "If some passage is obscure, I consider whether it treats of grace or of law, whether wrath or the forgiveness of sin, and with which it agrees better . . . for God divides his teaching into law and gospel."[96]

Luther's most extended response to his critics came in his work *On Translating: An Open Letter* (1530). At issue was especially the Pauline teaching of justification by faith in the New Testament. Luther freely acknowledges that his enemies have charged that "in many places the text has been modified or even falsified" to the shock of Christian believers. The most controversial place is Paul's doctrine in Rom. 3:28, which Luther rendered, "We hold that a man is justified without the works of the law, by faith alone." He explains:

> Here, in Rom. 3:28, I knew very well that the word "alone" (*solum*) is
> not in the Greek or Latin text; the papists did not have to teach me

that. At the same time they do not see that it conveys the sense of the text; it belongs there if the translation is to be clear and vigorous. . . . It is the nature of a German language that in speaking of two things, one of which is offered and the other denied, we use the word "alone" (*solum, allein*) along with the word "not" (*nicht*) or "no" (*kein*).[97]

Luther moves beyond philology (*particula exclusiva*) to soteriology when inserting the word "alone" (*solum*) at the heart of the Pauline gospel. "Actually the text itself and the meaning of St. Paul urgently require and demand it. For in that very passage he is dealing with the main point of Christian doctrine, namely, that we are justified by faith in Christ without any works of the law. . . . The matter itself, as well as the nature of the language, demands it."[98]

It is freely acknowledged that what Rome fears in Luther's translation is the inference that "people need not do any good works" at all. Nevertheless, Paul himself says literally "by faith" and "without the works of the law." The point of Paul (and Luther) here is certainly not to discourage a Christian's ethical love, but to deny firmly that such subsequent ethical activity is in any way co-redemptive. Of course, faith is never "alone" or without works of love, yet it is "only" by faith in Christ that we are saved. God does not judicially impute our unrighteousness to us (Ps. 32:3; Rom. 4:8), but graciously reckons Christ's righteousness to the faithful instead. "People must know that they are not saved by their good works but only by Christ's death and resurrection. . . . Faith alone, indeed, all alone, without any works, lays hold of this death and resurrection when it is preached by the gospel."[99]

In the next year, Luther composed a complementary work on the Old Testament, *Defense of the Translation of the Psalms* (1531). Once again, he emphasized the need to make the Scriptures available to the general public, completing his own first translation of the Psalter in 1524. Here again, the combination of philological skill and theological competence is considered imperative.

Luther begins by repeating his opponents' public charges that "at many places we have departed rather freely from the letter of the original." He openly acknowledges that he has done so "knowingly and deliberately."

No one should be surprised if here in Psalm 65 and in similar passages we occasionally differ from the rabbis and grammarians. . . . This is what all schoolmasters teach, that words are to serve and follow the meaning, and not the meaning the words. We know this, too, and St. Paul informs us in 2 Cor. 3:13-15, that the face of Moses is hidden from the Jews and that they seldom catch the meaning of the Scriptures, especially in the prophet.[100]

Luther extolled his contextual translation principle of "at times retaining the words quite literally, and at times rendering only the meaning." Recognizing realistically that he would likely "irritate Master Know-it-all" by his refusal simply to "stick to the words scrupulously and precisely," Luther's Christocentric interpretations were finally captive to the gospel "because we know that this psalm is singing of Christ and his kingdom."[101]

Of all the books of the Bible, the Psalter provides perhaps the strongest case for the necessity of translating not woodenly but pastorally by conveying what the text means spiritually to witness. In other words, to say the same in another language, one must often have to say it differently. This is preeminently true of such personal and intimate expressions of the believer's heart as in Psalm 5. Luther's earlier *Preface to the Psalter* (1528) sought to capture this spirit.

> A human heart is like a ship on a wild sea, driven by the storm winds from the four corners of the world. Here it is struck with fear and worry about impending disaster; there comes grief and sadness because of present evil. Here breaks a breeze of hope of anticipated happiness; there bears security and joy in present blessings.
>
> What is the greatest thing in the Psalter but this earnest speaking and these storm winds of every kind? Where does one find former words of joy than in the psalms of praise and thanksgiving? . . . On the other hand, where do you find deeper, more sorrowful, more pitiful words of sadness than in the psalms of lamentation. . . . And that they speak these words to God and with God, this, I repeat, is the best thing of all.[102]

It is this deep reverence for the Spirit's power in the Word to bring us into direct communion with the loving God that marks Luther's faithful handling of the Holy Scriptures. The Psalter of the Old Testament rightly enjoys a universal appeal "because it relates not only the works of the saints, but also their words, how they spoke with God and prayed, and still speak and pray." But most of all, as conveyed by the Holy Spirit, it is a gospel that "promises Christ's death and resurrection so clearly—and pictures his kingdom and the condition and nature of all Christendom—that it might well be called a little Bible."[103]

With these words we conclude our introduction to Luther as an evangelical catholic expositor of Holy Scripture. We have attempted to describe the biblical basis for Luther's theology in general and his theological ethics in particular. "Does it urge Christ?" is always his chief concern. "For this much is beyond question: that all the Scriptures point to Christ alone (John 1:46)."[104]

This Christocentric view of God's Word experienced by sinner and righteous as both law (curse) and gospel (promise) within both the Old and New Testaments is at once biblically simple and doctrinally complex. On the one hand, Luther's pictorial description of Scripture as "the swaddling cloths and manger in which Christ lies" can never be forgotten by even a seven-year-old child.[105] Yet, on the other hand, its theological profundity also challenges current Christian practitioners of historical-critical biblical scholarship to acknowledge the inspired and transcendent uniqueness of Holy Scripture as the church's written Word of God. "The Holy Scripture is God's Word, written, and, so to speak, lettered, and put into the form of letters, just as Christ, the eternal Word of God, is clothed in the garment of his humanity."[106] When so considered, the normative impact of Genesis on Luther's mature theological ethic is enormous, beginning with his Christocentric depiction of created humanity in its original state of righteous integrity before God (*iustitia originalis coram Deo*).

Part Two

The World's Two Kingdoms
(God or Satan)

Chapter 3

◀━━━▶

Adam and Eve: God's Command of Love

O ur previous chapter introduced Luther's Christocentric interpretation of the Bible with various examples taken at large from
his *Lectures on Genesis* (1535–45). This chapter will focus directly
on Luther's exposition of Genesis 1–2, covering God's primal creation by
loving command, before concluding with its New Testament fulfillment in
Matthew 5–7 and Romans 12–13.[1]

In this text on the biblical-theological ethos of Christian ethics, we will
highlight the divine creation of persons in God's loving image for life in
community. Only then can we rightly interpret such related texts as "You
shall be holy, for I the LORD your God am holy" (Lev. 19:12). Moreover, it
was only because the holy Lord "loved your ancestors" that ancient Israel
was elected and delivered out of bondage in Egypt (Deut. 4:37). We shall
also coherently seek to discern the Creator's purpose for human life, as
originally created through Christ (John 1:3) and later redeemed by Christ
(John 3:16), following humanity's fall into sin. The church's Christocentric
focus is not arbitrary; it is prompted by Luther's own evangelical understanding of what vital center makes theology uniquely Christian: "The
proper subject of theology is man guilty of sin and condemned, and God
the Justifier and Savior of man the sinner. Whatever is asked or discussed in
theology outside this subject is error and poison. Scripture points to this."[2]

Created in God's Image

Luther begins his commentary on the first creation account (Gen. 1:1—2:3)
by noting that it is of the "upmost importance" and yet "very difficult to
understand." Fundamental is the scriptural affirmation "that the world had
a beginning and that it was created by God out of nothing (*ex nihilo*)."
Then, in a single sentence, Luther observes in passing that Augustine's
"opinion" was that the six-day creation account was allegorical or figurative, while "what seems right to us" is rather that "Moses spoke in a literal
sense." Leaving the thorny subject immediately, Luther simply counsels, "If

58

we do not comprehend the reason for this, let us remain pupils and leave the job of teacher to the Holy Spirit."

Clearly, who and why and not how and when are the Reformer's primary concern in God's primal creation. He has absolutely no interest in cosmological speculation. His sole purpose is to praise the Creator: "The very simple meaning of what Moses says, therefore, is this: Everything that is, was created by God."[3]

Moreover, as a creedal Christian, Luther identifies the Creator God as being Triune from all eternity. While exegetically unfounded here, it is a lucid example of Luther's reading of the Bible with the eyes of faith as the church's written Word of God.

> Indeed, it is the great consensus of the church that the mystery of the Trinity is set forth here. The Father creates heaven and earth out of nothing through the Son, whom Moses calls the Word. Over these the Holy Spirit broods. As a hen broods her eggs, keeping them warm in order to hatch her chicks. . . . For it is the office of the Holy Spirit to make alive. . . .
>
> Of course, Moses does not say in so many words that the Father, the Son, and the Holy Spirit are the one true God; this was to be reserved for the teaching of the Gospel.[4]

Hence, though there was a time when the world was not, there never was a time when God was not. "In the beginning" (Gen. 1:1) should not raise such unanswerable speculations as "What was God doing before the beginning of the world? Was he in a state of rest or not?" Augustine relates in his *Confessions* that someone had answered to this effect: "God was making hell ready for those who pried into meddlesome questions."[5] Clearly enjoying the story, Luther draws the important doctrinal conclusion that God is wholly incomprehensible apart from divine self-revelation.

> God also does not manifest Himself except through His works and the Word. . . . It is folly to argue much about God outside and before time, because this is an effort to understand the Godhead without a covering, or the uncovered divine essence.
>
> The works of God are set before us so that we can grasp them. Such works are: that He created the heaven and the earth, that He sent his Son, that He speaks through His Son, that He baptizes, that He absolves from sin through the Word. He who does not apprehend these facts will never apprehend God.[6]

When God says, "Let there be," immediately "there was" (Gen. 1:3). As Paul later testified, "He calls the things which are not that they be" (Rom. 4:17). It is "through his speaking that God makes something out of nothing."[7] Words among us are realities with God. This is because God's Word is creative and omnipotent. Paul witnesses to the same Creator who commands light out of darkness in both the old and the new creation: "For it is the God who said, 'Let light shine out of darkness,' who has shone in our hearts to give the light of the knowledge of the glory of God in the face of Jesus Christ" (2 Cor. 4:6). For Luther, this confirms the Christian faith: "that Christ is true God, who is with the Father from eternity, before the world was made, that through Him, who is the wisdom and the Word of the Father, the Father made everything."[8]

Luther concludes that amidst all the ambiguities of biblical interpretation ("the rest of the ideas are without profit and uncertain"), the central message of the Holy Spirit is clear: "that God, by speaking, created all things that are worked through the Word, and that all His works are some words of God, created by the uncreated Word."[9] Why? It was all due to "the divine solicitude and benevolence toward us, because He provided such an attractive dwelling place for the future human being before the human being was created. . . . And all this generosity is intended to make man recognize the goodness of God and live in the fear of God."[10]

It is then and only then that God "summons Himself to a council" and climactically announces, "Let us make a man according to our image and likeness" (Gen. 1:26). This text introduces the concluding section of Genesis 1, and Luther's theologically profound meditation on God's creation of primal humankind in the state of original righteousness (*iustitia originalis*).

"In the first place, there is indicated here an outstanding difference between man and all the other creatures."[11] Unlike the beasts, humans are alone created in God's image (*imago Dei*) by God's special plan and providence. Along with a physical life shared by some other creatures, persons in God's image are also uniquely gifted with an eternal and spiritual life in communion with God. They have a personal and communal hope that transcends history. Christians may especially "believe in a spiritual life after this life and a destination for this life in paradise, which was devised and ordained by God, and that we confidently look for it through the merit of Christ."[12]

"In the second place, the word 'Let us make' is aimed at making sure the mystery of our faith, by which we believe that from eternity there is one God and that there are three separate persons in one Godhead: the Father, the Son, and the Holy Spirit."[13] Luther does not believe that God is speaking with angels, or the earth, or even in the royal plural grammatical form. Acknowledging that some will consider these evidences "too dark to prove so important an article of faith," Luther simple retrojects his New Testament faith back into the creation account.

"In the third place, there is stirred up here, as it were, a sea of questions."[14] The central issue is, just what is this "image and likeness of God"?

For example, Augustine's "image" keeps Aristotle's philosophical classification of the powers of the soul: memory, the mind or intellect, and will. The "likeness" lies in the gifts of grace that perfect human nature: memory is provided with hope, the intellect with faith, and the will with love. However, Luther holds that these "not unattractive speculations" contribute very little toward "the correct explanation" of the image of God. Moreover, such theories can also become the basis for "the very dangerous opinions of the [early church] fathers," as when the human free will that is attributed to God's image allegedly "cooperated as the preceding and efficient cause of salvation."[15]

At this critical point, Luther intentionally reverses his field and proceeds to interpret Genesis 1 (creation of Adam in God's image) in the subsequent light of both Genesis 3 (the fall) and 1 Corinthians 15 (restoration of God's image in Christ). In his Christocentric commentary on the Old Testament, Luther does not move logically forward from the sickness to the cure, but theologically backward from the remedy to the malady. In the order of salvation, he does not measure Christ in terms of Adam, but Adam in terms of Christ.

For Luther, therefore, it is not Plato and Aristotle (via Augustine and Aquinas), but rather Jesus Christ, the last Adam, true human as well as true God, who alone reveals what God originally intended the first Adam to image (Rom. 5:12-21). Faith confesses that God's image is truly reflected only in "the manifestation of the glory of God in the face of Jesus Christ" (2 Cor. 4:5-6). To glorify this Christ aright as Lord and Savior requires that we also acknowledge retroactively both the gravity of Adam's original sin and the corollary loss of Adam's original righteousness in the presence of God (coram Deo). "In this way," he contends, "a very beautiful and very accurate picture of original righteousness can be inferred from the deprivation we now feel in our own nature."[16]

> Since the loss of this image through sin, we cannot understand it to any extent. Memory, will, and mind we have indeed; but they are most seriously weakened, yes, to put it more clearly, they are utterly leprous and unclean. . . . Therefore when we speak about that image, we are speaking about something unknown. Not only have we not experience of it, but we continually experience the opposite; and so we hear nothing but bare words. . . . What we are stating faith and the Word teach, which, as if from a distance, point out the glory of the divine image.[17]

Proceeding, then, by way of dramatic "comparison with our present weakness," Luther grandly depicts the image of God, according to which Adam was created before the fall, as a "unique work of God" both in Adam's physical life and in his spiritual life. The former is embellished with fanciful and extravagant imagination. Living within a Paradise in which allegedly "the sun was brighter, the water purer, the trees more fruitful, and the fields more fertile," Adam's intellect was the clearest, his memory the best, his will the most straightforward, suffering no pain of anxiety or fear of death. His eyesight surpassed that of an eagle, and he was stronger than lions and bears. In short, fantasized Luther, Adam must have enjoyed inner qualities "of the purest kind" and the most "beautiful and superb qualities of body."[18]

Turning more seriously to the spiritual image of God, Luther describes Adam relationally (*in relatione*) in communion with both God (*coram Deo*) and Eve (*coram hominibus*). Created in holy love for sharing holy love ("not good that the man should be alone"), Adam's cohumanity is never to be solitary (Gen. 2:18). In this way, Adam enjoyed a life of "supreme pleasure . . . in obedience to God and submission to his will."

Moreover, engulfed by God's goodness and justice, Adam and Eve together enjoyed "a singular union of hearts and wills." Luther also contends, "In Adam there was an enlightened reason, a true knowledge of God, and a most sincere desire to love God and his neighbor, so that Adam embraced Eve and at once acknowledged her to be of his own flesh." Indeed, Luther is satisfied to conclude:

> Therefore my understanding of the image of God is this: that Adam had it in his being and that he not only knew God and believed that He was good, but that he also lived a life that was wholly godly; that is, that he was without the fear of death or of any other danger, and was content with God's favor (*favor Dei*).
>
> What is original righteousness (*iustitia originalis*)? Some make it a quality; others make it something else. If we follow Moses, we should take original righteousness to mean that man was righteous, truthful, and upright not only in body but especially in soul, that he knew God, that he obeyed God with the utmost joy, and that he understood the works of God even without prompting.[19]

"After the fall," in vivid contrast, Adam is no longer blessed "with a will obedient to God, and without any evil thought." His will, reason, and senses are now impaired and confined in bondage to sin, death, and the devil. It is a "serious and pernicious leprosy" that results in "great dangers" and "execrable lust and other sinful passions and inordinate emotions that arise in the hearts of all." These evils are rather "the image of the devil, who stamped them on us." In light of the need for the cross of Christ, Luther cannot "minimize original sin (*peccatum originale*)." Both from "the sins it produces (*peccata actualia*) and from the punishments it incurs," Adam's original sin "is by far the greatest sin." For Luther, it is enough to cite "hatred against God and blasphemy" as the "outstanding moral failing which truly demonstrates that the image of God was lost."[20]

Once again, it is imperative to note that original sin is a cross-determined affirmation of faith for Luther. It is Calvary that reveals both who God is and who humans are in relation before God. How great was the evil that necessitated the atoning death of the Son of God in human history? Its enormity is perceived only with the eyes of faith opened by the gospel. "Until this is accomplished in us, we cannot have an adequate knowledge of what that image of God was which was lost through sin in Paradise." God's image "was something most excellent, in which were included eternal life, everlasting freedom from fear, and everything that is good. However, through sin this image was so obscured and corrupted that we cannot grasp it even with our intellect."[21]

It is also noteworthy that Luther's spontaneous commentary here on original sin (based on Gen. 3) takes place already in the context of the Bible's very first mention of Adam's creation in the image of God (Gen. 1:26a). This is *before* the biblical narrative has even had the chance in the very same verse to introduce the dominical mandate for male and female humankind to exercise "dominion" over nonhuman creation (Gen. 1:26b). Nevertheless, Luther goes on to praise the Creator God who has previously assigned Adam and Eve the awesome responsibility to become the co-rulers of the earth with his holy and loving command: "Have dominion" (Gen. 1:28). God's gracious and loving command to be the Creator's coworkers is foundational for our ethical life here on earth. Our lives are to be lived "according to the command of the eternal God, to bring about the obedience of faith" (Rom. 16:26). Even if this is now a "marred blessing" because of the "enormity of original sin," humanity is lovingly called to image God's very nature in society through God's shared dominion of justice and wisdom. "Here the rule is assigned to the most beautiful creature, who knows God and is the image of God, in whom the similitude of the divine nature shines forth through his enlightened reason, through his justice and his wisdom. Adam and Eve become the rulers of the earth, the sea, and the air. But this dominion is given to them not only by way of advice but also by express command (*mandatum*)."[22]

In brief, the interpersonal and bi-dimensional setting commanded dominically for humanity in Genesis 1 is at once both religiously before God (*coram Deo*) and ethically in society (*coram hominibus*). In their disobedience and unrighteousness (*coram Deo*), sinful persons certainly cannot earn their own salvation "in obedience to God and submission to His will." Nevertheless, their "intellect and will indeed have remained," however impaired, and they are still able to generate much beneficial peace, freedom, and justice in society (*coram hominibus*). Our enlightened rationality is to serve our faithful and loving relationality. Notably God's command (*mandatum*) for us to become God's responsible coworkers in society "remains till now" to govern all human beings, especially faithful Christians aided by the Holy Spirit. Our human vocation is to share in God's historical dominion to God's eternal glory.

This bi-relational responsibility is also emphasized by Luther as he
moves on to declare that "the gospel has brought about the restoration of
that image." On the basis of the promise proclaimed by Paul (1 Cor. 15:45),
Luther affirms that the new person in Christ will be renewed into the life-
giving spirit of the risen Christ, the last Adam, "that is, he will be a spiritual man when he reverts to the image of God. He will be similar to God
in life, righteousness, holiness, wisdom, etc."[23]

In direct opposition to any and all forms of privatistic ethical quietism,
Luther insists that the reborn Christian's restoration of God's holy and loving image involves her or him simultaneously in both eternal life and historical service. We are made and being remade for life in communion with
both God and other persons, as we faithfully fulfill God's loving command
to "have dominion" through the responsible exercise of our "enlightened
reason, justice and wisdom."

> The Gospel has brought about the restoration of that image. . . . We
> are born again into eternal life or rather into the hope of eternal life
> by faith, that we may live in God and with God and be one with him,
> as Christ says (John 17:21).
>
> And indeed, we are reborn not only for life but also for righteous
> ness, because faith acquires Christ's merit and knows that through
> Christ's death, we have been set free. From this source our other righ
> teousness has its origin, namely, that newness of life through which
> we are zealous to obey God and we are taught by the Word and aided
> by the Spirit.[24]

Yet Luther is a biblical realist with no perfectionistic illusions. Only the
Savior is sinless. While no longer reigning (*regnans*), sin still persists in the life
of the redeemed, "so the godly have within themselves that unfinished
image which God will on the Last Day bring to perfection in those who
have believed His Word." Luther teaches that like the kingdom of God
itself, the Christian's righteousness (*iustitia Christiana*) is already inaugurated,
but not yet consummated. "This righteousness has merely its beginning in
this life, and it cannot attain perfection in this flesh. . . . The image of the
new creature begins to be restored by the gospel in this life, but it will not
be finished in this life."[25]

It is in this unsentimental spirit that Luther concludes his commentary
on Genesis 1. During the lifelong discipleship of being restored by the
Spirit to the image of God, our new life in Christ finds meaning and direction only in our own free and joyful obedience to God's loving command.
Through our responsible use of Spirit-enlightened reason, justice, and wisdom, so today, too, Christians are called to obey the gracious command to
cooperate with a dominion-sharing God as accountable vicegerents of cre-

ation (*cooperatio hominum cum Deo*). Hence, we are not to plunder, but to nurture nature, as God's loaned property. We are to demonstrate the same kind of delegated "dominion" (not domination) over nonhuman creation as the Lord *(dominus)* exercises over those human creatures who alone are made in God's holy and loving image. Therefore, God's loving command calls for humanity's accountable responsibility: responsible for God's creation while accountable to creation's God. In short, "God saw everything that he had made, and indeed, it was very good" (Gen. 1:31).

Mandated for Life in Community

Luther begins his exposition of Genesis 2 by extolling God's ongoing care of the earth after its creation through the creative power of God's Word. Since God is not time-bound, the Word spoken in the beginning is still operative in existence: "He spoke, and it came into being (Ps. 33:9); and as Christ says, "My Father is working still, and I work" (John 5:17). Consequently, the omnipotent God "governs and preserves the heaven and earth through the effectiveness of his Word. He has, therefore, ceased to establish, but He has not ceased to govern. . . . Almighty is the power and effectiveness of the Word which thus preserves and governs the entire creation."[26]

This paean of praise to humanity's Creator and Preserver affords Luther the opportunity to clarify the temporal limits of human free will (*voluntas und liberum arbitrium in externis*). He employs the Scriptures to distinguish what is beneath us (*coram hominibus*) from what is above us (*coram Deo*). In historical and ethical matters, persons enjoy limited free will; in eternal and religious matters, God's will alone rules. Luther thereby rejected both ethical quietism and religious synergism. This is a contentious issue "with which our opponents concern themselves so extensively," and therefore we shall also revisit it at far greater length below. Our chief concern here is to cite its inner coherence with Luther's Genesis 1 treatment of the ethical implications of our obedient freedom as persons made together for cooperative service in the image of God.

> In a certain way we indeed have a free will in those things that are beneath us. By the divine commission we have been appointed lords of the fish of the sea, of the birds of the heavens, and of the harts of the field. . . . But in those matters that pertain to God and are above us, no human being has a free will; he is indeed like clay in the hand of the potter, in a state of merely passive potentiality, not active potentiality. For there we do not choose, we do not do anything; but we are chosen, we are equipped, we are born again, we accept, as Isaiah says (64:8): "Thou art the Potter; we Thy clay."[27]

Having established both the basis and the limits of our ethical responsibility, Luther is now ready to analyze those divinely decreed patterns of life in human community within which persons co-created in God's image might properly worship their Creator and serve their fellow creatures. They are the societal embodiments of the Triune God's sovereign command. For humans are lovingly commanded to "have dominion" in divinely ordained "mandates" or "ordinances" (*mandata Dei*) that require our faithful obedience in both Christian and civil righteousness.

Reflecting these theological origins in Luther, but in the more nuanced anti-Nazi terminology of Lutheran Dietrich Bonhoeffer, "we speak of divine mandates rather than of divine orders because the word 'mandate' refers more clearly to a divinely imposed task rather than to a determination of being."[28] It recalls Luther's dynamic view of God's "continual creation" (*creatio continua*), for him "to create is always to do something new" (*creare est semper novum facere*). By thus explicitly highlighting the governing will of a righteous God behind all concrete and changing institutional forms, Christians intentionally avoid any uncritical capitulation to or endorsement of any and all alleged ontological "orders of creation" (nineteenth-century German Lutheranism). Consequently, Christian citizens are not commanded to obey the unjust governments of sinful tyrants and dictators when they become wholly divorced from the essential purposes of the Creator as ideologically secularized and demonically autonomous public institutions (for example, "governing authority," yes; but racist, dictatorial, and imperialistic Nazi Fascism, no!).

Following the narrative development of Genesis, Luther deals sequentially with "God's mandates" of the church, marriage, family, and labor before the fall, and then with armed civil government ("the sword") only after the fall. They are "God's institution, work, and ordinance" for the redemption, creation, and preservation of human righteousness (*iustitia*). Since our focus is on Luther's perennial theological ethics, rather than his own dated (and inevitably flawed) sixteenth-century social ethics, we will concentrate on their basic biblical foundations. Current reapplications of this normative material (as later necessary in opposing Nazism) may then be repeatedly developed and critically evaluated by others elsewhere.

1. God's first mandate for humankind is the church (*ecclesia*). It is established by the Word as a God-centered form of worship. Luther contends that "from the beginning of the world the Sabbath was intended for the knowledge and worship of God."[29] Moreover, "while Genesis does not say so in so many words, it does say that 'God blessed the seventh day and sanctified it'" (2:3).

Significant for Luther is that "to sanctify" means "to set aside for sacred purposes, for the worship of God." Therefore, if Adam had remained in the state of holy innocence, he would have held the seventh day sacred. For Adam, "this Word was Gospel and Law together." That is, "on this day he would have given his descendants instructions about the will and worship of God; he would have praised God; he would have given thanks; he would have sacrificed, etc."[30] For unlike the beasts, humans were co-created uniquely in the image of God for God's praise and communion.

> Because the Sabbath command remains for the church, it denoted that spiritual life is to be restored to us through Christ. . . . On the seventh day he wanted men to bring themselves both with His Word and with the forms of worship established by Him, so that we might give first thought to the fact that this nature was created chiefly for acknowledging and glorifying God.
>
> Moreover, this is also written that we might preserve in our minds a sure hope of the future and eternal life. . . . Therefore that God gives His Word, that He commands us to occupy ourselves with the Word, that He issues orders for sanctifying the Sabbath and for His worship—all this clearly proves that there remains a life after this life and that man was created not for this physical life only, like other animals, but for eternal life, just as God, who has ordered and ordained these practices, is eternal. . . . This is the real purpose of the seventh day: that the Word of God be preached and heard.[31]

Luther reinforces these Sabbath meditations by considering God's creation of "the tree of knowledge of good and evil" in the midst of the Garden of Eden. Noteworthy is that such knowledge must be faithfully and continually sought for from God, for it is not an inherent part of the human's natural endowment. As the Sabbath encouraged Adam's inner spiritual worship, so the tree is put before Adam in order that he might have some physical way of "indicating his worship of God and of demonstrating his obedience by an outward work . . . as it were, of worshiping God by not eating anything from it." Similarly, just as Christ instituted Baptism and Holy Communion as external signs of God's Word for the New Testament church, so too "this tree of knowledge of good and evil was Adam's church, altar, and pulpit. Here he has to yield to God the obedience he owes, give recognition to the Word and will of God, give thanks to God, and call upon God for aid against temptation."[32]

As in the Priestly narrative (Gen. 1:28), so here in the Jahwist (Gen. 2:16), Adam is personally addressed by the accountable form of a divine command (*mandatum*). In the first, he is appointed God's coworking vicegerent over the earth; in the second, he is warned that his delegated authority has boundaries that dare not be trespassed. In commanding Adam not to eat from this one tree in the garden, the Creator God is symbolically reinforcing the limits of the creature Adam's finite freedom. It is God alone, not Adam and Eve, who dominically decrees "the knowledge of good and evil." Nevertheless, this is also the site where this loving and communing God whom Adam is called to image could also be adored in the beauty of holiness as the beneficent Lord of life.

> Here we have the establishment of the church before there was any
> government of the home and of the state . . . without walls and with-
> out any pomp, in a very spacious and delightful place. . . . The church
> was established first because God wanted to show by this sign as it
> were, that man was created for another purpose than the rest of the
> living beings. Because the church is established by the Word of God,
> it is certain that man was created for an immortal and spiritual life.[33]

It is highly characteristic of Luther to portray God as a preacher: "Here
the Lord is preaching to Adam and setting the Word before him." This
short sermon of a "single command" proclaims the sovereign lordship of
the God whose holy and loving will is the God-imaging basis of all human
good and evil.[34] This is again foundational for Luther's theological ethics.

Had Adam not fallen into sin, he surely also "would have praised God
and lauded him for his dominion over all the creatures on the earth which
had been given to mankind." Moreover, "Psalms 148 and 149 suggest a
kind of liturgy for such thanksgiving, where the sun, the moon, the stars,
the fish, and the dragons are commanded to praise the Lord." This alone
God commands of Adam: "that he praise God, that he thank Him, that he
rejoice in the Lord, and that he obey Him by not eating from the forbidden tree." As for his later descendants, Adam the preacher would certainly
have admonished them "to live a holy and sinless life, to work faithfully in
the garden, to watch it carefully, and to beware with the greatest care of the
tree of knowledge of good and evil."[35]

2. God's second mandate for humankind is marriage (oeconomia),
extended medievally to include family, labor, and business. "After the
church has been established, the household government is also set up, when
Eve is added to Adam as his companion."[36] For Luther, it is theologically
essential to note that in this holy order and estate, "Eve, too, was made by
God as partaker of the divine image and of the divine similitude, likewise
of the ruler over everything." Indeed, it follows for Luther that just like
Adam, Eve was also set apart by God as a coworker both for parenthood
and for ministry. "Adam and Eve are not only parents, nor do they merely
provide for their children and educate them for this present life; but they
also perform the office of priests. Inasmuch as they are filled with the Holy
Spirit and are enlightened by the knowledge of Christ, who is to come,
they set before their children this very hope of a future deliverance and
exhort them to show their gratitude to so merciful a God."[37]

By unlovely contrast, however, Luther can cite no biblical warrant to
support his own late-medieval personal opinion that the female sex "is
inferior to the male sex," since obviously there is none. Had the woman
not sinned, of course, Eve would have been "the equal of Adam in all
respects." At the same time though, Luther does immediately condemn

Aristotle and other pagans who slander woman as a "necessary evil," a "maimed man," or even as a "monster." As a decade-long husband himself since 1525, Luther fumes, "Let them themselves be monsters and sons of monsters—these men who make such malicious statements and ridicule a creature of God in which God Himself took delight as in a most excellent work, moreover, one which we see created by a special counsel of God."[38]

Following at once God's initial command of the first human beings is the accompanying divine mandate, "Be fruitful" (Gen. 1:28). This added blessing is a related "command of God" to the husband and wife "in which the begetting of offspring is linked with the highest respect and wisdom, indeed with the knowledge of God."[39]

Once again, reflecting his own (and Paul's) patriarchal familial structure, Luther centers the value served by God's creation of Eve as Adam's wife in the "common good" of bearing children. "For God makes a husband of lonely Adam and joins him to a wife, who was needed to bring about the increase of the human race. . . . God is speaking of the common good or that of the species, not of Adam's personal good."[40] Indeed, it is only after creation is "corrupted by sin" that it is also benightedly acknowledged by Luther that women are also providentially necessary for other purposes. "Woman is needed not only to secure increase but also for companionship and for protection. The management of the household must have the ministration of the dear ladies. In addition—and this is lamentable—woman is also necessary for an antidote against sin. . . . In this respect Paul says (1 Cor. 7:2): 'Because of fornication let each one have his own wife.'"[41]

To be sure, Luther clearly does go far beyond his own age's "callous and inhuman attitude, worse than barbarous," which results in "aspersions against the female sex, aspersions which ungodly celibacy has augmented. . . . This is a doctrine of demons." In opposition, Luther is robustly supportive of the intentionality of God in creating sexual persons for the intimate "one flesh" relationship of husband and wife, which would have been both "most sacred" and "most delightful." Luther can even wax eloquent in his insistence: "For truly in all nature there was no activity more excellent and more admirable than procreation. After the proclamation of the name of God, it is the most important activity Adam and Eve in the state of innocence could carry on—as free from sin in doing this as they were in praising God."[42]

Luther elsewhere presents his more balanced social ethical position on marriage for Christians after the fall as both a "remedy against sin" of persisting lust (under God's law), as well as an "office of faith" for loving service (under God's gospel).[43] Basic to our primary purpose here in theological ethics is Luther's biblical affirmation that "the lawful joining of a man and a woman is a divine ordinance and institution." That God brought Eve to Adam is a "sort of description of a betrothal" (Gen. 2:22) that is "established by God Himself" and later reaffirmed by Christ's word, "What God has joined let no man part" (Matt. 19:6).[44]

Coupled with marriage and the family in Luther's late medieval ethos are labor and business. "The LORD God took man and placed him in the Garden of Eden to work it and to guard it" (Gen. 2:15). However, in these particular lectures on Genesis, Luther deals at far greater length with the tedious nature of work after the fall rather than, as elsewhere, with labor as an earlier expression of "man's greatest delight" in Paradise. For Adam, "work would have been a supreme joy, more welcome than any leisure." As a matter of ethical principle, Luther also insists that "man was created not for leisure but for work, even in the state of innocence. Therefore the idle sort of life, such as that of monks and nuns, deserves to be condemned."[45]

3. God's third mandate for humankind is civil government (*politia*). Decisive for Luther's chiefly negative depiction is his basic affirmation that "there was no government of the state before sin, for there was no need of it. Civil government is a remedy required by our corrupted nature (*remedium peccati*)."[46] Of course, as we have already seen, central to Adam's creation in God's image was his own commanded commission by God to "have dominion" or governance over nonhuman creation through the faithful exercise of his "fair and equitable reason in promoting the common good." That command for our responsible rule still holds after the fall. However, what Luther means additionally here by "civil government" is the determinative Pauline view of the coercive power of the armed state, backed by "the sword," for compelling the compliance of evil persons in human society.

> This is the one and foremost function of government, to hold sin in check, as Paul says (Rom. 13:4): "Government bears the sword for the punishment of the wicked." Therefore if men had not become evil through sin, there would have been no need of civil government; but Adam, together with his descendants, would have lived in utmost serenity and would have authorized more by moving one finger than all the swords, instruments of torture, and axes can achieve now.[47]

Later, in chapter 6, we will have ample opportunity to develop and evaluate Luther's view of God's third mandate for the armed might ("sword") of civil authority. This can be presented most effectively, however, only after our chapter 4 first develops Luther's analysis of humanity's fall into original sin in Genesis 3. Throughout he remains faithful to the authoritative biblical and cultural realism formed by Paul and traditioned by Augustine in the Western church.

Before that, however, Luther's treatment of God's two basic mandates before the fall (church and marriage) enables us even at this early stage to emphasize one important conclusion, especially in anticipation of subsequent interconfessional and even intraconfessional controversies in theological ethics. We have amply documented that there is absolutely no basis in Luther for any kind of nonbiblical natural theology, which would support any allegedly autonomous "order of creation" (for example, the state) that could rightly claim to be a naturalistic "law unto itself" (for example, Nazified *Eigengesetzlichkeit*), and therefore not morally accountable as one of the scripturally revealed mandates of the universal will of God the Creator (*mandata Dei*). It is freely acknowledged that society-at-large is not to be subjected to any intrusive clericalism from the institutional church. Nevertheless, the divinely ordained mandates of humanity *are* institutionally accountable to the moral direction (not legislated directives) of the universal will of God the Creator and Preserver for the common good, as revealed in Holy Scripture and solemnly proclaimed by the church of Jesus Christ.

We recall Luther's continuing ethical stress on Adam's "obedience to God and submission to his will" in joyful response to God's holy and loving "command." This provides the salutary reminder that already in the primal state of original righteousness (*iustitia originalis*), human creatures who were made (and now also Christians who are being remade) in God's holy image, were/are *never* divinely intended to be ethically autonomous. Indeed, we shall see below that it was precisely the creature's vain quest for such godless autonomy that was at the core of the human fall into sin (Gen. 3). Rather, all interdependent humans are called to image God's holy and loving will for societal peace, justice, and freedom as God's righteous coworkers in the "obedience of faith" (Rom. 1:5). That is why Christ always lived by teaching "Your will be done" (Matt. 6:10), and also prepared to die by praying, "Not my will but yours be done" (Luke 22:42). What, then, constitutes the abiding ethical coherence within God's commanded will before the fall of the first Adam and after the resurrection of Jesus, the final Adam?

God's Command before the Law

In this chapter's concluding two sections, we will explore God's loving adaptations in dealing with human creatures simultaneously both as righteous saints under God's gospel and as unrighteous sinners under God's law (*simul justus et peccator*). Why? Because as a trinitarian Christian, Luther let Scripture interpret itself, and he reads Genesis 1–2 before the fall as deduced from its later New Testament fulfillment in Matthew 5–7 and Romans 12–13.

After the Christ-event, God's original intention for humankind is most clearly inferred from its realization in the message and mission of Jesus

Christ. As the source of the church's authoritative Word of God, how does the biblical witness to the climactic final Adam of God's new creation both radically correct and fulfill its testimony to the first Adam of primal creation? To provide Luther's understanding of this central biblical issue, we delve more deeply into his evangelical catholic exposition of God's will for Adam in the primal state of creation. "And he commanded him, saying: Eat from every tree in Paradise, but from the tree of the knowledge of good and evil do not eat" (Gen. 2:16-17).

Had Adam remained righteous, Luther teaches, this "single command" (paralleling God's personal address in Gen. 1:28) would have revealed to him "as if written on a tablet," the goodness of a gracious and loving God.[48] Luther's anachronistic allusion here to the later form of the Mosaic Law ("written on a tablet") compels us to face a major theological ethical issue at hand: What are God's people required to do ethically, whether before the fall, after the fall, or since the Christ-event?

Even more concretely from Luther's Christocentric biblical perspective, how are Christians to reconcile Paul's post-Mosaic and especially post-exilic depiction in Galatians 3 of God's cursing law (*nomos*) with this Genesis 1–2 account of God's primal, gracious and loving command (*mandatum*)? Legalistically, need the later apostle's "faith apart from works prescribed by the law" (Rom. 3:28) inevitably lead to immoral license? We recall Paul's own spirited response to such contemporary attacks: "For sin will have no dominion over you, since you are not under law but under grace. What then? Should we sin because we are not under law but under grace? By no means!" (Rom. 6:14-15).

To introduce us to the complexities of this profound issue, the older Luther recalls "an instance from my own life, when I was shaken by a fanatic (*Schwaermer*) with a similar antinomian [Luther's designation for "lawless"] interpretation of God's gracious will for the unregenerate Adam." This was the Protestant fanatic's ahistorical and simplistic syllogism: "Both statements are Paul's: that no Law has been given to the just (1 Tim. 1:19), and that where there is no Law, there is also no transgression (Rom. 4:15). . . . No Law has been given for the just; Adam was just; therefore no Law has been given to him, but only a sort of exhortation."[49] Luther laments that such antinomians "do not quote Scripture in its entirety," and that they thereby can easily mislead simple Christians to accept "the awful conclusion that eating from the fruit was not even a sin, inasmuch as there was no Law."[50]

For Luther, it is incumbent on a good dialectician to make the proper theological and ethical distinctions regarding the New Testament and especially Pauline view of the various epochs within God's salvation history (*Heilsgeschichte*). "What Paul says about the Law which came in after (Gal. 3:17), they [the antinomians] deceitfully and blasphemously apply to the Law which was given in Paradise. . . . Paul is speaking strictly of a Law for which there was need after nature had become corrupted by sin."[51]

Luther warns that fanatics abuse the Scriptures whenever they tear a truncated text out of its distinctive historical and theological context. Paul's fuller text (1 Tim. 1:9-10) actually reads: "The law has not been given for the just person, but for murderers, adulterers, etc.," that is, for confronting humanity in sin after the fall. Yet it was *before* the fall that Adam and Eve had already received God's loving command (Gen. 1:28; 2:16), and it was precisely this divine command (*mandatum*) that they sinfully disobeyed.

Prompted by this self-serving display of exegetical license, Luther is keen to rescue God's pre-fall command from antinomianism without resorting himself to an unevangelical legalism in treating the primal and eschatological law of creation (*lex non scripta*). Since the Word of God must now be normed through the words of the Scriptures, evangelical discernment is imperative. Ethical confusion inevitably arises when different parts of the Scriptures use the same rich and traditional term "law" to depict God's eschatological will for humanity in theologically distinguishable, but not always pastorally separable, ways in historical narrative and doctrinal discourse. For Luther:

1. Inclusively, *law* (*Torah*) in the Old Testament can broadly cover both God's gracious command (*mandatum*) in primal creation and God's judging accusations in fallen creation.

2. Exclusively, *law* (*nomos*) in the Pauline New Testament can also refer narrowly and strictly to God's "strange work" (*opus alienium*) as sin's accusing Judge, in contrast to God's "proper work" (*opus proprium*) in the gospel as sin's forgiving Redeemer.

3. Figuratively (*synecdoche*), the law can substitute a part for the whole and designate either the Old Testament (especially its first five books) in general or any uniformly acting force that controls the human will—for example, used to contrast those who no longer live sinfully under the "the law of sin and of death" but rather obediently under "the law of the Spirit of life in Christ Jesus" (Rom. 8:2).

Hence, one's contextual understanding of the law in God's plan of salvation can dramatically alter the proper meaning of Paul's awesome claim that "Christ is the end of the law" (Rom. 10:4). Does this properly mean the historical termination (*finis*) or the eschatological goal (*telos*) or both of the Mosaic formulations of God's holy will for baptized Christians? Or is it just the judging "office of Moses" but not the ethical guidance of the post-exilic law that has been fulfilled by Christ for his righteous believers? (See the Afterword of this volume.)

To illustrate more concretely, various biblical authors commonly use such important ethical terms as *claim, mandate, command, commandments, law, precept, demand, admonition,* and *exhortation.* However, they are frequently employed in differently nuanced ways to indicate the multiple forms of God's eternal will to different persons in different situations in different epochs of the biblical drama of salvation.

In this case, Luther's Genesis 2 commentary aims to defend the binding nature of God's pre-fall command against the antinomian ("lawless") denial of original sin, but without thereby capitulating to its replacement by the retrojected legalism of any alleged eternal law (*lex aeterna*). In doing so, however, Luther can also spontaneously engage in some rather passionate linguistic imprecision. He distinguishes between "that law" after sin and "this law" before sin, or law as "one thing" before sin and as "something else" after sin, or "this command" before sin and "another law" after sin, or "not the same law" before sin and "a different law" after sin (*alia lex*).[52]

Luther's major theological intention here is to highlight the grievous impact of the fall on Adam's perception of God's holy and loving will: (1) the Genesis account of the original command's guiding instruction for a human creature's godly life (*mandatum*) and (2) the later Pauline witness to the subsequent law's condemning accusations (*nomos*) for Adam and Adam's seed as rebellious sinners (1 Tim. 1:9-10). Therefore, Luther concludes, "Paul is speaking here of another Law; for he clearly states that he is speaking about the Law which was not given to the just but to the unjust."

Clearly, Luther is struggling hard to pour New Testament wine into the ancient Genesis wineskins. His terminological consistency has not caught up with his doctrinal clarity. At heart, Luther wants to be faithful to Paul's law-free gospel of salvation. Yet it must also be freely acknowledged that there is considerable diversity among the various biblical witnesses to both the eschatological continuity and the historical discontinuity both within and between the Old and New Testaments. Nevertheless, Luther's basic theological ethical stance means to reflect Paul's distinctively Christocentric reading of God's Word. The result: God's eschatological command of love both precedes and follows the historical and interim "curse of the law" from which the cross of Christ has redeemed us (Gal. 3:13).

God's Command after the Law

We are not yet ready to analyze the crucial importance for Christian theological ethics of both the eschatological mission and message of the Lord Jesus and the congruent proclamation of the apostle Paul (chapters 7 and 8). We must first briefly anticipate some of that material if we are properly to present Luther's highly influential view of the difference in God's perceived will toward humankind before and after the fall in the biblical saga of salvation (Genesis 1–3).

In brief, Christian saints are redeemed creatures who are called to live in the Spirit under the same eschatological command of love that God originally revealed to Adam and Eve before they became sinners under God's historical judgment: "for the law brings wrath" (Rom. 4:15). First, in response to the fall of the first Adam, God the Creator becomes humankind's Judge, and the divine command of love in primal creation (*mandatum*) becomes the divine law of wrath in fallen creation (*nomos*). Then later, in the person and work of the final Adam, Jesus Christ, the Judge also becomes humankind's Savior. The historically interim divine law of wrath in fallen creation is thereby replaced by the eschatologically restored divine command of love in primal and redeemed creation (*mandatum*). Insofar as they are righteous, baptized Christians are thus "restored to Paradise and created anew" in Luther's memorable biblical promise.

Of course, God's holy will remains inherently and eternally one, but righteous persons perceive it historically in terms of grace, command, and love, while the unrighteous feel confronted by God's wrath, law, and judgment. Applied concretely to his commentary on Genesis, Luther seeks (theologically if not linguistically, synthetically if not analytically) to extol God's blessed command of love (*Gebot*) to the righteous Adam of Genesis 1–2 and to restrict God's cursed law of wrath (*Gesetz*) to the unrighteous Adam of Genesis 3 and thereafter. Moreover, he feels evangelically constrained to do so on the basis of the negative appraisals of the Mosaic law in the eschatological teachings of Jesus and Paul in the New Testament.

For example, "From the beginning [of creation] it was not so," teaches Jesus, and so he boldly interprets the Mosaic law (*lex*) on divorce, for example, as a divine accommodation to "hard-hearted" sinners (Deut. 24:1–4; Matt. 19:8). This remedial law is surely not the original form of God's holy and loving will that was revealed to the righteous in the primal order of creation ("the beginning"). Instead, it is humanly perceived as God's modified or altered will for initially judging and accusing before eventually forgiving and saving the repentant part of humankind.

Consequently, in his analysis of the marital infidelity exposed by "the Law which was given after sin," Luther sharply contrasts domestic life as originally intended for human creatures under God's blessed command and as later actually experienced by sinners under God's punishing law.

> If Adam had continued in his innocence, the children that were born would have married. Then, after leaving the table and dwelling place of their parents, they would have had their own trees and they would have lived separately from their parents. At times they would have come to their father Adam to sing a hymn and praise God, and then they would have returned to their own homes.
>
> But where something different happens, as when married people mutually forsake each other, this is not only against this command; it is also an indication of the awful depravity which has come into

human beings through sin and gets support from Satan, the father of all dissensions. . . . Christ, too, states that divorce was granted by Moses because of the hardness of the hearts of the Jews, but that it had not been so from the beginning (Matt. 19:8).[53]

So, too, in his Sermon on the Mount, Jesus repeatedly contrasts "what was said to those of ancient times" with his own Messianic claim, "But I say to you" (Matthew 5). Thereby he exposes the radical cleavage between the intended gracious governance of God's holy will in primal and redeemed creation, and the law's sin-opposing restraints and constraints in fallen creation. The law (*lex*) that is helpless in transforming personal character accommodates itself by punishing public misconduct: moving from anger to murder, from lust to adultery, from no oaths to false oaths, from nonresistance to retaliations. Law imposed from without can only check but not eradicate the sin expressed from within the human heart.

To be sure, Christ has come "not to abolish but to fulfill" the law and the prophets, but that kind of fulfillment requires a new righteousness that "exceeds that of the scribes and the Pharisees" (Matt. 5:17-20). This is manifest not merely quantitatively in the multiplication of legalistic deeds, but qualitatively in the righteous spirit of faith and love. This is the (figurative) law of the Spirit that ends all the (substantial) law of Moses in setting us right with God (*coram Deo*).

Of course, the law also still remains politically necessary in its civil form within society to prevent and to punish the criminal expressions of spiritual sin (*coram hominibus*). The followers of Jesus are thereby freed from the curse of the law as the way of salvation; however, they still remain obliged to fulfill its conduct through the assistance of the Spirit as the way of service. Jesus was no anarchist in proclaiming the unconditional character of God's grace. In his own words elsewhere, "Give to the emperor [Caesar] the things that are the emperor's, and to God the things that are God's" (Luke 20:25).

As with Jesus, so it is with Paul. In his letters to the Romans and Galatians, the law (*nomos*) represents only the sin-responsive and sin-disclosing form of God's divine will. For the apostle to the Gentiles, "by one man's [Adam's] disobedience the many were made sinners. . . . Law came in, with the result that the trespass multiplied" (Rom. 5:19-20). Why and when did the law come? Paul consistently contends that the later law came remedially only "four hundred and thirty years after" (the interval between Abraham and Moses) and "was added because of transgressions." Moreover, reflecting later Jewish belief, the law was not even given directly by God but only "through angels by a mediator [Moses]" (Gal. 3:17-18).

Undoubtedly, the essential *content* of the law, as reflecting God's pre-fall command (*mandatum*), remains "holy and just and good" (Rom. 7:12). At its inclusive core, the law still echoes the holy will of God (*Torah*), whose tough love now shapes its accusing and remedial forms (*nomos*) in addressing the unrighteous. It is only in this primal sense (Genesis 1–2) that God's gracious will remains truly worthy of the Torah piety of the faithful psalmist: "Happy are those [whose] delight is in the law of the LORD. . . . The law of the LORD is perfect, reviving the soul. . . . Happy are those whose way is blameless, who walk in the law of the LORD" (Ps. 1:1-2; 19:7; 119:1).

At the same time, however, Paul is equally convinced that when addressed accusingly to unrighteous persons (Genesis 3), God's will in the exclusive form of law serves only to disclose and to incite humanity's further sinful rebellion and subsequent judgment, condemnation, and death (Rom. 5:12-17). Indeed "all who rely on the works of the law are under a curse" (Gal. 3:10). Therefore, paradoxically it is from God's sin-killing "strange work" (*opus alienum*) as Judge in wrath and law that sinners need to be redeemed by God's obedience-enlivening "proper work" (*opus proprium*) as Savior in grace and gospel (1 Sam. 2:6-7; Isa. 28:21).

This same eschatological tension in God's revealed will before and after the fall of the first Adam is also revealed reciprocally in reverse before and after the resurrection of the last Adam, Jesus Christ. This likely explains why Paul generally *avoids* all references to God's law as such for providing the primary norms for the ethical obedience of righteous Christians. This is most notable throughout all the ethical exhortations (*parenesis*) of his epistles to the Romans, Galatians, Philippians, Thessalonians, or Corinthians. Consequently, Galatians intentionally refers to love as the figurative "law of Christ" (6:2), and 1 Corinthians speaks only derivatively and illustratively of "the commandments" (7:19). Similarly in the rest of the New Testament, there is once again not a single endorsement of God's Spirit-empowered law as normative for the Christian's new obedience in the books of John, Ephesians, Hebrews, Peter, the Johannine epistles, or Revelation. As Mosaic law (*lex*) replaced the eschatological command of love with the fallen first Adam, so now eschatologically commanded love replaces law with the resurrected last Adam—solely for Christians, and then only insofar as they are already righteous. "While the Law was given through Moses, grace and truth came through Jesus Christ" (John 1:17).

Most decisive for Luther's own theological ethics in his *Lectures on Romans* (1515–16) is how the apostle Paul sets out "to teach Christian ethics" in his epistle.[54] After eleven long chapters that proclaim "the mercies of God" in Jesus Christ, Paul's twelfth chapter introduces the consequent ("therefore") ethical norms for the baptized Christian's new life in Christ. Evangelically, this consists not in demanding obedience to new rules and regulations of the law. Rather, Paul exhorts spiritual transformation and renewal in fidelity to "the will of God" (12:1-2), along with the corollary ethical assurance that "love is the fulfilling of the law" (13:10). In brief, insofar as the gospel replaces the law as the Christian's way of salvation, so too the "fruits of the Spirit" replace the "works of the law" as the Christian way of service. In the "obedience of faith" under God's eschatologically restored primal command, Christians are called to be saints (*hagiois*) who are consecrated as coworkers for God's dominion-sharing service (1:5-7).

"I appeal to you, brethren" (12:1). Paul's characteristic word of ethical guidance in Romans takes not the judgmental form of accusation but rather the counsel of pastoral exhortation (*parenesis*). Luther here notes that Paul always appeals, never threatens, in the nurturing sections of his epistles (for example, Phil. 2:1ff.; 2 Cor. 6:1; 6:4). Moreover, Christians are gently and lovingly encouraged to believe that the Holy Spirit is truly at work "by reason of progress (*progressus*)" in their inaugurated, but not yet consummated, new life in Christ (*non sanus set curandus*). "For he is speaking of those people who have already begun to be Christians. Their life is not a static thing, but in movement from good to better, just as a sick man proceeds from sickness to health, as the Lord also indicates in the case of the half dead man who was taken into the care of the Samaritan."[55]

For those whose being as Christians is continually in a state of becoming, Luther declares that there are five dynamic stages that are "always in motion" in the life of baptized saints who are temples of the Holy Spirit: (1) nonbeing is a person in sin, (2) becoming is justification, (3) being is righteousness, (4) action is living righteously, and (5) being acted upon is to be made perfect and complete. Luther understands Paul's admonitions, "Be not conformed . . . be transformed" (12:2), to mean that a Christian is "always in becoming or in potentiality"; paradoxically, one's justified and sanctified being (*sein*) is precisely in one's state of perpetual becoming (*werden*):

> Man is always in nonbeing, in becoming, in being, always in privation, in potentiality, in action, always in sin, in justification, in righteousness, that is, he is always a sinner, always a penitent, always righteous. For the fact that he repents makes a righteous man out of an unrighteous one.
>
> Therefore if we are always repentant, we are always sinners, and yet thereby we are righteous and we are justified; we are in part sinners and in part righteous, that is, we are nothing but penitents. . . . The apostle teaches renovation of the mind from day to day, more and more, in accord with the statement in 2 Cor. 4:16: "our inner nature being renewed every day," and Eph. 4:23: "Be renewed in the spirit of your minds," and Col. 3:10: "You have put on the new man, which is being renewed."[56]

We shall have frequent occasion to return to Luther's Pauline teaching here on the paradoxical nature of the two realms of Christian existence and consequently also on its importance for Christian theological ethics. While it dare never become dualistic, it must always remain dialectical. For Luther, legalism and antinomianism are both anti-Pauline attempts to resolve prematurely the radical dichotomy in Christian anthropology: "So, then, I of myself serve the law of God with my mind, but with my flesh I serve the law of sin" (Rom. 7:24). For Luther, God's sanative grace in healing is "the most expressive statement of all."

> Note that one and the same man at the same time serves the law of God and the law of sin, at the same time is righteous and sinner (*simul iustus et peccator*)! . . . The saints at the same time as they are righteous are also sinners; righteous because they believe in Christ, whose righteousness covers them and is imputed to them, but sinners because they do not fulfill the Law, are not without concupiscence, and are like sick men under the care of a physician; they are sick in fact (*in re*) but healthy in hope (*in spe*) and in the fact that they are beginning to be healthy, that is, they are "being healed" (*sanificati*).
>
> The saints are always sinners in their own sight, and therefore always justified outwardly. But the hypocrites are always righteous in their own sight, and thus always sinners outwardly.[57]

"A living sacrifice" (12:1). A God-pleasing sacrifice of "our bodies" replaces dead animals and dead works; "it is we ourselves." Christians are "holy" not in the philosophical sense of "something firmly established as inviolate," but in the biblical sense of "something separated, or set apart, kept away from the profane, something which is removed from other uses and applied only to holy purposes worthy of God," as in Josh. 3:5: "Sanctify yourselves; for tomorrow the LORD will do wonders among you."[58]

> In brief, then, "holy" is the same as "sacred," to be pure and clean before God, whereby it is different from the cleanness which is observed before men. Yet in a strange way there is a confusion about the difference between the holy and the sacred, between holiness and sanctification. . . . For it is nothing that we perform good works and live a pure life, if we thereby glorify ourselves; hence the expression follows "acceptable to God."[59]

"That you may prove what is the will of God, what is good and acceptable and perfect" (12:2). Faith is "nothing else than obedience to the Spirit," which helps to explain why, for Paul, "faith itself transforms the thinking and leads us to acknowledge the will of God." This transformation of our mind is "the most useful knowledge that believers in Christ can possess," as scripturally demonstrated by Abraham, David, and the Virgin Mary. Yet God's will is often hidden and "comes in a form contrary to our own thinking (*sub contrario*)," thereby making the saints "do most willingly what they most strongly do not will to do." Scripture continually testifies that "the wisdom of God is hidden under the appearance of stupidity, and truth under the form of lying."[60] That makes Luther very suspicious of those community leaders who too easily confuse eternal righteousness with temporal justice.

> This is the reason (if I may speak of myself) why even hearing the word "justice" nauseates me to the point that if someone robbed me, he would not bring me much grief. And yet the word is always sounding in the mouths of the lawyers. There is no race of men upon the earth who are more ignorant about this matter than the lawyers and the good-intentioners and the intellectuals. For I in myself and many others have had the experience that when we were righteous, God laughed at us in our righteousness.[61]

While fully granting Luther's insistence on the false identification of justice with righteousness, the modern reader cannot help balking as the early Luther then goes on here (against Rome) seemingly to separate human justice from divine righteousness. The absolute judgments wholly appropriate to persons before God (*totus iustus et totus peccator*) are then uncritically applied by him to the relative judgments necessary for persons in society (*partim iustus et partim peccator*). That we are all equally sinful before God should not obliterate the fact that we are not all equally criminal in society. We should never forget that even while insisting that we are all unrighteous as sinners before God, Paul also rightly insisted on his own justice as a Roman citizen before Caesar (Acts 22:25ff.). Although the mature Luther was later to become far more politically active and socially responsible himself, the sheltered monk in the Romans commentary (1516) still contends:

> Therefore since before God no one is righteous, absolutely no injustice can be done to a person by any other creature, even though he may have justice on his side. Thus all cause for contention is taken away from men. Therefore, to whomsoever injury is done or an evil comes in return for his good actions, let him turn away his eyes from this evil and remember how great his own evil is in other respects, and then he will see how good the will of God is even in this evil which has come upon him; for this is what it means to be renewed in one's mind and to be changed into another state of mind and to be wise in the things of God.[62]

Having dealt first with "how we ought to conduct ourselves to God," namely, through the "renewal of our mind and the sanctification of our body" (Rom. 12:1-5), Paul is seen by Luther to refocus, and "from here to the end of the epistle, he teaches how we should act toward our neighbor and explains at length this command to love our neighbor."[63] Paul guides the human response to God's eschatological command of love by admonishing us to cultivate the "gifts that differ according to the grace given to us"; for example, for ministering, teaching, exhortation, generosity, diligence, cheerfulness, etc. (12:6-8).

Decisive for Luther's theological ethics is Paul's exclusive stress on God's gracious command of love for Christians who are "hidden" at work within their societal vocations, callings, offices, stations, and walks of life. These are the "masks of God" (*larvae Dei*) as the "hands, channels, and means" beneath which the Creator hides and through which he accomplished his law-determined and law-embodied preserving will. As already noted, neither in Paul nor in Luther is there any reliance upon the late medieval church's legalistic advocacy of the double-standard morality of (1) maximal obedience to "counsels of perfection" (*consilia*) in the Sermon on the Mount for the professionally religious in monastic life, as meritoriously superior to (2) minimal obedience to only the "general commandments" (*praecepta*) in the Mosaic Decalogue for ordinary Christians in daily life. No, *love alone in all its various forms* is God's universal command to all saints everywhere, and "the apostle, and indeed the whole Scripture, understands the term *saints* to apply to all who are faithful believers in Christ."[64] In no way are righteous Christians to resubmit to the spiritual servitude of the law, for "against this he [Paul] contends on behalf of the Christians with all of his might." Luther explains:

> This is a matter of being subjected to the Law and all of its burdens, that is, to believe that it is necessary for salvation to fulfill all the external works of the Law. For they who think and believe this remain slaves and will never be saved. . . . To be sure, the apostle and spiritual men also performed these works, and still do so, but not because they have to but because they want to; not because the works are necessary but because they are permitted.[65]

"Love is the fulfilling of the law" (13:10). Luther concludes his analysis of Paul's discussion of ethical norms in Romans by clearly recommitting righteous Christians to God's universal command of love in the redeemed creation (*Gebot*), after their having been liberated by Christ from all distrustful reliance on the law in the fallen and sinful creation (*Gesetz*). Character determines conduct; motivation governs demonstration. The decisive difference is between a loveless and calculating compliance with, or a loving and joyful fulfillment of, the eternal will of God "not because they have to, but because they want to." In the power of the Spirit, the truly authentic good deeds of Christians occur as willing and spontaneous "fruits of faith" within God's law-governed mandates (structures, establishments, and institutions) in society.

In fidelity to the teachings of Jesus and Paul, Luther therefore treats the relation of love and law dialectically, both in terms of spiritual correction and of ethical fulfillment. On the one hand, God's command of love is solely an imperative of law-free grace. "God's love has been poured into our hearts through the Holy Spirit that has been given to us" (Rom. 5:5). Therefore, God's eschatological command of love in primal creation, after doing its "strange work" as Mosaic law against sin in the interim of fallen creation, is again restored to its "proper work" of vocational sanctification within redeemed creation. As Jesus declared in Luke 22:34-40, all the teachings of the law and prophets "hang on" as dependent applications of the "greatest" of the summarized commandments, the normative twofold love of "the LORD your God" (Deut. 6:5) and of "your neighbor as yourself" (Lev. 19:18).

In like fashion, Paul reminds the Christians in Rome that the ethical commandments of the second table of the Mosaic Decalogue "and any other commandment" are all finally "summed up" in the primal command to love your neighbor "as yourself" (13:9). However, Luther also immediately reminds us as forgiven but still imperfect sinners that

> this most profound commandment . . . does not endorse the human self-love ("as thyself") which it clearly presupposes. The commandment . . . is understood in a twofold manner. First, we can understand it in the sense that both the neighbor and the self are to be loved. But in another sense it can be understood that we are commanded to love only our neighbor, using our love for ourselves as the example. This is the better interpretation because man with his natural sinfulness does love himself above all others, seeks his own in all matters, loves everything else for his own sake, even when he loves his neighbor or his friend for he seeks his own in him.[66]

On the other hand, God's command of love is universal in scope. In Christ's corrected expansion of post-exilic Judaic law, it is no longer limited to fellow Jews. Luther's concentration on the uniqueness of love in God's sovereign rule does not preclude its also taking on a multitude of variegated forms, as culturally adapted and legally compromised in different peoples, times, places, including even juridical and public policy. "Although this commandment when viewed in a superficial and general way seems quite a small matter, if we apply it to particular cases, it pours forth infinite salutary teachings and gives us faithful direction for all of our dealing."[67] As we shall have many concrete occasions to note later in Part Three, by contextual expressions both personally tender and socially tough, it is God's universal command of love that dialectically norms and unites God's twofold rule as humanity's Creator and Redeemer. This is true for Luther everywhere, whether it be variously and historically expressed in the Holiness Code (Leviticus 17–26), the Decalogue (Deut. 5:6-21), natural law (Rom. 2:14-16), the Sermon on the Mount and its Golden Rule (Matthew 5–7), or the love of neighbor in apostolic exhortations (Rom. 13:9).

As a trinitarian Christian, Luther is no narrow ethical sectarian. God's command of love is addressed to all persons created in God's own loving image. Indeed, strictly speaking, there is likely no specifiable "Christian" ethic as such; there are only Christians who act ethically and contextually in love and justice. For Luther, the evangelical uniqueness lies solely in the ground and goal of the ethical actors and not in the length and breadth of their ambiguous actions. As he repeated continually in his catechetical explanations of the Ten Commandments for Christians, "We are to fear and love God so that" fruits of faith nurture real neighbors in all areas of life.

> For this reason the apostle describes the essence of this commandment when he says in Phil. 2:4: "Let each of you look not only to his own interests but also to the interest of others," and in 1 Cor. 13:5: "Love does not insist on its own way." That is, it causes man to deny himself and to affirm another, to put on affection for the neighbor and put off affections for himself, to place himself in the person of his neighbor and then to decide what he wants him to do for him himself and what he and others might do for him. And then he will discover by this infallible teaching what he ought to do. But when this process is omitted, then commandments multiply and yet a man will not arrive where he is going. . . . Behold how deep and wide this commandment![68]

Luther is clearly convinced from this preponderance of evidence in biblical ethics that God's judging and accusing law (*nomos*) was never God's first word and therefore can also never be God's last word. Instead, it is God's gracious and eschatological command (*mandatum*) for righteous love that comes both before and after the interim demands of God's sin-conditioned Mosaic office. In keeping with his Christocentric view of the Scriptures, Luther's history of the church as the people of God is centrally governed by trinitarian soteriology: (1) God's primal command for creation, (2) God's law and gospel for redemption, and (3) God's renewal command for sanctification.

So despite all the evident linguistic diversity in usage within the Scriptures themselves, Luther aims to maintain strict Pauline theological consistency. On the one hand, God's will converts from eschatological command to historical law through Adam's unrighteous rebellion. Luther's exposition of the primal creation in Genesis 1–2 presents God's will positively in addressing righteous persons with a gracious and guiding command (*Gebot*). This contrasts strongly with his post-fall and especially post-exilic usage following Genesis 3, where the will of God is usually presented negatively in the form of the judging and accusing "law" (*Gesetz*) for disobedient sinners.

On the other hand, God's will reverts from historical law to eschatological command through Christ's righteous obedience. The Son of God is "no new Moses." He and his apostles exhort the loving behavior of righteous but imperfect Christians who are enlightened and empowered by the gracious gifts and fruits of the Holy Spirit *(parenesis)*. Baptized believers, whom God is now conforming to his true human image, Jesus Christ, the final Adam, are being transferred and called to fulfill in the "new creation" the same kind of loving lifestyle that God had originally intended for his primal image, the first Adam, "from the beginning" of pristine creation. Hence, God's unique filial exemplar commands by example, "I give you a new commandment, that you love one another. Just as I have loved you, you also should love one another" (John 13:34).

> The holy orders and true religious institutions established by God are these three: the office of priest, the estate of marriage, the civil government. . . . These three religious institutions or orders are found in God's Word and commandments and whatever is contained in God's Word must be holy, for God's Word is holy and sanctifies everything connected with it and involved with it.
>
> Above these three institutions and orders is the common order of Christian love, in which one serves not only the three orders, but also serves every needy person in general with all kinds of benevolent deeds, such as feeding the hungry, giving drink to the thirsty, forgiving enemies, praying for all men, suffering all kinds of evil on earth, etc. Behold, all of these are called good and holy works.[69]

We have completed Luther's depiction of the original righteousness *(iustitia originalis)* of Adam and Eve in the primal creation that is both conferred in Genesis 1–2 and inferred from the teachings of Jesus and Paul in the New Testament. As created in God's holy and loving image and mandated for God-ordained life in community, a coworking humankind was (and still is) intended to live and serve together righteously, under God's dominion-sharing universal command of love. God lovingly wills human freedom, justice, and peace through ministry, marriage and labor, and civil authority. Why the fulfillment of God's will remains such a perennial challenge for Luther's theological ethic is the subject of the next chapter on our primal parents' sinful rebellion against God and consequent unethical behavior toward each other.

Chapter 4

━━━◆━━━

Satan: God's Foe, Human Woe

I
N THIS CHAPTER we will concentrate on Luther's interpretation of the Genesis account of the fall of Adam and Eve into the original and ever-recurring sin of humankind (*peccatum originale*), and the emergence of what was later to be variously called "two ages" or "two cities" of God versus Satan, in the authoritative Scripture of Paul and the patristic tradition of Augustine.[1] The later unsentimental realism of Luther's congruent two kingdoms (*zwei Reiche*) was likewise predicated on a primary affirmation of Christian faith grounded in the Genesis witness to the fatal flaw in a fallen humanity. It is always either/or in the presence of God (*coram Deo*); there are allowed "no other gods" to worship.

> The kingdom is either God's (*regnum Dei*) or the devil's (*regnum diaboli*).
>
> I was baptized. Therefore I must maintain that I was translated from the kingdom of Satan into the Kingdom of God.
>
> Whatever is flesh is ungodly and under the wrath of God and a stranger to the Kingdom of God. And if it is a stranger to the Kingdom and Spirit of God, it necessarily follows that it is under the kingdom and spirit of Satan, since there is no middle kingdom between the kingdom of God and the kingdom of Satan, which are mutually and perpetually in conflict with one another.
>
> I have been hammering away at the distinction between the two kingdoms . . . because Satan, the evil one, never ceases to stew and brew these two kingdoms together.[2]

We will now develop the biblical (Paul) and patristic (Augustine) foundation for Luther's eschatological treatment of these two kingdoms of God versus Satan. Only afterward, in the following four chapters of Part Three, will we then fully expound the Reformer's corollary historical treatment of the twofold rule (*zweierlei Regimente*) of God versus Satan through both Christ and Caesar in church and society. In fidelity to all the manifold dynamics of Holy Scripture, it is ultimately this cosmic struggle between the world's two kingdoms (God versus Satan) that prompts the living Lord's twofold rule (Christ and Caesar) through the twofold functions of both law and gospel for empowering salvation and service within human history. For Luther, the purity of the gospel itself was at stake in the church's not mixing or confusing these various forms of God's temporal and spiritual rule (*mixtura regnorum*).

Our own book's structural division between Parts Two and Three is intended to highlight this radical advance made in Luther's own theological ethics. Historically, it was in meeting the challenges of the chaotic mid-1520s that Luther expanded—not replaced—his earlier dualistic model (the two kingdoms of God versus Satan) as in Augustine's *City of God* with his later dialectical model (the twofold rule of the one Triune God against Satan through both Christ and Caesar, as in Paul's Romans). The latter interpenetrated the former. Luther's modified ethical structure corresponds conceptually to his growing strife with the license of Protestant sectarians in addition to his initial struggles against the legalism of Roman semi-Pelagians. So what "faith alone" meant for Luther's doctrine, the two kingdoms and God's two regiments came to mean for Luther's theological ethics.

It is only the doctrinal rejection or historical ignorance of this later development in Luther's ethical outlook that can explain the persisting caricatures of his theological ethic as being "conservative," "dualistic," "quietistic," or "defeatistic" (see chapter 1). In contrast, we will contend that Luther's balanced mature position on God's twofold rule intersecting the world's two kingdoms, granting major cultural modifications, remains essentially a trustworthy scriptural guide for Christian theological ethics in our day.

Fallen Humanity

Luther develops his view of humanity's original sin in a detailed verse-by-verse analysis of Genesis 3. It was Paul's characteristic Christocentric exegesis and expansive exposition of this chapter that made so strong an impression on Luther. His opening words summarize just "how horrible the fall of Adam and Eve was."

> Through it we have lost a most beautifully enlightened reason and a will in agreement with the Word and will of God. We have also lost the glory of our bodies. . . . The most serious loss consists in this, that not only were those benefits lost, but man's will turned away from God. As a result, man wants and does none of those things God wants and commands. Likewise, we have no knowledge about what God is, what grace is, what righteousness is, and finally what sin itself is. These are really terrible faults, and those who do not realize and see them are blinder than a mole.[3]

This plight of humankind after the fall of its primal and prototypical parents (*status natura corruptae*) is pitted in stark contrast to its creation according to the image and likeness of God in the state of childlike innocence (*innocentia puerilis*). Luther considers it "a cause for great errors" when the evil of sin is minimized and our depraved nature is not acknowledged. Arguing "in the manner of [Aristotelian] philosophers," some of Luther's Ockhamistic opponents state that "the natural endowments have remained unimpaired." Luther counters, "the will that is good and righteous, that pleases God, obeys God, trusts in the Creator, and makes use of the creatures with an expression of thanks, has been lost to such an extent that our will makes a devil out of God and shudders at the mention of His Name, especially where it is troubled by God's judgment. . . . The more you minimize sin, the more will grace decline in value."[4]

Luther recalls Aristotle's statement in his *Nicomachean Ethics* (III, 4–5), "Reason pleads for the best," and the sentiment of the Sophists that "sound reason is the cause of all virtues." Luther does "not deny" that this is certainly true of such mundane matters (*coram hominibus*) as "managing cattle, building a house, and sowing a field." But in "higher matters" (*coram Deo*), it is certainly not true. Sin presupposed, it is antiscriptural to teach that "practice makes perfect" when it comes to love, faith, and humility before God.

> How can a reason which hates God be called sound? How can a will that resists God's will and refuses to obey God be called sound? . . . Therefore in theology let us maintain that reason in men is most hostile to God and that the respectable will is most opposed to the will of God. From this source arise the hatred of the Lord and the persecution of godly ministers. For this reason, and I said, let us not minimize this evil which human nature has contracted as a result of the sin of our first parents; rather let us emphasize it.[5]

It is of theological significance, however, that while Luther brings creation and sin into very close proximity, he also refuses to identify them. Creation still remains God's good and gracious gift to an innocent and obedient humanity, which only later rebelled under Satan. Hence, Luther states his opinion that "this temptation appears to me to have taken place on the Sabbath," indeed, on the very first "following Sabbath" after the creation of Adam and Eve on the sixth day. Early on that day, they first glorified their gracious Creator for all the blessings of life and love in Paradise: "In this way Adam and Eve, resplendent with innocence and original righteousness, and abounding in peace of mind because of their trust in God, who was so kind, walked about naked while they discussed the Word and command of God and praised God, just as should be done on the Sabbath. But then alas, Satan interfered and within a few hours ruined all this."[6] To be sure, Luther immediately acknowledges that here, too, "a sea of questions arises." Nevertheless, he refuses to engage in "wicked curiosity" or idle speculation. Negatively, "why do we not rather learn with Job that God cannot be called to account and cannot be compelled to give us the reason for everything He does or permits to happen?" Positively, "this account is so obscure in order that all things might be held over for Christ and for His Spirit, who was to shed light throughout the entire world like the midday sun and to open all the mysteries of Scripture."[7]

Satan is portrayed as a primordial personal power, the archenemy of God and God's people, who seeks to govern the sinful heart. What is preeminently clear for Luther is the theological profundity of the nature of satanic temptations. God is mocked as God's sovereign command is challenged: "Did God really command you not to eat from every tree in Paradise?" (Gen. 3:1). Scripture confirms that "Eve is simply urged on to all sins, since she is being urged on against the Word and the good will of God. . . . These Satan attacks and tries to destroy. . . . Truly, therefore, this temptation is the sum of all temptations; it brings with it the overthrow or the violations of the entire Decalogue. Unbelief is the source of all sins; when Satan brought about this unbelief by driving out or corrupting the Word, the rest was easy for him."[8]

For Luther, it is crucial to profess that one is a sinner before one commits sins. The unfaithful actor precedes and determines the disobedient actions. "The outward act of obedience follows sin, which through unbelief has fully developed in the heart." Hence, each of the first persons originally "became a rebel" because the devil's corrupted word had effected in them a corrupted will and reason, governing both mouth and hand (*opus diaboli*). "Before the desire to eat of the fruit arose in Eve, she lost the word which God spoke to Adam." Unbelief (*Unglaube*) in God and doubt of God's Word are therefore the original or primal sin, "and so later on, the fall is an easy matter." Once a new god is invented by Satan, our willful idolatry sets the stage for murder, adultery, and all other human sins. The devil began original sin "when he led Eve away from the Word of God to idolatry." Apart from God, humans are manufacturers of gods (*fabricatores deorum*).

> Satan was the contriver of this affair. . . . Through the enlightenment of the Holy Spirit, the holy Fathers and prophets readily saw that this was not an affair of the serpent, but that in the serpent there was that spirit, the enemy of innocent nature, of whom Christ said clearly in the Gospel that he did not stand in the truth and that he is a murderer and liar (John 8:44). It remained for the Gospel to present all this with greater clarity and to point out this enemy of God and men.[9]

It is also important that Luther emphasizes the pre-fall eschatological command of God that governs human worship; "it was his service and the obedience he could offer God in his state of innocence." At the same time, the disobedience to God's command is said (anachronistically) to bring with it "the violation of the entire Decalogue" and an idolatry that is "contrary to the First, the Second, and the Third Commandments."

Once again, we note Luther's preference, theologically and terminologically, for correlating command (*Gebot*) with God's will before the fall and the Decalogue or the law (*Gesetz*) with God's will after the fall. Luther does not suggest any essential difference at all between the religious and ethical content of both. What does decisively change, however, is the human creature's unrighteous disobedience to the Creator and its subsequent unjust effects when moving from the state of grace to the state of sin. When the Creator becomes Judge, God's command becomes law.

In the original state of integrity (*status integritatis*), "this command was given to Adam's innocent nature that he might have a directive or form for worshiping God, for giving thanks to God, and for instructing his children." Here it was a positive, loving, guiding expression of God's grace (*favor Dei*). By way of contrast in the state of sinful depravity (*status corruptionis*), "There is nothing more grievous, nothing more wretched, than a conscience frightened by the Law of God and by the sight of its sins." Here it is a negative, accusing expression of God's wrath (*ira Dei*). This corroborates our analysis of Luther's earlier contention that "the Law before sin is one thing and the Law after sin is something else (*alia lex*)."

In reciprocal fashion, this will also prove to be of ethical importance in our subsequent discussion of the role of God's command in the life of redeemed persons, insofar as they righteously "return Paradise-like" to the even greater glories of God's kingdom (chapter 8). In ethically responsible opposition to all simplistic forms of antinomianism, "it was God's intention that this command should provide man with an opportunity for obedience and outward worship, and that this tree [of good and evil] should be a sort of sign by which man would give evidence that he was obeying God."[10]

Satan's assaults on faith in God (the later Mosaic law's "First Table") is followed by loveless deeds against neighbors, disclosed by its "Second Table." The realization of their nakedness by the shame-filled Adam and Eve prompts Luther to return to the critical issue of just what original sin actually destroyed in the human's original righteousness. The Scholastics encountered by Luther employed their mistaken exegesis of Hebrew grammatical parallelism to maintain a qualitative difference between Adam's image (*imago*) and likeness (*similitudo*) of God (Gen. 1:26). In the fall, they held, humans did lose God's "superadded gift" (*donum superadditum*) of original righteousness (faith, hope, charity), but not their essential, natural endowments (justice, courage, prudence, temperance). The former had to be restored by the church's infusion of sacramental grace; the latter could be exercised through free will and uncorrupted reason as the natural foundation, awaiting supernatural perfection, of Christian ethics.

Luther argues that "this idea must be shunned like poison, for it mini-mizes original sin." Original righteousness was truly part of human nature, inseparable from the other so-called perfect natural endowments. Hence, "after man has fallen from righteousness into sin, it is correct and truthful to say that our natural endowments are not perfect but are corrupted by sin. . . . These Satan has corrupted through sin; just as leprosy poisons the flesh . . . so that the will and reason have become depraved through sin, and man not only does not love through sin God any longer but flees from Him, hates Him, and desires to be and live without Him."[11]

Luther's textual argumentation posits the holistic nature of humans (*totus homo*) as sinners before God in need of the Savior, Jesus Christ. Admittedly, it is based again on his Christocentric retrojection of the salvific purpose of God's mighty act in Christ. "All these thing we have lost through sin to such an extent that we can conceive of them only in a negative and not a positive way. From the evil which we have with us we are forced to infer how great the good is that we have lost." Human nature "indeed remains," but its universal corruption (*massa perditionis*) is marked by the loss of confident trust in God.

> When you declare that righteousness was not a part of the essence (*essentia*) of man, does it not also follow that sin, which took its place, is not part of the essence of man either? Then there was no purpose in sending Christ the Redeemer, if the original righteousness, like something foreign to our nature, has been taken away and the natural endowments remain perfect. What can be said that is more unworthy of a theologian?[12]

Along with the recognition of their nakedness and need for clothing, Adam and Eve now also feel compelled to "hide from the face of the Lord"—all guilty signs of the shameful loss of their original righteousness. "Only after the Law has come, does it become clear what we have done. But when sin has been brought to light, it appears to carry with it such great disgrace that the mind cannot bear having it looked at." Here Luther sees the immensity of original sin "with which we are born and which has been planted in us through the sin of our first parents."

Sinful humankind lives now in fear, shame, and guilt under God's law (*Gesetz*). "After their conscience has been convicted by the law and they feel their disgrace before God and themselves, Adam and Eve lose their confidence in God and are so filled with fear and terror that when they hear a breath or a wind, they immediately think God is approaching to punish them; and they hide." Characteristically, Luther can conceive of nothing "more horrible" than Paradise lost: to descend from "walking with God" in the cool of the evening to "hiding from God" in the midst of the trees.[13]

Law and Gospel

Then follows the Genesis 3 description of the trial and the judgment of the unfaithful and disobedient first human rebels against God. "Where are you?" are identified as "words of the Law" that God directs to the conscience of Adam. Adam frantically judges himself by his vain excuses. He accuses God for his fright and tries to "transfer his guilt from himself to the Creator." Roused by the "real sting of the Law," Adam is accused of disobeying God's command not to eat of the tree of good and evil. Again, Adam blames God for giving Eve to him, and then also blames Eve for deceiving him. Luther concludes, "Such is the working of the Law that, when the Law stands alone without the Gospel and the acknowledgment of grace, it leads to despair and ultimate impenitence."[14]

Eve is also questioned by God and "corrupted by sin, she is not one whit better than Adam." She, too, indirectly accuses God by accusing God's deceiving creature, the serpent. "This is the last step of sin, to insult God and to charge Him with being the originator of sin. Unless hearts are given courage through trust in mercy, this nature cannot be urged on beyond this point if there are successive steps of sin."[15]

Then follows the execution of God's sentence in accord with the heinous deeds committed. Luther sharply distinguishes between God's merciful judgment of Adam and Eve and God's wrathful cursing of the serpent taken over by Satan.

> "Where are you? Who told you that you are naked?" These words reveal God's love toward the whole human race; even after sin the human being is sought and called, and God converses with him and hears him. This is a sure indication of His mercy. Although these are words which deal with Law and judgment, they nevertheless indicate a clear hope that Adam and Eve were not to be condemned eternally.
>
> With the serpent and Satan He deals more harshly. . . . It is as if He were saying, "you, Satan, have already committed sin previously, and you were condemned when you fell from heaven. To this sin you have now added another, in order to bring man into sin through your misuse of the serpent. For this reason the serpent will bear this punishment, that now it alone will lie under the curse, when previously it shared in the blessing which all other beasts had."[16]

On this basis, Luther then interprets God's word in Gen. 3:15 in so Christocentric a manner that it was later called the *Proteuangelion*, the proclamation of the "earliest gospel" in the Old Testament that proleptically anticipates the gospel in the New: "I shall put enmity between you and the woman and your seed and her seed. And I will crush your head, and you will crush its heel."

As biblical background for this gospel proclamation, Luther first takes with utmost seriousness the "enmity" and "crushing" that Genesis reveals about the cosmic strife between God and Satan. The judgment of Satan was traditionally interpreted allegorically in terms of a rebellious angel's celestial banishment: "Satan has been hurled from heaven and has been condemned because of this sin." Luther prefers to read the Old Testament more soberly in the light of its New Testament fulfillment. Actually, Scripture never reveals sin's origin but only its divine defeat: "When we make statements about Satan, let us fall back on other Scripture proofs that are pertinent, sure and strong. Of this sort are John 8:44: 'The devil is a murderer and the father of lies'; 'He did not abide in the truth'; 1 Peter 5:8: 'He goes about like a roaring lion, seeking whom he may devour'; and John 16:11: 'The prince of the world is judged.'"[17] For the benefit of Adam and Eve, however, God speaks here to Satan "that they may hear this judgment and be comforted by the realization that God is the enemy of that being which inflicted so severe a wound on man. Here grace and mercy begin to shine forth from the midst of the wrath which sin and disobedience aroused." It is this simultaneous interaction of God's mercy and wrath that so fascinates the dialectical mind of Luther.

Significantly, Luther follows the stress on strife and struggle between God and Satan in Genesis 3. He faithfully employs the ancient military metaphor of *Christus Victor* in proclaiming a warring Christ who will deliver God's children from Satan in a divinely led "victory against the enemy that deceived and conquered human nature."[18]

> For Adam and Eve not only do not hear themselves cursed like the serpent; but they even hear themselves drawn up, as it were, in battle line against the condemned enemy, and this with the hope of help from the Son of God, the Seed of the woman. Forgiveness of sin and full reception into grace are here pointed out to Adam and Eve.
>
> Although this enemy fights with cunning and treacheries, the Seed will be born who will crush the head of the serpent. These words point to the ultimate destruction of Satan's tyranny, although it will not pass away without a most bitter conflict being fought for man.[19]

Amplifying the enmity between God and Satan, this patristic motif of God's mighty victory by "the Crusher," Jesus Christ, is afforded central place in Luther's portrayal of Gen. 3:15 as "a clear promise" and "a revelation of the depth of God's goodness." On the one hand, it trusts in the Son of God's humble incarnation. "What is born from Mary was conceived by the Holy Spirit and is the true Seed of Mary, just as the other promises given to Abraham and David testify, according to which Christ is called the Son of Abraham and the Son of David." On the other hand, it anticipates the Savior's bloody atonement. In "bruising His heel" in our stead at Golgotha, as it were, "The Son of God had to become a sacrifice to achieve these things for us, to take away sin, to swallow up death, and to restore the lost obedience. These treasures we possess in Christ, but in hope."[20]

Luther then moves on to "the second part of this sermon" in dealing with the bodily punishments of Eve and Adam. However, our own special concerns will best be served if we now conclude this opening section on Genesis 3 by highlighting two very Christocentric features of Luther's theological ethics. True God and true human, Jesus Christ reveals the depths of both divine love and authentically human (now Christian) love.

It is here in fallen creation that we first encounter the dialectical tension between the law and the gospel as the awesome weapons used against "the unholy trinity" of Satan, the flesh, and the world, in God's twofold rule of sinful humankind (*adversus Diabolum carnem et mundum*). Before their fall into original sin (Genesis 1–2), Adam and Eve were governed by God's gracious command of holy love. In the absence of any sin, strictly speaking, God's eschatological will as command was explicitly expressed neither as law (to condemn sin) nor as gospel (to conquer sin). At most, the law and the gospel were latently united in command and grace as the governing will of God for righteous human creatures. To cite again Luther's anachronistic description of the original state of humanity's pristine righteousness, "the Word which the Lord had spoken to Adam was 'Do not eat from the tree of knowledge of good and evil.' For Adam this Word was Gospel and Law; it was his worship; it was his service and the obedience he could offer God in this state of innocence."[21]

After their fall into original sin (Genesis 3), Adam and Eve were explicitly judged by God's law (the accusing form of God's will) and promised salvation by God's gospel (the redemptive form of God's grace). In other words, law and gospel had no necessary roles, as such, in God's primal creation; they only later became the sin-oriented expressions of God's gracious command, negatively and positively, that were personally experienced by rebels reflecting God's corrupted image. God's holy will was then paradoxically proclaimed and perceived as both hating sin while loving sinners. In God's mercy, Adam and Eve were enabled to live in the hope of the gospel: "Although their flesh must die for the time being, nevertheless, because of the promised Son of God, who would crush the head of the devil, they hope for the resurrection of the flesh after the temporal death of the flesh, just as we do."[22]

This historically grounded gospel, centered in "Jesus Christ and him crucified," must now also be proclaimed in Pauline opposition to the law as the sole way of salvation for sinners (2 Tim. 2:15). Here we recall Luther's employment of the law's nuanced terminological uses in the Holy Scripture: Law (*Torah*) can be the virtual equivalent of command as an expression of God's grace in the Psalms of the Old Testament; law (*nomos*) can also be among the chief enemies of the gospel as an expression of

God's wrath in the Pauline New Testament. "By faith the Christian is made the victor over sin, over the Law, and over death so that not even the gates of hell can prevail against him (Matt. 16:18). This statement [the seed of the woman] includes the redemption from the Law, from sin, and from death; and it points out the clear hope of a certain resurrection and of renewal in the other life after this life."[23]

We need to emphasize again that Luther's championing of especially Paul's law-free gospel is never intended to be "immorally antinomian." After all, "God is no antinomian!" Indeed, Luther insists that a vital result of the gospel's right proclamation is "to restore the lost obedience" to God's gracious command, the loving fulfillment of God's will that we joyously serve our neighbors. However, the Spirit-empowered renewal and righteous motive are all-decisive: Under God's law (*Gesetz*), we serve under duress and selfishly in order to be saved, whereas following God's command (*Gebot*), we serve voluntarily and selflessly because we have already been saved. We are no longer merely doing the right thing for the wrong reason; sanctifying renewal always accompanies justifying faith in Jesus Christ. Luther's biblical conviction is stated thus: "If the serpent's head is to be crushed, death certainly must be done away with. If death is done away with, that, too, which deserves death is done away with, that is, sin. If sin is abolished, then also the Law. And not only this, but at the same time the obedience which was lost is renewed."[24]

Along with God's law-gospel dialectic on the divine side, Luther's analysis of Genesis 3 also introduces us on the human side to an ethical realism that is deeply aware of the perennial traces of original sin (*reliquum peccati*). Christ's glorious victory on the cross has already dethroned sin, but it has not yet fully destroyed it (Col. 2:15). The sin of the baptized Christian is decisively vanquished by Christ's imputed and imparted righteousness, but it is not yet eliminated. The age of grace is no longer the age of sin, but it is not yet the age of glory. So there is absolutely no room for any moral perfectionism, ecclesial triumphalism, lax antinomianism, or societal utopianism in Luther's theology of the cross (*theologia crucis*).

Only on the Last Day will Satan's condemnation of God and defeat by Christ be made manifest to all (1 Cor. 15:28). In the historical interim, "Only this happens: that Adam and Eve are set into conflict with this enemy to keep them busy."[25] Christians are therefore called to follow the examples of Adam and Eve in living a life of faith and hope in Christ— they in the Christ to come and we in the crucified and resurrected Christ who has come—and thereby become truly holy and righteous. Without Christ, the world has no final hope.

> The world is like a drunken peasant. If you lift him into the saddle on one side, he will only fall off on the other side. One can't help him, no matter how one tries. He wants to be the devil's.

Thus we also live in the same hope. And, because of Christ, when we die, we keep this hope, which the Word sets before us by directing us to put our trust in the merits of Christ. It is vain to long for such perfection in this life that we become wholly righteous, that we love God perfectly, and that we love our neighbor as we love ourselves. We make some progress; but sin, which was in our members (Rom. 7:23) and is present everywhere, either corrupts or altogether obstructs this obedience. . . . Meanwhile, our life is in the midst of death.[26]

This study's eventual ethical goal (chapter 8) will be to explore Luther's quoted acknowledgment here that despite original sin, "we make some progress." Indeed, our entire Part Three will meet that moral challenge. First, however, we must continue to fulfill our prior theological task to demonstrate how this Genesis 3 cosmic struggle (God versus Satan) is congruently depicted in the New Testament witness of Paul and in the subsequent theological ethics of Augustine. Together they institute the biblical and patristic backbone for Christian realism in the Western church.

The remainder of this chapter will therefore develop those characteristic ways by which Paul and Augustine served to prepare Luther to magnify God's sin-forgiving grace by first excoriating humanity's God-distrusting sin, as uniquely revealed in both the necessity and the gift of the cross of Jesus Christ. Whether in terms of "two ages" (Paul), "two cities" (Augustine), or "two kingdoms" (Luther), the trio's common dichotomy amplified the realistic testimony to the desperate plight of sinful humanity dualistically embroiled in the cosmic struggle between God and Satan (Genesis 3).

Paul on the Two Ages

Luther's lifelong preoccupation with the depths of human sinfulness was already evidenced in his early *Lectures on Romans* (1516). While it is certainly the comforting gospel about Christ that is the central message of Paul as God's apostle to the Gentiles, the distinctive nature of this eschatological gospel as God's forgiving and renewing love requires that it be addressed to persons who have already been compelled to confess their desperate need for such a Savior. "From this text of the apostle it is clear that in this letter he is not speaking primarily against those who are open sinners, but against those who appear righteous in their own eyes and trust in their own works for salvation. For he is trying to encourage these people to magnify the grace of God, which cannot be magnified unless the sin which is forgiven through this grace is first acknowledged and magnified."[27]

Of special interest to Luther was Paul's contention that the Genesis account of the fall of Adam, when interpreted typologically and Christocentrically, has profound universal significance for both the church and the world. The cosmic dualism between God and Satan is set in stark relief for New Testament Christians by the apostolic testimony to Christ as the last

Adam, the gracious progenitor of a new humanity whom God has sent to regenerate and renew the fallen humanity of the first Adam. Therefore, Paul's universal gospel involves not only one but two "antitypical" Adams and ages.

While the most significant features of Paul's gospel of salvation and service in Christ will be analyzed below in chapters 7 and 8, we must first focus our attention on its sinful background in the universal guilt of a faithless and disobedient humankind ("Adam"). It is the ensuing dualistic strife between Satan and God for human allegiance that Paul eschatologically contrasts in the New Testament between the old age of the first fallen Adam and the new age of the final redeemer Adam, Jesus Christ. Indeed, this life and death struggle is at the very heart of the Christian message for Luther: "This is the principal theme in Scripture. For God has arranged through Christ whatever the devil brought in through Adam. And it was the devil who brought in sin and death. Therefore God brought about the death of death and the sin of sin, the poison of poison, the captivity of captivity. . . . These are the 'delights of Christ.'"[28]

Following the teachings of Christ (Mark 1:15; Luke 4:16-21; 7:22; 24:25-27; Matt. 11:4-5), Paul often interpreted events in the Old Testament as "types" or illuminating foreshadowings of contemporary experiences in New Testament times, whether by way of similarity or contrast. This non-allegorical tradition meant to witness to the diversified unity of God's redemption history throughout the Scriptures, with pivotal events in ancient Israel anticipating the final victory of God's righteousness now manifested in Jesus Christ. Illustratively, for Paul, the Israelites in the wilderness, their crossing of the sea, their protecting cloud, their miraculous food and drink, and the rock from which their needed water sprang (cf. Exodus) were all to be regarded by faith as "types to come" of Christian baptism, the Lord's Supper, and Christ himself, respectively.

Where strictly defined by the uniqueness, newness, and finality of the Christ-event that is proclaimed in the New Testament, this hermeneutical method can both respect Old Testament history for itself and also underscore the deep spiritual bond between the two testaments. When read in faith, there are divine promises and fulfillments within and between both parts of the church's one Holy Bible. Nowhere is this mode of Christocentric biblical interpretation more powerfully presented than in the epistles of Paul, as notably highlighted in the opening chapters of Luther's *Lectures on Romans* (1516).

In Romans 1, Paul announces that the gospel of God's righteousness is "the power of God for salvation to everyone who has faith, to the Jew first and also to the Greek" (Rom. 1:16). This good news (*Evangelium*) is inseparably linked with the bad news (*Gesetz*) that in God's sight, all persons, Jew and Gentile, are unrighteous in God's sight and in desperate need of forgiving pardon and renewal. For Luther, then, Paul's initial task was to compel unrighteous and self-righteous persons to view themselves in the judging presence of God (*coram Deo*):

> The chief purpose of this letter is to break down, to pluck up, and to destroy all wisdom and righteousness of the flesh. This includes all the works which in the eyes of people or even in our own eyes may be great works. No matter whether these works are done with a sincere heart and mind, this letter is to affirm and state and magnify sin, no matter how much someone insists that it does not exist, or that it was believed not to exist.[29]

Luther was highly aware of the radicality of Paul's view of human sin because he had already lectured in Wittenberg on Aristotle's *Nichomachean Ethics* during 1508 and at Erfurt on Peter Lombard's standard medieval theological textbook, the *Sentences,* during 1509, the years just prior to his own intensive biblical research and lectures on the Psalms and Romans. In the former two, a humanistic and semi-Pelagian spirit prevailed in the Aristotelian-governed ethics of the "rancid philosopher" (III, 7): "we become just by doing just acts." In the latter two, the gospel message promised rather that sinners are declared to be righteous solely through their faith in Jesus Christ and that they then witness lovingly to others through the power of the Spirit in the "obedience of faith" (Rom. 1:5, 16-17).

> The righteousness of God is so named to distinguish it from the righteousness of man, which comes from works, as Aristotle describes it very clearly in Book III of his *Ethics*. According to him, righteousness follows upon actions and originates in them. But according to God, righteousness precedes works, and thus works are the result of righteousness, just as no person can do the works of a bishop or priest unless he is first consecrated and has been set apart for this.[30]

Paul's affirmation of the universal guilt of humankind is grounded in his conviction that God judges conduct by character, not character by conduct. The various levels of human perdition lead from ingratitude, vanity, spiritual blindness, and finally to idolatry itself, whereby sinners worship and serve some creature rather than the Creator (1:25). Luther avers with Paul: "This is the worst. To have arrived at this point means to have arrived at the abyss. For when a person has lost God, nothing remains except that he be given over to every type of turpitude according to the will of the devil. The result is that deluge of evils and blood-letting of which the apostle goes on to speak."[31]

Religious unrighteousness is therefore the spiritual root of the inseparable ethical fruit of societal disobedience. Love of God always precedes and governs love of neighbor. Therefore Luther contends that for Paul,

Unrighteousness is the sin of unbelief (*Unglaube*), the lack of the righteousness that comes from faith, for as we read in Rom. 1:17, Mark
16:16, and in many other passages, he who believes is righteous, he
who does not believe also does not obey, and he who does not obey is
unrighteous. For disobedience is the essence of unrighteousness and
the essence of sin, according to the statement of Ambrose, "sin in disobedience to the heavenly commandments."[32]

In Romans 2, our sinful "disobedience to the heavenly commandments" is further elucidated in depth by contrasting our external obedience to the letter of the law and our internal fulfillment of its loving spirit.
One may literally comply with the demands of the law out of the fear of
punishment or the hope of reward. That kind of legalistic obedience,
however minimally acceptable to civil society, is not pleasing to the God
who searches the heart. It is only in faith and with love that we can truly
fulfill God's will in the power of the Holy Spirit. Luther interprets Paul as
teaching "that no one is looked upon as righteous except the one who fulfills the Law in deed, and no one fulfills the Law except the man who
believes in Christ. Thus the apostle intends to conclude that outside of
Christ no one is righteous, no one fulfills the Law."[33]

In other words, the "works of the Law," merely externally and faith-
lessly performed as such, are in no way comparable before God to the
"fruits of the Spirit" that are eschatologically commanded and accepted by
God as authentic expressions of faith active in love and justice. Only the
Holy Spirit makes human works good. Sin presupposed, clean hands may
well hide a corrupted heart. Consequently, Paul concludes realistically that
no one is righteous and that "no human being will be justified in his
[God's] sight by deeds prescribed by the law, for through the law comes
knowledge of sin" (Rom. 3:20).

This is well expressed by blessed Augustine in the eighth chapter of
On the Spirit and the Letter, where he says, "They do the works of the
Law according to the Letter without the Spirit, that is, from fear of
punishment and not from love of righteousness. With their will they
would want to do something different if they could get by with it
without punishment, but they do so with a guilty will. What advantage can external works have when before the will is sinful, even
though the hand may be righteous before men?"

[Augustine also teaches], "The Letter is nothing but Law without
grace." We, on the other hand, may say that the Spirit is nothing but
grace without Law. Whenever the Letter is, or Law without grace,
everything remains dead in the Letter.[34]

By way of stark contrast, Romans 3 and 4 are chiefly devoted to Paul's
spirited proclamation of "the gospel of the righteousness of God through

faith in Jesus Christ for all who believe. . . . For we hold that a man is justified without the works of the law, by faith alone" (Rom. 3:22,28). Integrally interspersed, however, is Paul's profound analysis of the contrasting original sin of humankind, its perduring impact on all subsequent human history, and the resultant struggle between Satan and God as represented by the opposing forces of the fallen Adam and the risen Christ.

In commenting on Paul's quotation of Psalm 32 regarding "the blessedness of those to whom God reckons righteousness apart from works" (4:6-8), Luther is reminded of the related message of Psalm 51: "This verse speaks most explicitly of original sin, according to the Hebrew text: 'Behold, I was conceived in iniquities,' that is, in unrighteousness, and 'in sin did my mother bear me' (Ps. 51:5). For the meaning is that this unrighteousness and sin do not refer to the mother who conceives and bears but to the child who is conceived and brought forth."[35]

Luther goes on to explain further that "through Adam" one is conceived in a state of corporate unrighteousness before God. All the sin which belongs to all of fallen humanity now becomes their own, too.

> This iniquity exists whether I perform it or even know about it. I am conceived in it, but I did not do it. It began to rule in me [*peccatum regnans*] before I began to live. It is simultaneous with me. . . . Therefore the sin is now my own, that is, by my will it has been approved and accepted by my consent, because without grace I have been unable to overcome it in myself; therefore it has overcome me, and I am, because of that same tinder and evil lust, through my work also an actual sinner and not merely under original sin.[36]

Luther is quick to insist that we not moralize self-righteously about this universal human condition. We are each born into and willingly perpetuate the corporate condition of fallen humanity. We are not sinners because we commit sinful deeds; we commit sinful deeds because we are sinners.

When it comes to evaluating "righteousness," therefore, we dare not confuse our relative moral standing in a godless society (*coram hominibus*) with our absolute religious standing before Almighty God (*coram Deo*). In the Scriptures, "righteousness" is an exclusive category that designates my being rightly or wrongly related to the God in whose holy and loving image I have been interdependently created. Human righteousness is therefore not so much intrinsic as it is relational. It is determined not by our moral computation but by God's sovereign imputation, whether negatively in wrath or positively in mercy. In the eternal tribunal, God judges as sinners all those who are born in sinful solidarity with the fallen Adam, of whom some may also be faithfully acquitted through their baptismal interchange with the righteous Christ.

> Scripture uses the terms "righteousness" and "unrighteousness" very
> differently than the philosophers and lawyers. This is obvious, because
> they consider these things as a quality of the soul (Aristotle).
>
> But the "righteousness" of Scripture depends upon the imputation
> of God more than on the essence of a thing itself. For he does not
> have righteousness who only has a quality, indeed, he is altogether a
> sinner and an unrighteous man; but he alone has righteousness whom
> God mercifully regards as righteous because of his confession of his
> own unrighteousness and because of his prayer for the righteousness
> of God and whom God wills to be considered righteous before Him.
> Therefore, we are all born in iniquity, that is, in unrighteousness, and
> will die in it, and we are righteous only by the imputation of a mer-
> ciful God through faith in His Word.[37]

Luther's interpretation is clearly based here on Paul's proclamation of
the gospel in Romans, where, without exception, it is consistently affirmed
that "all have sinned and fall short of the glory of God" (3:23), and "to one
who without works trusts him who justify the ungodly: such faith is reckoned as righteousness" (4:5). To document that this teaching is not merely
peculiar to Paul alone, however, Luther explosively treats over twenty other
illustrative passages in turn from both the Old and New Testaments, from
Genesis through Revelation, that corroborate his view "that we are all in
our sins": Gen. 8:21; Exod. 34:7; Rom. 3:20; 1 Kings 8:46; 2 Chron. 6:36;
Eccles. 7:20; Job 7:20-21; 9:2,15; 27:6; Pss. 32:6; 72:14; 130:8; 143:2; Isa. 64:6;
Jer. 30:11; 1 Tim. 1:15; Rom. 7:19; Phil. 3:13, James 3:2; 1 John 1:8; 5:18;
Rev. 22:11. Indeed, it was Christ himself who commanded his followers to
pray daily, "forgive us our debts" (Matt. 6:12).[38]

Finally, in Romans 5, Luther views our inherited original sin (*concupiscentia*) as inherently self-serving and lifelong both in duration and corruption. In opposition to the semi-Pelagian anthropology so widespread in the
church piety of his day, Luther held with Paul that God's response to our
prayer, "Search me, O God, and know my heart" (Ps. 139:23), serves only
to disclose a rebel engaged in idolatrous self-worship.

> The reason is that our nature has been so deeply curved in upon itself
> (*incurvatus in se*) because of the viciousness of original sin that it not
> only turns the finest gifts of God in upon itself and enjoys them (as is
> evident in the case of legalists and hypocrites), indeed it even uses God
> Himself to achieve these aims; but it also seems to be ignorant of this
> very fact, that in acting so iniquitously, so perversely, and in so
> depraved a way, it is even seeking God for its own sake. Thus the
> prophet Jeremiah says in Jer. 17:9: "The heart is perverse above all
> things, and desperately corrupt; who can understand it?"[39]

As a result, Luther's reading of Paul compelled him to favor the church's
"ancient doctors" (Augustine and Ambrose) over its "newer doctors"

(John Duns Scotus, William Ockham, and Gabriel Biel) on sin and grace, because the latter Scholastics "speak without the testimony of Scripture, they speak with little authority." In contrast, "the ancient doctors in agreement with the apostles are saying the same things and much more clearly."[40] In this spirit, Luther favored Augustine's position that the scriptural foundation for the church's doctrine of original sin is centered in the Pauline teaching that "sin came into the world through one man [Adam], and death came through sin, and so death spread to all because all have sinned" (5:12).

The early Western church (Tertullian, Cyprian, Ambrose, and especially Augustine) taught the solidarity of humanity with Adam not only in the consequences of his sin, but in the sin itself, which was universally transmitted through natural generation. In dealing with the Vulgate Latin translation of the Pauline Greek text (*in quo* being "unclear in Greek" as either masculine or neuter), they referred the key phrase directly to Adam, "*in whom* all have sinned" (5:12). This decision results, of course, in a pessimistic view of fallen humanity, since it entails the radical corruption (though not total destruction) of one's reason, will, and passions among all guilty human persons before God.

Luther believed for many reasons that this Western patristic view of original sin comported best with the teaching of Paul in Romans 5: (1) "through one man" means that sin originated in the disobedience of Adam, not imitation of the devil; (2) "through one man" also means the original sin of Adam, not actual sins of his many human followers; (3) "sin came into the world" means that human beings became guilty through the imitating rebellion of Adam; (4) "death through sin" means that human death was not the original intention of God the Creator; (5) "death spread to all men" means that it comes upon all guilty sinners; (6) "sin" in the singular means the uniqueness of this fallen state; (7) "in which all men sinned" means that each sins are one's own; (8) "sin was in the world before the Law was given" means that actual sins were practiced but original sin as such was unknown until Moses revealed it in Genesis 3; (9) "sins were not like the transgression of Adam" means that they were not an exact simulation of Adam's original infidelity; and (10) that "Adam is a type of the One who was to come" is reserved because of its importance for more extruded explication below.[41]

Luther summarizes his understanding of Paul's view of original sin in polemical opposition to those Scholastics and Sophists whom he castigates as "O fools, O pig-theologians (*Saw theologen*)," namely, Duns Scotus, Pierre d'Ailly, and especially Gabriel Biel.[42] Referring to the standard late medieval church teaching of Peter Lombard's *Sentences,* Luther insists that original sin,

> according to the apostle and the simplicity of meaning in Christ Jesus, is not only a lack of certain quality in the will, nor even only a lack of

> light in the mind or of power in the memory, but particularly it is a total lack of uprightness and of the power of all the faculties both of body and soul and of the whole inner and outer man. On top of this, it is a propensity toward evil . . . the universal concupiscence by which we become disobedient to the commandment. As the ancient holy fathers so correctly said, this original sin is the very tender of sin, the law of the members, the weakness of our nature, the tyrant, the original sickness.[43]

It will best serve our primary purpose if we now conclude this section on Paul's view of original sin in Romans 5 by sketching his eschatological contrast between the two ages of Adam and Christ, as centered respectively in the first Adam's fall and the second Adam's cross (5:12-21). That Paul considered Adam as a "type of the One who was to come" (5:14) was to prove to be decisive for the theological worldviews and ethics of both Augustine and Luther. In the authentic tradition of the gospel, Luther recollects Augustine's quotation of St. John of Chrysostom's exegesis of this Pauline passage:

> . . . in the likeness of the transgression of Adam, who is "a type of the One who was to come," because Adam is also a figure of Christ. And how is he a figure? The answer is that just as Adam has become a cause of death to those who are born of him, even though they have not eaten of the tree, the death brought on by the eating, so also Christ was made a provider of righteousness for those who belong to Him, even though they are entirely lacking in righteousness, and He has given it to us through His Cross.[44]

Here in one of the most profound passages of the New Testament, Paul boldly encompasses all of human history by contrasting two opposing ages that are typologically represented by Adam and Christ. Adam heads the old age of death and sin; Christ heads the new age of life and righteousness.

Three theological convictions undergird Paul's position here. First, God's mighty act in Christ has cosmic significance. The cross and resurrection inaugurate a whole new aeon for humanity and not merely for individual persons in Christianity. Second, every person's life is linked inseparably with the lives of other human beings in corporate solidarity. Through natural birth all of God's sinful creatures are united before God "in Adam"; through spiritual rebirth all righteous saints are united before God "in Christ." Third, sin and death are interrelated enemies of humanity that are provoked and exposed by God's law (*nomos*). Persons die because persons sin; both are constitutive of the old age in Adam to be overcome by the life and righteousness reckoned to forgiven and renewed sinners baptized into the new age in Christ.

Paul is interpreted by Luther as personifying sin, death, the devil, along with God's wrath and law, as demonic powers that curse humanity in its faithless distrust and sinful rebellion. Creatures become like those whom they worship, whether like God in Christ (*imago Dei*) or like Satan in Adam (*imago diaboli*).

> Thus the likeness of Adam's transgression is in us, because we die, as if we had sinned in the same way he did. And the likeness of Christ's justification is in us, because we love, as if we had produced the same kind of righteousness that He did. Therefore, because of this likeness, Adam is the type of the One who was to come; that is, Christ, who came after Him. Indeed, in order that He might take away this likeness and give us His own, "He was born in the likeness of men" (Phil. 2:7) and sent by the Father "in the likeness of sinful flesh" (Rom. 8:3). And thus, "as in Adam all die, so also in Christ shall all be made alive."[45]

Christians today who do not accept the literal historicity of the first Adam can still appreciate the theological significance of designating Christ as the final Adam. Paul is lauding the personal and direct intervention of God in history to offer humankind a fresh start, a new beginning, a second chance. Adam depicts humanity as it is—in sin, under law, trespass, judgment, and death. Christ represents humanity as it was meant to be—in righteousness, under grace, freedom, love, and life. True human, as well as true God, Jesus Christ has come so that "grace might also reign through righteousness to eternal life" (Rom. 5:21).

Luther notes particularly Paul's contention that all this human regeneration and renewal takes place only through "the grace of God and the free gift of that one Man, Jesus Christ" (5:15).

> The meaning is "the grace of God" (by which He justifies us, which actually is in Christ as in its origin, just as the sin of man is in Adam) "and the free gift," namely, that which Christ pours out from His Father upon those who believe in Him. The gift is "by the grace of that one Man," that is, by the personal merit and grace of Christ, by which He was pleasing to God, so that He might give this gift to us. This phrase "by the grace of that one Man" should be understood as the grace of Christ, corresponding to personal sin of Adam which belonged to him, but the "gift" is the very righteousness which has been given to us.[46]

Later in this epistle (and so below in chapter 5), Paul will also develop the eschatological tension between the present and future dimensions of Christian hope. On the cosmic level, the new age in Christ (elsewhere, the kingdom of God) is already inaugurated but not yet fully consummated. It has already intersected the old age in Adam but not yet replaced it. In like fashion on the human level, the Christian is at once righteous and sinful, already fully justified ("grace") but not yet fully sanctified ("gifts"). The baptized believer is simultaneously a sinful creature in the "old age" of Adam and also a redeemed saint in the "new age" of Christ. At present, however, we must be satisfied to present this "two ages" typology in Paul as foundational for the later coherent teachings of the "two cities" in Augustine and then still later for the "two kingdoms" in Luther.

Augustine on the Two Cities

In view of the subsequent wake of church history, it should never be forgotten that Luther's young adult piety was decisively shaped by the strict discipline of the hermit wing of German Augustinian monasticism. When admonished by his general vicar "to renounce this world and consecrate yourself to God and our order," Brother Martin freely vowed "to live until death without worldly possessions and in chastity according to the *Rule of St. Augustine of Hippo.*" Of course, Luther later turned sharply against the "meritorious pretenses of monkery," that is, its specious late-medieval theological rationale in contributing to salvation. Nevertheless, the ardent German monk whose very baptismal name was consecrated by the father of Western monasticism, St. Martin of Tours, consistently expressed life-long gratitude for his monastic life of prayer, study, and work, as such.

Our limited concern here is to document briefly how Luther's world-renouncing vow as a "seriously pious," indeed serupulant (*pusilanimitas*), Augustinian monk was initially cultivated in an ecclesial and theological ethos decisively governed by one of the immensely influential texts of the Western Christian church, St. Augustine's *City of God* (413–26). This classic deserves our special consideration as an intermediary bridge between Paul's earlier "two ages" and Luther's later "two kingdoms." Each in his own day and way, these three kindred "Christian realists" grappled with the complex eschatological relations of God and Satan, kingdom and history, Christ and culture, church and world.

The *City of God,* at once theological, philosophical, historical, and political, depicts our corporate human destiny with broad strokes on a massive literary canvas. The affinities with Genesis are immediately apparent. Certainly one major goal of Augustine's rich and many-faceted work was to refute the pagans' charge that Rome had been ignominiously sacked by the barbarian Goths under Agaric (410) because the empire had officially become Christian. Hence, the fall of Rome provided Augustine with a strategic point of departure for analyzing the dualistic relation of two cities—what he symbolically called the "city of God" (*civitas Dei*), the heavenly city, the new Jerusalem, in mortal combat with the "city of man," the earthly city, the evil Babylon (*civitas diaboli*).

In variously nuanced presentations, colored vividly by Augustine's own personal experiences, these two antithetical powers portray the unique calling of "the City of God, that is to say, God's Church," in a temporal world governed ultimately by the devil (*regnum diaboli*). At the same time,

Augustine also freely acknowledges that not all in the church will be saved and not all in the world will be damned. Highly mysteriously, the world remains God's good creation, despite its polytheistic idolatry. It can therefore "be used" (*uti*) prudently for God's providential purposes by God's people during their temporal "pilgrimage in this world" toward eternal life. Their chief social concern is to secure "freedom to worship the true, one God." Ultimately and ecclesiologically, there is only the world's final judgment; penultimately and ecclesiastically, however, the two cities are "interwoven and mingled with one another."[47]

Nevertheless, the massive work's full title, *Concerning the City of God against the Pagans,* also signals Augustine's prevailing dualistic disposition. So does its bifurcated structure. Part One is divided into two divisions: the first five books (1–5) deplore the pagan polytheism of ancient Rome; the second five books (6-10) scrutinize pagan worship and Greek philosophy, anticipating Augustine's ringing trinitarian response to his culture's basic challenge: "How is this God you tell of, and how is it proved that he is the only one to whom the Romans owed obedience, and that they should have worshiped no god besides him?"[48]

Part Two is likewise subdivided into three major divisions that develop differing features of the two cities: the first four books (11–14) deal theologically and philosophically with creation, time, and eternity; the next four books (15–18) sketch biblically the city of God after Adam's fall from Abel to Christ, the corresponding city of man from Cain through the great ancient empires drunk with the lust for power (*libido dominandi*); and then the final four books (19–22) conclude teleologically with resultant consideration of war and peace, law and order, and the beatific vision of God.

Our central interest for theological ethics is Augustine's organizing principle of the two cities as such. His inspiration is not merely political but explicitly biblical: "Glorious things are said of thee, O city of God" (Ps. 86:3; cf. Pss. 87:3; 48:1,2,8; 46:4-5). By *city,* Augustine means a "society or community" or a "house, temple, or family." He then also refers to "these two diverse and opposed communities of angels, in which we find something like the beginnings of the two communities of mankind."[49] A city is therefore an association of persons held together by a common bond, in this ultimate case by love of God or of self.

> This is assuredly the great difference that sunders of the two cities of which we are speaking: the one is a community of devout men, the other a community of the irreligious, and each has its own angels attached to it. In the one city love of God has been given first place, in the other, love of self.
>
> We see then that the two cities were created by two kinds of love: the earthly city was created by self-love reaching the point of contempt

for God, the Heavenly City by the love of God carried as far as contempt of self. In fact, the earthly city glories in itself; the Heavenly City glories in the Lord (1 Cor. 10:17).[50]

The cities are allegorical or mystical in character, originating with faithful and unfaithful angels in heaven. The citizens of these two cities are separated and in conflict with one another by virtue of their relation to God: either "a love inspired by its founder" (city of God) or "a preference for their own gods" (city of humanity). This is the great divide that results on earth from the disobedient transgression prompted by Adam's evil will: "Pride is the start of every kind of sin" (Eccles. 10:13). The two cities have two leaders. The humility that is so highly prized in the city of God

> receives particular emphasis in the character of Christ, the king of that City. We are also taught by the sacred Scriptures that the fault of exaltation, the contrary of humility, exercises supreme dominion in Christ's adversary, the Devil. . . .
>
> I classify the human race into two branches: the one consists of those who live by human standards, the other of those who live according to God's will. I also call these two classes the two cities, speaking allegorically. By two cities I mean two societies of human beings, one of which is predestined to reign with God for all eternity, the other doomed to undergo eternal punishment with the Devil.[51]

While no compromise is possible between worship of the true God in Jesus Christ and competing pagan gods and goddesses, Christians and their non-Christian neighbors must nevertheless realistically share their civil lives together prior to the Final Judgment. "Both kinds of men and both kinds of households alike make use of the things essential for this mortal life; but each has its own very different end in making use of them."[52]

This means very practically for Augustine that the Christian community must critically work together with other people with whom it cannot worship together. The church should neither identify with the world nor separate from the world. "Since the life of a city is inevitably a social life," realistic accommodations are required:

> Thus even the Heavenly City in her pilgrimage here on earth makes use of the earthy peace and defends and seeks the compromise between human wills in respect of the provisions relevant to the mortal nature of man, so far as may be permitted without detriment to true religion and piety. In fact, that City relates the earthly peace to the heavenly peace . . . for this peace is the perfectly ordered and completely harmonious fellowship in the enjoyment of God, and of each other in God.[53]

Augustine's dual proposals for theological condemnation of, and yet cultural accommodation with, pagan Rome were both, in varying degrees, to have their eventual impact on Luther's theological ethics. Yet very different historical circumstances shaped the marked one-sidedness of Luther's eventual Augustinian inheritance. For example, where are the defined boundaries between the two cities after the Roman empire becomes officially "Christianized" by Emperor Constantine the Great after A.D. 312? Moreover, the thousand years between the death of Augustine and the birth of Luther also witnessed the rise and fall of the subsequent church-state-culture medieval synthesis of Western Christendom. Whereas Augustine's projected protagonist was the political secularism of ancient Rome ("instruments of Satan"), Luther's was rather the ecclesial clericalism of late medieval Romanism.

To illustrate: In the papal bull *Unam Sanctam* (1302), Pope Boniface VIII had marked the zenith of medieval papal hegemony by declaring that Rome was the only "One Holy Catholic and Apostolic Church" (outside of which there was "neither salvation nor remission of sin"). God has allegedly committed the "two swords" of spiritual and temporal power to Rome, the former of which was to be exercised directly by the clergy of the church, and the latter of which was to be delegated by the church to secular authorities, to be wielded on behalf of the Roman church and under its direction (cf. Luke 22:38). All this neo-theocratic papal ideology claimed the implicit blessing of Augustine's opposing two cities.

It is historically understandable that the beleaguered leader of the Reformation was far more impressed by Augustine's pessimistic depiction of the earthly city than by his mentor's uncritical linkage of the Catholic Church with the city of God. Therefore, in his own Christocentric interpretation of the fall in Genesis 3, Luther once again demonstrated that he was primarily a Paulinist and only secondarily an Augustinian.

To be sure, Luther always strongly endorsed Augustine on the radical nature of human sin against the semi-Pelagian tendencies of late medieval Scholasticism. At the same time, however, Luther felt increasingly compelled to challenge even Augustine on the secular power of the church, which he judged to be unfaithful to "the clearest Gospel of all" in Paul's Romans. For in this epistle, Paul goes on to complement his dualistic doctrine of the two ages between God and Satan (Romans 5) with God's twofold rule against Satan, as simultaneously and dialectically exercised through both Christ and Caesar (Romans 12–16). It was only through his deeper study of Romans amid the chaotic societal challenges of sixteenth-century Germany that Luther, the former Augustinian monk, uncovered his own biblical vocation to reform and amplify Augustine's dualistic two cities, encompassing also Paul's depiction of God's twofold rule within the world's two ages in the two-stage development of his own complex teaching of the two kingdoms.

Part Three

God's Twofold Rule
(Caesar and Christ)

Chapter 5

Cain and Abel: Law Judges before God

I N PART ONE, we concentrated on establishing the biblical character of Luther's ethics. We then examined, in Part Two, the biblical foundations in Genesis and Romans for the world's "two ages" (Paul) or "two cities" (Augustine) in the cosmic struggle between God and Satan, which resulted from the fall into sin of Adam and Eve.

In Part Three, we will now develop at length Luther's paradoxical biblical teaching on God's sovereign but highly dialectical response to all of this cosmic evil and human sin. After emulating the cosmic dualism of Paul and Augustine with his own early teaching on what later became identified as the "two kingdoms" (*zwei Reiche*), Luther went on to *complement* this inaugurated eschatology with a very dialectical historical corollary. It is God's twofold rule or governance/governments (*zweierlei Regimente*) both within and between the two intersecting realms of creation and redemption through Caesar and Christ with law and gospel for Christian service and salvation.

Moreover, this grand paradigm of God's twofold rule throughout the world's two kingdoms deftly integrates the Reformer's holistic view of Christian faith and life. As a professor of Scripture, Luther was never vocationally called to write a systematic theology or theological ethic as such. Nevertheless, his comprehensive biblical teaching on God's twofold rule does provide us with a coherent trinitarian scope and Christocentric shape for functionally interrelating all the tension-filled elements of the total scriptural witness to the mighty acts of the Triune God against Satan in human salvation.

Luther on the Two Kingdoms

We shall continue our survey of Luther's *Lectures on Genesis* (1535) in order to initiate our coverage of God's varied responses to the willful seduction of Adam and Eve by the wiles of Satan, and the subsequent murder of their son Abel by his older brother, Cain.[1] Dominating the fall to flood narrative of Genesis 3–7 is the awesome display of God's righteous wrath, demonstrating the total absence of any divine permissiveness in the face of human sin.

Created in God's image, persons are both responsible and accountable. In reaction to human distrust and disobedience, however, God's holy love takes on and is humanly perceived in the strange and fearsome forms of wrath, accusations, condemnation, and judgment. While God's proper work (*opus proprium*) is to comfort, his strange work (*opus alienum*) is simultaneously to terrify (cf. Isa. 28:61). When applying this dialectical stance to the tragic breach between Abel and Cain, God's pious friend and idolatrous enemy, Luther explicitly acknowledges his personal indebtedness to his Pauline-influenced, dualistic teacher, Augustine, whose two cities are now intentionally transmuted into Luther's two churches.

Here (Gen. 4:3-4) the church begins to be divided into two churches: the one that is the church in name only but in reality is nothing but a hypocritical and bloodthirsty church, and the other one, which is without influence, forsaken, and exposed to suffering and the cross, and which before the world and in sight of that hypocritical church is truly Abel, that is, vanity and nothing. "For Christ also calls Abel righteous and makes him the beginning of the church of the godly, which will continue until the end (Matt. 23:35). Similarly Cain is the beginning of the church of the wicked and of the bloodthirsty until the end of the world. Augustine treats this story in a similar way in his book *The City of God*."[2]

Immediately after the Genesis account of the fall, there follows "the second part of the sermon, in which God threatens bodily punishments, first for the woman, then also for the man."[3] Tempered by the earlier promise of Eve's future "seed" (Christ) who will crush the head of the serpent (3:15), God's "fatherly anger" toward Adam and Eve should not be confused with the "wrath of the Judge" against Satan, who has no hope of deliverance. "This is why until the Last Day he will rage with such great fury against the church and against the Son of God."[4]

Luther cites the word of Christ (John 8:44) that Satan "was a murderer from the beginning and is . . . a liar and the father of lies." This is "the light of the Gospel" by which the darkness of the Old Testament is made clear. The created innocence of Adam and Eve was destroyed by Satan in Paradise when he "weakened the authority of the divine command" (*mandatum*) and tempted that they would be like gods if they ate from the forbidden tree of the knowledge of good and evil.

The "chief meaning of this passage" is that the devil is the "originator of this catastrophe," and that, reflecting Paul's teaching, God's good creation is forever divided in a permanent breach:

> Adam is a figure of Christ. . . . Just as through Adam sin came to all, so also Christ's righteousness comes to all who believe in Him. . . .
>
> Dealt with in this manner, what else can the closed Paradise and the cherubim with their swords stationed to guard Paradise signify than that without faith in Christ man can endure neither the Law nor the Gospel? The tree of death is the Law, and the tree of life is the Gospel, or Christ. Those who do not believe in Christ cannot draw near to these trees.[5]

Chapter 4 of Genesis introduces the story of Cain and Abel against the background of their fallen parents, Adam and Eve. Luther emphasizes again that originally Adam and Eve "are not only parents . . . but they also perform the office of priests." They were filled with the Holy Spirit, enlightened by the knowledge of the Christ to come, and led their children in worship, exhorting them "to show their gratitude to so merciful a God." It follows for Luther that soon after Cain and Abel are introduced they are likewise depicted as "bringing offerings" to God of the fruit of the earth (Cain) and of the animal flocks (Abel). Each is thereby destined to become "an example of the twofold church, the true and the hypocritical one."[6]

The main feature of these dualistic two churches (elsewhere "realms" or "kingdoms") is that they are composed of two different kinds of people, believers and unbelievers. They represent for Luther the two *spatial* force-fields within which God's intersecting twofold rule is *temporally* exercised against Satan in radically different ways. All depends on the state of righteousness of the human inhabitants, who follow either the "faithless and bloodthirsty Cain" or the "faithful and righteous Abel." Consequently, the true church is always "hidden," known only to God by its faithful sign: "conformity to Christ" (Rom. 8:29) in his suffering and death. "Their blood will be regarded precious in His sight" (Ps. 72:14). "But there is a judgment coming between the full and the hungry, between the goats and the sheep, and between Abel and Cain. In it, God will announce His approval of that suffering and hungering church, and also His condemnation of the hypocritical and bloodthirsty ones. This is our comfort and, as it were, the sugar with which our present hardships must be flavored and overcome."[7]

Significantly, Luther centers the conflict between the two churches of Cain and Abel in this "outstanding passage" on the evangelical "essence of our teaching." It is the primal biblical witness to the doctrine of justification by faith. "We teach and confess that a person rather than his work is accepted by God and that a person does not become righteous as a result of righteous work, but that a work becomes righteous and good as a result of a righteous and good person, just as the text here proves. Because God has no regard for Cain, He has no regard for his offering either."[8]

Luther proclaims that the "the true church" bases its life on the divine grace embodied in Christ that is apprehended by human faith. This is "the basic issue": that nothing is pleasing to God unless it is done in faith. This is in agreement with the profound statement of Paul (Rom. 14:23): "Whatsoever is not of faith is sin." Additionally, the second basic issue is that "sin is so enormous that it cannot be blotted out by sacrifices and other works but only through God's mercy, which must be accepted by faith . . . nor does faith, as a work, make just; but it makes just because it apprehends the mercy which is offered in Christ."[9]

Following his loveless murder of Abel in jealousy and rage, Cain, clearly "possessed by Satan," ironically accuses himself by excusing himself before God. He denies his guilt, even as he also flaunts God's universal command of love, as implanted in the human heart (Rom. 2:15) and then also later written into the "natural (moral) law" (*lex naturae, lex moralis*) of the Old and New Testaments.

> He does not say: "Lord, I confess it. I have killed my brother. Forgive me!" But he himself, who should be accused, even accuses God: "I am surely not the keeper of my brother, am I?" What does he accomplish by this haughtiness? This, that he freely admits that this Law (Lev. 19:18), "Love your neighbor as yourself," is no concern to him; and likewise the command (Matt. 7:12), "What you do not want done to yourself, do not do to one another." This Law was not promulgated for the first time in the Decalogue, but is written in the hearts of all men.[10]

Unlike earlier, when Adam was not personally cursed, but only the earth (Gen. 3:17), now Cain is himself cursed by God where Abel's blood has been spilled (Gen. 4:10). God's forensic judgment, "Cursed are you," changes forever the future of humanity. "Here is the beginning of the two churches that are utterly opposed to each other: the one, the church of Adam and the godly, which has the hope and promise of the blessed Seed; the other, the church of Cain, which has lost this hope and promise through its sin and cannot regain it."[11]

To be sure, God mercifully moderates the sentence and commands that no one should kill Cain (Gen. 4:15). Nevertheless, Cain is compelled to bear a permanent sign as an indication of the wrath of God that marks his exile, curse, and other penalties.

Symbolically, the world's first murderer was also destined to become the primal progenitor of opposition to the world's gracious Creator: "At the very beginning there were two kinds of churches: the one, that of the children of Satan and of the flesh, which quickly makes great increases; the other, that of the children of God, which makes slow gains and is weak."[12]

Then, in chapters 6 and 7 of Genesis, Luther's attention turns finally to the story of the flood. This climactic section is governed by Luther's earlier explanation of the "strange work" (*opus alienum*) of God's grieving wrath in response to human infidelity. "The LORD saw that the wickedness of humankind was great in the earth . . . and the LORD was sorry that he had made humankind on the earth, and it grieved him to the heart" (Gen. 6:6). "God is not mocked," and his wrath was certainly not like Cain's "capricious anger." Rather, it expressed "the utmost clemency and the utmost fairness," prompted by the righteous quality of God's holy love. "In this instance there is no wrath except that of judicial authority; for it is directed at the crime, not at the person."[13]

Even when inflicting punishment, destruction, and condemnation, "God remained constant." The Lord was most severe with sinners "when they began to misuse His gifts," but he also intentionally promised deliverance to Noah and his righteous family in order "to frighten the ungodly and to awaken us with many awe-inspiring examples of His wrath, that we may learn to despair of ourselves and to put our trust in His grace alone."[14]

Noah was God's "greatest prophet," who preached for the longest time about "the universal punishment of the entire world." Nevertheless, his preaching was despised among both the Cainites and the descendants of Adam. It serves only to demonstrate that "the church of Satan is everlastingly at war with the church of God."[15]

It is the "true church" that demonstrates it is "always a wall against the wrath of God." It "grieves, it agonizes, it prays, it pleads, it teaches, it preaches, it admonishes, as long as the hour of judgment has not yet arrived but is impending."[16] In other words, the "true church" (as its living Lord in Mark 1:15), proclaims to sinners the judging law of God ("repent") only in order to prepare them to receive aright the saving gospel of Christ ("believe in the good news . . . the kingdom of God has come near").

Luther considered God's law-gospel dialectic of such importance after the fall that he explicitly structured his commentary on the Genesis narrative accordingly: first God's command of love (Adam), then God's judging law (Cain), and only afterward God's saving gospel and renewed exhortations of love (Abraham). "In this way Moses describes the first and original world. . . . In the beginning there was that most holy and, in truth, that golden age which the poets also mention, without a doubt as the result of the traditions and statements of the patriarchs. But when sins prevailed, God did not spare the first world but destroyed it with the Flood. Neither did he spare the second world, which was under the Law."[17]

In other theological contexts, Luther would more usually speak not about two churches or two worlds (as here in the Genesis setting of Cain and Abel), but rather of two realms or two kingdoms (*zwei Reiche*), thereby intentionally stressing the New Testament witness to Christ's proclamation and inauguration of the in-breaking kingdom of God amid its faithless and loveless enemies. However, the basic dualist motif remains eschatologically the same: Satan versus God, along with their respective followers.

In *The Bondage of the Will* (1525), for example, Luther concludes his entire work by speaking boldly of God's division "of the entire race of men into two, giving the righteousness of God to believers and denying it to unbelievers." Therefore in Romans, Paul denies that "anything outside this faith is righteous in the sight of God, and if it is not righteous in the sight of God, it must necessarily be sin." The result is that, "With God there is nothing intermediate between righteousness and sin, no neutral ground."[18]

To cite a "crowning touch from Paul," Luther recalls the conflicting powers of "flesh" and "spirit" that had earlier made such a deep impression on Augustine:

> In Romans 8:5, where Paul divides the human race into two types, namely, flesh and spirit (just as Christ does in John 3:6), he says, "Those who live according to the flesh set their minds on the things of the flesh, but those who live according to the Spirit set their minds on the things of the Spirit." . . . Thus the twin statements of Paul are confirmed, that the righteous live by faith (Rom. 1:17), and that whatever is not of faith is sin (Rom. 14:23).[19]

For Luther, so also is it in Paul and in John. Whether cast in the contrasting terms of light or darkness (John 1:15), church or world (1 John 5:19), and from above or from below (John 8:23), the Johannine gospel is proclaimed in dualistic images of "division," "absolute distinction," or "antithetically." Illumined by the Spirit, Christians see that "Scripture everywhere preaches Christ by contrast and antithesis, putting everything that is without the Spirit of Christ in subjection to Satan."[20]

> For unless everything said about Christ and grace were said antithetically, so as to be said over against its opposite—for instance, that outside of Christ there is nothing but Satan, apart from grace nothing but wrath, apart from light nothing but darkness, apart from the way only error, apart from the truth only a lie, apart from life only death—what, I ask you, would be the point of all the discourses of the apostles and of Scripture as a whole?[21]

Luther typically characterizes this biblical cleavage of fallen humankind in the eschatological terms of two kingdoms. On the one side is the trinitarian power of God, the Father, Son, and Holy Spirit; on the other side are the antitrinitarian forces of sin, death, and the devil, to which are added, paradoxically by Paul, God's own wrath and law. Before God (*coram Deo*), humans must let God alone be God. "These things are, I think, sufficiently established by that one saying of Christ's from Matt. 25:34: 'Come, O blessed of my Father, inherit the Kingdom prepared for you from the foundation of the world.'"[22] Outside God's kingdom of grace and love is only Satan's antikingdom of sin and death. "For what is the whole human race without the Spirit but the kingdom of the devil, a confused chaos of darkness, hell (*infernum*). That is why Paul calls the demons "the rulers of this darkness" (Eph. 6:12), and says in 1 Cor. 2:8: "None of the princes of this world knew the wisdom of God."[23]

Luther therefore believes that he is bound by his fidelity to the Scriptures to teach the reality of the two kingdoms within creation this side of the fall. Here his eschatological realism remains essentially coherent with the Pauline and Augustinian re-traditioning of the testimony of Genesis. God's one kingdom in Paradise has been severed into two ages/cities/kingdoms that are destined to suffer in eschatological conflict until Christ's return in glory.

> For Christians know that there are two kingdoms in the world, which are bitterly opposed to each other. In one of them Satan reigns, who is therefore called by Christ "the ruler of this world" (John 12:31) and by Paul "the god of this world" (2 Cor. 4:4) He holds captive to his will all who are not snatched away from him by the Spirit of Christ, as the same Paul testifies.
>
> In the other Kingdom, Christ reigns, and his Kingdom ceaselessly resists and makes war on the kingdom of Satan. Into this Kingdom we are all transferred, not by our own power but by the grace of God, by which we are set from the present evil age (Gal. 1:4) and delivered from the dominion of darkness (Col. 1:13).
>
> Constantly I must pound and squeeze in and drive in and wedge in this difference between the two kingdoms, even though it is written and said so often that it becomes tedious. The devil never stops cooking and brewing these two kingdoms into each other. . . . Thus the devil is very busy on both sides, and he has much to do.[24]

What is truly biblically distinctive about Luther is the dialectical way in which he witnesses to God's temporal twofold rule by law and gospel *within each* of these two kingdoms of fallen creation and renewed redemption. Therefore, our own study will now follow Luther's lead as we move across the divide of the two kingdoms after the flood: from the "first world" of original creation governed by God's "proper work" (*opus proprium*) through the grace of love to the "second world" of fallen creation governed by God's "alien work" (*opus alienum*) through the wrath of the law. All this movement begins spiritually in the anguished pangs of conscience experienced by sinners, whether as righteous or as unrighteous. Before God (*coram Deo*), "the law accuses and puts to death" (*lex accusans et condemnatrix*).

Law's Theological Function

We return now to Paul's *Lectures on Romans* (1516) in order to complement the apostle's earlier analysis of human sin by focusing more sharply on his parallel development of the law's "theological function" (*usus theo-*

logicus/spiritualis/elenchticus) as both uncovering and even inciting the fallen creature's unbelief and disobedience in one's direct accountability to the Creator. In order of importance, not merely civilly but spiritually, it is the cumulative witness of Romans 3, 5, and 7 that God's universal law compels us to judge ourselves in depth as God judges us in the heavenly court (*in loco forensi*). The forensic verdict: guilty!

In chapter 3, we first recall Paul's universal indictment of Jew and Gentile alike as being "under the power of sin." He quotes with approval the judgment of Psalm 14: "None is righteous, no, not one; no one understands, no one seeks for God" (Rom. 3:9-11). Of special interest to us is the way Paul then grounds the standard for human accountability solely in the sovereign law of God. Here before God every self-justifying mouth is stopped: "For no human being will be justified in his sight by works of the law since through the law comes knowledge of sin" (Rom. 3:20).

There is no more illuminating scriptural passage than Rom. 3:20 to initiate our discussion on Luther's understanding of the theological (or spiritual) function of the law before God. For Paul it is the inseparable prelude to the gospel: whatever is said positively by the gospel (*Evangelium*) always presupposes what has already been said negatively by the law (*Gesetz*). Luther paraphrases Paul: "For we are not righteous because we act according to the Law, but because we are first righteous, therefore we then fulfill the Law; since through the Law comes, or is, the knowledge, but not the forgiveness, and thus not justification, of sin, so that proud men who do not know their sins may be humbled."[25] That summarizes Luther's consistent Pauline answer to "the purpose of the law": "That it may humble the proud."[26] Or in his cited comments from Augustine on this very passage: "For through the Law He has shown man his weakness, so that through faith he may flee to His mercy for cleansing."[27]

Luther cites Paul distinguishing between law and faith, or between the letter and grace, and also their reflective works. The law "either forces obedience through fear or allures us through the promise of temporal benefits." In contrast, the works of faith are done "out of the Spirit of liberty and solely for the love of God."

Properly understood, Scripture is evangelically consistent. Consequently, when both "St. James and the apostle" say that a person is justified by works (Rom. 2:13; James 2:24), they are refuting those who contend that faith suffices without any works at all. No, what they both teach is that faith justifies "without the works of the Law." Therefore it follows that "justification does not demand the works of the Law but a living faith which produces its own works."[28] Or in other words, faith alone justifies, but justifying faith is never itself alone without the Spirit's accompanying works of love (*fides sola iustificat, sed non est sola*).

This "knowledge of sin" comes by the law both through biblical proclamation (Rom. 7:7) and through daily experience. The law is not merely a codified collection of dead, codified edicts, but also a living reality that is universally embodied in the threatening demands of rulers, parents, teachers, neighbors, occupations, and so forth everywhere in life. For Luther, both sources disclose to a person "how deeply sin and evil are rooted in time, which he would not have understood if he did not have the Law and had not attempted to work in accordance with it." Whenever a person is confronted by an ethical precept or prohibition and feels hostile to it, one's sinfulness is thereby exposed "since a man is not a sinner unless he is unwilling to fulfill the Law, which prescribes good works and forbids evil." Luther explains:

> For if we were righteous and good, we would consent to the Law
> with ready will and delight in it, just as we now delight in our sins and
> evil desires. Hence: "Oh, how I love Thy Law" (Ps. 119:97) and again
> "But his delight is in the Law of the Lord" (Ps. 1:2). Behold, thus it
> has come to pass that through the Law there is knowledge of the sin
> which is in us, that is, of our evil will which inclines toward the evil
> and abhors the good. How useful the knowledge is![29]

In light of his own current semi-Pelagian doctrinal controversies, Luther stresses that by "works of the Law," he means "those which are regarded in themselves as being self-sufficient for righteousness and salvation." Unrighteous people who "have worked according to the outward form of the Law" have not truly "fulfilled the Law" as expressions of faith active in love and justice to one's neighbors. "For the 'works of the Law' are one thing and the 'fulfilling of the Law' another. For grace is the fulfilling of the Law, but not works. Well does he say 'works of the Law' and not 'will of the Law' for they do not will what the Law wills, although they do perform what the Law commands. But the Law wills and demands our will."[30]

Beyond the technical terminology is the decisive doctrinal issue: "We are not made righteous by doing righteous works, but rather we do righteous works by being righteous. Therefore grace alone justifies. . . . It is what Blessed Augustine in the thirteenth chapter of his *On the Spirit and the Letter* says: 'What the law of works commands by its threats, this the law of faith accomplishes by believing.'"[31]

God's law brings "the knowledge of sin" to different persons in different ways; it drives both the weak into despair and the strong into vanity. Luther cites corroborating scriptural testimony from Paul's claim in Rom. 3:23 that based on God's law, "all have sinned and fall short of the glory of God." He offers a random sample: "Let the righteous still do right" (Rev. 22:11); "I will confess against myself my unrighteousness" (Ps. 32:5); "I know my transgression, and my sin is always before me. Against Thee, and Thee only,

have I sinned, and done what is evil in Thy sight" (Ps. 51:3-4); "If we say
we have no sin we deceive ourselves and the truth is not in us" (1 John.
1:8); "For there is no man who does not sin" (1 Kings 8:46); "There is not
a righteous man on earth who does good and never sins" (Eccles. 7:20);
"There is none righteous. All have turned aside" (Ps. 14:3). Thus we pray,
"Forgive us our debts" (Matt. 6:12), and so forth.[32]

Therefore, when Paul then goes on to claim that "we uphold the law"
as we "overthrow the law" by this faith (3:31), his paradoxical proclamation
elicits Luther's immediate support. Intrinsically, "carnal people could get
the idea that the apostle is overthrowing the Law because he says we are not
justified by the Law." Extrinsically, however, "we assert that it is fulfilled
and confirmed by faith." In other words, the law is to be championed precisely for its nonsalvific purpose of exposing sin before God. In this way
the law is truly upheld for the limited judging function that "God the Law-
giver" intended it to perform with sinners after the fall. It is realized both
"in itself, when it is promulgated; in us, when we fulfill it with our will and
our works. But apart from faith, no man does this."[33]

In brief, this is Luther's basic reason in highlighting the "knowledge of
sin" that is brought by the law as God's intentional prelude to the gospel's
forgiveness of sin. In fidelity to Paul, he wants to insure that the spiritually
sick patient discontinues his compulsive dependence on impotent and
counterproductive home remedies. Before God, "works of the law" and
"works of grace and faith" are not interchangeable but antithetical: not
law but grace is the basis for the ethical actor's good works. Truly God-
pleasing persons "do not do these works, therefore, in order to seek justification, but that they may glory in the righteousness which they already
possess"—by grace through faith in Christ alone.[34]

Paul also warns that, along with conveying this "knowledge of sin,"
"the law brings wrath" (4:15). God's righteous ire, "wrath," is prompted by
human idolatry ("against their turning away from the true god") and
wickedness ("on account of their turning to idol worship").[35] It is God's
tough love at its toughest.

Rebels are therefore given up to their sinful lusts so that each one "may
recognize how great the wrath of God's severity is that is hanging over his
head, that God would rather let that be done which He hates most, just to
punish him. For there is nothing worse than sin!"[36] All wrath comes about
when God's law works it. Therefore, as demonstrated here by Paul himself,
sinners need to hear clearly the uncompromising law of God: "Do you not
realize that God's kindness is meant to lead you to repentance? But by your
hard and impertinent heart you are storing up wrath for yourself on the
day of wrath, when God's judgment will be revealed" (2:4-5). "Thus the
law works wrath, that is, when it is not fulfilled, it shows the wrath of God

to those who have failed to provide for its fulfillment. Thus the law is not evil, but they are evil to whom it was given and to whom it works wrath, but to the others (that is, the believers) it works salvation; actually it is not the Law that works this but grace."[37]

Of course, it is our sinful transgression of God's holy law that incites God's wrath. "But that would not be the case if there were no law. For the law, as long as it is without faith that fulfills it, makes all people sinners and establishes the fact that they are guilty and thus unworthy of the promise, indeed worthy of wrath and desolation, and in consequence it turns the promise into a threat."[38]

In Romans 5, Paul finally adds "increase of sin" (5:20) to the "knowledge of sin" and the "bringing of wrath" to the law's major contributions to the "strange work" (opus alienum) of God in the face of human sin. This refers, says Luther, to our actual sins ("trespasses") beyond Adam's original sin, "which began without the Law and before it." Unless God's law had come in, "there would have been no sin, and it would not have abounded." Moreover, according to Augustine, sin is increased in the twofold sense that (1) it is now "exposed and imputed" to us by God, and (2) it works through "increasing concupiscence by prohibiting it, and increasing our loathing for the Law by commanding it."[39]

Original sin presupposed, Luther agrees that the law's disclosure of sin serves only to arouse it by prescribing things against it and by prohibiting the very things that sin wishes to do. "The meaning is: the Law came and without any fault on the part of the Law or in the intentions of the Law-giver, it happened that it came for the increasing of sin, and this happened because of the weakness of our sinful desire, which was unable to fulfill the Law." Quoting favorably from Augustine's Propositions, Luther concludes: "By this very word, he [Paul] has shown that the Jews did not understand the purpose for which the Law was given. For it was not given that it might give life—for grace alone through faith gives life—but it was given to show by how many tight bonds of sin they are held who presume to fulfill the Law by their own powers."[40]

Paul's deep insights into the sinful and even death-dealing powers of God's law reach their climax in the dense dialectics of Romans 7. It has subsequently given rise to some of the most heated controversies in New Testament interpretation down to the present day (for example, W. G. Kuemmel, E. Kaesemann, R. Bultmann, R. Hays, E. P. Sanders, J. D. G. Dunn, H. Raisaenen, S. Westerholm, T. R. Schreiner, U. Wilckens, K. Stendahl, P. Stuhlmacher). Luther grapples mightily with the provocative text and concludes that Paul's chief intention is "to explain that remarkable proposition which he has stated in chapter 4:15: 'The Law brings wrath, but where there is no Law, there is no transgression.'"[41]

Moreover, Luther contends that "a wonderful and profound summary of this chapter of the apostle" is to be found in his extrapolated words of Rom. 7:4:

> Likewise, my brethren . . . you who have died to the Law (Rom. 6:14), that is, to the dominion of the Law through the body of Christ, that is through His time and mystical body which was also put to death, so that you may belong to another, and not to the Law, which lords over its bond servants by fear, but to Him who has been raised from the dead, who rules His children in love, in order that you may bear fruit for God: that is, that you may produce good works.[42]

For our purposes, the paradoxical promise of the Christian's liberation from the law through the gospel for ethical service ("belong to another, and not to the Law . . . that you may produce good works") must provide the central focus. Paul declares that the baptized Christian's sinful nature ("old man") has been crucified with Christ in faith and is therefore now no longer "under the law" (Rom. 6:14), that is, enslaved to the "dominion of the Law." This means, dialectically, that the Christian is free from obeying God's law (*Gesetz*) zealously as a way of salvation (the "old man" in Adam), in order to fulfill God's command (*Gebot*) lovingly as a way of service (the "new man" in Christ).

The sinful passions of the unregenerate ("our old man and man in his unconverted state") are first "aroused" and "increased" by the Law (7:5) to sin even more, because the fulfillment-insuring elements of grace and faith are still lacking. Thereafter, however, "When grace is given . . . we die to the power and dominion of the Law, but not to the Law in its proper and simple sense, that is, we are not under the Law, even though we have the Law." So, once the regenerate appropriate God's grace through faith, says Luther, "we are in the Spirit, we are discharged from the law of death, that is, from the dominion of the Law . . . so that we serve, so that we are worshipers of God, in the new life, which is through the grace of regeneration of the Spirit" (7:5-6).[43]

Paul's polemic against the law is grounded in his belief that ultimately at stake is a life-and-death struggle between two opposing ways of salvation. In the original passage (7:1-3), Paul has just employed a somewhat strained marital analogy to illustrate his chief point that death cancels a person's obligation to the law. Christ has died, and baptized Christians have also died with him. The result is that reborn Christians are now free from the law as a way of salvation. They do not serve their neighbors "under the old code" of the law in order to be saved. Instead they lovingly serve their neighbors "in the new life of the Spirit," because they have already been saved by grace through faith alone. "Works of the law" and "fruits of the Spirit" are inherently antithetical: the external acts may even be identical, but the basis, motives, power, and goals of the ethical actors are radically different.

The paradox of the law for Paul is that it can never empower the fulfill-ment of its own demands. In the end it commands the impossible of sin-ners, that spontaneous love as "fruits of faith," which can never be delivered on demand (*impossibilitas legis in statu corruptionis*). The written law is composed of the codified forms of God's holy will in confrontation with human sin. Its "you-shall-nots" are generally expressed negatively because our unfaithful disobedience is already divinely presupposed. For Paul, therefore, the law fulfills its God-pleasing role only when it "arouses our sinful passions" and exposes our need for a sin-forgiving Savior.

This capacity of the law to fulfill God's alien work as Judge is clearly illustrated by Paul in the sin of coveting. If our excessive desire for that which is another's were not explicitly forbidden by God's written law ("You shall not covet"), Paul confesses (7:7) that "I should not have known, but should not have escaped, sin, as we read above in 3:20: 'through the Law comes the knowledge of sin,' if it had not been for the Law."[44] There is absolutely no question in Paul's (or Luther's) mind that "the Law is holy . . . just and good, in itself and in them who are holy and just and good" (7:12). Nevertheless, it is this same law that in action "made me understand and became the occasion" for sin, through the law, to arouse all kinds of cov-etousness and death in him (7:13).[45] To summarize: In normative content, the law revealing God's holy will is purely righteous. However, in forma-tive practice, the law accomplishing God's work paradoxically prompts more evil consequences among the unrighteous.

Paul concludes this weighty chapter with a graphic description of inner spiritual conflict between Spirit and faith presented in terms of a first per-son singular, present tense confession (7:14-20):

> For we know that the law is spiritual; but I am of the flesh, sold into slavery under sin. I do not understand my own actions. For I do not do what I want, but I do the very thing I hate. Now if I do what I do not want, I agree that the law is good. But in fact it is no longer I that do it, but sin that dwells within me. For I know that nothing good dwells in me, that is, in my flesh. I can will what is right, but I cannot do it. For I do not do the good I want, but the evil I do not want is what I do. Now if I do what I do not want, it is no longer I that do it, but sin that dwells within me.

At the heart of many issues relating to this familiar passage is the ques-tion of identity: Who is the "I" speaking here? Is it really Paul witnessing to himself, and if so, is it before or after he became a Christian? Or is Paul speaking merely stylistically of the plight of the human race as a whole? The answer is likely finally determined by one's view of the gravity of original sin and the subsequent intrinsic effects of baptismal grace on the persistence of sin in the life of the redeemed.

Luther takes the bold position that Paul is speaking here in the present tense autobiographically and, as such, representatively of all forgiven Christian believers who coexist both in the "old age in Adam" and the "new age in Christ." Paul the apostle is personally confessing here "about himself" that "I am at the same time a sinner and a righteous man (*simul iustus et peccator*)." In testimony whereof, Luther quotes Augustine approvingly: "This warfare is characteristic of faithful Christians. . . . The law of sin contends against the law of the mind, and the law of sin which was present in the members of even the great apostle is forgiven in Baptism, but it does not come to an end."[46]

The war between the flesh and the Spirit takes place within the heart of every Christian. Consequently, Luther continually insisted here and elsewhere, "He is like a horseman. When his horses do not trot the way he wants them to, it is he himself and yet not he himself who makes the horse run in such and in such a way. For the horse is not without him, and he is not without the horse. But because a carnal man certainly consents to the law of his members (v. 20), he certainly himself does what sin does. For now it is the mind and flesh not only of one person but also of one will."[47]

Luther's position opposed the conventional wisdom and piety within the Roman church of his day. To be sure, Augustine could still be cited, at least qualifiedly, on the side of Pauline realism: "Warfare is characteristic of faithful Christians. In Baptism there is a remission of all sins. And there remains with those who have been baptized a kind of civil war against their weaknesses."[48] However, this pessimistic anthropology was certainly not at all representative of his local opponents, the semi-Pelagian Sophists. Significantly, Luther located the source of the problem in the theological function of the law. He warned:

> At this point we must not think, as Lyra and others say, that the apostle is speaking regarding the person of some degraded man and not of his own person. Likewise he is not speaking of that crass darkness of the mind, as if he does not know the Law except in a very superficial way. But he [Paul] is speaking of his own person and of all the saints and of that abysmal darkness of our heart, by which even the saints and the wisest men have nothing but an imperfect concept of themselves and thus of the Law.[49]

Luther's evaluation was based on his profound understanding of the law's very different theological function before God (*coram Deo*) and ethical function within society (*coram hominibus*). In Romans 7, as over against 12–16, Paul is clearly "dealing with the Law as it applies to the inner man and the will and not with respect to the works of the outer man."[50] This double dialectic ("inner" and "outer" within both the "old" and "new") is the complex eschatological anthropology that must be strictly observed in

Pauline theology: "Once we have understood his customary presuppositions and his bases and principles, all the rest is easy."[51]

Applied to the issue at hand, Romans 7 is dealing with the residual ves-
tiges of the sinful "old man" within the religious "inner man" before God
and not at all with the ethical activity of the righteous "new man" that
issues from the "outer man" in society. Even more pointedly, Paul is affirming the lifelong tension within the heart of every spiritually already reborn
but ethically still imperfect Christian, as disclosed by God's holy law.

Cutting through the density of Paul's rhetoric, Luther also wants to
repudiate any moralistic misinterpretation of the Christian faith. Since
one's being determines doing, it is faith alone that governs works. Paul
aims to show that when the "old man" (sinner) dies to the law and sin, then
"that man is purged from sin rather than the opposite, though the human
mind says the contrary." Since original sin radically corrupts human character religiously, it will not do simply to change human conduct ethically.
One's personal transformation into the "new man" in Christ must spiritually precede one's moral renewal within society.

Luther then traces and exegetes the dozen Romans 7 expressions "which
prove that these are the words of a spiritual man," not an unbeliever, in this
Pauline reorientation: "But I am carnal" (v. 14); "I do not understand my
own actions" (v. 15); "For I do not do what I want, but I do the very thing
I hate" (v. 15); "I agree that the Law is good" (v. 16); "It is no longer I that
do it, but sin that dwells within me" (v. 20); "For I know that nothing good
dwells within me, that is, in my flesh" (v. 20); "I can will what is right, but
I cannot do it" (v. 18); "So I find it to be a law that when I want to do
right, evil lies close at hand" (v. 21); "For I delight in the law of God in my
inmost self" (v. 22); "I see in my members another law at war with the law
of my mind" (v. 23); "Wretched man that I am! Who will deliver me from
the body of this death? (v. 24); "So then, I of myself serve the law of God
with my mind, but with my flesh I serve the law of sin" (v. 24).[52]

Luther concludes his running commentary on Paul's spiritual self-
examination with an expanded reaffirmation of the ambivalent nature of
Christian personhood before God: already righteous but not yet sinless.
"Note that one and the same man at the same time serves the law of God and
the law of sin, at the same time is righteousness and sins! . . . I, the whole man,
the same person, I serve a double servitude."[53] Already freed in heaven from
the reign of sin (*peccatum regnans*) but on earth not yet morally sinless (*peccatum
regnatum*), the Christian lives in a "double servitude" to both the "old age" in
Adam and the "new age" in Christ (cf. Rom. 5). "In the Spirit" he already
wills God's will; "in the flesh" he still acts in bondage to the enemies of God.

Paul's description of the tension-filled character of Christian existence
now reaches its paradoxical climax: The baptized Christian is both free from
God's accusing, judging law insofar as he is already righteous in heaven and

yet bound to it insofar as he still remains sinful on earth. He lives by faith in God's promise while on the way to becoming a righteous Christian. Little wonder that Paul cries out in mixed tones of anguish and joy: "Wretched man that I am! Who will deliver me from this body of death? Thanks be to God through Jesus Christ our Lord!" (Rom. 7:24-25).

At this decisive point we leave Luther's theological commentary on the judging role of God's holy law in Genesis and Romans in order to examine more fully just how badly his controversial views fared under the critical scrutiny of two of his chief rival contemporaries, Latomus and Erasmus. Luther, of course, was greatly aroused by such semi-Pelagian strife, personally convinced that the purity of Christ's law-free gospel was theologically at stake.

Sin's Indelible Character

Luther knew that God's nonsalvific law is terrifying in its spiritual function ("office") as the bearer of God's wrath against human sinfulness (Rom. 4:15). This was an offensive Pauline view that found little positive response among the theologians of the late medieval church. There the common and opposing teaching was that the gospel was simply the church's new law (*nova lex*). It refined Moses by offering a Christ to imitate and the infused grace to empower believers to satisfy the perennial demands of God's old law for eternal salvation. Between 1515 and 1521, therefore, Luther was compelled to develop from an unknown university lecturer on Romans into a biblical church reformer who challenged the authority of both the pope and the emperor, only to be excommunicated by the former and outlawed by the latter.

Among the many attacks published against Luther's alleged doctrinal unorthodoxy and papal disobedience was a tract by that "prickly and thorny sophist," Jacobus Latomus.[54] He was a Roman theologian at the University of Louvain, Belgium, where some of Luther's books had earlier been burned. In seven sections, Latomus challenged Luther's views regarding the massive effect of sin on such matters as good works, free will, and idolatry, and of offenses against the First Commandment.

Luther responded promptly and vigorously in his *Answer to Latomus* (1521), though he was hampered by the absence of any theological library ("I have only my Bible with me") in his forced exile at the Wartburg ("in my Patmos"). However, all that he really needed was his Bible, which he was in the midst of translating into German. Part One refutes the major condemnation of Luther by Latomus; Part Two concentrates on the nature of sin; and Part Three discusses the relative authority of Scripture and tradition with reference to law and gospel.

In Part One, "The first of the condemned propositions is this: God commands the impossible."[55] Latomus had conveniently disregarded Luther's two published qualifications—"for us" and "without the grace of God." It is unscriptural, charges Luther, for the "modern theologians" (that is, Duns Scotus, William of Ockham, and especially Gabriel Biel) to contend that a sinful person can, solely on the basis of one's free will, "actually do" the will of God if he would but "do what in him lies" (*facere quod in se est*).[56]

Luther counters that "many important pronouncements of Scripture have been forced to yield to this scandalous doctrine" (for example, Rom. 8:3ff.; Acts 13:38ff.; 15:10; Matt. 19:24-26). Consequently, he insists that "all the commandments of God are fulfilled, not by our perfect deeds, but in the abundantly forgiving grace of God."[57] Determinative for him is Paul's supporting testimony:

> Paul, and after him Augustine, loudly thundered that man through the Law, without grace, only becomes worse, because the Law "brings wrath" (Rom. 4:15) and, "came in to increase the trespass" (Rom. 5:20). Thus they have canceled the whole New Testament by this blasphemous opinion, and have led us unfortunates, now only nominal Christians, to the place where Christ is of absolutely no use except to teach us.[58]

"The second thesis: Sin remains after baptism."[59] Here there is a clash of authorities: "Latomus condemns this proposition—which I have proved on the authority of Paul (Rom. 7)—by the authority of Gregory." Postponing substantive discussion until later, Luther pointedly remarks that "the [early church] fathers were but men."[60] "The third thesis: It is not necessary to confess all mortal sins to the priests." Once again the problem is a conflict of authorities. Latomus cites a general council of the church; Luther repeats his appeal to a higher authority: "What Scripture supports that council?"[61]

Finally, Part One ends with a fourth thesis: "Every good work of the saints while pilgrims in this world is sin."[62] Luther turns again to Holy Scripture and insists with Isa. 64:6: "We have all become like one who is unclean, and all our righteousness are like filthy rags." While this Old Testament prophetic passage obviously refers originally to faithless Jews, Luther holds that God intends it also for the New Testament people of God, the saints of all ages, whom he intends to create and renew in Christ. (Cf. Rom. 3:11-12; Ps. 14:3; Rom. 4:7-8; Ps. 32:1-2; Lam. 2:2; and Ps. 28:5.)

In brief, Luther contends that such statements refer to the faithful as well, for "our good works are of such sort that they cannot bear the judgment of God, as is said in Psalm 143:2: 'Enter not into judgment with thy servant, for no man living is righteous before thee.'"[63] He concludes his running analysis of such further supporting texts as Job 9:22; Ps. 44:17ff; and Jer. 49:12 and 30:11 with the paradoxical thesis on the Christian's simultaneous sinfulness and righteousness that recalls his earlier lectures on Romans: "What else, then, does He do but so deal with those who are just that He makes it appear they are not just? Nevertheless, because He judges truly and righteously, it must be that those who are under this judgment are at the same time righteous, and yet unclean. In this way He shows that no one ought to rely on his own righteousness, but solely on His mercy."[64]

At this critical point, in Part Two we shall focus our attention on Luther's remaining analysis of the relation of the law to the gospel of God's grace, as initially prompted by Paul's passage in 2 Cor. 3:10: "What once had splendor has come to have no splendor at all, because of the splendor that supports it." Luther clarifies: "Many are persuaded that Paul deals in the above text with the ceremonial righteousness which is now repealed; yet he is speaking of the whole law, and comparing law with grace, not law with law. This error comes from the fact that they suppose the gospel is the teaching of laws."[65]

Luther's chief point is that God's grace in Jesus Christ is the sole basis for human salvation. Or put negatively, the law since Adam's fall does not save; it condemns. This side of the fall, God's ministries of the law and the gospel are radically different with regard to salvation: The law exposes sin; the gospel forgives it. "In brief, then, let us point out that there are two ministries of preaching; one of the letter, the other of the Spirit. The letter is the law, the spirit is grace. The first belongs to the Old Covenant, the second to the New. The glory of the law is the knowledge of sin; the glory of the Spirit is that revelation, or knowledge, of grace which is faith. Therefore the law did not justify."[66]

Paul is immediately cited as providing apostolic authority for the claim that viewed in the mirror of God's law, "all men are under the power of sin" (Rom. 3:9), and that the law works wrath and death in carrying out its accusing and judging role. "The whole law was holy, just and good, as Paul says in Rom. 7:12; but because of our fault, that which is good cannot be good to us, nor does it make alive, but kills."[67] It is clear for Luther that while the whole law is the letter that kills, the life-giving Spirit is the grace conveyed to faith in Christ. To secure salvation before God (*coram Deo*), law cannot replace "grace alone" and works cannot replace "faith alone."

> I say, therefore, that just as the law of the Decalogue is good if it is observed—that is, if you have faith, which is the fullness of the law and righteousness—so also it is death, and wrath, and no good to you if you do not observe it—that is, if you do not have faith. This is so, no matter how many good works you do—for the righteousness of the law, that is, of the Ten Commandments is unclean and abolished by Christ even more than is the righteousness of ceremonies.[68]

Even though Augustine can be quoted by Latomus to claim that it is not really sin, but only "lust (*concupiscentia*) and the motions of sin that remain after baptism," Luther pleads boldly, "Here I entreat you, dear reader, be free and a Christian. Do not swear allegiance to any word of man, but be a steadfast believer of the Holy Scripture."[69]

Sin is essentially "that which is not in accord with God's law." This is the "single and very simple" way in which Scripture describes sin. It should not be confused with "an imperfection, a penalty, or a fault," and thus "weaken and mock the Word of God, for none of these terms are found in Scripture." Luther flings down the gauntlet:

> The issue between myself and the sophists is whether or not this sin which remains (*reliquum peccati*) must be truly considered sin. . . . It cannot be denied, as they would like to do, that is called sin by the Apostle; and so they take refuge in the interpretations and distinctions of the fathers.[70]
>
> Hence, in order to reintroduce the use of the Pauline word "sin," we here reject once and for all everything that all of the fathers have said when they called this remainder lust, weakness, penalty, imperfection, fault, or whatever else they supposed it to be. To them we oppose Paul, the Gentiles' apostle. . . . For not even Augustine, even though he is of all the fathers the best, was free to change the expression Paul used and to invent another.[71]

This particular disagreement notwithstanding, Luther does still conclude Part Two, after analyzing "five clear passages in which Paul describes sin" (Rom. 8:3ff.; 8:2; 6:12; 6:14; 6:6) by reaffirming Augustine's final dictum in his *Retractions*, "All sin is forgiven in baptism, not so that it no longer exists, but so that it is no longer imputed."[72]

That is the scriptural truth for Luther: "Sin is truly sin, but because grace and the gift are in me, it is not imputed." Sin is not totally eradicated by baptism, but it is nevertheless redemptively covered by the righteousness of Christ that God mercifully reckons to the faithful (*iustitia alienum*). In God's sight, Christ's "extrinsic" righteousness (*extra nos*) is imputed to us; our own "intrinsic" unrighteousness (*in nos*) is not imputed to us. The gospel is the good news that a forgiving God wills to see his faithful only "in Christ." "What, then, are we sinners? No, rather we are justified, but by grace. Righteousness is not situated in those qualitative forms, but in the mercy of God."[73]

Luther's final Part Three centers on "the chief point of disagreement." Is it only by forgiving mercy, or is it by its very nature, that this sin is not opposed to God and his law? The scriptural solution rests in its witness to the twofold rule of God by the law and the gospel throughout the two kingdoms of fallen and redeemed creation.

> The divine Scriptures deal with sin in two ways: in one way, through the law of God, and in another way, through God's gospel. These are two Testaments of God which are ordained for our salvation so that we may be freed from sin.

> The law deals with sin only to reveal it, as Paul says in Rom. 3:20:
> "Through the law comes knowledge of sin." The knowledge teaches
> two things: [inwardly] in the corruption of nature (Rom. 7:7) and
> [outwardly] in the wrath of God (Rom. 4:15). The gospel, on the
> contrary, deals with sin so as to remove it, and thus most beautifully
> follows the law. It also teaches and preaches two things, namely,
> [inwardly] the righteousness of God (Rom. 3:21) and [outwardly] the
> grace of God (Rom 5:15).[74]

Recalling Paul's typology of the first and last Adams in Rom. 5:15,
Luther here contrasts both God's wrath and grace and also distinguishes
between "grace" as God's justifying favor for eternal life and the Spirit's
"gifts" as God's sanctifying healings of persisting pockets of spiritual sickness in our temporal lives. For Christians, the former is already accomplished by Christ (justification); the latter are begun by the Spirit but not
yet complete (sanctification). Sin persists (Rom. 6:12), but it no longer
reigns (*peccatum regnans*) after it is itself reigned by grace through faith (*peccatum regnatum*), as the Holy Spirit impels its expulsion and determines the
believers' ethical conduct.

> Now we have finally come to the point. A righteous and faithful man
> has both grace and the gift. Grace makes him wholly pleasing so that
> his person is wholly accepted. . . . Everything is forgiven through
> grace, but as yet not everything is healed through the gift.
>   In the meantime, while this is happening, it is called sin, and is truly
> such in its nature; but now it is sin without wrath, without the law,
> dead sin, harmless sin, as long as one perseveres in grace and his gift.[75]

In this "simple and Pauline way," Luther claims to have shown Latomus
that "God saves real, not imaginary, sinners, and he teaches us to mortify
real rather than imaginary sin." He rehearses again his earlier portrait of
"carnal," sin-scarred Christians from Romans 7. It is a realistic but not
morbid portrayal of the indelible human situation this side of the fall.
Therefore, the "spiritual or theological function" of God's law is not to
save, but to reveal the universality of human infidelity and its lifelong persistence, however sublimated, even in the earthly pilgrimage of the
redeemed. Yet Christian hope remains confident of God's ultimate will:
"He does not want us to halt in what has been received, but rather to draw
near from day to day so that we may be fully transformed into Christ."[76]

Bondage of Will and Reason

In his later years, Luther ranked *The Bondage of the Will* (1525) next to the
Large Catechism (1529) as among his best theological works.[77] He wrote it
as a biblically grounded response to an attack on him published a year earlier by Erasmus of Rotterdam. While Luther remained totally at odds with
his adversary's position, he nevertheless concluded his work by addressing

Erasmus as a worthy opponent who had cut to the quick: "I praise and commend you highly for this also, that unlike all the rest you alone have attacked the real issue, the essence of the matter in dispute, and have not wearied me with irrelevancies about the papacy, purgatory, indulgences, and such like trifles. . . . You and you alone have seen the question of which everything hinges, and have aimed at the vital spot, for which I sincerely thank you."[78]

This "real issue" at stake, as Luther perceived, was whether it was truly biblical for Erasmus to assert that humans still enjoyed "free will" (or better, "free choice") to earn salvation before God after the fall. "It is essentially salutary and necessary for a Christian, to find out whether the will does anything or nothing in matters pertaining to eternal salvation. Indeed, as you [Erasmus] know, this is the cardinal issue between us."[79]

Actually, Luther's Latin title (*De servo arbitrio*) would be rendered more accurately as "unfree choice" in direct opposition to his opponent's earlier work (*De libero arbitrio*) in which Erasmus affirmed, "By 'free choice' in this place we mean a power of the human will by which a man can apply himself to the things which lead to eternal salvation, or turn away from them."[80] In brief, the controverted issue for Erasmus was not so much metaphysical as it was ethical. That is, "free choice" here relates practically to human "good works" and their purported meritorious contribution to one's earning of salvation (*lex iustificatrix*). Not so for Luther, who taught from Scripture that sinners could not freely do good out of love: "God gave man a free will. But the question here is whether this freedom is in our power. One ought properly to call it a changeable, mutable will because God works in us and we are passive. . . . Our free will is passive, not active, because it doesn't lie in our power."[81]

Significantly, Erasmus's affirmation focuses on a free will as the base for human ethical responsibility. However, it refers neither to humanity's fallen state nor to God's grace—determinate factors for theological ethics in Luther. Both want Christian renewal, but Erasmus pursues it prudently in a theological vacuum, whereas Luther champions it passionately as a righteous by-product. Our own special interest will be to highlight Luther's dialectical treatment of God's law and gospel, along with human will and reason, within the Reformer's designated two kingdoms of sin and grace.

From this perspective, the debate between Luther and Erasmus really centered on the "theological function" of God's law (*usus theologicus*) in challenging the place of human free will and reason in contributing to salvation. Erasmus's work, *A Diatribe or Discourse concerning Free Choice,* showed that Luther clearly did not have the predominant support of most of the early church fathers for his radical rejection of synergistic salvation. The debate was therefore restricted to the proper interpretation of the

Word of God in Holy Scripture, the only final authority that Luther would accept.

On this basis, Erasmus argues that human freedom of choice is inferentially necessary on two grounds: (1) It is the moral presupposition for our earning any God-pleasing merit, and (2) it is the volitional presupposition for satisfying God's law and commandments. The imperative "You shall" implies the indicative "You can." For Luther to teach persons that they have no such moral choice, contends Erasmus, leads inevitably to moral irresponsibility and disregard for God's law. Without such freedom there can be no just ground for divine punishment or reward, and neither salvation nor damnation can be justly merited. In short, both for a righteous God and for responsible human moral agents, persons need freedom of choice: choice for works, works for merit, and merit for salvation.

In response, Luther exegetes literally dozens of biblical passages to demonstrate that there is no such human "merit" that determines either salvation or damnation in the Christian faith. To be sure, there is both reward for the righteous and punishment for the unrighteous, but that kind of perfect goodness—the kind of selfless love revealed and commanded by Jesus Christ as God's eternal will—cannot and will not be merited by anyone this side of the fall. "Merit" is therefore not even a biblical category. The sole ground of the salvation of sinners is God's freedom to act graciously in Christ for the unmerited benefit of faithful persons.

Consequently, in this exclusively evangelical orientation to salvation before God (*coram Deo*)—whatever else must surely be said in our own chapter 6 about ethical choices and service in society (*coram hominibus*)—the sole office of God's law here is to reveal what a sinner does not and cannot do before one is first radically rectified and transformed by God's grace. With regard to allegedly meriting salvation, a sinner's will is bound and reason is blind.

Luther employs the convicting function of God's law to refute Erasmus's arguments in support for free choice/will. He complains that Erasmus's "superficial arguments," typically "equivocal and evasive," have in principle "been refuted already so often by me."[82] We may quickly recall his *Lectures on Romans* (1516), *Disputation against Scholastic Theology* (1517), *The Heidelberg Disputation* (1518), and his *Defense and Explanation of All the Articles Condemned* (1521).

Luther complains, "Erasmus, you go too far" in affirming that "our will accomplishes anything in things pertaining to eternal salvation . . . and yet the papists pardon and put up with these enormities of yours simply because you are writing against Luther."[83] Nevertheless, since Scripture clearly claims that "it is God who works everything in everyone" (1 Cor. 12:6), it compels us "to be very certain about the distinction between God's power and our own, God's work and our own, if we want to live a godly life."[84]

Luther's interest is not at all speculative; ultimately it goes to the trustworthiness of God to fulfill his gracious promises to those who trust in Christ for forgiveness and salvation. Therefore, we must "treat Holy Writ with sufficient reverence."[85]

> For if these things are not known, there can be neither faith nor any worship of God. . . . For if you doubt or disdain that God foreknows all things, not contingently, but necessarily and immutably, how can you believe his promises and place a sure trust and reliance on them? How will you be certain and sure unless you know that he knows and wills and will do what he promises, certainly, infallibly, immutably, and necessarily?[86]

Nor will Luther allow the clear testimony of Holy Scripture to be subjected to the critical judgment of human reason, as if reason itself were not corrupted by sin when it comes to issues of faith and salvation. Reason and human traditions cannot be trusted as authoritative substitutes for the Word of God in the kingdom of redemption. This the true God cannot tolerate, and so the Word of God and the traditions of men are irrevocably opposed to one another, precisely as God himself and Satan are mutually opposed, each destroying the other like two kings laying waste to each other's kingdoms. "'He who is not with me,' says Christ, 'is against me'" (Matt. 12:30).[87]

Moreover, it is vital that God's convicting law be proclaimed as an expression of his holy will for two reasons: "the first is the humbling of our pride, and the knowledge of the grace of God; and the second is the nature of Christian faith itself."[88] On the one hand, Scripture teaches that it is to those who lament and despair of themselves that God has promised his forgiving and renewing grace (1 Pet. 5:5). The pastoral concern thus becomes: How best can this divine humbling of sinners be effected? Answer: Allow the Holy Spirit to drive persons away from trust in self to trust in God.

> No man can be thoroughly humbled until he knows that his salvation is utterly beyond his own powers, devices, endeavors, will, and works, and depends entirely on the choice, will, and works of another, namely, of God alone. . . . When a man has no doubt that everything depends on the will of God, then he completely despairs of himself and chooses nothing for himself and chooses nothing from himself, but waits for God to work; then he has come close to grace, and can be saved.[89]

On the other hand, Scripture also teaches that faith has to do with things that are not seen (Heb. 11:1). If faith is to have room, that which is to be believed must be hidden. Indeed, the best place for hiding the spiritual truth is "under an object, perception, or experience which is contrary to it."

This "strange work" (*opus alienum*) of the "hidden God" (*Deus absconditus*) is perceptible only to the eyes of faith, however paradoxical it may appear to be (*sub specie contrario*). "Thus when God makes alive he does it by killing, when he justifies he does it by making men guilty, when he exalts to heaven he does it by bringing down to hell, as Scripture says, 'The LORD kills and brings to life; he brings down to Sheol and raises up' (1 Sam. 2:6). Thus God hides his eternal goodness and mercy under eternal wrath, his righteousness under iniquity."[90]

In terms of our theme's major development, Luther incorporates his "free will" debate with Erasmus fully within his overarching construct of the two kingdoms of fallen and redeemed creation. Ultimately, all persons are either under Satan or God; our wills are either in disobedient bondage to God's cosmic enemy or in obedient service to God's Holy Spirit. In neither case, however, are we human creatures the free and autonomous captains of our own destiny.

> In short, if we are under the god of this world, away from the work and Spirit of the true God, we are held captive to his will, as Paul says (2 Tim. 2:26), so that we cannot will anything but what he wills. . . . But if a Stronger One comes who overcomes him and takes us His spoil, then through his Spirit we are again slaves and captives—though this is royal freedom—so that we readily will and do what he wills.
>
> Thus the human will is placed between the two like a beast of burden. If God rides it, it wills and goes where God wills, as the psalm says, "I am become as a beast (before thee) and I am always with thee" (Ps. 73:22). If Satan rides it, it wills and goes where Satan wills; nor can it choose to run to either of the two riders or to seek him out, but the riders themselves contend for the possession and control of it.[91]

To avoid potential confusion, we must again clearly distinguish between the vertical and horizontal expressions of human freedom. Luther's total rejection of free will (this chapter) is exclusively limited to salvation before God (*coram Deo*), that is, being rightly or wrongly related to God or Satan. This absolute spiritual bondage is not to be confused with Luther's simultaneous affirmation of our relative free choices (next chapter) in facing challenges of unjust relations with fellow human beings in society (*coram hominibus*). The same Triune God deals with us in both these relational dimensions of human existence through the theological and political functions of the law, respectively.

In opposing Erasmus, Luther draws this same distinction between what is "above us" (theologically vis-à-vis God the Creator) and what is "beneath us" (politically vis-à-vis other human creatures). Persons are relatively free as subjects/citizens to do some moral good in history; they are absolutely bound as sinners to do no saving good for eternity.

> Free choice is allowed to man only with respect to what is beneath
> him and not what is above him. That is to say, a man should know that
> with regard to his faculties and possessions, he has the right to use, to
> do, or to leave undone, according to his own free choice, though even
> this is controlled by the free choice of God alone who acts in what-
> ever way he pleases. On the other hand, in relation to God, or in mat-
> ters pertaining to salvation or damnation, a man has no free choice,
> but is a captive, subject, and slave either of the will of God or the will
> of Satan.[92]

Moreover, what is salvifically impossible for a sinner's free will in general is likewise true of his sin-corrupted reason in particular. Luther reminds
Erasmus that "Lombard clearly thinks with Augustine that free choice by its
own power can do nothing but fall and is capable only of sinning."[93] It is
not able not to sin (*non posse non peccare*). Not so by Erasmus and others,
especially when fortified by their misinterpretation of Eccles. 15:14-17: "If
thou wilt observe the commandments, they shall preserve thee, and so
forth." Luther here draws the line: "It is therefore at this point, 'If thou
wilt,' that the question of free choice arises. . . . Here *Diatribe* will retort that
by saying, 'If thou wilt keep,' Ecclesiasticus indicates that there is in man a
will capable of keeping and not keeping commandments, otherwise, what
point is there in saying to one who has no will, 'If thou wilt'?"[94]

Luther replies that this represents the unfaithful response of sinful
"Madame Reason," autonomous human self-rationalization, in trying to
elude God's Word with an unauthorized and corrupting inference ("for
Reason interprets the Scriptures of God by her own preferences and syllo-
gisms, and turns them in any direction she pleases . . . especially when she
starts playing her wisdom on sacred objects").[95]

Referring to his earlier two-kingdom dualism, Luther teaches that
human reason "sound and fair" is a wonderful gift of God for adjudicating
the claims and counterclaims of truth and justice in "things beneath us"
within Satan's kingdom of fallen creation. When enlightened by the Spirit,
it resonates with human goodness and communal well-being. It has
absolutely no authority or competence, however, in the "things above us,"
in God's kingdom of redemption.

Here the "whore reason" (*Hure Vernunft*) tries to tempt humans away
from faithfulness to the Scriptures. Here it can only pose ("Madame Reason") as a counterfeit substitute for faith in plying seductive solutions for
solving the mysteries of God's will and the unfathomable depths of God's
grace. In matters of salvation, prideful and autonomous reason "would
make the Spirit and Scriptures unnecessary," overlooking her own "spiritual blindness and diseases" and showing only "how foolish she is in tack-
ing her inferences onto the Scriptures." To cure this pride and blindness of

human reason, "God has no readier remedy than the propounding of his Law."[96]

Luther demands that "we everywhere stick to the simple, pure and rational sense of the words of Scripture," whenever the authors intend us to do so. God's Word dare not be disturbed beyond recognition by Erasmus's all-too-clever inferences, similes, word plays, and "tropes" (figures of speech or figurative and allegorical literary interpretations). No, it is not antiscriptural reason but intra-scriptural law that Luther proposes "for the confrontation of the foolish, mundane, [Sophist] wisdom: 'If thou wilt,' therefore 'thou canst' will freely."

> God says: "Do, hear, keep," or "If thou shalt hear, if thou wilt, if thou shalt do." Will the correct conclusion be drawn from this be: "Therefore we can act freely, or else God is mocking us"? Why does it not rather follow: "Therefore God is putting us to the test so as to lead us by means of the Law to a knowledge of our impotence if we are his friends and truly and deservedly to trample on and mock us if we are his proud enemies? That is the reason God gives laws, as Paul teaches (Rom. 3:20).[97]

It is precisely the "theological function" of God's law to judge and convict slaves of Satan of their faithless and loveless hearts. Luther insists, "Here is the truth of the matter in a nutshell. As I have said, by such sayings man is shown what he ought to do, not what he can do."[98]

God's will in the Old and New Testaments, whether expressed in the imperative, future indicative, optative, or conditional tenses, addresses a sinner in such ways that "he is warned and aroused by it to see his own impotence." God's law reveals in depth the heart as well as the acts of the moral actor (totus homo). Whenever we reach the juncture of two ethical roads, "by means of the Law it is shown how impossible one of them is, namely, the way to the good, unless God gives the Spirit, and how broad and easy the other is if God allows us to take it."[99]

It follows for Luther that the words of the law are decreed by God "not to affirm the power of the will, but to enlighten blind reason." It commands the kind of obedient love of which sinners are no longer able or willing. Thereby it conveys the "knowledge of sin" (Rom. 3:20), but not its abolition or avoidance. "The whole meaning and purpose of the law is simply to furnish knowledge, and that of nothing but sin; it is not to reveal or to confer any power. For this knowledge is not power, nor does it confer power, but it instructs and shows that there is no power there, and how great a weakness there is."[100]

As Paul taught in Gal. 3:24, this is the negative function of God's law in preparation for the positive function of God's gospel to lead to Christ (pedagogus ad Christum). However, the chief hermeneutical problem in Erasmus's

Diatribe is that it "makes no distinction between expressions of the law and the gospel."[101] Despite the testimony of Paul and John, Erasmus simply will not accept that the law convicts of sin and the gospel acquits with grace.

Therefore, without this qualitative differentiation, Erasmus cannot acknowledge that passages such as "Thou shalt love the LORD thy God with all thy heart (Deut. 6:5)" are "nothing but law, the law at its peak," as it commands the impossible "and shows what we ought to do and cannot do."[102] Though both lie side by side in the Scriptures, God's laws and threats are not to be confused with his gospel's promises and exhortations. Luther's debate with Erasmus centers on "free choice precisely as it is without grace, and arguing that by laws and threatenings, or the Old Testament, it is brought to knowledge of itself, so that it may run to the promises set forth in the New Testament."[103] Luther further writes: "God gives commandments in order to instruct and admonish men as to what they ought to do, so that they may be humbled by the knowledge of their wickedness and attain to grace. . . . This passage, too, therefore, still stands invincible against freedom of choice (Gen. 8:21)."[104]

Luther concludes his rebuttal of Erasmus's critique of his own *Assertion of All the Articles Condemned* (1520) by reasserting the central focus of this debate: the evangelical difference between divine operation and divine-human cooperation in achieving eternal salvation and community service.

> For what we assert and contend for is this, that when God operates without regard to the grace by the Spirit, he works all in all, even in the ungodly, inasmuch as he alone moves, actuates, and carries along all things by the motion of his omnipotence.
>
> Then when he acts by the Spirit of grace in those whom he has justified, that is, in his Kingdom, he actuates and moves in them in a similar way, and they, inasmuch as they are his new creation, follow and cooperate. . . . But that is not our subject here. We are not discussing what we can do through God's working but what we can do of ourselves.[105]

This summarizes Luther's Christocentric denial of any divine-human cooperation for eternal salvation ("without the Spirit"), while he also simultaneously endorses the ethical obligation of God's dominion-sharing Christians to engage in divine-human cooperation for societal service ("with the Spirit"). However, where does that then leave the moral lives of non-Christians, along with ethically imperfect Christians, who are still under God's universal law? Luther meets this corollary challenge by once again emphasizing the distinction between "fruits of the Spirit" (motivated by obedient Christian love under the gospel), and "works of the law" (prompted by enlightened self-interest under the law).

Clearly, human free choice cannot "fulfill" the law by the Spirit in its loving depths before God. Nevertheless, it can still "do" or perform moral works that externally obey the letter of God's law at the surface level of the requirements of civil society. Qualitatively, such works are inferior to God's religious righteousness; yet quantitatively, they are still superior to society's civil unrighteousness. To recall Augustine's realistic appraisal of the moral activity of people's corrupted, but not destroyed, remnants of God's image after the fall, "pagan virtues are splendid vices."

Moreover, by these nonredemptive but socially beneficial "works of the law," the apostle of the law-free gospel to the Gentiles means inclusively "all the laws written in the Book of the Law—ceremonial, juridical, and moral."

> Paul's division is confirmation enough of what we teach, for he divides men as doers of the Law into two classes, putting those who work according to the Spirit in one, and those who work according to the flesh in the other, and leaving none in between.
>
> And suppose I allow that free choice can by its own endeavor achieve something—good works, let us say, or the righteousness of the civil or moral law—yet it does not attain to the righteousness of God; nor does God regard its efforts as in any way qualifying it for his righteousness. . . . For Paul clearly distinguishes the two righteousnesses, attributing one to the law and the other to grace.[106]

Two of Luther's formulations are especially noteworthy as ethical links to our next chapter. First, in conscious conformity with Paul's clear affirmation of both a "righteousness of law" and a "righteousness of grace," Luther has developed his own teaching on God's twofold rule through law and gospel within both the two kingdoms of fallen creation and redemption. Each of these two kinds of righteousness, in turn, also has two focused expressions, both a spiritual function for eternal life (*coram Deo*) and an ethical function for historical life (*coram hominibus*).

In this volume, chapters 5 and 6 explore the two functions of God's law while chapters 7 and 8 will develop the complementary two functions of God's gospel. Consequently, this initial chapter has consistently amplified the law's totally negative "theological function" (*usus theologicus*) to expose sin within the eternal realm of redemption. In the next chapter, we will develop the law's relatively positive "political function" (*usus civilis/politicus*) to promote the general welfare and common good within the historical realm of fallen creation.

Second, Luther's endorsement of this "righteousness of the civil or moral law" also serves to break out from his internal conscience debates with Latomus and Erasmus on the law's spiritual relation to sin, into the external arena of the law's other vital function: the preservation of society, despite prevailing sin, through the public struggles for order, freedom, and justice.

To keep his presentation biblical, it is imperative for Luther to emphasize that both these remedial functions of the law still paradoxically represent the "strange forms" of God's love: judging sin by wrath and preserving justice by force. They dialectically prepare us for God's parallel twin blessings of granting salvation and inspiring service as the "proper forms" of God's love, yet to be revealed by the twofold gospel of Christ's grace and the Spirit's gifts. On this side of Adam's fall, moreover, promoting "civil righteousness" (*iustitia civilis*) is necessarily a form of "tough love" that is ultimately directed against Satan as mediated through the "least worst" means that are publicly and effectively available. In sin-opposing societal realism, Luther explains, "It is just as if a carpenter were cutting badly with a chipped and jagged ax."[107]

Chapter 6

Noah and Moses: Law Preserves in Society

WE HAVE SHOWN THAT LUTHER'S VIEW of the two kingdoms (*Reiche*) substantially reconfirmed the eschatological dualism of God versus Satan in Genesis, the two ages in Paul's Romans, and the two cities in Augustine. Moreover, for the first half of the 1520s, his early dualistic views on God's twofold rule (*Regimente*) of unbelievers with the law and believers with the gospel were coextensively incorporated within this cosmic cleavage. As in Augustine, the unfortunate societal result in the early Luther's theological ethic was a bifurcated humanity: (1) in the temporal kingdom, there was the law's realm of Satan, the fallen world, sin, death, and the temporal sword of Caesar; (2) in the spiritual kingdom, there was the gospel's realm of God in Christ, the redeemed church, faith, new life, and the sword of the Spirit. Consequently, in this exclusively dualistic model, there was no coherent room for God's dialectical governance of human history by the law and the gospel for Christians also characterized by Paul as at once both righteous and sinful. In so sharply severing creation from redemption, it virtually identified Caesar's realm (negatively) with Satan.

By the mid-1520s, however, Luther began to benefit from deepened scriptural study of both theological and social ethics. God's dialectical two governments increasingly *interpenetrated* the world's dualistic two kingdoms in such biblically based studies as *Temporal Authority* (1523), *Sermons on Exodus* (1524–27), *Whether Soldiers, Too, Can be Saved* (1526), climaxing in his *Sermons* (1530–32) and *Commentary on Matthew 5–7* (1532).

This exegetical work was prompted not least by the socially isolated, former monk's unprecedented public challenges (often now experienced firsthand): rulers' piety and profligacy, knights' uprising, free-church iconoclasm, limited youth education, competitive trade and usury, emptying of monastic cloisters, peasants' rebellions, sectarian theocratic romanticism, and threatened wars against the Turks—in short, the disintegration of medieval feudalism within an institutionally integrated Western Christendom. Luther's original and abiding focus on the theological reformation of the church—itself a monumental calling—was increasingly in danger of being eclipsed by the host of nontheological agendas of political, social, economic, and military forces that were anxious to co-opt the Reformation-recovered gospel to support their own ideological self-interest. Preeminently, the eschatological teachings of Jesus in the Sermon on the Mount needed somehow to be reconciled with Paul's and Peter's ethical admonitions for Christian societal involvement; for example, when to "turn the other cheek" and when to "take up the sword."

Luther's nuanced response was paradoxically both theologically conservative and ethically radical: Theologically, he permanently retained the dualistic two-kingdom motif as the Bible's essential eschatological backdrop; ethically, he also newly refocused his complementary public witness on the dynamically intersecting powers of the Triune God's twofold "right-hand and left-hand rule" both within and between each of the two kingdoms of fallen creation and inaugurated redemption. Thereafter, the spiritual two kingdoms (*Reiche*) still refer to the dualistic results of the fall (Satan versus God), whereas God's temporal twofold rule (*Regimente*) now highlights God's dialectical responses to the fall (Caesar and Christ), both as the world's Preserver (with his left hand) and Redeemer (with his right hand). The Triune God thereby works both temporally and eternally with a different function of the law and the gospel intersecting each of the two kingdoms.

Luther's mature paradigm reflects more coherently the inaugurated, but not yet realized, eschatology of the New Testament. He thereby paradoxically avoids both the activism of those zealots who would publicly identify the church and the world (opposed by creation's two kingdoms) and the quietism of those pacifists who would privately divorce them (challenged by God's twofold rule).

Our goal in this chapter is to trace those biblical and theological resources that led Luther in his *Lectures on Galatians* (1535) to the double use of the law (*duplex usus legis*). Therein it consistently stresses that in addition to the law's theological function (*usus theologicus/spiritualis*) to "increase transgressions" of sin in one's conscience, there is also its complementary civil or political function (*usus civilis/politicus*) to "restrain transgressions" of injustice and disorder in everyday life.

> Here one must know that there is a double use of the law. One is the civil use (*usus civilis*). God has ordained civic laws, indeed all laws, to restrain transgressions. I do not do this voluntarily or from the love of virtue but because I am afraid of the sword and the executioner. . . . This is why God has ordained magistrates, parents, teachers, laws, shackles, and all civil ordinances, so that, if they cannot do more they

will at least bind the hands of the devil, and keep him from raging at will.[1]

Finally, to protect Christian ethical freedom from the continual unbiblical threats of moralism and legalism, Luther concludes his development of the law's theological and political functions with the magisterial edict: "And that is as far as the law goes (*Da hort lex auff*)."[2] We will return at the end of Part Three (chapter 8 and the Afterword) to a much fuller examination of Luther's evangelical fulfillment of the post-fall historical law (*Gesetz*) with God's pre-fall, eschatological command (*Gebot*), in order to exhort and guide the ethical life of regenerated Christians being sanctified within the law-preserved structures of society, in obedience to God's loving will.

Now, however, in order to begin to trace this "left hand" breakthrough of God's law from its (vertical) theological to its (horizontal) political or societal function, we will purposely revert once again to the thematic narrative of the Genesis saga. In its two-front war against Satan, God's law moves out from the cursing of Cain to the nurturing of Noah. In the Holy Scriptures, the same God whose judging law convicts the "spiritual unrighteousness" of sinners under Cain then also lawfully protects their "civil righteousness" (*iustitia civilis*) as political subjects/citizens who live under God's providential covenant with Noah. (The modern democratic notion of a politically responsible citizenry with civil rights, of course, was still totally unknown in both the ancient and German late medieval worlds.)

The Noachic Covenant

Postponing until the next two chapters our consideration of God's salvific covenant of grace "within the loins of Abraham," we turn now to God's universal covenant of law with post-Noachic humanity after the flood. This material is most fully developed in Genesis 6–9 and highlights God's remedial action against "despisers of God" who had already (anachronistically) transgressed the Decalogue's first table of God's law ("contempt of God and of His Word") and who afterward "offend most flagrantly against the Second Table also."[3] Significantly for Luther, this pre-Mosaic violation of God's pre-codified will is ethically marked by humanity's "disregard of natural and positive law . . . despising the laws of nature" as written universally by God on the human heart in creation.[4]

> Therefore the true sin of the original world was the disorganization of all classes of men. The church was undermined by the idolatrous and ungodly forms of worship as well as by tyrants who cruelly persecuted the godly teachers and holy men; government was destroyed through their tyranny and acts of violence; and the home was ruined

by their perverse lusts. This worldwide corruption was the unavoid-
able result of the downfall of godliness and decency. Men were not
only evil; they were utterly incorrigible.[5]

In commenting on the biblical approach to the political sins of rulers
(*Obrigkeit*), Luther notes the "strange counsel of God, who directs us to
respect the government, to obey it, to serve it, and to give it honor." Yet
biblical threats are directed most frequently against unjust rulers "as if God
pursued them with a special hatred." The irony, therefore, is that "Scripture commands us to honor the government, but it itself does not honor
the government." For Luther, the only plausible explanation is that "the
Lord Himself wants to be the only one to punish them, has reserved punishment for Himself, and has not granted it to their subjects." Yet their days
are numbered; as the German proverb says, "A prince is a rare bird in the
kingdom of heaven."[6]

So universal is human guilt that God in righteous wrath determines "to
make an end of all flesh. . . . I will destroy them with the earth" (6:13). In
the flood, God destroys all that he has created, with the exception of eight
souls led by the patriarch Noah, whom God loves. Together with his faithful family, Noah is chosen by the Lord God who "preserves the church,"
that is, God's faithful, in order to provide humankind with a fresh start.
"Thus in this passage we observe the providence of God, according to
whose counsel the ungodly are punished but the good are preserved. This
takes place in an amazing manner; while God punishes the ungodly, He
nevertheless does not destroy nature in its entirety but graciously makes
provision for future generations."[7]

Following the awful sign of God's wrath, Noah and his family are
blessed by the Holy One "who has been changed from an angry God to a
merciful one."[8] God promises, "I will never again curse the ground because
of man" (8:21). Then God speaks words of comfort that are intended to
transform his beloved. "He now begins to be a different God from the one
He has been thus far. Not that God changes, but that He desires a change
in the people, who are now swallowed up, as it were, in contemplation of
His wrath."[9]

Luther sees God's mercy grounded in the realization that "the imagination of man's heart is evil from his youth" (8:21). This corroborating biblical testimony to the radicality of original sin is later illustrated civilly by
Aristotle and Cicero, "who are the most eminent men in this class [of
philosophers], teach many things about the virtues and bestow superb
praise on them because of their civil purpose; for they see that they are
beneficial both in public and private life." However, regarding God "they
teach nothing," and therefore "the virtues of the heathen must be distinguished from the virtues of Christians."[10] Indeed, regarding faith and life,

"all Aristotle is to theology as darkness is to light." Luther's twofold reason for religiously rejecting heathen morality: "the formal cause, that is, right reason, is lacking, inasmuch as there is no knowledge of God and no right will toward God"; moreover, "the final cause is corrupt; for the true goal, obedience to God and love of one's neighbor, receives no consideration."[11]

Yet after this clear and unequivocal rejection of any saving benefits of natural revelation and rational morality ("to prescribe and desire what is right before God"), Luther goes on in Genesis 9's depiction of God's covenantal blessings to Noah and his kin to support "civil righteousness" (*iustitia civilis*), a real but relative public morality that is of universal significance for believers and unbelievers alike. For as we have already seen, rational and honorable people, however godless, can still outwardly "do" the just works of the law that they will never inwardly piously "fulfill." Structural bulwarks of social justice include the divinely mandated ordinances of marriage, ministry, and magistrates. However, this side of the fall, they are in this aeon at best "emergency orders" (*Notordnungen*), by which the Creator now preserves humankind from its own sinful self-destruction.

At the outset, God reconfirms marriage (9:1), "for through His Word and command God joins the male with the female, and that for the definite purpose of filling the earth with human beings."[12] Marriage is deemed God-pleasing and divinely ordained as "the source of both the family and the state, and the nursery of the church."[13]

Human dominion over the animal world is also accentuated (9:2), when beasts, birds, and fish are now designated for human food and nourishment as "God sets Himself up as a butcher." Here we also see some of the residual ethical benefits of our creation in God's image: "that the human being is endowed with reason, which has the advantage over all the animals."[14]

Then Luther turns to a highly important section in which the Lord "adds a commandment that concerns the *state*."[15] God gives a new law (9:4) about not shedding human blood, and he also restricts people's liberty to eat meat until it has first been cleansed of its blood. In Gen. 9:5, Luther understands "for your lifeblood I will surely require a reckoning" to mean "God's prohibition of murder in general, in accordance with the Fifth Commandment, which says (Exod. 20:13): 'You shall not kill.'"[16] However, Gen. 9:6 also then continues with the divine decree, "whosoever sheds the blood of man, by man shall his blood be shed," that heralds a new era in the history of fallen humanity.

After the flood, "the Lord establishes a new law and wants murderers to be killed by men." Even though Cain was not to be killed by anyone for the murder of Abel (Gen. 4:15), God now delegates the civil "sword" of punishment to the state within fallen creation, in order to maintain an officially authorized modicum of civil order and justice. For Luther, this provides the biblical foundation in principle (whether or not exercised prudently in practice) for the state's capital punishment internally and defensive warfare externally. The Commandment "You shall not kill" (that is, in Hebrew, *murder*) is addressed to private persons, not to official governments, which are now divinely mandated (*mandata*) to preserve law and order. Persons may not personally murder, but state authorities or soldiers may officially kill if authorized as a last resort to do so in order to maintain the common good. "Here God shares his power with man and grants him power over life and death among men, provided that the person is guilty of shedding blood."[17]

Three critical reflections are immediately necessary at this point. First, although there was some "household government" in the domestic clan of Adam and Eve in the Garden (Gen. 1:26-28), now armed "civil government" is for the first time divinely instituted by God "as a remedy required by sin; cf. Rom. 13:4."[18] Its "foremost function is to hold sin in check (*remedium peccatorum*)"; indeed, "here God establishes government and gives it the sword, to hold wantonness in check, lest violence and other sins proceed without limit."[19]

Second, if might is the state's ground, then right is its goal. "Here we have the source from which stem all civil laws and the law of nations." The magistrates' official power over life and death is necessarily extended "to punish all sins forbidden in the law's Second Table": for example, disobedience of children, theft, adultery, and perjury. The guilt of personal "sin" is still governed directly by God in the church (*coram Deo*); the guilt of societal "crime," however, may now be governed indirectly by God through the state within the world (*coram hominibus*). "For this reason courts have been established and a definite method of procedure has been prescribed."[20]

Third, the establishment of civil authority that is grounded in might and aiming at right is to be seen by believers as "a proof of the supreme love of God toward man." God provides these "walls as outward remedies against sin," in order to provide "protection for our life and possessions." After all, humans alone are made by God "in His own image" (9:6), and God wills that our sin-corrupted image might fully "be restored through the Word and the Spirit."

Hence, we are all called "to show respect for this image in one another," and an armed civil government provides another strange form (*opus alienum*) of God's preserving love in order to set limits on Satan's opposing injustice. The unbelieving world may not agree with all this, "but we who have the Word are aware that the counter argument must be the command of God, who regulates and establishes affairs in this manner. Here it is our duty to obey the divine regulation and to submit to it."[21]

The Genesis testimony is that God established a new covenant with Noah and his kin (Gen. 9:9), as a further sign that "He wanted to protect, defend, and preserve them."[22] Clearly "this is an indication of God's extra-ordinary affection for mankind . . . like a mother who is caressing and pet-ting her child in order that it may finally begin to forget its tears and smile at its mother."[23]

All these developments lead Luther to meditate further on "the ministry of the Law" after the flood within the temporal twofold rule of God over a fallen creation. By now his dialectical approach is quite familiar to us. On the one hand, before God (*forum theologicum*), the law's theological function is "a ministry of death and sin." Thus Paul calls the ministry of the law "the ministry of death" (2 Cor. 3:7); he says "the law kills" (2 Cor. 3:6), "the law brings wrath" (Rom. 4:15), and "the law causes sin to increase" (Rom. 5:20). This scriptural approach (*ad modum scripturae*) is clearly endorsed by Luther: "It bears witness against us through our conscience, because we have not done the will of God revealed in the Law, but we have even done the opposite."[24] His somber conclusion: "by the works of the Law we are not justified."[25] He states that Christian righteousness "is opposed to, or above, Aristotle, who taught that righteousness is produced by actions, especially extended and frequent actions. But this civil righteousness is reprobate before God. True righteousness comes into being by believing the words of God with the whole heart (Rom. 4:3)."[26]

On the other hand, within everyday life (*forum politicum*) and even from non-Christian moralists in society, a person can learn from the law "what he ought to do" in legal righteousness (*iustitia civilis*). Indeed, Luther can praise Aesop over Cato as "the better teacher of morals to say nothing of the ethical masters of rational, reasonable, and equitable moral conduct, Cicero and Aristotle" (*ad modum Aristotelis*).

Luther can easily shock biblicistic sensibilities by boldly asserting:

> So far as moral precepts are concerned, we cannot find fault with the industry and correctness of the heathen. . . . God wants the Law to be taught, and He Himself reveals it; nay, He even writes it upon the hearts of all human beings, as St. Paul demonstrates in Rom. 2:15.
>
> From this natural knowledge have originated all the books of the more sensible philosophers, such as Aesop, Aristotle, Plato, Xenophon, Cicero, and Cato. It is a good idea to set such books before uneducated and unruly individuals, that their wicked impulses may in some mea-sure be counteracted through this training.[27]

When completing his commentary on Genesis 11, Luther reaffirms his primary commitment to the Christian reader: "Now you have a history of the first world. This has been faithfully presented by Moses as proof of the misinterpreted transmission of the promise concerning Christ . . . as you marvel of those holy rulers of the first church, Adam, Seth, Noah and Shem," prior to his climactic saving covenant with Abraham, "with whom a new world and a new church began . . . with a clear promise concerning Christ who was to bless all nations."[28]

These passages are cited to support our view that Luther's primary concern was never ethical but theological and that even when he dealt with ethics it was never narrowly biblicistic. Not humanly autonomous, but ethically ordered "right reason" and "natural law" were acknowledged to be humanity's universal norms for civil righteousness (cf. Rom. 2:15). Yet sin has badly corrupted both (Rom. 1:21), so that "the noble gem called natural law and reason is a rare thing" among unrighteous human beings. Hence, the law's "civil function" is at best remedial and cannot ever hope to produce more externally than moral hypocrisy: doing the right thing for the wrong reason toward a morally mixed goal. Nevertheless, human struggles for societal justice do serve as powerful, though buffeted, "dikes" against the ever-threatening floods of sinful humanity's civil unrighteousness.

As Luther preached consistently, "You cannot rule a fallen world with the gospel!" This is a realism that alienates all starry-eyed idealists, be they Christians or secular humanists alike, who either covet or fear the alleged Christianization of the world and all its values through the moral performance of the alleged good works of the law. His is a hopeful realism, however, that Luther learned directly from Paul's Romans, in the apostle's sanctified analysis of the sin-corrupted means and ends of God's natural moral law, that is, the law of creation that forbids evil and commands good.

Pauline Natural Law

We have earlier developed Luther's understanding of Paul's claim in the opening chapters of his *Lectures on Romans* (1516) that all of humanity is in need of the saving gospel of Christ because all have been found guilty of sin by God's holy law ("theological function"), whether it is written in the Old Testament (Jews) or the human heart (Gentiles). Shifting our focus from spiritual unrighteousness (sin) to civil unrighteousness (crime), we will now explore more fully Paul's complementary scriptural position on the "political function" of God's law, that is, God's gracious provision of universal law and civil authority, with societal structures and statutes for the benefit of preserving fallen humanity against public injustice, economic corruption, and social disorder.

Luther's deliberations are centered on the classical Pauline texts that are located in Romans 2 and 13. Let it be said clearly at the outset, therefore, that both of these texts are basically corollaries or illustrations of Romans 1 and 12 respectively. That is to say, the primary attention of both the apostle Paul and later the reformer Luther rested on the church's gospel and personal love (Romans 1 and 12) rather than on the world's universal law and public justice (Romans 2 and 13), not least because sinful perversions of the latter had perennially threatened the righteous purity of the former. However, it was precisely as church leaders that both unexpectedly also became theological and even social ethicists.

Both Paul and Luther were writing pastorally for fellow Christians: Paul for small pockets of believers in local congregations whose members held no public leadership in an overwhelmingly pagan society, and Luther for late medieval believers whose church leadership had also often co-opted civil authority within a nominally Christian society. In short, in addressing their own distinctive situations (to say nothing of their mutually mistaken expectations of the imminent end of the world), both church teachers gave primary attention to the law's theological rather than its (underdeveloped) political function, to the subsequent detriment of both their dependent social ethics. Nevertheless, the valid theological foundations still remained there for the later church's further study and modified social application (*applicatio*).

After the announcement of his forgiving and life-giving gospel in Rom. 1:17 ("the righteous shall live by faith"), Paul goes on to analyze the universal guilt of humanity, Jews and Gentiles alike. In the case of the Gentiles, Paul deals in Romans 2 with their accountability to the essentials of God's law that is "written on their hearts."

> When Gentiles, who do not possess the law do instinctively what the law requires, these, though not having the law, are a law to themselves. They show that what the law requires is written on their hearts, to which their own conscience also bears witness; and their conflicting thoughts will accuse or perhaps excuse them on the day when, according to my gospel, God through Jesus Christ, will judge the secret thoughts of all. (Rom. 2:14-16)

Though the Gentiles have not had the added benefit of the Jews' written Mosaic law, "they can instruct themselves" by virtue of the law that is "written by the finger of God" on their hearts through their creation in the image of God (*scriptum in cordibus suis*). "By nature and indelibly the law of nature is imprinted on their minds, while their conscience bears witness to their good and evil works."[29]

Of whom is Paul speaking here? Luther asserts that they are the people who are "in the middle" between the ungodly Gentiles and the believing Gentiles. They engage in "some good action directed toward God as much as they are able"; they are "people who gladly want to do the will of God, but they are pusillanimous and tremble when they hear of the teachings."[30] The gracious Creator has provided such persons with "the law that is written in letters concerning the works that have to be done but not the grace to fulfill this law."[31] Nevertheless, they do "show what the law requires" by "doing those things that are of the law" and by hearing their conscience give "a good witness of good deeds and an evil witness about evil deeds" in evaluating their ethical lives.[32]

Luther rejected any "analogy of being" (*analogia entis*) between the Creator and rational human creatures. He likewise repudiated any ontological basis in an autonomous natural theology for this cited natural law (*lex naturalis*) in Romans or of related teachings in the Stoic philosophy of the pagan Greeks. While he accepted a limited general revelation of God's law (*revelatio generalis*) in reason, conscience, and nature, he also believed that the resultant law of sinful people (*lex gentium*) needed the corrected fulfillment of God's revealed law in Holy Scripture (*lex divina*). Nevertheless, he frequently refers to this influential passage from Romans 2 for illuminating his concept of "civil righteousness" from a variety of different perspectives. Imperative for its proper interpretation within Luther's governing theology of the cross is his dialectical emphasis on the natural law's metaphysical abuse within the world's spiritual two kingdoms (*coram Deo*), along with its ethical benefits within God's twofold rule of temporal humanity (*coram hominibus*).

On the one hand, what is "natural" in an unnatural world after the fall? Luther's view of the radical impact of original sin on the image of God, free will, and human reason necessarily rejects any synergistic way of salvation that allegedly both supplements the human cardinal virtues of justice, courage, temperance, and prudence with the divine theological virtues of faith, hope, and charity. This Roman view also incorporates civil law and natural law (*lex naturae*) with divine law and eternal law (*lex aeterna*) into a legalistic ladder of meritorious moral obedience that climbs up from implicit faith (*fides implicita*) through good works to the "highest good" of a beatific vision (*summum bonum*). For Luther, the fallen creation in Holy Scripture challenges this primary presupposition of the late medieval scholastic version of the majestic Thomistic metaphysical synthesis of Paul and Aristotle: "grace does not destroy nature, but perfects it (*gratia non tollat naturam, sed perficiat*)." For Luther, *natural law* (*lex naturae*) means solely the revealed law of God the Creator (*lex creationis*), ultimately love in its various expressions.

On the other hand, what is "law" for God's preservation of the fallen world? It is essential for Luther's scriptural position that God's law remain unified. God's will is also one, and it is the one loving will of the one loving God that paradoxically governs the law's twofold use, theologically or politically. That unitive will is ultimately love in both its "strange" and "proper" forms. Luther contends that the Creator's natural law of love is the one law that runs through all ages. Through conscience and right (*humane*) reason, it norms all human laws and governs all of God's mandated societal structures for justice, fairness, and equity (*epieikei, clementia, comoditus, gelindigheit*), among Christians and non-Christians alike. It moderates the severity of unjust laws as rigidly applied to individual cases in different circumstances. It is universally known (however corrupted by sin), because it is written by God the Creator on the hearts of all people.

The most radical by-product of this recognition of God's universal law of love, even among the Gentiles, is Paul's corollary endorsement of the nontheocratic rule of a pagan Caesar in forcefully compelling its public compliance ("sword") for the sake of civil righteousness. Therefore, the interrelated interpretation of Genesis 3 and 9 with Romans 2 and 13 became the classical scriptural test case for Christian ethical realism. "Let every person be subject to the governing authorities; for there is no authority except from God, and those authorities that exist have been instituted by God. . . . If you do what is wrong, you should be afraid for the authority does not bear the sword in vain. It is the servant of God to execute wrath on the wrongdoer (Rom. 13:1-4)."

In exegeting Romans 13, Luther cites both John 19:11 and 1 Pet. 2:13ff. for dominical and apostolic authority to corroborate Paul's view that "subjects should obey their superiors by assisting them and loving them." Paul declares that the governing powers (*exousiais*) "have been instituted by God," although Luther does add here the important qualification, "even though those who possess the authority may not have been instituted by Him. . . . Natural law is a practical first principle in the sphere of morality; it forbids evil and commands good. Positive law is a decision that takes circumstances into account and conforms with natural law on credible grounds. The basis of natural law is God, who has created this light, but the basis of positive law is civil authority."[33]

Nevertheless, Luther considers it foundational that "here the apostle is instructing the people of Christ how they should conduct themselves over against the higher powers," and in contrast to the Jewish idea he teaches that they should be "obedient even to evil and unbelieving rulers." As in the previous chapters of Romans, where Paul taught that civil power should not upset the church order, so here he admonishes the same reciprocally of the church. "For both orders are of God; the one to give guidance and peace for the inner man and his concerns; the other for the guidance of the outer man and his concerns." This corresponds, significantly, to the Christian's "two citizenships; he is subject to Christ in faith, to the emperor [Caesar] in his body."[34]

Luther keeps reiterating "for the sake of emphasis" that the armed civil authorities are the "ministers of God." He recalls that King Cyrus of Babylon, a godless idolater, is also deemed a "servant" of God in the writings of the Old Testament prophets. So this is not his novel idea and believers are duly warned: "Do not think that because of your Christianity you are above punishment." This is because Christians themselves remain sinful and continue to live and work among sinful non-Christians. For the sake of public justice and the common good, they are therefore reminded, "the gospel does not abrogate this natural law, but confirms it as the ordinance and creation of God."[35]

Indeed, our obedience to God's universal law and its civilly armed enforcers is to be seen by Christians as a very concrete way by which they may illumine their darkened and sin-corrupted reason by faith (*christiana et libera ratio*), love their neighbors, and so "fulfill the law." Therefore, the second part of the Lord's great commandment, "You shall love your neighbor as yourself" (Matt. 22:37-39), is specifically cited by Paul as "a summary or recapitulation" of the various commandments of the second table of the Mosaic Decalogue (Rom. 13:8-10) to govern civil life in society.

For Luther, Paul's teaching is clear: Both Christians and non-Christians are called to "obey" God's universal moral law, but only faithful Christians can "fulfill" it in love as intended by the Spirit. The proper fulfillment of Romans 13 is wholly predicated on the "spiritual worship" of the governing apostolic admonition: "Be transformed by the renewal of your minds" (Rom. 12:2).[36] Luther is here endorsing the apostolic teaching that this "spiritual worship" is action that is empowered by the Holy Spirit, whether it be carried out under civil or ecclesiastical auspices. The institutional church has no monopoly on "the spiritual"; indeed, it may even wrongly hinder the legitimate piety of one's civic duties.

> For my part, I do not know, but it seems plain to me that in our day the secular powers are carrying on their duties more successfully and better than the ecclesiastical rulers are doing. For they are strict in their punishments of thefts and murders, except to the extent that they are corrupted by insidious privileges. . . . So much so that perhaps it would be safer if the temporal affairs also of the clergy were placed under secular power.
>
> Satan, "the father of lies and a murderer" (John 8:44) occupies both realms, the spiritual and the temporal: the former through the lies of wicked teachers . . . and the latter through the tyrant's sword.[37]

In making such contextually conditioned social ethical judgments ("in our day"), Luther recognizes that he is "speaking under the compulsion of my sorrow and the demands of my office." Yet ethically, he considers it "most important to make an application to our present life of the doctrine that is taught." Providing "moral direction" for all of God's societal estates and offices is an "auxiliary service" (*vikarischen Dienst*) of the holy office of preaching. He repeatedly claims to do so "by apostolic authority," for "it is my duty to speak of whatever I see not being done correctly, even in the case of those in high places."

> There are also countless important matters in worldly affairs that need improvement. There is a disunity among the princes and the estates.

Greed and usury, wantonness, lewdness, extravagant dress, gluttony, gambling, conspicuous consumption with all kinds of vice and wickedness, disobedience—of subjects, servants, laborers, extortion by all the artisans and peasants (who can list everything?) have so gained the upper hand that a person could not set things right again with ten councils and twenty imperial diets.

Now if a preacher in his official capacity says to kings and princes and to the world, "Thank and fear God, and keep His commandments," he is not meddling in the affairs of secular government. On the contrary, he is thereby serving and being obedient to the highest government. Thus the entire spiritual authority does nothing else than serve the divine authority, which is why they are called servants of God and ministers of Christ in the Scriptures.[38]

What is truly deplorable, however, is that so many politically apathetic, modern Lutheran church leaders both have refused to exercise that same apostolic authority for their own public ethical leadership and have been unable or unwilling to *re-contextualize* Paul's (and Luther's) social ethical admonitions after secularism had so decisively replaced clericalism and human justice and freedom were far more threatened by twentieth-century state rather than church dictatorships. In short, evangelical biblical fidelity should never confuse the culture-conditioned social ethics of any past era with the Scripture's normative theological ethic of faith-activated love and justice.

Finally, Luther does properly reiterate the unique way in which the Spirit-worked love of Christians fulfills the law of the Creator (Rom. 13:10; cf. Gal. 5:14; Matt. 19:19 or Lev. 19:18). Especially here, one must avoid the egocentric misinterpretation that neighbor love is merely an extension of self-love, or that "love begins at home." What do the admonished words "as yourself" really mean? We recall:

First, we can understand it in the sense that both the neighbor and one's own self are to be loved. But in another sense it can be understood that we are commanded to love only our neighbor, using our love for ourselves as the example. This is the better interpretation, because man with his natural sinfulness does love himself above all others, seeks his own in all matters, loves everything else for his own sake, even when he loves his neighbor or his friend, for he seeks his own in him.[39]

Luther finds scriptural support for this view of love-grounded law in Christ's "Golden Rule" (Matt. 7:12). God's law "contains many ways of applying to life the principle of love." Indeed, Luther freely cites the authority of Christ's word to teach here that the whole transmitted law is nothing but the natural law, "which cannot be unknown to anyone and on

account of which no one can be excused." As a fundamental expression of
God's command of love, natural law serves as the source and norm under
which all human laws are to be held accountable. It is this natural law—as
summarized in the (de-Judaized) Decalogue—that provides the normative
ethical criteria for both informing and assessing our social, political, economic, and military judgments based on our limited and selfish human reason. Through the natural law's political function, love may employ reason
and power to achieve justice and good order in society. In its absence, justice becomes heartless, and power becomes ruthless.

> It is the heart and empress of all laws, the fountain from which all laws
> flow forth. . . . But wise and understanding "miracle-workers" (*Wun-
> derleute*) for its social applications are few and far between. . . . There-
> fore we need written laws and public regulations to govern the people.
>   However, there is no greater unhappiness and injustice on earth than
> when people are governed by laws without love. Therefore the proverb,
> "the most law, the most injustice" (*summum ius, summa iustitia*).[40]

Consequently, it is not enough for people to be "content with their good
intentions." Rather, we should emulate the way Moses taught the children
of Israel in Deut. 6:6ff. that "all their efforts and thoughts and senses must
be applied and directed to this end."

> For this reason the apostle describes the essence of this commandment
> when he says in Phil. 2:4: "Let each of you look not only to his own
> interests but also to the interest of others," and in 1 Cor. 13:5: "Love
> does not insist on its own way," that is, it causes man to deny himself
> and to affirm another, to put on affection for the neighbor and put off
> affection for himself, to place himself in the person of his neighbor.[41]

In the lifelong pursuit of this restored selflessness before God (*coram Deo*),
Christians should not be discouraged so long as they follow the Spirit and
try and try again. "To stand still on the way to God is to retrogress, and to
progress is always a matter of beginning anew (*semper a novo incipere*)." As
Paul also says in 2 Cor. 6:1-2: "Working together with Him, then, we
entreat you not to accept the grace of God in vain."[42]

Luther complained that humanistic and polytheistic philosophers have
perennially composed so many speculative "fables" (*multa fabulamur*) about
natural law. However, when governed properly by scriptural foundations,
the "natural law" is really our sin-conditioned apprehension of God's pre-
fall command of love (*mandatum*) that reveals both the Creator God's original intention for humanity and the Redeemer God's abiding purpose for
the inaugurated renewal of humanity. Therefore Luther insists:

> No less carefully must one understand that very popular distinction
> which is made among natural law, the written law, and the law of the

gospel. For when the Apostle says here [Gal. 5:14] that they all come together and are summed up in one, certainly love is the end of every law (1 Tim. 1:5). In Matt. 7:12 Christ, too, expressly equates that natural law, as they call it—whatever you wish that men would do to you, do so to them—with the law and the prophets.[43]

Christ's organic correlation of "the law and the prophets" with the Golden Rule of the natural law of love in the Sermon on the Mount prompts us now to examine Luther's distinctive understanding of the character and scope of the "political function" (*usus politicus*) of God's law for Christians in pivotal texts of the Old Testament, most especially in the Mosaic Ten Commandments.

Mosaic Natural Law

What is the binding authority, if any, of the Mosaic law for the moral life of Christians? We have seen that Luther's early testimony to the Christ promised in the law and prophets of ancient Israel—"the manger of Christ"—was intended to restore the Christocentric authority of the Old Testament. Consequently, his earliest scriptural protests were primarily directed against the allegorical interpretation of late medieval Roman Catholic exegetes and commentators. Their nonscriptural speculation obeyed no binding apostolic norms and therefore resulted in a wide variety of incompatible beliefs and practices that were themselves in continual need of equally nonscriptural adjudication by casuistic canon lawyers. Scriptural authority was thereby arbitrarily subjugated to the teaching office (*magisterium*) of the Roman church.

Within a decade, however, Luther also had to respond to liberal opponents on the Protestant side. In their bitter anti-Romanism, overzealous "fanatics" contended that the Holy Spirit was given directly to each individual Christian apart from the church's mediating Word and sacraments of grace. They reacted, lamented Luther, as if they had "swallowed the Holy Spirit, feathers and all!" They rejected the Reformer's churchly teaching that "it has pleased God to impart the Spirit, not without the Word, but through the Word so as to have us as cooperators with God (*cooperatores Dei*; cf. 1 Cor. 3:9; 2 Cor. 3:18; 8:23) when we sound forth outwardly what he himself alone breathes inwardly whenever he wills (John 3:8), thus doing things that he could of course do without the Word, though he does not will to do."[44]

Ironically, the first victim was once again the normative authority of the Word of God in witnessing to the mighty acts of God for human salvation. Luther consistently charged both religious fronts with this same basic error:

I have had this year [1525] and am still having, a sharp enough fight with those fanatics who subject the Scriptures to the interpretation of their own spirit. It is on this account also that I have hitherto attacked the pope, in whose kingdom nothing is more commonly stated or more generally accepted than the idea that the Scriptures are obscure and ambiguous, so that the spirit to interpret them must be sought from the Apostolic See of Rome. Nothing more pernicious could be said than this, for it has led ungodly men to set themselves above the Scriptures and to fabricate what they pleased, until the Scriptures have been completely trampled down and we have been believing and teaching nothing but the dreams of madmen.[45]

Luther's indictment here is made at the outset of his celebrated debate with Erasmus of Rotterdam, *The Bondage of the Will* (1525). We have already analyzed this magisterial work in connection with Luther's discussion of the enslaved condition of the human will and reason after the fall. Here our major concern centers on his parallel claims of the clarity of the Holy Scripture as the authoritative basis for making such doctrinal affirmations as Christians.

Indeed, it is the "evasive and equivocal" neutrality of Erasmus ("I take no delight in assertions") that fires Luther's initial ire. Having been censured by Erasmus for his own "obstinate assertiveness," Luther counters with the insistence that "a man must delight in assertiveness or he will be no Christian," and especially regarding "assertions of those things which have been divinely transmitted to us in the sacred writings."[46] Such public confession has been commanded of Christians by Christ (Matt. 10:32), the apostle Paul (Rom. 10:10), and St. Peter (1 Pet. 3:15). "Take away assertions and you take away Christianity. . . . The Holy Spirit is no skeptic."[47]

Luther's willingness to make doctrinal assertions is based on his conviction of the essential clarity of the Holy Scripture. While many things are certainly still hidden in God, "the subject matter of the Scriptures is all quite accessible. It enjoys both an "inner clarity" illumined by the indwelling of the Holy Spirit (*testimonium Spiritus Sancti internum*), and an "external clarity" by which "nothing at all is left obscure or ambiguous, but everything there in the Scriptures has been brought out by the Word into the most definite light, and published to all the world."[48]

This external judgment "belongs to the public ministry of the Word and to the outward office, and is chiefly the concern of leaders and preachers of the Word." The Scriptures themselves are replete with passages showing that they are neither obscure nor ambiguous (for example, Deut. 17:8; Psalms 19 and 119; Isa. 8:20; Rom. 1:2; 1 Cor. 3–4; 2 Pet. 1:19; John 5:39; Acts 17:11). Therefore, all human spirits are to be tested "in the presence of the church at the bar of Scripture." For it ought above all to be settled and established among Christians that "the Holy Scriptures are a spiritual light far better than the sun itself, especially in things that are necessary to salvation."[49] Luther concludes:

It may suffice for a beginning to have laid it down that the Scriptures
are perfectly clear, and that by them such a defense of our position
may be made that our adversaries will not be able to gainsay it. . . .
But if there are those who do not perceive this clarity, and are blind or
blunder in the sunlight, then they only show—if they are ungodly—
how great is the majesty and power of Satan over the sons of men,
to make them neither hear nor take in the very clearest words of
God.[50]

Building on this claimed clarity of the Scriptures, Luther went on to
reassert some very provocative Pauline doctrinal assertions as "the clearest
gospel." On the basis of his Christocentric reading of Hebrew Scriptures,
Luther taught, dialectically, that the Old Testament is (1) still binding on
Gentile Christians where it theologically promises the coming Christ, but
(2) no longer binding on Gentile Christians where it historically served the
ancient theocracy of Israel alone with the interim laws of Moses. Then it
was a "disciplinarian until Christ came, so that we may be justified by faith.
But now that faith has come, we are no longer subject to a disciplinarian, for
in Christ Jesus you are all children of God through faith" (Gal. 3:23-24).
This was massively reinforced by the Johannine dictum: "The law indeed
was given through Moses; grace and truth came through Jesus Christ"
(John. 1:17).

Luther developed this dialectical position on Scripture in his publication
How Christians Should Regard Moses (1525). Originally included within a
long series of articles of seventy-seven sermons on Exodus preached by
Luther from October 1524 to February 1527, its general character com-
mended itself to later editors as a fitting hermeneutical introduction to the
1527 printed volume of Luther's earlier series of sermons on Genesis,
preached from March 1523 through September 1524. In short, it is the
"Moses" of the entire Septuagint that is under homiletical analysis here,
especially offered by Luther as pastoral guidance amid the turmoil of the
mid-1520s (the biblicistic legalism and theocratic violence of such radical
enthusiasts as Andreas Karlstadt and Thomas Muenzer).

Here it must be frankly acknowledged that Luther's earlier-praised
"clarity of Scripture" was not always aided by his own loose and hyper-
bolic formulations of some very subtle theological distinctions. For
instance, he can almost immediately follow the theological claim that
"Moses does not pertain to us" with the pastoral advice that sixteenth-
century rulers should "follow the example of Moses." In our own quest
for scriptural clarity, we more prosaically need to refer such former
statements to the distinctive 613 regulations in the law codes of Moses
and the theocracy, and the latter to the leadership style modeled justly by
Moses the lawgiver. Indeed, Luther can use the generic term *Moses* quite

inexactly to refer (1) theologically, to a preparatory stage in God's plan of salvation, (2) historically, to the political times of ancient Israel, and (3) personally, to the chosen recipient of the old covenant between God and the Jews (to whom Luther also wrongly attributed the solitary authorship of the first five books of the Bible).

Luther begins his work with the arresting comment that there have been only two public sermons "from heaven": (1) God's giving of the law to Moses atop Mt. Sinai (Exodus 19–20), and (2) God's exposition of the gospel through the Holy Spirit at Pentecost (Acts 2:2-4).

> These two sermons are not the same. . . . The law commands and requires us to do certain things. The law is thus directed solely to our own behavior and consists in making requirements. The gospel . . . reverses the approach of the law, does the very opposite, and says, "This is what God has done for you; he has let his Son to be made flesh for you, has let him be put to death for your sake!" So, then, there are two kinds of doctrine and two kinds of works, those of God and those of men.[51]

Here the theocratic law of Moses has its peculiar historical place. It binds "only the Jews and not the Gentiles."[52] These legal, moral, and ceremonial rules and regulations, mediated to Moses by angels (according to Paul, Gal. 3:19), are not to be confused with the universal law of nature, written into all human hearts, Jews included, by God the Creator (Rom. 2:14-15). The claim that the Mosaic law is historically addressed solely to ancient Israel is demonstrated for Luther by both the preface and the Jewish Sabbath (Third) Commandment of the Ten Commandments.

> That Moses does not bind the Gentiles can be proved from Exod. 20:1, where God himself speaks, "I am the Lord Your God, who brought you out of the land of Egypt, out of the house of bondage." This text makes it clear that even the Ten Commandments do not pertain to us. For God never led us out of Egypt, but only the Jews. . . . We will regard Moses as a teacher, but we will not regard him as our lawgiver—unless he agrees with both the New Testament and the natural law.
>
> Again one can prove it from the Third Commandment that Moses does not pertain to Gentile Christians. For Paul (Col. 2:16) and the New Testament (Matt. 12:1-2, John 5:16) abolish the Sabbath, do show us that the Sabbath was given to the Jews alone, for whom it is a stern commandment.[53]

Why, then, does Luther still preach and teach about Moses? "In the first place, I dismiss the commandments given to the people of Israel." While they are not obligatory for Gentile Christians, they nevertheless provide historical models and "examples for us to be free to follow him in ruling as he ruled" (for example, tithing, jubilee year statutes, dress codes, circumcision). "The Gentiles are not obligated to obey Moses. Moses is the Saxon code of law (*Sachsenspiegel*) for the Jews. But if an example of good government were to be taken from Moses, one could adhere to it without obligation as long as one pleased."[54]

Luther's liberating conclusion is that Christians are bound only by God's universal natural law, some of which, however, is also embodied in the Mosaic moral law, but none of which is to be found in the legal and ceremonial codes peculiar to ancient Israel. In much the same way as Paul later incorporated pre-Christian ethical exhortations of natural law into the uniquely Christian revelation of the will, power, and goal of the gospel of Jesus Christ (for example, Eph. 5:3-5; Phil. 4:8-9), so too had Moses still earlier "Judaized" non-Jewish morality in the ancient world (cf. treaties of Hittite kings) as appropriate responses of obedience to the sovereign Lord God who led his people out of Egyptian bondage. Christians are to obey the moral law of Moses only when he agrees with the universal natural law of the Creator (Rom. 2:14-15) and provides us with a "mirror of our life" in the Ten Commandments (cf. Matt. 7:12; Rom. 13:8-9). Then they reveal the eternal love of God's will (*Decalogus est aeterna*).

> What God has given the Jews from heaven, he has also written in the hearts of all men. Thus I keep the commandments which Moses has given, not because Moses gave the commandments, but because they have been implanted in me by nature, and Moses agrees exactly with nature. But the other commandments of Moses, which are not implanted in all men by nature, the Gentiles do not hold. . . .
>
> Thus we read Moses not because he applies to us, that we must obey him, but because he agrees with the natural law and is conceived better than the Gentiles would ever have been able to do. Thus the Ten Commandments are a mirror of our life, in which we can see wherein we are lacking.[55]

The second thing to notice in Moses are "the promises and pledges of God about Christ." Of course, this is "the best thing"; it is "the most important thing in Moses which pertains to us"; here Christ is promised and I can "find strength for my weak faith. For things take place in the kingdom of Christ just as I read in Moses that they will."[56]

It is this crucial distinction between "Christ as promised" in Moses (gospel) and "Christ as preceded" by Moses (law), that the radical sectarians are unable or unwilling to make. It is not enough for radical preachers to shout, "Here God is speaking!" and again, "God's Word, God's Word!" while all they do is "mislead the poor people and drive them to destruction." The critical question is whether it was said *to you*. We must "pay attention and know to whom God's Word is addressed." Just because

God's people were once ordered to beat Amalek to death (Exod. 17:8-16) does not mean that Gentile Christians are now likewise ordered to wipe out all their enemies. This is what was being publicly advocated by the Anabaptist revolutionary, Muenzer, before he was himself captured and executed after the battle of Frankenhausen (1525).

> Misery and tribulation have come out of this sort of thing. The peasants have arisen, not knowing the difference, and have been led into this error by those factious spirits. . . . One must deal cleanly with the Scriptures. From the very beginning the Word has come to us in various ways. It is not enough simply to look and see whether this is God's Word, whether God has said it; rather we must look and see to whom it has been spoken, whether it fits us.[57]

Finally, we should read Moses for the "beautiful examples of faith, of love, and of the cross, as shown in the fathers, Adam, Abel, Noah, Abraham, Isaac, Jacob, Moses, and all the rest." There are also "examples of the godless, how God does not pardon the unfaith of the unbelieving; how he can punish Cain, Ishmael, Esau, the whole world in the flood, Sodom and Gomorrah, and so forth. . . . Nowhere else do we find such fine examples of both faith and unfaith."[58]

Law's Political Function

Against this background of the natural law of love in the Pauline and Mosaic Scriptures, we turn finally to Luther's systematic analysis of God's rule of everyday life through the "political function" of the law (*usus politicus*). Luther concluded from Scripture that God governs humanity in a twofold way: (1) his "proper" way of giving (via the gospel), and (2) his "strange" way of demanding (via the law). Fidelity to God and his Word means that we neither separate nor equate the law and the gospel, for their equation leads to clericalism as surely as their separation leads to secularism. Luther held that it is fatal both to our religion and to our ethics if we do not properly distinguish the realm of faith (under the gospel) from the realm of life (under the law).

In maintaining this crucial distinction, however, he never relinquished his primary assertion of the fundamental unity of worship and service in the eternal strategy of the Creator God's love in the daily lives of people. Only by asserting both their provisional diversity (versus clericalism) and their ultimate unity (versus secularism) could Luther arrive at an evangelical theology of society that freely renders what is due both God and Caesar. His doctrine of God the Preserver's rule through the "political function" of the law exposed the prevailing clericalism of late medieval Rome and provided the biblical and theological foundations for a just and responsible society under God.

The early Luther's most impressive attempt to correlate his traditional eschatological view of the world's two kingdoms (Satan versus God) with his deepening historical view of God's twofold rule (Caesar and Christ) may be found in *Temporal Authority: To What Extent It Should be Obeyed* (1523).[59] Whatever its persisting shortcomings, this interim position still made a singular contribution to a perennial dilemma in Western church-state relations. It implicitly disavowed Augustine's dualistic relegation of all temporal authority to Satan in his *City of God* and dialectically sought to defend a loving God's providential provision of the civil "sword of Caesar" to regulate law and order, along with justice and equity, in a fallen human society. It was arguably the first biblically grounded defense of temporal government against Roman ecclesial hegemony, which also simultaneously championed the active participation of Christians in political affairs as a godly calling.

In his letter of dedication to Duke John of Saxony, Luther recalls what a thorny problem the relation of civil to religious authority has been for the Christian church throughout its turbulent history. More concretely, should the civil authority's sword ever be used by regenerated Christians? The apparent contradiction between religious perfection and ethical responsibility—both of which are enjoined upon Christians in Scripture—seems virtually irreconcilable. The neuralgic point centers on the appropriate boundaries for obeying Christ's command, "Give to the emperor [Caesar] the things that are the emperor's, and to God the things that are God's" (Luke 20:25).

For example, Matthew 5–7 and Romans 13 / 1 Peter 2 seem to talk about "the sword" in two different languages to two different worlds. Yet to sever the two does violence to the unity of God's Word and God's people. Such a tactic leads inevitably to the double-standard morality of late medieval Rome between obeying clergy ("counsels") and laity ("precepts"). Luther soundly condemned this ethical dualism within Christ's one church.

Essentially, Luther's task was to purify the state of the dualistic stench *(odium)* with which it was invested as the "city of the devil" *(civitas diaboli)* within Augustine's *City of God,* prior to the late medieval church's subsequent program of subordinating the civil to the religious sphere. The uniqueness of Luther's formulation, however, lies in its implicit rejection of any kind of biblical-philosophical synthesis (as with Plato in Augustine or with Aristotle in Aquinas), and his explicit correlation of the totality of human experience with the strictly biblical categories of God's twofold rule of humankind, "with his left hand" by law and "with his right hand" by gospel, as the two-edged sword of the Word. Ultimately, Luther's background doctrine of the two kingdoms was grounded firmly in the New Testament eschatology of the two ages (aeons) in Adam and Christ.

However, the pressing need was to integrate God's historical twofold rule properly into the world's eschatological two kingdoms of fallen creation and inaugurated redemption.

Luther devotes the first part of *Temporal Authority* to an emphasis on the divine character of the establishment and maintenance of armed civil authority in God's preservation (*conservatio*) of the world. He does so in conscious opposition to the views of both the medieval Romans and the sectarian radicals (*Schwaermer*), who alike depreciate the civil realm as religiously inferior and contaminating to a truly Christian life. While Luther does still affirm in 1523 that "if all the world were composed of real Christians, that is, true believers, there would be no need for or benefit from prince, king, lord, sword, or law" (cf. 1 Tim. 1:9), his biblical realism already then convinces him that "there are few true believers, and still fewer who live in a Christian life."[60] As a "remedy against the sin" (*remedium peccatorum*) of the world, therefore, God has ordained "that the temporal sword and law be used for the punishment of the wicked and the protection of the upright."[61]

> We must provide a sound basis for the civil law and sword so that no one will doubt that it is the world by God's will and ordinance. The passages which do this are the following: Rom. 13:1-2, "Let every soul be subject to the governing authority, for there is no authority except from God; the authority which everywhere exists has been ordained by God. He then who resists the governing authority resists the ordinance of God and he who resists God's ordinance will incur judgment." Again in 1 Pet. 2:13-14: "Be subject to every kind of human ordinance, whether it be to the king as supreme, or to governors, as those who have been sent by him to punish the wicked and to praise the righteous."[62]

It would be difficult for us to overemphasize the decisive influence that such biblical passages played in the formative stages of the expansion of Luther's theological ethics. The more Rome neglected them, the more Luther stressed them, often forcing both into rigid positions that did not always take the totality of the biblical witness (for example, Revelation 13) into more balanced consideration. Nevertheless, Luther could present an impressive array of biblical citations to document his contention that "this penal law existed from the beginning of the world."

Actually, and more accurately, none of Luther's cited biblical sources refer to God's institution of temporal authority in creation itself before the fall of Adam. As he himself later declared in his *Lectures on Genesis* (1535), "There was then no need of civil government, since nature was unimpaired and without sin."[63] The remedial character of the armed state is there traced back to Cain's fear of the sword of civil punishment. Its validity is then continually "reestablished and confirmed" throughout biblical history, says Luther, by God (Gen. 9:6), the law of Moses (Exodus 21), John the Baptist (Luke 3:14), and Christ himself (Matt. 26:52).[64]

Yet parallel with all these affirmations, Luther recognizes that other passages like Matthew 5–7 and Romans 12 "would certainly make it appear as though in the New Testament Christians were to have no temporal sword."[65] Luther's classical reconciliation of this abiding Christian predicament is grounded in his masterful delineation of the world's two kingdoms (*zwei Reiche*), throughout which humanity's living God rules dialectically (*zweierlei Regimente*) as both Creator-Preserver and as Redeemer-Sanctifier. Luther boldly drives the mystery of the tension between the two ages of Scripture back into the diversified activities of the one Triune God. Since Christians live on earth by faith and not sight, Luther's doctrine is intended as a confession of faith in the lordship of God over all of creation, rather than as either a political program or a metaphysical system. It views humanity from the perspective of eternity (*sub specie aeternitatis*), seeking out the handiwork of a God whose mighty acts in history as "masked" through human instruments (*larvae Dei*) are perceptible only to the eyes of faith.

Luther charges that it is blasphemous for us to designate some realm of God's creation as "secular" or "profane" if we thereby judge it to be unworthy of divine activity or self-sufficient in its own autonomy. God rules temporally everyone and everywhere. It is God alone in whom "we live, and move, and have our being" (Acts 17:28). And yet because not all of God's creatures acknowledge God's lordship, the same Triune Lord rules persons differently as their Creator and as their Redeemer.

> Here we must divide all the children of Adam and all mankind into two classes, the first belong to the kingdom (*Reich*) of God, the second to the kingdom of the world. Those who belong to the kingdom of God are all the true believers who are in Christ and under Christ . . . and the gospel of the kingdom . . . as Psalm 2:6 and all the Scripture says. . . . All who are not Christians belong to the kingdom of the world and are under the law. There are few true believers, and still fewer who live a Christian life, who do not resist evil and indeed themselves do no evil. For this reason God has provided for them in a different environment beyond the Christian estate and the kingdom of God. He has subjected them to the sword so that, even if they would like to, they are unable to practice their wickedness.
>
> For this reason God has ordained two governments (*Regimente*): the spiritual, by which the Holy Spirit produces Christians and righteous people under Christ; and the temporal which restrains the un-Christian and wicked so that—no thanks to them—they are obliged to keep still and to maintain an outward peace.
>
> One must carefully distinguish between these two governments. Both must be permitted to remain; the one to produce righteousness the other to bring about external peace and to prevent evil deeds.[66]

The key points in Luther's 1523 position are these: (1) God is the hidden Lord of both opposing kingdoms, although he rules by different means (law and gospel) for different ends (peace and piety) in each; (2) every Christian lives in both of these kingdoms simultaneously—in the kingdom of God insofar as one is already righteous, and in the kingdom of the world insofar as one is still sinful; and (3) God's two governments within these two kingdoms are to be sharply distinguished from one another, which means that the functions of the law and the gospel are to be neither separated (in secularism) nor equated (in clericalism), but both permitted to coexist in harmonious interaction and coordination as complementary expressions of God's creative and redemptive activity against Satan among all human beings everywhere.

We shall now further explore Luther's comparison of both these kinds of interacting human righteousness: (1) "Christian righteousness" under God's right-hand rule by the Christocentric gospel (*iustitia Christiana*) and (2) "civil righteousness" under God's left-hand rule by the universal natural law (*iustitia civilis*). God's twofold rule by law and gospel thereby intersects and contravenes the opposing forces of the kingdom of Satan against the kingdom of God. The former righteousness of the gospel, building on Abraham, will be developed in fuller theological fashion below, both in Christ's justification of saved sinners (chapter 7) and the Holy Spirit's sanctification of serving saints (chapter 8). The civil righteousness of the law, building on Noah, Moses, and Paul, will be concluded later in this chapter.

1. *Christian Righteousness*. Here Luther lays chief emphasis upon faith and love, that is, the righteousness of God in Christ and its fruit, Christian righteousness, as the constitutive elements in the realm of God's redemptive and sanctifying work. The graciousness of God and his law-free gospel of Christ are essential both for eternal salvation (by faith alone) and for the temporal service of our neighbors (by faith active in love). Luther contended, "Christ is not a law-giver but the fulfiller of the law" (Matt. 5:17). The Lord of grace is certainly not some kind of *Mosissimus Moses* (Moses quadrupled) seated atop a new Mount Sinai, who proclaims merely an intensified new law (*Gesetz*) in his own Sermon on the Mount. Rather, when led by the Holy Spirit of the living God, the Christian—as righteous—knows no law but the faithful transmission of divine love (1 Tim. 1:19). In Luther's view, ethical spontaneity distinguishes our life of love in the power of the Holy Spirit.

> A good tree needs no instruction or law to bear good fruit; its nature causes it to bear according to its kind without any law or instruction. I would take to be quite a fool any man who would make a book full of laws and statutes for an apple tree telling it how to bear apples, and not thorns, when the tree is able by its own nature to do this better

than the man with all his books can describe and demand. Just so, by the Spirit and by faith all Christians are so thoroughly disposed and conditioned in their very nature that they do right and keep the law better than anyone can teach them with all manners of statutes; so far as they themselves are concerned, no statutes or laws are needed.[67]

It is on the strength of God the Spirit's twin gifts of faith and love that Luther is able to repudiate both legalistic options in theological ethics that are common in his day, as preeminently illustrated in their conflicting interpretations of the Sermon on the Mount (Matthew 5–7), so-called since the new law (*nova lex*) construal of St. Augustine. On the one hand, Luther repudiated the late medieval Roman Catholic separation of "general precepts" of the Decalogue for the baptized laity, and "counsels of perfection" in the Sermon on the Mount (for example, poverty, chastity, and obedience) only for the ordained clergy. The ethical chasm inherent in this double-standard morality is unbiblical and therefore illegitimate for Christian ethics. On the other hand, Luther also rejected the current Protestant sectarian views that Christ's born-again saints were either to separate themselves from the sinful world by retreating into enclaves of moralistic perfectionism or to strive to re-theocratize the fallen world, as God's elect, armed with both the military sword of divine judgment and the ethical legal absolutes of the Sermon on the Mount. This, too, struck Luther as alien to the apostolic admonition to live and serve "in, but not of" this world.

Contrariwise, Luther's *Commentary on the Sermon on the Mount* (1532) dealt with Matthew 5–7 as the revelation of God's eschatological grace in Christ, which, although inclusive of the "Golden Rule" (Matt. 7:12), also goes behind and beyond Moses, "in order to open up the true meaning of God's commandments." Even when Christ also employs the law's theological function here, it is solely as part of his "strange work" as accusing Judge that is both preliminary and subservient to his "proper work" as gracious Savior, by embodying and proclaiming the salvific and parenetic functions of the gospel. However, because of the textual unverifiability of this anonymously edited commentary (cf. chapter 8), we shall prudently limit our brief comments to its general doctrinal orientation in Christian righteousness as so often also corroborated by Luther elsewhere.

As we have already noted above, Luther viewed the Decalogue as a codified summary of natural law of love of God and neighbor, written on the hearts of all human creatures (Matt. 22:34-40; Rom. 2:14-16). In the Sermon on the Mount during his earthly ministry, the same Christ whom Matthew depicts as the "Son of God" and "risen Lord" (Matt. 16:16; 28:17) also authoritatively deepens, intensifies, radicalizes, and even partially abolishes some parts of the Mosaic Decalogue (Exodus 20) and other parts of Israel's "Holiness Code" (Leviticus 19). He does so, eschatologically, in order to reaffirm God's gracious command (*Gebot*) for righteous disciples (Christians) as they are now called to witness to the Redeemer's inbreaking kingdom, in fulfillment of the Creator's original intention for humanity as created in God's image ("from the beginning," Matt. 19:8).

To be sure, the Mosaic law (*Gesetz*) remains a valid expression of God's will for non-Christian and Christian sinners, and it will not pass away until God's salvific work is completed at the end of time (Matt. 5:19). Nevertheless, as accompanying comfort and guidance for truly faithful disciples, the Sermon on the Mount combines God's eschatological and unconditional promises of grace (Beatitudes, Matt. 5:1-12) with expressions of the kind of radical moral obedience required of those forgiven and renewed sinners who are graciously incorporated into God's sovereign rule in Christ ("But I say to you": Matt. 5:21-22, 27-28, 31-32, 33-34, 38-39, 43-44). Thereby, both the empowering indicatives and corollary imperatives of God's grace encompass the new church's corporate discipleship (Christ's addressed "you" is always in the plural) of those who faithfully trust in God's truthworthiness, as revealed in the Savior's person and passion. Thereby, the "higher righteousness" of the kingdom (Matt. 5:20) reveals the lived faith of Christian believers. "You therefore, must be perfect [in faith and love] as your heavenly Father is perfect" (Matt. 5:48). This Christian righteousness fulfills God's primal command (*Gebot*) for humanity that underlies the later, sin-conditioned Mosaic and post-exilic codified commandments (*Gesetz*).

Hence, concluded Luther, the Sermon on the Mount is best understood in terms of God's twofold reign within the world's eschatological two kingdoms. In opposition to Satan's kingdom of sin, it graciously describes the "Christian righteousness" of God's inbreaking kingdom in Christ. Weak and fearful disciples (in all ages) are being inspired and admonished by the Holy One, who proclaims in self-revelation, "the kingdom of heaven has come near" (Matt. 4:17). The "good news of the kingdom" in Christ's preaching, teaching, and healing is elsewhere addressed generally to all persons, most of whom sinfully reject it. Here, however, it is intentionally concentrated and addressed directly to the faithful (insofar as they are righteous). In terms of the world's opposing two kingdoms of Satan and God, the fundamental eschatological boundary is marked by our righteous or unrighteous response to Christ the Lord's personal and primary challenge: "Who do you say that I am?" (Matt. 16:15). The apostles do not accentuate penultimate differences among Christians, but they do distinguish them all ultimately from nonbelievers. One the one hand, "There is neither Jew nor Greek, there is neither slave nor free, there is neither male nor female; for you are all one in Christ Jesus" (Gal. 3:28). On the other hand, "For I tell you [plural], unless your righteousness exceeds that of the scribes and Pharisees, you will never enter the kingdom of heaven" (Matt. 5:20).

In concrete terms, this means for Luther that natural law's "civil righteousness" in the Ten Commandments is enjoined upon all of God's human creatures, while the Christian righteousness of the Sermon on the Mount is addressed exclusively to Christ's disciples; that is, as Christians "who are under another government (*Regiment*)."[68] It goes without saying, of course, that insofar as Christians remain sinful, they still fall with all other persons under the "theological function" of the you-shall-nots of the Ten Commandments. Therefore, it is of the greatest importance for our understanding of the totality of Luther's later expanded theological ethic, that we clearly distinguish this twofold human righteousness that corresponds to the twofold rule of God within the world's two kingdoms of redemption and creation: (1) *Christian righteousness* is the piety generated by the Holy Spirit in the hearts of renewed Christians in the form of faith active in love; (2) *civil righteousness* is the morality of which all God's rational creatures are capable—Christians included—in the form of law-abiding social justice.

Required of imperfect Christians living "in the midst of wolves," therefore, is both a calculating love that takes the form of justice ("wise as serpents") and a sacrificial love that "exceeds" the demands of the law ("gentle as doves," cf. Matt. 10:16). Thereby, one and the same Christian acts both privately in faithful love as a "Christian person" (*Christperson*) and publicly in loving justice as an "official person" (*Amtperson*) within God's mandated structures of society. So, for example, I am called to forgive my repentant neighbor personally for some grievous sin (in conscience under the gospel of love), and then may also go on to punish that same person for that same deed officially as soldier to soldier or as judge to criminal or as parent to child (in society under the law of justice). However, since both the gospel of love and the law of justice are complementary expressions of the same sovereign will of God, they are not to be perverted—as in some later forms of Lutheranism—into just another ethical double standard that virtually divorces private and public morality.

Luther's primary concern in *Temporal Authority* is still with the Christian righteousness that believers exercise for their many neighbors' benefit in the public realm of civil and temporal affairs. Significantly, it is not as though they were to perform different functions or to engage in different activities from those of their nonbelieving fellow humans. The decisive difference between God's universally mandated and society's officially sanctioned "stations" or "offices" (*Staende*) which all persons hold, and the "callings" or "vocations" (*Berufe*) which only believing Christians acknowledge, is that of the Spirit's motivation, power, and goals. It is not merely what we do or where we do it, but rather why and how it is done, that pleases God. Once again, the ethical fruits are judged by the religious roots, as God's will is not merely outwardly obeyed but inwardly fulfilled.

> Externally there is not much difference between the Christian and another socially upright human being (*hominem civiliter bonum*). The works of the Christian are cheap in appearance: He does his duty according to his calling; he rules the commonwealth; he runs the household; he tills the field; he helps, supports, and serves the neighbor. The unspiritual man does not praise these works but thinks of them as common and of nothing, as something that laymen and even heathen do . . . but they are good and acceptable to God when they are done in faith, a joyful spirit, obedience, and gratitude to God.[69]

Applied concretely to the military ethical issues at hand, this means for Luther that Christians are voluntarily to submit themselves to the authority and demands of civil officers and rulers for the sake of the general welfare of the community. Believers and nonbelievers alike are all created children of God whom Christians are to look upon as "neighbors" in need of personal love expressed through social justice. "Since a true Christian lives and labors on earth not for himself alone but for his neighbor, he does by the very nature of his spirit even what he himself has no need of, but is needful and useful to his neighbor."[70]

The question of whether a Christian may bear arms on behalf of the civil community—in the light of the nonresistance (and not merely nonviolent resistance) demands of the Sermon on the Mount—is thereby settled in terms of God's twofold rule of law and gospel within the world's two kingdoms of wrath and grace. Personally, no person may take up the sword on one's own behalf as one Christian believer acting among other Christians (*persona privata* under God's gospel). But officially, he may disavow pacifism and justly bear arms as a Christian subject acting on behalf of others in the larger community of non-Christians (*persona publica* under God's law). In a fallen and sinful world, Christian love will often have to do some strange and even dirty work (*opus alienum*) in order to protect the good and punish the wicked against the public assaults of Satan. "Therefore, if you see that there is a lack of hangmen, constables, judges, lords, or princes, and you find that you are qualified, you should offer your services and seek the position, that the essential governmental authority may not be despised and become enfeebled or perish. The world cannot and dare not disperse with it."[71]

Luther's biblical realism has forced him to come forward with a stirring cry for persons to assume their Christian social responsibility. Since civil occupations serve God's creating and preserving rule over humanity, all Christians are to become involved in public affairs for the sake of the commonwealth. Addressed originally to "his disciples" (Matt. 5:1), the ethical absolutes of the Sermon on the Mount relate only to disciples in personal relationships with their fellow believers in the kingdom of God (*Gebot*).

They do not seek to prescribe moral conduct for a sinful and unjust society-at-large (*Gesetz*). There, civil jurisdiction remains under the just and prudent governance of humane reason (*regnum rationis*) for the common good. Nor should the refusal of Christ and his apostles to take up the sword discourage us from our own responsible citizenship. The apostles' calling was the unique one of establishing the kingdom of God, yet never once did they forbid, but rather always strongly encouraged, the active participation of their followers in the exercise of loving justice in society. Neighborly service does not endanger salvation by grace; it is rather its responsible by-product.

> In this way the two propositions are brought into harmony with one another: at one and the same time you satisfy God's Kingdom inwardly and the kingdom of the world outwardly. In one case, you consider yourself and what is yours; in the other you consider your neighbor and what is his. In what concerns you and yours, you govern yourself by the gospel and suffer injustice toward yourself as a true Christian; in what concerns the person or property of others, you govern yourself according to love and tolerate no injustice toward your neighbor.[72]

2. *Civil Righteousness.* Luther's purpose in *Temporal Authority* is clearly emphasized by its subtitle as providing pastoral guidance on just limits for Christian subjects (or citizens): *To What Extent It Should Be Obeyed.* This characteristically contextual approach to concrete demands of societal justice are never relativistically situational, however, because the Redeemer's norming love is always related directly to the universal structures (*mandata*) mandated by the Creator God's natural law for fallen humanity. Luther asserts with Paul that the ethical dimensions of human existence are properly under the reign of God's law, whose theological function of judging sin before God (*usus theologicus*) is always coupled with its civil function of promoting justice and punishing crime in society (*usus politicus*).

> To put it as briefly as possible, Paul says that the law has been laid down for the sake of the lawless, 1 Tim. 1:9, that is, so that those who are not Christians may through the law be restrained outwardly from evil deeds. . . . In addition, Paul ascribes to the law another function in Romans 7 and Galatians 2, that of teaching men to recognize sin in order that it may make them humble unto grace and unto faith in Christ.[73]

The indispensable key to Luther's 1523 understanding of "civil righteousness" within the "kingdom of the world" is his conviction that God has ordained civil authorities "to restrain the un-Christian and wicked so that they must keep the peace outwardly, even against their will."[74] This means that God in his loving providence (*conservatio*) has so structured daily life in the civil community that all persons—"even against their will"—are constrained to live in conformity with at least a minimal standard of social morality if only out of the fear of punishment or hope of reward.

In comparison with Christian righteousness, of course, this civil righteousness (*iustitia civilis*) comes off a very poor second. Whereas Christian righteousness springs forth from faith and is therefore joyful and willing, civil righteousness is forced out of unbelief and is consequently "murmuring" and "involuntary." Since "all that does not proceed from faith is sin" (Rom. 14:23), civil righteousness has absolutely no justifying value—no matter how enlightened its self-interest might be. It is "reprobate before God" and "inherently vicious" at the core, however attractive its surface appearance.[75] Luther remains unequivocal in his religious condemnation of all social ethical behavior that is not fired by the loving heart of one who has confessed Christ as his or her Lord and Savior. "Now where temporal government or law alone prevails, there sheer hypocrisy is inevitable, even though the commandments be God's very own. Without the Holy Spirit in the heart no one becomes truly righteous, no matter how fine the works he does."[76]

Yet parallel with the many statements that condemn all civil righteousness as sinful in the sight of God, there are important writings of Luther that consider the moral efforts of unregenerate persons to be relatively "righteous" in the realm of creation. For instance, although hating and killing might be considered equally sinful in heaven, it is clearly the lesser of two evils if society can at least compel a person to control one's murderous actions even if not one's hateful thoughts. In a fallen and sinful world, ethics must usually be satisfied with the imperfect second best.

Consequently, God punishes sin with sin and employs sinful individuals and institutions as imperfect "dikes" against the even more demonic floods of our unfaithful rebellion against our Maker. Eternally and historically, "God is himself the founder, lord, master, protector, and rewarder of both spiritual and civil righteousness. There is no human ordinance or authority which is not a godly thing."[77] Therefore the righteous are called in love to do justice in critical cooperation with all the unrighteous with whom they coinhabit God's good earth.

Works of civil righteousness, therefore, fall on the boundary line between the two kingdoms as ultimately evil but provisionally good; they are products of sin that are at once remedies against it, flawed but still necessary. To reapply Luther's basic distinction between the law's theological function before God (*coram Deo*) and its political function (*coram hominibus*): "Learn here to speak of the law as contemptuously as you can in matter of justification [*in causa iustificationis*] . . . but apart from justification [*extra locum iustificationis*], we ought with Paul to think reverently of the law, to commend it highly, to call it holy, righteous, good, spiritual, and divine."[78]

Perhaps the most cogent illustration of Luther's ambivalent attitude toward civil righteousness is the unexpected way in which he lauds the social expressions of goodness that natural human reason and common sense can effect—apart from the gospel—for a just and peaceful society. Luther was convinced that all God's rational creatures—despite sin—are still capable of a high degree of civil righteousness by virtue of the divine law that God has written "with his own finger" into their hearts at creation.[79] Even the most cursory reading of Luther's writings reveal a surprising number of references, even in his own officially designated Christian society, to the distinction between God's twofold rule by law and gospel in the world's two kingdoms, and the admirably high position afforded human reason when it is employed in the service of neighbors and limited to managing the technical affairs of everyday life.[80]

> Here you must separate God from man, eternal matters from temporal matters. Involving other people, man is rational enough to act properly and needs no other light than reason. Consequently, God does not bother to teach men how they are to build houses, or make clothes, or marry, or make war, or sail a boat. For all such matters, man's natural light is sufficient. But in divine matters, such as man's relation to God and how God's will is fulfilled for our eternal salvation, here man's nature is completely stone-blind.[81]

In marked consistency with his earlier teaching is Luther's systematic portrayal of the proper exercise of reason and force to achieve social order and civil justice in his *Sermons on Exodus* (1524–27). In the first place, there must be a clear distinction between the spiritual and political expressions of God's twofold rule: "You have often heard of the differences between religious and civil authority. In the spiritual realm men are ruled by God through Christ as the head of all believers, although neither Christ nor the believers are ever openly seen. In the civil realm Christ does not exercise his rule directly, for he has delegated his powers to human rulers who are to govern their citizens in moderation, justice, and equity."[82]

In the second place, the nonredemptive rule of the sword in the human kingdom is aimed at the establishment of a just and orderly society in which persons may live in peace and the gospel might be proclaimed unto the ends of the earth.

> Here we have described for us how the people of Israel were united together under a civil government and how that government was organized. [Moses] attends first to the civil authority before ordering the religious authority. . . . This is because the civil sword must first be exercised to secure peace and order on earth before anyone can preach with the necessary time, place, and tranquility. When men are compelled to take up spears, guns, and swords in time of strife, there is little opportunity to preach God's Word.[83]

In the third place, the nonredemptive rule and maintenance of the civil realm should be governed by a judicious use of reason and common sense that is implanted by God into every human being created in God's image. In public office, personal piety is no substitute for political produce. As Luther was so often characterized as saying later, "Better a wise Turk than a foolish Christian," when it comes to running the state for the social welfare of all.

> God has placed man's civil life under the dominion of natural reason which has ability enough to rule physical things. Reason and experience together teach man how to govern his wife and family, how to care for his livestock, and how to do everything else that belongs to sustaining a life here on earth. These powers have been graciously bestowed by God upon man's reason, and we need not look to Scripture for advice in such temporal matters. God has seen to it that even the heathen is blessed with the gift of reason to help him live his daily life.[84]

Finally, Christians should be vigilant and not mix God's twofold rule (*mixtura regnorum*) in the two kingdoms by demanding of pagans in the kingdom of the world what is possible only sometimes among imperfect Christians in the kingdom of God. Centuries before the repeal of the ill-fated Eighteenth Amendment to the U.S. Constitution, Luther insisted that "the world cannot be run by the gospel. . . . The sheep, to be sure, would keep the peace and would allow themselves to be fed and governed in peace. But they would not live very long."[85] Rather than attempt any naive and fruitless "Christianization" of the fallen social structures in the community, Christ's followers should dedicate their consecrated brains to learn even from conscientious pagans how best to live their daily lives so as to achieve the most equitable society possible under human reason, justice, law, and order.

> Pagans have been found to be much wiser than Christians. They have been able to order the things of this world in a far more capable and lasting way than have the saints of God. As Christ said, "The children of this world are wiser in their own generation than the children of light." They know how to rule external affairs better than St. Paul or the other saints. It is because of this that the ancient Romans had such glorious laws and ordinances . . . without any counsel or guidance from Holy Scripture or the apostles.[86]

Consequently, without at all weakening the radical distinction between Christian and civil righteousness, Luther can gratefully view all the provisional victories of socially responsible people over hunger, sickness, crime, and public evils in general as proleptic "signs" and foretastes of the coming kingdom of God when the rule of Christ will be all in all. Political peace and social justice remain qualitatively inferior to the peace of God and his righteousness, but—like the long finger of John the Baptist in Mathias Grünewald's "Crucifixion"—they can point to the coming kingdom even while not yet a part of it. Many a critic of Luther's alleged "cultural quietism" would do well to read Luther himself to challenge their unexamined prejudices. "Civil government is an image, shadow or figure of the lordship of Christ . . . a glorious ordinance and splendid gift of God, who has established it and will have it maintained as something men cannot do without. . . . It is the function and honor of worldly government to make men out of wild beasts and to prevent men from becoming wild beasts."[87]

Through this dynamic interpretation of Christian and civil righteousness, Luther believed that his theological ethic fulfilled the dialectical requirement of Holy Scripture, while at the same time maintaining the crucial distinctions among God's twofold rule by the law and the gospel within the kingdom of Satan and the kingdom of God. At heart, Luther's whole presentation is a brilliant application in societal terms of his earlier 1520 description of the paradoxical stance of the liberated Christian who is personally free in faith to serve others in love (*libertas Christian*).

In 1526 Luther could look back and boast, "Not since the time of the apostles have the temporal sword and temporal government been so clearly described or so highly praised as by me."[88] At the same time it should also be acknowledged in far longer hindsight today that Luther's 1523 liberation of society from illegitimate church control was achieved at considerable cost to the delicate civil balance between power and justice both to his current and later generations. While rightly championing temporal authority, Luther's own culturally conditioned patriarchal spirit admittedly also led him to oppose social disorder far more fervently than either political or economic injustice. His one-sided tilt needs major current correction.

Luther's early biblical approach to God's temporal rule in society was contextually limited almost exclusively to the post-fall civil realm in general ("Caesar") and its absolute obedience to civil rulers ("temporal sword and government") in particular. That 1523 characteristic emphasis on political power and military might (at the expense of societal freedom and justice) was only egregiously reinforced by Luther's similar pre-1530 social ethical responses to current public affairs in such works as *A Sincere Admonition by Martin Luther to Christians to Guard Against Insurrection and Rebellion* (1522), *Against the Robbing and Murdering Hordes of Peasants* (1525), and *On War against the Turk* (1529).

It was only later in less turbulent times that Luther's comprehensive public ethical stance finally caught up with his biblical theology, begun in the further clarifications of his organizing principle of the "temporal" (*weltlich*) beyond the civil "sword" to include also "everything that belongs" to the pre-fall divine ordinances of marriage and family, economic affairs, religious and educational life, and the community-enhancing contributions of unarmed civil authority, as we have already learned of these primal societal mandates of God in Luther's later-written *Lectures on Genesis* (1535ff.). These are all essential expressions of the more wholesome "political function" of God's providential will, as surely protected by, but not solely limited to, the sword of Caesar, in public obedience to the natural law of love for the common good. Here, for example, is Luther's typical later counsel from the late 1520s onward for the "proper behavior of a pious prince among his people or subjects":

> The spiritual government or authority should direct the people vertically toward God that they may do right and be saved; just so the secular authority should direct the people horizontally toward one another, seeing to that body, property, honor, wife, child, house, home, and all manner of good remain in peace and security and are blessed on earth. God wants the government of the world to be a symbol (*Vorbild*) of true salvation and of his kingdom of heaven, like a pantomime or mask (*larva Dei*).[89]
>
> To put it briefly, this petition [in the Lord's Prayer] includes everything that belongs to our entire life in this world, because it is only for its sake that we need daily bread . . . food and clothing . . . peace and concord . . . in short, in everything that pertains to the regulation of both our domestic and our civil or political affairs.
>
> It would therefore be fitting if the coat of arms of every upright prince were emblazoned with a loaf of bread instead of a lion or a wreath of rue, or if a loaf of bread were stamped on coins, in order to remind both princes and subjects that it is through the princes' office that we enjoy protection and peace and that without them we could neither eat nor preserve the precious gift of bread.[90]

We note in conclusion that Luther's *Temporal Authority* (1523), as further refined already in *Whether Soldiers, Too, Can be Saved* (1526), certainly did begin to distinguish more properly and clearly between (1) the world's eschatological two kingdoms (God versus Satan) and (2) God's interacting two governments (the temporal through Caesar and the spiritual through Christ), by means of which the united forces of God's kingdom struggle for righteousness against the demonic forces of Satan's kingdom. Hereafter, the earlier cited "two divisions of humankind" are correlated solely with the world's conflicting "two kingdoms." Also, within God's providential rule of temporal justice, God-ordained good offices are more realistically contrasted with their frequently evil office holders. Additionally, he soon refused to reprove the juridically approved armed self-defense of suffering Christians against the tyranny of unjust "political bloodhounds" in *Dr. Martin Luther's Warning to His Dear German People* (1531). Thereby the revised foundation of his theological ethic was substantially established for incorporating future contextual refinements.

Nevertheless, it should likewise be clearly acknowledged for historical accuracy that the older Luther in his own officially Christian society often continued conveniently to interchange such terms as "kingdom" (*Reich*) and "rule" (*Regiment*) or "estate" (*Stand*) and "vocation" (*Beruf*) in theological shorthand. This has prompted much confusion and even mischief among Luther researchers living in more secularized societies ever since (cf. chapter 1). We dare not continue to repeat these errors today when applying doctrinal norms to radically different societal situations.

Since we have thoroughly explored the theological and political functions of God's judging and preserving law in the previous two chapters, we will now devote the next two chapters to highlight the redeeming and sanctifying functions of God's saving and serving gospel in the work of Christ and the Holy Spirit.

Chapter 7

Jesus Christ: Gospel Justifies before God

IN FAITHFULLY ANSWERING THE CALL OF GOD, Abraham begins the third age of humanity for Luther, following the first two ages before and after the flood. God bestows on him an outstanding distinction: "With Abraham a new world and a new church began, for with Abraham God begins once more to separate His church from all nations, and He adds a very clear promise concerning Christ, who was to bless all nations."[1] So as we begin to trace the Genesis 12 and 15 witnesses to the Old Testament source of God's salvific work in the gospel, the Lord's covenantal promise to Abraham that is later uniquely fulfilled in Jesus Christ must first receive central prominence. For this gospel is the direction-setting "north" by which Luther faithfully boxes all the other points of his theological and ethical compass.

Abraham's Covenantal Righteousness

While Luther believed that Abraham was undoubtedly "a very honorable man if one considers his civil virtues," his importance for humanity in Genesis 12 rests exclusively in God's saving grace. "God elects as patriarch an idolater, who is estranged from God and a prisoner of Satan." Thereby Abraham embodies "a rule that is universally true. . . . Of himself man is nothing, is capable of nothing, and has nothing except sin, death, and damnation; but through His mercy Almighty God brings it about that he is something and is freed from sin, death, and damnation through Christ, the Blessed Seed."[2] God's covenantal promise to Abraham, "I will make of you a great nation" (12:2), is clearly "a most outstanding passage and one of the most important in all Holy Scripture." In the light of Sarah's barrenness, what the Lord promises Abraham here is "altogether impossible, unbelievable, and untrue if you follow reason." Though God the Creator rules the remaining kingdom too, "He does this in a hidden manner" (*Deus absconditus*). Moreover, its reception is corrupted by sin. Now the Triune God's general revelation as Creator will have to be coupled and clarified with his special revelation as Redeemer (*Deus revelatus*).

God promises that this chosen people of Abraham will be special ("I will bless you") by virtue of his personal self-disclosure to them as the Holy One who "dwells in its midst, reveals Himself in the Word, in the worship, and in the holy prophets, who were filled with the Holy Spirit and gave this people instruction concerning the will of God."[3]

> In these few simple words the Holy Spirit has thus encompassed the mystery of the incarnation of the Son of God. The holy patriarchs and prophets explained this more fully later on in their sermons, namely, that through the Son of God the entire world would be made free, hell and death would be destroyed, the Law would be abrogated, sins would be forgiven, and eternal salvation and life would be given freely to those who believe in Him. This is the day of Christ about which He discourses in John 8:56, the day which Abraham did not see with his bodily eyes but did see in the Spirit, and was glad.[4]

Luther is convinced that "this passage is in agreement with the first sermon about the Seed who crushes the head of the serpent" (Gen. 3:15).[5] This is the "earliest gospel" (*Proteuangelion*) in the Old Testament that is divinely promised to Eve, the wife of the first Adam and fulfilled through Mary, the mother of the final Adam. God's old covenant/testament with Abraham is gloriously fulfilled in his new covenant/testament personally embodied in Jesus Christ.

"So Abraham went, as the Lord had told him" (12:4). Here is an "outstanding example of faith . . . in the legend or the account of the most holy patriarch." Abraham's action is an expression of the obedience of faith: "Promise and faith belong together naturally and inseparably." Abraham's faith appropriates God's promise, "wrestling with doubt and against reason." This faith is "a change and a renewal of the entire nature"; it is "the work of the Holy Spirit, fashions a different mind and different attitudes, and makes an altogether new human being."[6] Thus the rectified believer is also personally transformed through internal change by the Holy Spirit. As an undeserved present of the Holy Spirit, faith is a theonomous divine gift, not an autonomous human work; it belongs to God and empowers us to trust that we belong to him, too.

> Therefore faith is an active, difficult, and powerful thing. If we want to consider what it really is, it is something that is done to us rather than something we do; for it changes the heart and mind. And while reason is wont to concern itself with things that are present, faith apprehends the things that are not present and contrary to reason, regards them as present. This is why faith does not belong to all men, as does the sense of hearing; for few believe.[7]

Luther maintains that this is the "true order: that outward obedience follows upon inward obedience." That is to say, the same faith that first receives God's loving grace then performs loving deeds to the neighbor. Reflecting a major dispute in the Reformation, Luther holds:

> We refuse to maintain that Abraham was justified because he forsook everything when he went out from the Chaldeans. He had already been justified when he believed the promise of God that was revealed through the holy patriarchs. If he had not been righteous, he would never have gone out and would never have obeyed God when he called. Therefore he heard the Word and believed the Word; and later on, after he had been justified thereby, he also became a righteous doer of works by wandering about and following Christ, who had called him.[8]

The complementary ethical obedience of Abraham demonstrates that true obedience is not legalistic adherence to a moral code but rather "doing what the Lord has commanded you through His Word." Moreover, it is necessary "that He speaks *to you*." God did once command Abraham to sacrifice his son, Isaac, as a test of patriarchal faith, but that was intended solely for him, not for us. In other words, we are not to imitate Abraham's deeds, but Abraham's covenantal faith, in carrying out our own obedient deeds. "Obedience deserves to be praised as obedience only if it proceeds from the promises or the commands of God . . . otherwise it is the obedience of Satan."[9] Only in this way, by distinguishing the vocation of the gospel from the imitation of the law, may "the example of the holy patriarch who died so many thousands of years ago serve as a pattern for the church to this day."[10] In this way, Abraham may be "rightly considered the chief of all the saints," indeed, an "inimitable example of great faith toward God and of perfect justice and love to men."[11]

This evangelical orientation is biblically corroborated for Luther by Gen. 12:4: "Abram was seventy-five years old when he departed from Haran." Paul affirms that "the law was given four hundred thirty years after the promise was given to Abraham" (Gal. 3:17); Luther adds that "from this year it is exactly four hundred and thirty years to the departure of the Children of Israel from Egypt." Not merely the chronology, but the theology is decisive for Luther: "Therefore it follows that the Law does not justify, since Abraham was just long before the Law was given, in fact, even before he was circumcised and before he built an altar."[12] In such comforting passages of Scripture, "God reveals that He will be the trustworthy Protector of all who believe in Him and put their trust in His mercy."[13]

Moving on to Genesis 15's account of Abraham's trust in God's trustworthiness, Luther praises as "one of the foremost passages of all Scripture (15:6): 'And he believed the Lord; and He reckoned it to him as righteousness.'" From this pivotal passage, Luther contends that Paul later constructed "the foremost article of our faith—namely, that faith alone justifies (*sola fides iustificamur*)." Moreover, he did it in so masterful a way, that "no one has treated this passage better, more richly, more clearly, and more powerfully than St. Paul in the third to the twelfth chapters of Romans." Therefore we are admonished: "Read Paul and read him most attentively."[14] His proclamation of the Christocentric gospel was eventually to become the gracious hallmark of the Lutheran Reformation's renewal of the Western church.

It was Paul's apostolic calling to "establish the universal statement," based on his commentary on Gen. 15:6, that all who believe the Word of God are just. He declared in Rom. 4:23: "The words 'it was reckoned to him' were written not for his [Abraham's] sake alone"—who later on died—but (Rom. 15:4) "for our instruction, that . . . we might have hope."[15] This is the gospel, the "power of God unto salvation" (Rom. 1:16), the promise of God, attested by the Holy Spirit, that the unrighteous may become righteous before God by their trust in his forgiving mercy that is personally embodied in Jesus Christ. "In order to comfort the church of all times, He is saying that those who, with Abraham, believe this promise are truly righteous. Here, in the most appropriate place, the Holy Spirit wanted to set forth expressly and clearly the statement that righteousness is nothing else than believing God when He makes a promise."[16]

At this point, Luther notes that Paul intentionally raised "an important debate concerning the Law and faith: whether the Law justifies, whether faith does away with Law, and so forth." Here Paul "stresses the matter of time"; that is, Abraham is reckoned as righteous or justified long before the law, the works of the law, the people of the law, or the lawgiver, Moses, was even born. Then consequently: "Is the Law useless for righteousness? Yes, certainly. But does faith alone, without works, justify? Yes, certainly. . . . How, then, did he obtain righteousness? In this way: God speaks, and Abraham believes what God is saying. Moreover, the Holy Spirit comes as a trustworthy witness and declares that this very believing or this very faith is righteousness and is regarded by Him as such."[17]

Relating this law-free gospel immediately to the doctrinal strife of his own day, Luther stresses that this passage makes no mention of any "preparation for grace, of any faith formed through works, or of any preceding disposition." No, the Hebrew verb used means solely "to impute" or "to think": "When the Divine Majesty thinks about me that I am righteous (*reputationem Dei*) . . . then I am truly righteousness, not through my works but through faith, with which I grasp the divine thought."

Therefore Paul properly translates the Hebrew with the Greek verb (*dikaioun*) meaning "to reckon as" or "to account" (Rom. 3:20; 4:4-5); indeed, marvels Luther, Paul repeats it ten times in Romans 4 alone! God's righteousness is granted "to one who does not work but trusts in Him who justifies the ungodly, his faith is reckoned as righteousness"; and again, "for

no human being will be justified in His sight by works of the Law."
Indeed, to sharpen the gospel's grace to its very extreme, not even our
Spirit-gifted faith may be considered a work of the law. Righteousness is
"not given to faith as a work of ours; it is given because of God's thought,
which faith lays hold of." Moreover, this biblical faith is not merely blind
speculation or acceptance of religious information (*fides historica*) but
rather Christ-centered trust (*fiducia*), "the firm and sure thought or trust
that through Christ God is propitious and that through Christ His thought
concerning us are thoughts of peace, not of affliction or wrath."[18]

The promise of God's grace, for Christ's sake, is the Spirit's gift, and the
faith that trusts in God's grace, revealed in Christ's cross, is God's work.
Baptized and faithful Christians may confidently trust that "your life is hidden with Christ in God" (Col. 3:3). That is the godly, salvific gospel that
Luther uncovers in the Genesis 15 source "from which Paul has drawn his
discussions in Romans and Galatians."[19]

Before we turn our attention more fully to Paul's Epistle to the Galatians, there is one final question to pose. What of our ethical lives, if our
sin-corrupted works of the law play no role in our being covenantally
reckoned and made righteous before God? For Luther, this immediately
follows: "After that there is also the Law (*lex*); for God not only promises,
but He also commands and enjoins. Moreover, it is the concern of the Law
that you conform your will to it and obey God's commands." Thereby
Luther anachronistically answers the chronic charge of his critics that his
theology is immoral: "When we declare that a man is not justified by
works, they assert that we are forbidding and condemning good works."[20]

The "faith alone" that saves, as we have seen, is itself "never alone."
Faith alone lays hold of the promise; its accompanying love carries out the
commands of the Creator who is no longer our accusing Judge. These
twin gifts of God—by Christ in the Spirit—are logically distinguishable
but not chronologically separable, both sequentially and consequentially.
"*Dann, damals, nachdem, hernach, darnach*": Faith lives in love; love is lived
faith. Luther is confident that this is "sound and true doctrine" because
these issues "have been decided on the basis of the sources." Indeed,
"everything is regulated in accordance with the norm of the Word."[21]

> This theology did not originate with us, as the blasphemous papists cry
> out; nor was it thought up or invented by us. St. Paul teaches it, and as
> a witness he calls Moses, who says that Abraham believed God and that
> this was reckoned to him for righteousness. . . . Therefore the only dif-
> ferent between Adam's faith and ours is this: Abraham believed in the
> Christ who was to be manifested, but we believe in the Christ who has
> already been manifested; and by faith we are all saved.[22]

Luther concludes by praising the hermeneutical key with which he unlocks the Scriptures: "It is truly wisdom above all wisdom to be able to distinguish properly between Law and Gospel and to be a good dialectician in this matter."[23] It is the chief calling and "highest art" of a Christian minister "to divide the Word of God rightly (2 Tim. 2:15), and not mix anything foreign with the sound doctrine."[24] Since there are two kinds of people, unrighteous and righteous, the church "presents a twofold Word" of God's wrath and promises, and now God's gracious promises will control on Paul's proclamation in Romans and Galatians of "the justification of the ungodly (*iustificatio impii*)."

Reconciled by Christ the Mediator

Luther's *Lectures on Galatians* (1535) were devoted to one of his highly valued and favorite New Testament texts. As a decade-long evangelical husband once declared at his home table, "It is my epistle, to which I am betrothed. It is my Katie von Bora."[25]

Paul's letter to the Galatians provides us with a very lucid presentation of his Christocentric gospel of justification by faith. Luther's focus will therefore be on Christian righteousness: a sinner's being both declared and made righteous by the gracious Triune God. This chapter will present its gracious theological ground in Christ's external salvific work of both reconciling us with God the Father and redeeming us from God's demonic enemies (Galatians 1–3). Chapter 8 will then be devoted to its ethical goal in our transformed inner renewal by the accompanying gifts of the Holy Spirit (Galatians 3–6). Again, distinguishable but inseparable, these two complementary dimensions of justification and sanctification, grace and gifts, regeneration and renewal, are conjoined by the ubiquitous risen Christ, who is himself personally present in the Christian's faithful union with Christ (*reputare iustum et efficere iustum*).

Luther initiates his discussion of reconciliation in Galatians 1 with a summary of Paul's argument: "Paul wants to establish the doctrine of faith, grace, the forgiveness of sins or Christian righteousness and all other kinds of righteousness." Alternative kinds of righteousness are political, ceremonial, and moral—all under God's universal law. "Over and above all of these is the righteousness of faith or Christian righteousness . . . which God imputes to us without works, and is neither political nor ceremonial nor legal nor works-righteousness, but is quite the opposite."[26]

These two kinds (not forms) of righteousness are designated by Luther as inherently contrary or antithetical. Whereas all the other forms are active (we work everything), Christian righteousness is "passive" ("we work nothing, that is, we only receive and permit someone else to work in us, namely, God").[27] We must note at the very outset that "passive" (*iustitia passiva*) is not to be understood here contextually as "personally uninvolved" but rather as "totally receptive," since there certainly is much human activity involved, but in its origin, faith is solely God's work in and through us (*ad iustificationem nihil cooperantur*).

First the law comes "to show us our sin"; then "we take hold of the promise of grace offered in Christ the Mediator. In other words, this is the righteousness of Christ and the Holy Spirit, which we do not perform but receive, which we do not have but accept, when God the Father grants it to us through Jesus Christ."[28]

Again we are presented with Luther's twofold relational perspectives of the same person living at once before God (*coram Deo*) and within society (*coram hominibus*). Here the focus is initially on the former. Christians are called "to live before God as though there were no law whatever." Contrariwise, "works and the performance of the Law must be demanded in the world as if there were no promise or grace."[29] The demands are addressed by the law to the sinner's "flesh" or "old man"; the promises are proclaimed by grace to the believer's "spirit" or "new man." "This is our theology, by which we teach a precise distinction between these two kinds of righteousness, the active and the passive, so that morality and faith, works and grace, temporal society and religion may not be confused. Both are necessary, but both must be kept within their limits."[30]

Luther is still very concerned, however, that he not be misinterpreted and that "no one may suppose that we reject or prohibit good works." It is solely the alleged saving merit of such human works that Luther rejects. His purpose is rather to "set forth two worlds . . . in which we place two kinds of righteousness": (1) the earthly "righteousness of the Law" by which we perform good works, and (2) the heavenly "Christian righteousness" which we accept by faith as the saving benefits of Christ's righteousness that God graciously reckons to us. The paradox of the Christian life is that "as long as we live here, both remain." Our persisting sinful flesh under Satan is continually ruled and crushed (*peccatum regnata*); our prevailing righteous spirit rules (*peccatum regnans*), rejoices, and is saved by Christ. Luther contends: "In this epistle, therefore, Paul is concerned to instruct, comfort and sustain us diligently in a perfect knowledge of this most excellent and Christian righteousness."[31]

The Christian life is a steady movement of continual struggle and transition (*transitus*) "from the law to grace, from active righteousness to passive righteousness; in short, from Moses to Christ." Yet the paradoxical and joyful discovery of the Christian life is that "when I have this passive righteousness within me . . . I perform good works whenever the opportunity arises."

If I am a minister, I preach, I comfort the saddened, I administer the sacraments. If I am a father, I rule my household and family, I train my children in piety and honesty. If I am magistrate, I perform this office which I have received by divine command. If I am a servant, I faithfully tend to my master's affairs.

In short, whoever knows for sure that Christ is his righteousness not only cheerfully and godly works in his calling but also submits himself for the sake of love to magistrates, also to their wicked laws, and to do everything else in this present life—even if need be, to burden and danger. For he knows that God wants this and that obedience pleases Him.[32]

Clearly this passive righteousness vis-à-vis God also prompts my Christian social responsibility vis-à-vis my neighbors. Only now I no longer autonomously do good works; I theonomously fulfill them. What God in Christ does *for me* (*pro me*) organically generates what God in the Spirit does *in and through me* (*in me*). In the former God necessarily operates alone; in the latter God enables me to cooperate (Phil. 2:12-13). In either case, I am the undeserving beneficiary of both the grace of Christ and the gifts of the Spirit that are efficaciously operative through faith for both my salvation and my service.

Chapter 1 of Galatians opens with the realistic recognition that a sinful world hates the gospel. "Paul an apostle (1:1) had no sooner planted the pure doctrine of the gospel and the righteousness of faith" among the Galatians than "false teachers" were seduced by the devil to destroy it. They charged the gospel with treason and libertinism: it "subverted commonwealths, principalities, kingdoms, empires and religions"; and it was also guilty of "abrogating the laws, of subverting morality, and of granting men the license to do whatever they please." This was the threatened response of fallen humankind to Paul's bold proclamation of Christ's lordship as "the apostle or ambassador of Jesus Christ . . . to the glory of God."[33] Paul's central purpose in this epistle is

> to discuss and to defend the righteousness that comes by faith, and to refute the Law and the righteousness that comes by works. . . . Thus at the very outset, Paul explodes with the entire issue he intends to set forth in their epistle. He refers to the resurrection of Christ, who rose again for our justification (Rom. 4:25). His victory is a victory over the Law, sin, our flesh, the world, the devil, death, hell, and all evils; and this victory of His He has given to us.[34]

Luther wants to speak about the Christian's holiness, but unlike Paul's legalistic enemies, the Judaizers, he also wants "to distinguish between Christian holiness and other kinds of holiness." The former is "not active but passive"; the latter is based on one's "way of life or of his works."

Before God (*coram Deo*), the former is based on the gospel about Christ; the latter is grounded on the law misused by Satan. The antithetical boundary is exclusively marked by the cross of Christ the Mediator (*crux sola*) and his suffering self-sacrifice for us. Therefore, "the most necessary and important thing is that we teach and repeat this doctrine daily. . . . For if we lose the doctrine of justification, we lose simply everything. . . . In short, whoever does not know the doctrine of justification takes away Christ the Propitiator." As precise as a "mathematical point" (*punctus mathematicus*), Christ for Luther is "the central point of the circle" around which everything in the Holy Bible revolves.[35]

Paul's salvific gospel therefore centers at once in the crucified Christ "who gave himself for our sins" (1:4). This alone is the proper doctrinal location for the "joyous exchange" (*froehliche Wechsel*) between sinners and Jesus their Savior: "You have taken upon yourself what is mine and have given to me what is yours." Consequently, Luther's dialectic of the law and the gospel as the strange and proper forms of God's Word and work (Isa. 28:21) provides us with the indispensable lens through which to discern the depths of the mission and ministry of Jesus Christ. When the issue is righteousness and new life, "you must pay attention only to this Man, who presents Himself to us as the Mediator."[36]

> I follow this general rule: to avoid as much as possible any questions that carry us to the throne of the Supreme Majesty. It is better and safer to stay at the manger of Christ the Man. For there is very great danger in involving oneself in the mazes of the Divine Being.
>
> Christ is, in the strictest of terms, not a Moses, a tormentor, or an executioner but the Mediator for sins and the Donor of grace, who gave Himself, not for our merits, holiness, glory, and holy life but for our sins. Christ also interprets the Law, to be sure, but this is not His proper and chief work.[37]

Moreover, the gospel's saving work takes place precisely where God's Son opposes the world's law-oriented demonic forces at their worst. It becomes eternally effective whenever believers "take hold of Christ, who by the will of the Father, has given Himself into death for our sins."[38] How? As Christ's righteousness is imputed to me (*imputatio iustitiae*), my sins are not reckoned to me (*non imputatio peccati*) but to him. While I remain totally sinful in self (*totus peccator in se*), before God and for Christ's sake I am now also totally righteous (*totus iustus in Christ*). This is the eschatologically unique office of Christ (*officium Christi*) in reconciling the world to the Father in the Spirit (2 Cor. 5:17).

The gospel includes the good news that the two kingdoms of God or Satan are not static and fixed in their human population. Through the intervention of God's redemptive rule in Christ, sinners may by grace through faith be transferred from the kingdom of Satan to the kingdom of Christ. Luther affirms, "the kingdom of the world that is the kingdom of sin, death, the devil, blasphemy, despair, and eternal death. But the kingdom of Christ is the kingdom of grace, forgiveness of sins, comfort, salvation, and eternal life, into which we have been transferred (Col. 1:13), by our Lord Jesus Christ, to whom be glory forever, Amen."[39]

Christ's glorious reconciliation of humanity with God can take place only when the law and the gospel are not confused. Only by faith in the promise (*promissio*) of the gospel about Christ's vicarious work for us can sinners be saved. Here our works of the law, sin-corrupted as they are, have no place. "With Paul we boast that we teach the pure Gospel of Christ" (Gal.1:7). Those who "pervert the gospel"—both in Paul's day and in ours—will be judged. Luther insists, "Because they confuse the Law with the Gospel, it is inevitable that they subvert the Gospel. Either Christ must abide, and the Law perish; or the Law must abide, and Christ perish. It is impossible for Christ and the Law to agree and to share the reign over a conscience (*coram Deo*)."[40]

As we close our review of the first chapter of Galatians, we must remind ourselves once again that Luther's tirade against the curse of the law here is limited exclusively to matters of justification before God (*in loco iustificationis*). It is here, and here alone, in exclusive fidelity to God's reconciling "rule" by the "sheer grace" of the gospel, that Luther may rightly lament, "Oh, if only one could distinguish carefully here and not look for the Law in the Gospel, but keep it as separate from the Law as heaven is distant from the earth!"[41] In Paul's Christocentric order of salvation, (1) before the gospel forgives, the law must spiritually judge, and (2) only after the gospel renews, may the law as command be fulfilled ethically in love (*supra et extra legem*).

In chapter 2 of Galatians, Paul's vivid description of his labors as the apostle to the Gentiles, entrusted with the message of God's law-free gospel, was read by Luther as both validation and vindication. "The basic issue was this: Is the Law necessary for justification, or is it not?" In Luther's understanding of Paul, "The truth of the Gospel is this, that our righteousness comes by faith alone without the works of the Law. . . . Therefore what the Scholastics have taught about justifying faith 'being formed by love' (*fides caritate formata*), is an empty dream. For the faith that takes hold of Christ, the Son of God, and is adorned by Him is the faith that justifies, not a faith that includes love. For if faith is to be sure and firm, it must take hold of nothing but Christ alone."[42]

The dispute between Paul and Peter at Antioch (2:11ff.) was therefore no esoteric matter for Luther: At stake was nothing less than "the truth of the gospel"; indeed, "the main doctrine of Christianity." It was the New

Testament message that "Jesus Christ, the Son of God, has suffered and
died to deliver me from sin and death (*misericordia salvans*)." The basic
problem was that "Peter had confused the distinction between the Law and
the Gospel, and thus he had persuaded the believers that they had to be justified by the Gospel and the Law together. This Paul refused to tolerate."[43]

> Therefore whoever knows well how to distinguish the Gospel from
> the Law should give thanks to God and know that he is a real theolo-
> gian. I admit that in the time of temptation I myself do not know how
> to do this as I should. The way to distinguish the one from the other
> is to locate the Gospel in heaven and the Law on earth, to call the
> righteousness of the Gospel heavenly and divine and the righteous-
> ness of the Law earthly and human.[44]

Those unacquainted with Luther's dialectical mind are likely to be confused by such paradoxical assertions: "There is a time to hear the Law and
a time to despise the Law. There is a time to hear the Gospel and a time to
know nothing about the Gospel." Not so his biblically guided students. In
terms of the distinctive functions of God's law and gospel, Luther is simply calling for Christians "to distinguish well between the two in his heart
and in his conscience." Here in the presence of God, the law's theological
function is solely "to terrify you," as the gospel's salvific function is solely
to promise God's unconditional righteousness in Christ against Satan for
the faithful.[45]

So when Peter no longer treated as "a matter of indifference whether
you eat pork or any other meat," he exposed himself to Paul and the Gentiles as one who had betrayed the gospel of justification by faith in Jesus
Christ, apart from works of the law.

> These words, "works of the Law," are to be taken in the broadest pos-
> sible sense and are very emphatic. . . . Therefore take "works of the
> Law" generally to mean whatever is opposed to grace: Whatever is not
> grace is Law, whether it be the Civil Law, the Ceremonial Law or the
> Decalogue. . . . For by the righteousness of the Law, Paul says, a man
> is not pronounced righteous in the sight of God; but God imputes the
> righteousness of faith freely through His mercy, for the sake of
> Christ.[46]

Luther takes pains here to explain "the true meaning of Christianity."
First, a person must acknowledge, through the law, "that he is a sinner, for
whom it is impossible to perform any good work." One cannot placate
God with sins. The law's function is to expose the sin of Satan, prepare us
for justification, and drive us to Christ. The second step is to accept the
gospel message that "God has sent His only Son into the world to die for
us . . . and He wants to give us forgiveness of sins, righteousness, and eter-

nal life for the sake of Christ." Stripped to the essentials, "this, in summary, is our theology about Christian righteousness."[47]

Luther's repeated phrase, "for the sake of Christ" (*propter Christum*), emphasizes that Christian faith, like God's grace itself, is centered objectively on the real presence and sacrifice of the crucified and risen Christ. This is vital: It is "for Christ's sake" alone that God accepts sinners and that sinners are declared and made acceptable to God. The New Testament's portrayal of Christ as mediator between God and humanity (1 Tim. 2:5; Heb. 12:24) requires both divine grace and human faith. Justification is by grace, through faith, for Christ's sake, unto good works. Luther's carefully chosen prepositions here are as important for him as are "in and under" to relate Christ's body and blood to the bread and wine of Holy Communion.

Luther contrasts his view with the currently prevailing Scholastic view (John Duns Scotus, Gabriel Biel, William of Ockham) that persons are justified by "faith-formed love," a "dangerous error" of law-gospel conflation that reduces Christian faith to "an idle quality or an empty husk in the heart, which may exist in a state of mortal sin until love comes along to make it alive." That, for Luther, is not the strictly imputational/forensic Pauline view that the only true faith is the justifying "faith that takes hold of Christ."

> If it is true faith, it is a sure trust and firm acceptance in the heart. It takes hold of Christ in such a way that Christ is the object of faith, or rather not the object, but so to speak, the One who is present in the faith itself (*in ipsa fide Christus adest*). . . . Therefore the Christ who is grasped by faith and who lives in the heart is the true Christian righteousness, on account of which God counts us righteous and grants us eternal life.[48]

In this gracious and justifying human encounter, Luther emphasizes that "these three things are joined together: faith, Christ, and acceptance or imputation." Faith takes hold of Christ and grasps his real presence in the heart "as the ring encloses the gem." Indeed, so intimate is this corporal union that faithful believers are said by Luther to be personally "baked" together as "a cake" with their Savior (*eyn kuchen mit Christo*). On this Christocentric foundation, "God accepts you or accounts you righteousness only on account of Christ, in whom you believe." This divine and juridical acceptance or imputation is imperative, "because we are not yet purely righteous, but sin is still clinging to our flesh during this life. . . . Nevertheless, we always have recourse to this doctrine, that our sins are covered and that God does not want to hold us accountable for them" (Romans 4).[49] This is all because of the "alien righteousness" of the mediating cross of Christ, which is at once never produced by us or belonging to us, but always shared with us and received by us in faith through the ministry of the church in Word and sacrament. In classical trinitarian terms: since God the Son now dwells in the hearts of faithful Christians through God the Spirit, God the Father also regards those Christian believers "in Christ," that is, in and through the bestowed righteousness of his crucified and risen Son.

Luther concludes his profound analysis of Gal. 2:16 on justification "by grace or by faith in Christ" by defining a Christian as "not someone who has no sin or feels no sin; he is someone to whom, because of his faith in Christ, God does not impute his sin . . . for the sake of Christ." Moreover, "to the extent that he is a Christian, he is above the Law and sin, because in his heart he has Christ, the Lord of the laws." Finally, to call a spade a spade, "here we are perfectly willing to have ourselves called *solafideists* ("faith alone"-ists) by our opponents, who do not understand anything of Paul's argument."[50]

> We concede that good works must also be taught; that this must be in its proper time and place, that is, when the question has to do with works [*coram hominibus*], apart from this chief doctrine. But here [*coram Deo*] the point at issue is how we are justified and attain eternal life. To this we answer with Paul: we are pronounced righteous solely by faith in Christ, not by the works of the Law or by love. . . .
>
> We are not disputing now whether good works ought to be done. But since we are now dealing with the subject of justification, we reject works . . . which take Christ's glory away from Him.[51]

Luther's intentional postponement of ethics here ("in due time") is not an empty rhetorical ploy, but a promise that he will soon fulfill in his upcoming commentary on Galatians 3–6 (covered in our own next chapter). To distinguish is not to separate; it is necessitated by the theological reality that the "alien righteousness" of the mediating Christ that is already fully reckoned to our faith is not yet fully realized or actualized in our own love. Ethics has an essential place in Christianity, but it remains penultimate to that which alone is ultimate. Service does inherently follow salvation when "the Lord, the giver of life," Christ's inseparable Holy Spirit, also enters the scene and begins to renew the regenerate.

> Having been justified by grace in this way, we then do works; yes, Christ himself does all in us.
>
> Therefore we conclude with Paul that we are justified solely by faith in Christ, without the Law and works. But after a man is justified by faith, now possesses Christ by faith, and knows that He is his righteousness and life, he will certainly not be idle but, like a sound tree, will bear good fruit (Matt. 7:17). For the believer has the Holy Spirit; and where He is, He does not permit a man to be idle but drives him

to all the exercises of devotion, to the love of God, to patience in affliction, to prayer, to thanksgiving, and to the practice of love to all men.[52]

In short, Luther drives the mystery of the relation of faith to love back
into the perichoretic interaction of the three persons of the Holy Trinity,
the external works of whom are indivisible within creation (*opera trinitatis
ad extra indivisa sunt*). God the Father sends God the Son into our hearts to
save us through faith, and Christ, in turn, brings God the Spirit with gifts
that drive us into the lives of others to serve them in love to the Father's
glory. The interrelated movements of salvation and service within the
evangelical part of the twofold rule of the one Triune God are not contradictory but complementary, so long as we respect the sequential ordering of God's earthly intervention that is provoked by human sin in history.
This is the Christocentric bottom line in Luther's theological ethic: Sanctifying love does not form or adorn our faith, but justifying faith does form
and adorn our love.

Redeemed by Christ the Victor
The gospel of God's salvific work in Jesus Christ was proclaimed by
Luther in a wide variety of biblical ways, since the church catholic in
council had never officially endorsed any one exclusive view of the atonement. Following Paul, Luther generally employed the biblical theme of *reconciliation* when speaking of Christ's mediating work between sinners and
their forgiving God and *redemption* with regard to Christ's victorious work
between sinners and the evil enemies of God's gracious love.

In the opening chapters of his *Lectures on Galatians* (1535), we have just
reviewed Luther's stress on Christ's saving work in reconciling a sinful
humankind to a Holy God. In the great doctrinal tradition of St. Anselm
of Canterbury's *Why Did God Become Man? (Cur Deus Homo?)*, Luther certainly emulated Paul's insistence that Christ revealed God's righteousness
by obediently suffering for us in his atonement. For Anselm, divine justice
was "satisfied" when Christ, the infinite and sinless God-human, paid God
the Father an infinite vicarious reparation on the cross, for the heinous
offense and dishonor caused by the sin of the world (*satisfactio vicaria
Christi*). This early medieval imagery, predicated on the eclectic basis of
God's eternal law (*lex aeterna*), also expanded on part of the Pauline forensic witness to Christ's perfect righteousness as being "imputed" or "reckoned" or "accounted" by God to faithful Christians (Romans 4; *iustitia
imputata*).

In review, however, we have also noted Luther's depiction of the Christian's faithful union with the risen Christ indwelling his heart as the holy
ground of his righteousness. This view couples Anselm with Athanasius:
That our imperfect faith in union with Christ is nevertheless graciously

reckoned by God as perfect righteousness does bear some formal resem-
blance to the Eastern Orthodox position on "deification" (*Theosis*), by
which Christians through union with Christ become by grace what God is
by nature, as they are renewed in God's image and likeness (cf. Rom. 8:30;
2 Cor. 3:18; Col. 2:9: 2 Pet. 1:14). Justification is no merely external legal
fiction that involves no real change in transforming human nature. For
Luther, justification is inseparable from sanctification in the same event, as
the reborn believer is faithfully united with the risen Lord, transformed
and empowered with the gifts of the Spirit for new obedience to God's
will and command of love.

Moreover, Luther can also employ the patristic fishing metaphor
employed by Gregory of Nyssa and others (rooted in Job 41:1) that on the
cross, the divine-human Christ tricked Satan to bite off more than he
could chew!

> The kingly authority of the divinity is given to Christ the man. . . .
> Nor did the humanity conquer sin and death; but the hook that was
> concealed under the worm, at which the devil struck, conquered and
> devoured the devil, who was attempting to devour the worm. There-
> fore the humanity would not have accomplished anything by itself;
> but the divinity, joined with the humanity, and it alone, and the
> humanity did it on account of the divinity.[53]

This vivid illustration serves as a transition to the second major biblical
metaphor of *redemption,* also employed by Luther in his development of
God's saving work in the gospel. Perhaps this was because he felt that the
medieval, eternal law-oriented template of "satisfaction" was "still too
weak to fully express the grace of Christ and does not adequately honor his
suffering" in redeeming us from God's foes.[54]

Along with his being the reconciling Mediator between God and
humanity, Christ can also be proclaimed by Luther as the redeeming Victor
over God's demonic enemies who hold humanity in captivity. Redemption
thereby complements reconciliation, when the church's teaching stress is
placed not on God's sovereign honor (reconciliation) but on God's evil
adversaries (redemption), whom Luther frequently personifies as being in
mortal combat with Christ and his salvific gospel. The chief of these
malevolent powers are sin, death, the devil, and most paradoxically along
with Paul, God's wrath and law.

Luther's commentary on Galatians 3 provides us with a concentrated
portrayal of those demonic powers that were united unsuccessfully against
the crucified Son of God. Characteristic is Gal. 3:13: "Christ redeemed us
from the curse of the Law, having become a curse for us—for it is written:
'Cursed is everyone who hangs on a tree.'"[55]

"For us" (*pro nobis*) is the salvific key to the mystery of why the innocent Christ became a curse. For Christ did "take all our sins upon Himself, and for them died on the cross." In that sense, "Christ has to become the greatest thief, murderer, adulterer, robber, desecrater, blasphemer, etc., there has ever been anywhere in the world (*summus, maximus et solus peccator*)." Thereby "he made satisfaction for them with His own blood."[56]

At the same time, however, "Christ thereby set us free from the curse of the Law." As death has "lost its sting," so the law's curse has had its accusations and condemnations removed through the gospel. By Christ's death, "the whole world is purged and expiated from all sins, and thus it is set free from death and from every evil."[57] In this historical duel with Christ, "it is necessary for sin to be conquered and killed, and for righteousness to prevail and live." The curse,

> which is divine wrath against the whole world . . . must yield to the blessing which is divine and eternal. . . . Therefore Christ, who is the divine Power, Righteousness, Blessing, Grace and Life, conquers and destroys these monsters—sin, death, and the curse—without weapons of battle, in His own body and in Himself, as Paul enjoys saying (Col. 2:15): "He disarmed the principalities and powers, triumphing over them in Him." Therefore they can no longer harm the believers.[58]

If you look at the victorious Jesus Christ (*Christus Victor*), "you see sin, death, the wrath of God, hell, the devil, and all evils conquered and put to death." Note that these powers are now already dethroned but not yet annihilated. The decisive victory has been won, but Christ's war against the "principalities and powers" (Eph. 6:12) continues to the end. Therefore, "to the extent that Christ rules by his grace in the hearts of the faithful, there is no sin or death or curse. But when Christ is not known, there these things remain. And so all who do not believe lack this blessing and this victory. 'For this,' as John says, 'is our victory, faith'" (1 John 5:4).[59]

The victory of Christ on the cross, vindicated by his glorious resurrection, remains hidden here on earth and is revealed only to the eyes of faith. For Paul declares that this has all taken place "in Himself" (Col. 3:3), that is, "such great things were to be achieved in the one and only Person of Christ," and to those with whom Christ shares the spoils of his victory in faith. Only they can know that Christ is the Victor over sin, death, and the eternal curse, "for they alone confess that He is God by nature."[60] In this Easter victory, the faithful are truly blessed: "By this fortunate exchange with us He took upon Himself our sinful person and granted His innocent and victorious Person. Clothed and dressed in this, we are freed from the curse of the Law, because Christ Himself voluntarily became a curse for us (Phil. 2:9)."[61]

Christ died for us, "but it was impossible for death to hold Him. Therefore he arose from death on the third day, and now He lives eternally."
Moreover, he promises eternal life to Christian believers as well. The salvific
gospel of Christ announces this "joyous exchange" through faith: his righteousness for our sins. "Faith alone grasps this victory of Christ. To the
extent that you believe this, to that extent you have it (so glaubstu, so
hastu)."[62]

> If you believe that sin, death, and the curse have been abolished, they
> have been abolished, because Christ conquered and overcame them in
> Himself; and He wants us to believe that just as in His Person there is
> no longer the mask of the sinner or any vestige of death, so this is no
> longer in our person, since He has done everything for us. . . . Accord-
> ingly, the victory of Christ is utterly certain. . . .
>
>   For in fact there is no sin any longer, no curse, no death, and no
> devil, because Christ has abolished all these. Accordingly, the victory
> of Christ is utterly certain; the defects lie not in the fact itself, which
> is completely true, but in our incredulity.[63]

That "incredulity" consists of far more than our refusal to accept the
correctness of doctrinal truths. At heart, we do not trust the gospel's
promise that we ourselves have been graciously redeemed. The gospel's
promise is that Christ "took sin, the condemnation of the Law, and death
upon Himself, not for Himself, but for us. Therefore the whole emphasis
is on the phrase 'for us.'"[64]

> For you do not yet have Christ, even though you know that He is God
> and man. You truly have Him only when you believe that this alto-
> gether pure and innocent Person has been granted to you by the
> Father as your High Priest and Redeemer, yes, as your Slave. Putting
> off His innocence and holiness and putting on your sinful person, He
> bore your sin, death, and curse; He became a sacrifice and a curse for
> you, in order thus to set you free from the curse of the Law.[65]

Hence, Galatians 3 witnesses that our redemption from demonic powers, along with our reconciliation with God the Father, is another powerful way by which Paul and Luther proclaim the salvific power of the gospel
about Jesus Christ. Sin, death, and the devil, along with God's wrath and
law: "Because He was the Son of God He could not be held by them. He
conquered them and triumphed over them!"[66]

Luther's emphasis here on redemption to depict the gospel's saving
function before God (coram Deo) may also be documented in his elucidation of the Apostles' Creed in both his Large Catechism (1529), addressed
didactically to the clergy, and his Small Catechism (1529), addressed more
devotionally to the laity. These texts are worthy of our special attention

now since both were eventually incorporated into the normative confessional authorities of the Lutheran church's *Book of Concord* (1580).

We feel here the soteriological pulse of Luther's confession of apostolic doctrine. Christianity is not to be confused with an alternate form of the philosophy of religion; it claims to be God's way of salvation, pure and simple. The Pauline gospel announces a salvific event that has been graciously carried out by the Holy One who "proves his love for us in that while we still were sinners Christ died for us. Much more surely then, now that we have been justified by his blood, will we be saved through him from the wrath of God" (Rom. 5:8-9).

Luther reflects on this Pauline "good news" in doxological praise: "We could never come to recognize the Father's favor and grace were it not for the Lord Jesus Christ, who is a mirror of the Father's heart. Apart from him we see nothing but an angry and terrible judge."[67] Yet theologically significant for our catechetical survey here is that Luther's teaching on redemption in the Second Article of the Creed does not even mention the Pauline legal metaphor of forensic justification as such, but rather develops its evangelical equivalent in other biblical imagery and terminology.

In the *Large Catechism,* Luther simplifies the traditional medieval subdivision of the Creed into twelve articles, allegedly contributed by each of the twelve apostles. For evangelical and pedagogical clarity, he chooses instead to highlight three articles, each of them concentrating on the preeminent work to which each of the three persons of the Holy Trinity is specially related. "Thus the first article, concerning God the Father, explains creation; the second, concerning the Son, redemption; the third, concerning the Holy Spirit, being made holy."[68]

The Second Article stresses "how [God] has given himself completely to us, withholding nothing."[69] Its substance teaches "how we are redeemed," namely, in Jesus Christ, our Lord. To confess Jesus Christ as Lord is to acknowledge "that he has redeemed and released me from sin, from the devil, from death, and from all misfortune."[70]

Luther develops this motif of redemption from evil forces with stark and graphic power. Prior to liberation by Christ, confesses the Christian, I was "captive under the power of the devil"; "condemned to death"; "entangled in sin and blindness"; "under God's wrath and displeasure"; "sentenced to eternal damnation, as we had merited it and deserved it." Following the victory of Christ, all this has changed.

> Those tyrants and jailers now have been routed. . . . He [Christ] has snatched us, poor lost creatures, from the jaws of hell, won us, made us free, and restored us to the Father's favor and grace. . . . Let this be the summary of this article, that the little word "Lord" simply means the same as Redeemer, that is, he who has brought us back from the

devil to God, from death to life, from sin to righteousness, and keeps us there.[71]

When the rest of the Article clarifies "how and by what means this redemption was accomplished," Luther freely mixes metaphors and interprets the cross of Christ in the economic images of satisfaction and payment: "how much it cost Christ and what he paid and risked . . . that he might make satisfaction for me and pay what I owed, not with silver and gold but with his own precious blood." Following the victorious resurrection, the defeated powers submit to defeat: Christ "devoured death," and "the devil and all his powers must be subject to him and lie beneath his feet."[72]

In the *Small Catechism,* Luther likewise summarizes the Christian gospel of Christ's person and saving work in masterful simplicity and power. Once again, the motifs of military victory and economic satisfaction are intertwined without the more technical forensic terminology of Paul's "imputation" categories. The evangelical meaning of "the second article: Redemption" is confessed to be:

> I believe that Jesus Christ, true God, begotten of the Father in eternity, and also a true human being, born of the Virgin Mary, is my Lord. He has redeemed me, a lost and condemned human being. He has purchased and freed me from all sins, from death, and from the power of the devil, not with gold or silver but with his holy, precious blood and with his innocent suffering and death. He has done all this in order that I may belong to him, live under him in his kingdom, and serve him in eternal righteousness, innocence, and blessedness, just as he is risen from the dead and lives and rules eternally. This is most certainly true.[73]

For Luther it is no accident that the Creed's summary of the Christian faith does not include a single word on the teaching (to say nothing of the miracles) of the historical Jesus. After all, "the kingdom of God has come near; repent, and believe in the good news" (Mark 1:15) is the recorded common message of both John the Baptist and Jesus of Nazareth. What is finally unique about the Savior in the apostolic gospel is his divine person and work centered on the cross: "Jesus Christ and him crucified" (1 Cor. 2:2). Paul proclaims that Christ and the cross "became for us wisdom from God, and righteousness and sanctification" (1 Cor. 1:30) in the organic communion of grace and faith to forgiven, reborn, and renewed Christians.

Calvary proves to be determinative for Luther as well. His doctrine has a soteriological center of gravity. As the Creed is the heart of the catechisms and as the Second Article on Christ is the heart of the Creed, so Christ's redemptive work on the cross is the heart of the Second Article. Luther's theology of the cross is governed by the apostolic gospel, which glories in the cross of the redeeming Lord. So important is Christ's victory to Luther that "the entire gospel that we preach depends on the proper understanding of this article."[74]

As construed by subsequent biblical scholarship, there are many diverse treatments of "righteousness" and "justification" within the New Testament (for example, Matthew 5–6; John 16; Hebrews 5, 10; and James 2). Moreover, even in Paul's letters, the gift of salvation is also metaphorically described in various ways, for example, freedom (Galatians 5), reconciliation (2 Corinthians 5), peace (Romans 5), new creation (2 Corinthians 5), new life (Romans 6), sanctification (1 Corinthians 1), sonship and heirs (Galatians 4; Romans 8), and redemption (Ephesians 1). It is primarily to Luther, however, that we owe the special prominence afforded Paul's construal of the courtroom-like drama of justification (Romans 3) as the doctrine regulating the gospel promise in terms of divine judgment, acquittal, and renewal (*in foro Dei*). While there are many equivalents, there are no real or adequate substitutes for its awesome profundity in proleptically anticipating the relation to the Final Judgment within biblical theology (*actus forensis Dei*). On the downside, however, an exclusive stress on Paul's single metaphor of forensic "imputation" can (and in later Lutheran orthodoxy has) undercut Christian sanctifying renewal in the Spirit (cf. Afterword).

Gospel's Salvific Function

As we now shift our attention from Luther's biblical teaching to his biblical preaching, there is no better text than the *Sermons on the First Epistle of St. Peter* (1522) to explore his views on God's redemptive rule through the gospel's salvific function. It will provide us with a valuable transition from this chapter's gospel proclamation in the church (*coram Deo*) to the next chapter's ethical application in the everyday life of society (*coram hominibus*).

In his foreword, Luther's first concern is to clarify the proper understanding of the gospel. Though there are four written Gospels, there is really only one gospel in its content: that is, "a sermon or report concerning the grace and mercy of God merited and acquired through the Lord Jesus Christ with his death."[75] This means that it is not "what one finds in books," and especially "not a book of laws" whose legal compliance merits salvation. "The Gospel . . . announces to us the grace of God bestowed gratis and without our merit, and tells us how Christ took our place, rendered satisfaction from our sins, and destroyed them, and that He makes us pious and saves us through His work."[76]

This Christocentric view of the gospel governs its redemptive character. The letters of the apostles, especially St. Paul and St. Peter, have this central evangelical purpose in mind: "Whenever it deals with Christ as our Savior and states that we are justified and saved through faith in Him without our works, then there is one Word and one Gospel; just as there is but one faith and one Baptism."[77] In this respect, "St. Paul's epistles are gospel to a greater degree than the writings of Matthew, Mark and Luke. Accordingly, this Epistle of St. Peter is also one of the noblest tools in the New Testament; it is the genuine and pure Gospel."[78]

At the outset of chapter 1, Peter identifies himself as an "apostle," a messenger whom Jesus Christ has commanded to preach about him. Of special interest to us is that the epistle is intentionally addressed to Christians who are "chosen and destined by God the Father and sanctified by the Spirit for obedience to Jesus Christ and for sprinkling with His blood" (1:2).

Luther at once acknowledges that Peter "expresses himself differently from St. Paul." At the same time, he asserts that "the purpose is identical with Paul's declaration that we are saved through faith in Christ."[79] To signal Luther's own position in relating to later controversies surrounding the relevant theological categories employed here, the original Reformer is freely asserting that in Paul's language on "justification" and Peter's language on "sanctification," the substance or purpose is identical regarding our salvation.

Peter first proclaims that we are "chosen and destined by God the Father." Luther sees this as strong confirmation that "the human doctrine of free will and of our own powers no longer amounts to anything." Additionally, Christians are then declared to be "sanctified by the Spirit." Christians are predestined by God to become "spiritually holy." In the late medieval church, "the precious words 'holy' and 'spiritual' have been perverted." External offices, clothing, and works do not make one holy; only inwardly are Christians made "sincerely holy in the spirit before God." Indeed, "nothing is holy but the holiness that God works in us."[80]

While the Scripture addresses all baptized Christians as "saints," the current late medieval church reserved that title for only its outstanding and exemplary members. Luther counters:

> We must get the noble name ["holy"] back. You must be holy. But you must be prepared not to think that you are holy of yourself or on the strength of your merit. No, you must be holy, because you have the Word of God, because heaven is yours, and because you have become truly pious and holy through Christ. This you must avow if you want to be a Christian. . . . You must believe and confess that you are holy, but by Christ's blood and not by reason of your own piety.[81]

This marks the biblical revolution in human ethics: Holiness is not the goal, but the ground, of our authentic piety before God. As we have been justified (Paul) by the legal imputation of Christ's righteousness, so have we also been sanctified (Peter) by our baptismal sprinkling by Christ's blood and death. Justification is not merely the present beginning of a lifelong process of moral improvement that climaxes in a future sanctification. No, the New Testament "calls us holy if we believe" right now. All of Peter's verbs regarding sanctification are cast here in the past (not the future) tense ("sanctified," "have become holy," "sprinkled with Christ's blood"). If, as Luther contends, this is "identical" with Paul's word, it is because Paul also promised the baptized Christians in Corinth that in the past (not the future), "You were washed, you were sanctified, you were justified in the name of the Lord Jesus Christ and the Spirit of our God" (1 Cor. 6:11). Indeed, Paul's epistle was addressed "to those who are sanctified in Christ Jesus" (1:2), when he went to admonish them about their sexual immorality, sectarian strife, and class struggles. Therefore they (and we) are called to grow in righteousness, not in holiness. In the New Testament, sanctification means to be (religiously) set apart from others by the Spirit—past, present, and future—and not to be (ethically) set above others by the church.

This is why "St. Paul says that we become holy if we obey and believe the Word of Christ and are sprinkled with His blood." It is not outstanding deeds of love, but simple faith in Christ and his blood shed for us (*pro nobis*), that saves us. Luther can therefore compare Peter with Paul and conclude, "To be submissive to the Word of God and Christ and to be sprinkled with His blood is the same as believing."[82]

In addressing different audiences with different images, the same many-splendored reality is conveyed by Paul with a juridical metaphor ("imputation") and by Peter with a ritual metaphor ("sprinkling"). Yet many churches in many centuries after the apostles have virtually severed imputed justification and imparted sanctification in a rigidly structured order of salvation (*ordo salutis*) to their mutual detriment. Therefore, Luther in essence is insisting on the reapplication of the biblical precept: "What God has joined together, let no one separate" (Mark 10:9)—in this case, righteousness and ethics, new life and new obedience.

In his epistle, Peter then goes on "to tell us what Christ is and what we have acquired through Him." We have been "born anew to loving hope through the resurrection of Jesus Christ from the dead" (1:3). He preaches in order that people may come to faith through such preaching and be saved through faith. "This is what it means to preach the genuine Gospel. . . . From this one can judge what true Christian doctrine or preaching is. For when one wants to preach the Gospel, one must treat only of the resurrection of Christ. He who does not preach this is no apostle."[83]

It is salutary to "go back to the Old Testament and learn to prove the New Testament from the Old." There we find "the promise concerning Christ," as Christ himself said (John 5:39). In this sense, "the books of Moses and the prophets are also Gospel, since they proclaimed and described in advance what the apostles preached or wrote later about

Christ." The chief difference is that the Old Testament was meant to be written, whereas the New Testament, or the gospel, "should really not be written but should be expressed with a living voice (*viva vox*) which resounds and is heard throughout the world."[84]

Another difference is that "in the Old Testament God carried on a twofold government (*Regiment*): external and internal." This ancient theocratic rule of Israel is no longer God's societal wish in the New Testament. "Now, however, God reigns only spiritually in us through Christ. He executes the physical and external rule through the civil government. Therefore the external rule was abrogated when Christ came. What belongs to the spiritual government, however, has not been repealed but always continues to be in force, as, for instance, the laws in Moses concerning the love for God and one's neighbor."[85]

Luther's description of God's twofold rule in creation and redemption emphasizes the permanent call for "everything the prophets say about faith and love. Therefore Christ also confirms this in Matt. 7:12: 'Whatever you wish that men would do to you, do so to them; for this is the law and the prophets.' In addition, Moses and the prophets bear witness to the Christ who is to come."[86] God's law and gospel must therefore be properly divided *within* each of the two Testaments and not improperly *between* them. So, for example, there may be more true gospel in Isaiah than in James for preaching and teaching the Word of God. "Thus you see how St. Peter teaches us to outfit and equip ourselves with the Scripture. Up to this point he has been describing what it means to preach the Gospel, and how the prophets proclaimed beforehand that it was to happen and was to be preached this way."[87]

Luther goes on to address the seeming paradox in Peter that God saves us solely through faith and yet judges us according to our works. Both are true; the gospel is the good news that, on account of faith in Christ, God acquits sinners who have also already been pronounced guilty. Yet we must also realize that where there is no faith, there can be no good works either. After all, "whatever life I live in faith, I live for my neighbor, to serve and help him." Consequently, the works of a Christian, activated by the Spirit, are "fruits of faith," and these God will mercifully judge as acceptable. God will ask, "If you are a Christian, then tell Me: where are the fruits with which you can show your faith?"[88]

Everything then depends on our redemption through "the precious blood of Christ, the Son of God. . . . Just one drop of this innocent blood would have been more than enough for the sin of the whole world."[89] St. Peter says, "You were ransomed . . . with the precious blood of Christ, like that of a lamb from the futile ways of your fathers" (1:18), "this without blemish or spot" (1:18-19). "This shows that it cost the Son of God His blood to redeem the people." Here Peter directs us to Isa. 53:7: "Like a lamb that is led to the slaughter," and to "the paschal lamb in Exod. 12:3ff."[90] "Peter declares that we 'have been born anew' (1:23). How does this take place? God lets the Word, the Gospel, go forth. He causes the seed to fall into the hearts of men. Now when it takes root in the heart, the Holy Spirit is present and creates a new man. There an entirely new man comes into being, other thoughts, other words and works. Thus you are completely changed."[91]

That a "new man" in Christ comes into being who is "completely changed" again belies all charges of our redemption being reduced in Luther to merely a "legal fiction" (cf. next chapter). Instead, Luther concludes his sermonic commentary on the epistle's first chapter with high praise and with no reservations. "In it you see how masterfully St. Peter preaches faith and treats of it. Hence one sees clearly that this epistle is the true Gospel."[92]

With this commendation, we complete our textual review of the Pauline foundation and Petrine reinforcement of Luther's predominant teaching of God's salvific gospel in terms of justification by faith. We have intentionally highlighted Luther's characteristic twofold construal: (1) as *reconciliation* in relation to God's gracious imputation of Christ's righteousness to the faithful, and (2) as *redemption* in relation to Christ's victorious liberation of believers from the demonic forces that have kept humanity in bondage since the fall. In short, through the gospel of Christ's cross and resurrection, the Holy One is vindicated, the evil powers are vanquished, and unrighteous but faithful Christians are inseparably forgiven and renewed.

Chapter 8

Holy Spirit: Gospel Sanctifies in Society

T HIS CHAPTER WILL SUMMARIZE THE ETHICAL DIMENSIONS and/or implications of Luther's multifaceted doctrine of justification by faith. While virtually all of the component parts have already been developed in the previous three chapters, the way in which they are coherently integrated within Luther's theological ethics has been the source of theological and ecclesiastical debate both during and since the Reformation, most especially in the twentieth century (cf. chapter 1 and Afterword).

In our own documented review of Luther's theological ethics, we have systematically elaborated his highly influential view of God's twofold rule by law and gospel of both fallen and redeemed humankind within the world's antagonistic two kingdoms. In Luther's reading of biblical and especially Pauline eschatology, the Triune God rules all of life by and for righteousness through the power of his sovereign Word. This takes place historically through the continual and dynamic and opposing interaction of God's law and gospel, each with its own two distinctive complementary functions.

As Creator and Preserver, God employs the law's theological function to judge the willful and perennial misuse of humanity's original righteousness in the primal creation (*justitia originalis*), cf. chapter 5, and its political function to prompt the civil righteousness of rational persons in the realm of fallen creation (*justitia civilis*), cf. chapter 6. As Redeemer and Sanctifier, God is at the very same time employing the gospel's salvific function in the cross to reckon the alien righteousness of Christ to faithful persons in the realm of regenerated redemption (*iustitia Christi*), cf. chapter 7, and its ethical function in the Spirit to empower the Christian righteousness of loving persons to break out into the realm of renewed creation (*iustitia Christiana*), expounded here in chapter 8.

We have already set the stage for this theological ethical conclusion with our earlier preliminary discussions of God's command of love before and after the fall in the world's successive states of pristine (*integritatis*) and sinful (*corruptionis*) creation (chapter 3). It remains for us now in this final chapter to support our academic claim that the biblically congruent climax of Luther's theological ethic is better expressed by God's gospel than by the law. It calls for reinstatement of God's sanctifying love command (*mandatum*) as the second or parenetic use of the gospel (*usus pareneticus evangelii*) rather than the later designated "third use of the law" (*tertius usus legis; see Formula of Concord, VI, in Afterword*). It would crown Luther's preferable evangelical (rather than legalistic or antinomian) approach to the Christian's ethical obedience to God's primal will in creation. Our proposal builds exclusively on Luther's societal application of God's primal command of love, the Spirit's ecclesial and vocational sanctification, and the renewed dominion-sharing service (Gen. 1:28) of the universal priesthood of baptized Christians within the divinely mandated ordinances of church and society.[1] It will thereby also fulfill our original paradigm and pledge (Preface) to demonstrate the increasingly acknowledged "reconciled diversity" within the ecclesially complementary forces of love and law (Lutheran-Reformed) along with justification and sanctification (Lutheran-Roman Catholic) for more coordinated Christian community involvement.

God's Command Renewed

As we return to Luther's *Lectures on Galatians* (1535), the focus now shifts in the latter half of Paul's text from doctrine to ethics and thereby in trinitarian plenitude from what God in Christ has done *for* us and our gracious salvation, to what God in the Spirit does *in* and *through* us for our neighbors' service. In simultaneous interaction, the twofold divine action is historically distinguishable but eternally inseparable, for the Lord is a "glowing oven of love" (*gluehende Backofen*).

The evangelical foundation remains, of course, "the most joyous of all doctrines: . . . In Christ all sin is conquered, killed, and buried; and righteousness remains the victor and the ruler eternally."[2] After all, this is "the chief doctrine of the Christian faith," because it witnesses to the gospel promise that "by this joyous exchange with us (*froehliche Wechsel*), He took upon Himself our sinful person and granted us His innocent and victorious Person."[3]

Without in any way compromising the gospel's unique salvific function in receptive (or passive) faith, Luther follows Paul in moving on now to its ethical or parenetic function in active (or transmitted) love. Faith and love are both divinely intended to be essential in the bi-dimensional Christian life (*vita Christiana*): "Faith alone justifies. But once we have been justified by faith, we enter the active life . . . in works of love toward the neighbor."[4]

Paul's advocacy of the Holy Spirit's calling to remove faithful Christians from "the curse of the law" to the "law of love" (*lex caritatis*) is clear and compelling. Luther first lays the negative foundation for the ethical "office"

of the Holy Spirit (*officium Spiritus Sancti*), by following Paul's allegorical
analogies in Galatians 3–4 of the interim (custodial) tenure and non-salvific
role that is assigned by God to the law of wrath in contradistinction to the
gospel of Christ. ("What then is the function of the Law? Transgression.")
Luther is untiring in his insistence, here as elsewhere, that "such a proper
distinction between the function of the Law and that of the Gospel keeps
all theology in its correct use."[5] Indeed, Luther draws the line very sharply:
"Whatever is outside Christ and the promise—with no exceptions,
whether it is the Ceremonial Law or the Moral Law or the Decalogue,
whether it be divine or human—is consigned to sin."[6]

Nevertheless, this radical contrast between law and gospel, or works and
faith, pertains only with regard to eternal salvation (*coram Deo*); for "apart
from the issue of justification (*extra locum iustificationis*), no one can adequately praise true good works."[7] The challenge is to make their proper distinction in daily life: "Anyone who would know this art well would deserve
to be called a theologian."[8] It is an art based on the eschatological divide
between the old age in Adam and the new age in Christ (Romans 5), yet
also radically complicated by the historical reality that the Christian coin-
habits both ages simultaneously as both righteous and sinful: "Therefore a
Christian is divided into two times. To the extent that he is flesh, he is
under the Law; to the extent that he is Spirit, he is under the Gospel."[9]

Consequently, Luther insists in 1535 that one may not draw the simplistic and dangerous inference that "the Law is worthless" at the expense of
"both uses of the Law." That was precisely the 1525 error of the "fanatical
spirits who prompted the peasants' revolt a decade ago by saying that the
freedom of the Gospel absolves men from all laws" (versus the law's valid
political function).[10] No, societal and sinful Christians remain in lifelong
need of the law, which is "good and necessary," insofar as they act civilly
in society (*coram hominibus*), and "most important and proper," insofar as
they act sinfully before God (*coram Deo*).[11]

In *Galatians 3,* Luther concludes his analysis of Paul's limited analogy of
the law as "our custodian until Christ came" (3:24) by asking rhetorically,
"But what does the Law do in those who have been justified through
Christ?" His paradoxical response: At once both righteous and sinful
before God, a Christian is at once free from the law in Christ as already
righteous but also bound by the law in one's self as still sinful.

> If you consider Christ and what he has accomplished, there is no Law
> anymore. Coming at a predetermined time, He truly abolished the
> entire Law. . . . But the law in our members is at war with the Law
> of our mind (Rom. 7:23), and it interferes so that we cannot take
> hold of Christ perfectly. . . . So far as we are concerned, then, we are
> partly free of the Law and partly under the Law. With Paul we serve

the Law of God with our mind, but with our flesh we serve the law
of sin (Rom. 7:25).[12]

Luther can also speak of the simultaneity of the Christian's righteousness and sinfulness either vertically, from the eschatological perspective of
qualitative justification (*totus-totus*), or horizontally, from the historical perspective of quantitative sanctification (*partim-partim*). That is, one and the
same Christian is (as justified) totally sinful in self and totally righteous
before God (*reputative totaliter iusti et revera totaliter peccatores coram Deo*),
while yet also (as sanctified) partially sinful and partially righteous within
society (*partim iustus et partim peccator coram hominibus*). Therefore any
Christian can and does morally improve (*progressus*) and develop into more
responsible service under the vocational dimension of God's twofold rule
(2 Cor. 3:18). There is where the already/not yet dialectic of God's inbreaking reign is painfully enacted within every newly baptized Christian.
Through our baptismal incorporation into God's kingdom, we are already
totally *regenerated* by the Spirit's grace but only partially *renewed* by the Spirit's gifts. Our residual sin is no longer reigning (*peccatum regnatum*) but
reigned (*peccatum regnans*) by God's indwelling Holy Spirit (Rom. 6:12).

Our paradoxical condition as morally imperfect Christians is therefore
not dualistically static. Having spiritually died in Baptism, we now ethically
"walk in newness of life" (Rom. 6:4-6). So there is, teaches Luther, a continual growth in grace, since "we have received the first fruits of the Spirit
(Rom. 8:23)." Because of the "remnants of sin" within us, however, we
will need to experience lifelong "daily mortification (*mortificatio*) of the
flesh, the reason and our powers, and the renewal (*vivificatio*) of our mind
(2 Cor. 4:16)." Reborn Christians will receive daily "new impulses" for
actualizing sanctification; there is certainly "true renovation of the forgiven."
Consequently, Christians may boldly live by hope that "we have the first
fruits of the Spirit, and that we shall be completely leavened when this sinful body is destroyed and we arise new with Christ, Amen."[13]

It is imperative to underscore that the Christian's daily progress (and
regress) is not aimed at demonstrable ethical perfection (pietism) but rather
toward hidden spiritual fidelity to the loving will of God (piety). These are
not our own autonomous works; they are the Spirit's "fruits" that evidence
fulfilling renewal by the indwelling Christ. After all, the apostolic admonition is that we "grow in the grace and knowledge of our Lord and Savior Jesus Christ" (2 Pet. 3:18). That is, our growth is by way of God's
grace and not by our works; we grow theonomously more and more (and
not autonomously less and less) in our total dependence on God's
unmerited favor. Moral autonomy is doctrinal heresy. As a "temple of the
Holy Spirit who is within you" (1 Cor. 6:19), the Christian moral agent
is, in the last analysis, "I, yet not I, but Christ in me" (Gal. 2:20). During

our daily sanctification, the indwelling Holy Spirit expels our persisting sinfulness through "purification, expurgation, and recuperation" (*purificatio, expurgatio, et sanatio*).

As Luther continually insisted, the Christian is always *in statu viatoris*, that is, on the way to becoming the saint that proleptically one has already been declared to be in Baptism and is already in heaven (Col. 3:3).

> Our justification is not yet finished. It is in the process of being made; it is neither something which is actually completed nor is it essentially present. It is still under construction.
>
> This life, therefore, is not godliness but the process of becoming godly, not health but getting well, not being but becoming, not rest but exercise. We are not now what we shall be, but we are on the way. The process is not yet finished, but it is actively going on. This is not the goal but it is the right road. At present, everything does not gleam and sparkle, but everything is being cleansed.[14]

Luther concludes his analysis of Galatians 3 by once again clarifying that the unity and equality that Christians already enjoy "in Christ, that is, in the matter of salvation" ("neither Jew nor Greek, slave nor free, male nor female") is graciously based on "the garment of Christ, which we put on in Baptism" (*coram Deo*).[15] There is, of course, "a distinction among persons in the Law and in the sight of the world (*coram hominibus*); and there must be one there, but not in the sight of God, where all men are equal, for 'all have sinned and fall short of the glory of God' (Rom. 3:23)." Therefore Luther's is also not an egalitarian liberation ethic, but a gracious liberation faith. He consciously counters "the fanatical spirits" in his own day with confident trust in our intimate union with the risen Lord: "Christ and faith must be completely joined." By actively renewing and rededicating our complementary and diversified gifts of the Spirit, "Christ must be, live, and work in us. However, He lives and works in us, not speculatively, but really, with presence and with power."[16]

In Galatians 4, it is an affirmation of biblical faith for Luther that "God has sent the Spirit of His Son into your hearts" (4:6). This takes place through the church's proclamation of the life-transforming gospel.

> This happens when through the spoken Word we receive fire and light, by which we are made new and different, and by which a new judgment, new sensations, and new drives arise in us. This change and new judgment are not the work of human reason or power; they are the gift and accomplishment of the Holy Spirit, who comes with the preached Word, purifies our hearts by faith, and produces spiritual salvation in us.[17]

The preeminent "fruit of the Spirit" is twofold: to trust in Christ for salvation and to live for neighbors in service. On the one hand, there is

Christian faith, where we are lords of all. "Let us be satisfied with the testimony of our conscience, by which we know as a certainty that it is a divine gift when we not only believe in Jesus Christ but proclaim and confess Him openly in the presence of the world."[18] It is biblical truth that "no one can say 'Jesus is Lord' except by the Holy Spirit" (1 Cor. 12:3).

On the other hand, there is Christian love, where we are called to become servants of all. "We also discipline ourselves in piety and avoid sin as much as we can."[19] Because "Christ did not establish a new Law to follow the old Law of Moses," there are no new rules and regulations of conduct to obey, and thereby to demonstrate to the world that one is a Christian.[20] In restoring the personalized preeminence of God's primal command on Maundy Thursday, Christ declared simply, "A new commandment I give to you, that you love one another; even as I have loved you, that you also love one another" (John 13:34). Through his freely willed death on the cross (*obedientia passiva et activa*), our exemplar Jesus Christ uniquely revealed and fulfilled God's forgiving and renewing will for humankind.

The world still scoffs, "Can anything good come out of Nazareth?" (John 1:46)—or the followers of the Nazarene? It cannot see ordinary things being done by extraordinary saints without the eyes of faith. These deeds are acceptable to God "when they are done in faith, a joyful spirit, obedience and gratitude to God."[21]

Only *in extremis* may the cost of discipleship lead to suffering and death in taking up one's own cross. In opposing the gospel-crusading Peasants' Rebellion (1525), for example, Luther counseled those who took up the sword in the name of Christ, "Suffering! Suffering! Cross! Cross! This and nothing else is the Christian law!" Then the Christian martyr's arcane allegiance becomes most publicly transparent. "In a time of tribulation or of the cross and the confession of faith (which is the proper and principal work of believers), when one must either forsake wife, children, property, and life or deny Christ, then it becomes evident that by the power of the Holy Spirit we confess the faith, Christ, and His Word."[22]

Through these normally undramatic but faithful and loving external signs, however, every Christian "may believe for a certainty that he is in a state of grace and that his person with its works is pleasing to God."[23] Moreover, faithful Christians may freely throw themselves into the vocational service of others and confidently trust in God's loving care. "It is a great comfort when Paul says here that the Spirit of Christ, sent by God into our hearts, cries: 'Abba! Father!' And when he says in Rom. 8:26 that He helps us in our weakness and intercedes for us with sighs too deep for words."[24]

This is "our foundation" for overcoming "the monster of uncertainty" and spiritual assaults (*Anfechtungen*) when engaging in Christian social action:

"The Gospel commands us to look, not at our own good deeds or perfection but at God Himself as He promises, and at Christ Himself, the Mediator."[25] With an air of accomplished finality, Luther declares: "This is the conclusion of Paul's argument. From here until the end of the epistle he will not argue very much but will set forth commandments about morality."[26]

In Galatians 5, Paul begins again with a spirited "defense of the doctrine of faith and of Christian liberty against the false apostles' advocating circumcision for Gentile Christians. He champions the law-free freedom of grace for which 'Christ has set us free'" (Gal. 5:1). This is the gospel's "freedom from the eternal wrath of God. Where? In the conscience." It is therefore not essentially political, "but theological or spiritual freedom." It is an eternal liberation "by which we are made safe and free through Christ from the Law, from sin, death, the power of the devil, hell, etc. . . . and in their place it establishes righteousness, peace, life, etc." Central is the evangelical conviction, prompted in response to the party of Christian Judaizers in Galatia, that "this freedom is granted to us, not on account of the Law or our righteousness but freely, on account of Christ."[27]

This elucidation of the salvific function of the gospel is coupled with a citation of the theological function of the law. For Luther, to trust in one's circumcision is to distrust in one's Savior before God (*coram Deo*). "Trust in works and righteousness on the basis of works causes Christ to be of no advantage." If one admits to the religious significance of circumcision, one is in principle "bound to keep the whole Law" (5:3). For before God, grace and law are mutually exclusive ways of salvation. "Therefore anyone who is a founder or a worshiper of the doctrine of works suppresses the Gospel, nullifies the death and victory of Christ, obscures His sacraments and their proper use, and is a denier, an enemy, and a blasphemer of God and of all His promises and blessings."[28]

Most pointedly, once Christ is the end of the law, that also excludes the redemptive value of all of Moses. This is declared to be Paul's "final conclusion: 'You must give up either Christ or the righteousness of the Law.'"[29] Before God, the law of Moses must bow to the gospel of Christ. "Therefore we do not allow ourselves to be oppressed by any law of Moses at all. We grant, of course, that we should read and listen to Moses as one who predicted Christ and witnessed to Him, also that we should look to him for examples of outstanding laws and moral precepts; but we do not grant him an authority over our conscience."[30]

In the face of the salvific dichotomy between grace and law, Paul contends that "through the Spirit, by faith, we wait for the hope of righteousness" (5:5). The tension between faith in a past event and hope for a future consummation is seen by Luther as a further biblical witness to the lifelong pilgrimage about which the "simultaneously righteous and sinful" Chris-

tian (*simul justus et peccator*) confesses: "I am righteous here with an incipi-
ent righteousness; and that in this hope I am strengthened against sin and
look for the consummation of perfect righteousness in heaven."[31] Hence,
Luther concludes: "We have indeed begun to be justified by faith, by
which we have also received the first fruits of the Spirit; and the mortification of our flesh has begun. But we are not yet perfectly righteousness.
Our being justified perfectly still remains to be seen, and this is what we
hope for. Thus as righteousness does not yet exist in fact (*in re*), but it still
exists in hope (*in spe*)."[32]

Luther goes on to encourage, "These things are correctly understood
when they are put into practice." Similarly, Paul goes on to develop our
own chief concern in this chapter, namely, the second or parenetic function of the gospel—"faith working through love" (5:6). Radically shifting
gears, forward from the "office of Christ" to the "office of the Spirit" (and
not back to the "office of Moses"), Luther teaches that "in this passage
Paul is not dealing with the questions of what faith is or of what avails in
the sight of God; he is not discussing justification. He has already done that
very thoroughly. But in a brief summary, he draws a conclusion about the
Christian life" (*coram hominibus*).[33]

"Faith works": The love of God received by faith is at once conveyed by
faith to needy neighbors (the lost, the last, and the least) in society. In the
power of the Spirit, a living faith "arouses and motivates good works
through love." This excludes not only the works-righteous but also the lazy,
the idle, and the sluggish. "'Not so, you wicked men' says Paul. 'It is true that
faith alone justifies, without works; but I am speaking about genuine faith,
which, after it has justified, will not go to sleep but is active through love.'"[34]
Luther joyfully declares that "Paul is describing the whole of the Christian
life in this passage: inwardly it is faith toward God, and outwardly it is love
or work toward one's neighbor." Love is provided its "impulse and motivation" by our confident trust in Jesus Christ, who is both God's gracious gift
for us to accept and God's ethical exemplar for us to emulate.[35]

At this point, there follow a number of apostolic admonitions and
exhortations about good morals (*parenesis*). They address Christians both in
the flesh as the goading of law and in the Spirit as the guiding of love. "For
the apostle makes it a habit, after the teaching of faith and the instruction
of consciences, to introduce some commandments about morals, by which
he exhorts the believers to practice the duties of godliness toward one
another. . . . [Christians] teach morals and all the virtues better than any
philosophers, because they add faith." Luther is building here on his earlier
explanation:

> The New Testament properly consists of promises and exhortations,
> just as the Old Testament properly consists of laws and threats. For in

the New Testament the gospel is preached, which is nothing else but a message in which the Spirit and grace are offered with a view to the remission of sins, which has been obtained for us by Christ crucified.

Then follow exhortations, in order to stir up those who are already justified and have obtained mercy, so that they may be active in the fruits of the freely given righteousness and of the Spirit, and may exercise love by good works and bravely bear the cross and other tribulations of the world. This is the sum of the whole New Testament.[36]

To add faith to morals is what the distinctive lifestyle of Christians is all about. It is the parenetic use of the gospel (*usus pareneticus evangelii*) that ensures the inseparability of "promises and exhortations" in the Christian's mode of sanctification (*in loco sanctificationis*). Following Paul very closely here, Luther will not resort to either the legalism of works-righteousness or the libertinism of unrighteousness. Paul insists, "for you were called to freedom, brethren; only do not use your freedom as an opportunity for the flesh, but through love be servants of one another" (Gal. 5:13). Luther deplores "the danger on both sides." Legalists revert to the bondage of the law; antinomians capitulate to the tyranny of the flesh. Regarding the latter, the anti-Roman Reformer feels at least indirectly responsible for the liberated "people of Gomorrah," the lax Lutherans who are now unwilling to be ruled "by the gospel of peace." "They all boast of being evangelicals and boast of their Christian freedom. Meanwhile, however, they give in to their desires and turn to greed, sexual desire, pride, envy, etc. No one performs his duty faithfully; no one serves another by love. This misbehavior often makes me so impatient that I would want such 'swine that trample pearls underfoot' (Matt. 7:6) still to be under the tyranny of the pope."[37]

Luther struggles to make clear the qualitative difference between Christian freedom and sinful license. For Christians to be liberated from the "curse of the law" (Rom. 10:4) means "faith added"—to be renewed in heart and mind for obeying God's primal command(ment) of love (John 13:34). Persons in God's holy and loving image are being recreated to transmit God-like love to others. Persons are not created with God's blanket permission to do "whatever we please" as a thinly disguised "opportunity for the flesh." (5:13).[38] The gospel is always against the law (*contra legem*) but never against God's primal command of love (*pro mandatum*).

Christians should remember that "while they are free before God before the curse of the Law," nevertheless, in the Spirit "the apostle imposes an obligation on them through this law of mutual love in order to keep them from abusing their freedom (Rom. 8:3-6). . . . Therefore let everyone strive to do his duty in his calling and to help his neighbor in whatever way he can."[39]

God's loving command is directed to our renewed will (*voluntas renatus*), not to our feelings, and requires radical obedience as our response. Moreover, our love is to be directed most especially toward "one of the least of those who are members of my family" (Matt. 25:40), for whom Christ died. Nor should we generally expect the world's adulation. Christians love because they are loving, not because their neighbors are particularly lovable. "You will find many mockers so inhuman and spiteful that they do not refer to the objects of their malice by their proper names, but describe them with some contemptuous nickname like 'Cockeyed' or 'Hooknose' or 'Big-mouth.' In short, the world is the kingdom of the devil, which, in its supreme smugness, despises faith and love and all the words and deeds of God."[40]

Luther freely acknowledges that "it is difficult and dangerous to teach that we are justified by faith without works and yet to require works at the same time. Unless the ministers of Christ are faithful and prudent here and are 'stewards of the mysteries of God' (1 Cor. 4:1), who rightly divide the Word of truth (2 Tim. 2:15), they will immediately confuse faith and love at this point. Both topics, faith and works, must be carefully taught and emphasized, but in such a way that they both remain within their limits."[41]

As the baptized believer's best ethical guide, Luther advocates the Pauline admonition, "walk by the Spirit" for you are "led by the Spirit and not under the law" (5:16,19). Christian freedom has love as its content and the gifts of the Spirit as its context. For imperfect Christians "on the way" to becoming true Christians, the ethical imperative "walk by the Spirit" is always based on the prior gracious indicative ("led by the Spirit"). Thereby, baptized Christians become on earth what God has already accepted them to be in heaven: saints.

In the Christian's faithful union with the indwelling risen Christ, the Spirit accompanies the Lord to nurture baptismal regeneration with ethical renovation (*Spiritus sanctificans*). Yet no moralistic or perfectionistic sanctification is advocated here by either Paul or Luther. Self-improvement bows to the Spirit's eschatological renewal of death and new life in Christ. Granting the burden of the persistence of sin in the life of the redeemed, the apostolic exhortation is to "receive the gift and the first fruits of the Spirit here (Rom. 8:23) . . . and begin to love."[42] What the law demands but never produces, the Spirit promises and always delivers (2 Cor. 3:18).

We are called and led by the Spirit ("grace") to join in the ongoing struggle against the flesh ("sin"). To walk by the Spirit means that "by the Spirit you battle against the flesh and follow your spiritual desires."[43] The Christian life requires taking sides between "two contrary guides in you, the Spirit and the flesh."[44] This does not generally mean speaking in tongues or sexual desire, but rather imperfect God-centeredness or total self-centeredness. "If we look at the flesh we are sinners; if we look at the Spirit we are righteousness. We are partly sinners and partly righteous. Yet our righteousness is more abundant than our sin, because the holiness and righteousness of Christ, our Propitiator, vastly surpasses the sin of the entire world."[45]

Therefore the apostle has established this as a general exhortation or "rule for the saints: that they should be servants of one another through love, that they may bear one another's weaknesses and burdens (6:2), and that they should forgive one another's trespasses (Matt. 6:12-15)."[46]

When faithful and loving Christians walk by the Spirit and fight back against the flesh, they certainly live under God's command of love. However, "you will not be under the Law." Baptized to die and eventually rise with Christ, Christians are "partly flesh and partly Spirit, but in such a way that the Spirit rules and the flesh is subordinate, that righteousness is supreme and sin is a servant."[47] By God's baptismal grace (Rom. 6:4), the sin that once ruled (*peccatum regnans*) is now itself ruled (*peccatum regnatum*) within our new life in Christ. Saints are forgiven sinners in the lifelong process of renewal (*iustitia actualis*).

Luther recalls poignantly that, as a monk, he "often had a heartfelt wish to see the life and conduct of one saintly man." He imagined "the sort of saint who lived in the desert and abstained from food and drink, existing on nothing but roots and cold water." He derived this notion about "unnatural saints" from the sophists and early church fathers before he learned about "ordinary saints" from the apostles.

> But now that the light of truth is shining, we see with utter clarity that Christ and the apostles designate as saints, not those who lead a celibate life, who are abstemious, or perform other works that give the appearance of brilliance or grandeur but those who, being called by the Gospel and baptized, believe that they have been sanctified and cleansed by the blood and death of Jesus. Thus whenever Paul writes to Christians, he calls them saints, sons and heirs of God, etc.
>
> Therefore saints are all those who believe in Christ, whether men or women, whether slaves or free. And they are saints, on the basis, not of their own works but of the works of God; which they accept by faith, such as the Word, the sacraments, the suffering, death, resurrection, and victory of Christ, the sending of the Holy Spirit, etc. In other words, they are saints, not by active holiness but by passive holiness.[48]

Luther finds such authentic Christian saints "hidden" among persons in all stations of life. While their lives are "hidden with Christ in God" (Col. 3:3), they quietly confess their redemption in Christ and "do their duty in their callings on the basis of the command of the Word of God." They are godly, however weak, because they resist the desires of the flesh and do not gratify them. When they sin they seek God's forgiveness, and when they prevail they sing God's praise. They struggle with sin continually in their vocations and obtain the victory by that very struggle. Indeed, "justified and sanctified by His death . . . all believers in Christ are saints. . . . Our work on the farm, or in the garden, in the city, or in our home, in battle or in government—what else is it but the work of a "mask" (*larva*) through which God wants to give us his good gifts? These occupations are the Lord's masks beneath which He hides Himself and through which He accomplishes His purposes."[49]

Commenting pastorally and profusely on each of the vices and virtues of character cited in Galatians by Paul (5:19-24), Luther makes one general observation worthy of special note: "Paul does not say 'works of the Spirit,' as he had earlier said 'works of the flesh,' but he adorns these Christian virtues with a worthier title and calls them 'fruit of the Spirit.' For they bring very great benefits and fruit, because those who are equipped with them give glory to God and by these virtues invite others to the teaching and faith of Christ."[50]

By way of concluding this commentary on the "fruit of the Spirit" that characterizes one's vocational sanctification in Christ, Luther strongly echoes Paul's dictum: "Against these there is no law" (5:24). The reason: "The Law is not laid down for the just" (1 Tim. 1:9). It also explains why the latter portion of Galatians, as other Pauline epistles, is filled not with rules and regulations but exclusively with loving admonitions, exhortations, and advice for the faithful Christian's ethical guidance (*usus parenesis evangelii*). It serves to confirm Luther's teaching on the ethical function of the gospel for Christians insofar as they are already righteous.

> For the just man lives as though he had need of no Law to admonish, urge, and constrain him; but spontaneously, without any legal constraint, he does more than the Law requires. And so the Law cannot accuse and condemn the just; nor can it disturb their consciences. It tries, of course, but when Christ has been grasped by faith, He dispels the Law with all its terrors and threats. Thus it is completely abrogated for them, first in the Spirit, but then also in works.[51]

In Galatians 6, Paul symbolically designates the normative command of love by which Christians in the Spirit are eschatologically "to bear one another's burdens," as the loving "law of Christ" (6:2), in fulfilled contradistinction to the law of Moses. Luther agrees in so many words: "The Law of Christ (*lex Christi*) is the law of love." He explains, "For after redeeming and regenerating us and constituting us as His church, Christ did not give us any new law except the law of mutual love (John 13:34)."[52] This fulfills the Johannine promise, "the law indeed was given through Moses; grace and truth came through Jesus Christ" (John 1:16). Throughout all the God-ordained structures of human life, whether in the institutional church, the state, the family, the arts, the military, business, and every other man-dated station of society, there are daily neighbors to be loved, justice to be done, and burdens to be borne. Luther reminds Christians that they are called to "let love be teacher and mistress, to regulate the laws and to turn them toward moderation" as their Spirit-empowered Christian righteous-ness breaks out into the temporal realm of civil righteousness, voluntarily going the "second mile" (Matt. 5:41). "Here let us not be unkind and severe; but following the example of Christ, who supports and hears such people, let us also support and bear them."[53]

So it is, contends Luther, deep in the midst of church and community—"in any area of life"—that we Christians are called to fulfill the loving law of Christ. Our deepest motivation: "The love of Christ urges us on" (2 Cor. 5:14) to provide a public "testimony of faith" (*testimonium fidei*). Moreover, the primary place where this service is to be enacted is in one's daily vocation. At the end of every day and life, the Christian's confession should be: "With my utmost faithfulness and diligence I have carried out the work of my calling as God has commanded me to; and therefore I know that this work, performed in faith and obedience to God, is pleasing to Him."[54]

Vocational Sanctification

We have seen consistently in Luther that justification and sanctification represent the bi-dimensional character of God's reckoned, and effective righteousness for and in us. Whether developed in terms of pardon and power, birth and growth, or declaration and actualization, it is the lifelong renewal of the believer's regenerated life in Christ that is here at stake. Var-ious interrelated elements of our being, indivisibly accounted and made righteous, can be theologically distinguished but never existentially sepa-rated. Against legalists, Luther emphasized the nuanced distinctions; against libertines, he stressed the essential unity. We have documented both.

Luther has little patience with those church leaders who were so preoc-cupied with eternal salvation in Christ (*vita aeterna*) that they virtually dis-regarded their Christian social responsibility for the very world in which Christ loved and for which Christ died. Faith in the Triune God must cou-ple both the justifying and sanctifying dimensions of the twofold rule of God in the world, exclusively otherworldly and socially irrelevant church leaders notwithstanding.

> They may be fine Easter preachers, but they are very poor Pentecost preachers, for they do not preach *de sanctificatione et vivficatione Spiritus Sancti,* "about the sanctification by the Holy Spirit," but solely about the redemption of Jesus Christ, although Christ (whom they extol so highly, and rightly so) is Christ, that is, he has purchased redemption from sin and death so that the Holy Spirit might transform us out of

the old Adam into new men—we die unto sin and live unto righteousness, beginning and growing here on earth and perfecting it beyond as St. Paul teaches (Rom. 6–7).[55]

Luther never viewed this sanctification in post-Enlightenment terms of humanistic perfectability through moral improvement. Rather, he remained biblically realistic in advocating the need for *remissio et sanatio,* that is, for a forgiven sinner's lifelong pardon and renewal by the Holy Spirit. As we have seen, the perpetual promise of growth is not in moral self but in God's grace (2 Pet. 3:18); that is, paradoxically, the more we grow, the more dependent we become on the gifts granted by the ethical governance of the indwelling Holy Spirit, who always accompanies the church's holy Word and blessed sacraments. Strengthened by the Lord's Supper, our new life in the Spirit "continually develops and progresses." Hence Luther taught: "It is well-known that the new obedience in the justified brings with it the daily growth of the heart in the Spirit who sanctifies us, namely, that after the battle against remnants of false opinions about God and against doubt, the Spirit goes on to govern the actions of the body so that lust is cast out and the mind becomes accustomed to patience and other moral virtues."[56]

In his treatise *On the Councils and the Church* (1539), Luther maintains that Christians, eschatologically, are a holy people who are "to remain on earth until the end of the world. . . . They love eternal life as their true fatherland and life, while they must yet remain and tarry here in exile."[57] Just as individual Christians are "at once righteous and sinful" (*simul iustus et peccator*), so too the church is "at once holy and sinful" (*simul sancta et peccatrix*). Therefore Luther characteristically treated sanctification both personally and corporately. It depicts the communal life of the baptized in the lifelong process of actualizing our gifted sanctification here on earth. "Saints" are always described in the plural in Scripture. This is true, whether they are gathered in worship as the church called out (*ek-klesis*) of this world or participating in service as the church sent into the world.

On the one hand, Luther first analyzes the chief marks of God's holy and catholic people, the church (*ecclesia sancta catholica*): God's Word, Baptism, Sacrament of the Altar, Office of the Keys, Public Ministry, Divine Worship, and the Sacred Cross. These are "the seven principal parts of the great holy possessions whereby the Holy Spirit effects in us a daily sanctification and vivification in Christ, according to the first table of Moses."[58]

More directly related to our more immediate concern in theological ethics are the "additional signs whereby the Holy Spirit sanctifies us accordingly to the second table of Moses." These are summarized in the Decalogue, "which we need not only to apprise us of our lawful obligations, but also to discern how far the Holy Spirit has advanced us in his work of sanctification and by how much we still fall short of the goal, lest we become secure and imagine that we now have done all that is required. Thus we must constantly grow in sanctification and always become new creatures in Christ. This means 'grow' and 'do so more and more' (2 Pet. 3:18)." Unlike works of the law, which are good in appearance but evil in the heart, fruit of the Spirit is created while lust resists, but the Spirit of grace is nevertheless victorious. Or again, in terms of the Christian's lifelong struggle between the "old man" in Adam and the "new man" in Christ (Rom. 5:12-21): "It mortifies the old Adam and teaches him patience, humility, gentleness, praise and thanks, and good cheer in suffering. That is what it means to be sanctified by the Holy Spirit and to be renewed to a new life in Christ."[59]

We shall now explore both the ecclesial and the societal dimensions of sanctification in turn. First, sanctification, or making holy the unholy, is the work of the Triune God preeminently attributed to the Holy Spirit (*officium Spiritus Sancti*) in Luther's interpretation of the Third Article of the Creed in his *Large Catechism* (1529). Luther's doctrine of the church here is governed by the sanctifying activity of the Holy Spirit through holy things, the divinely ordained means of grace. Christians are transformed by the gospel from without (*extra nos*), that is, when proclaimed from within the church. As in Christ, so in the church of Christ: The finite encompasses the infinite in the power of the life-giving Spirit (*spiritus vivificans*).

Luther treats "the holy Christian church" and "the communion of saints" as synonymous. The Holy Spirit makes "saints" (holy ones) by testifying about Jesus Christ: "He first leads us into his holy community, placing us in the church's lap, where he preaches to us and brings us to Christ."[60] What God has graciously done *for us* in Jesus Christ must now also be faithfully received *in us* through the Holy Spirit. "In order that this treasure might not remain buried but be put to use and enjoyed, God has caused the Word to be published and proclaimed, in which he has given the Holy Spirit to offer and apply to us this treasure, this redemption."[61]

So for Luther, the scriptural ordering of the affirmations of faith in the Third Article is pneumatologically ecclesiocentric: First the life-giving Holy Spirit proclaims the gospel; then is born the holy Christian church or the "communion of saints," who have been vivified by the gospel and granted God's gracious gifts of forgiveness, resurrection, and eternal life. In effect, the church is the "daughter of the Word" and embodies as proleptic "first fruits" the communal dimension of God's gracious justification and sanctification of an unrighteous world.

Luther summarizes his evangelical catholic understanding of salvation (*salus*) by the Holy Spirit within the Christian church under four headings. *First, the church is unique by virtue of its Head, Jesus Christ.* It is the incomparable "workplace of the Holy Spirit" who, with the Word of God, grants forgiven sinners the gift of faith to enable them to confess the saving lordship of Jesus Christ. It is the Holy Spirit who speaks "in, with, and under" the preacher's faithful proclamation of the living Word of God (*viva vox evangelii*). An evangelical sermon becomes a redeeming and sanctifying means of grace precisely because "faith comes from what is heard, and what is heard comes by the preaching of Christ" (Rom. 10:17). So, for Luther, no Spirit, no Word; no Word, no church; no church, no salvation. The Holy Spirit, Luther declares,

> has a unique community in the world, which is the mother that begets and bears every Christian through the Word of God, which the Holy Spirit reveals and proclaims, through which he illuminates and inflames hearts so that they grasp and accept it, cling to it, and persevere in it. . . . For where Christ is not preached, there is no Holy Spirit to create, call, and gather the Christian church, apart from which no one can come to the Lord Jesus Christ.[62]

Second, the holy Christian church is to be understood as a communion, or community, of saints. It is a holy Christian people gathered about God's Word in order to become strong in the faith and in the fruit of the Spirit. Here each baptized saint becomes a part and member, "a participant and co-partner" (cf. 2 Cor. 1:19) in all its divine blessings. "Until the last day," it is an anticipatory and efficacious sign of God's sanctifying reign in Christ through the power of the Spirit. This is the "sum and substance" of the "communion of saints" for Luther.

> I believe that there is on earth a holy little flock and community of pure saints under one head, Christ. It is called together by the Holy Spirit in one faith, mind, and understanding. It possesses a variety of gifts, and yet is united in love without sect or schism. . . . The Holy Spirit will remain with the holy community or Christian people until the Last Day. Through it he gathers us, using it to teach and preach the Word. By it he creates and increases holiness, causing it daily to grow and become strong in the faith and in its fruits, which the Spirit produces.[63]

Luther views the church here in eschatological conflict with God's created but fallen world. On the one hand, the church is certainly "a holy little flock" under its Head, Jesus Christ. It will not idolatrously pander to survive. On the other hand, God has raised Jesus from the dead and will continue to act as the Holy Spirit, "causing it daily to grow." So there are also divine grounds for churchly hope as God's people remain faithful. In a theology of the cross, however, we dare not confuse eschatological hope and ecclesiastical optimism. God's true church—as God's true Son—is hidden to all but the eyes of faith (*Deus absconditus*). In a theology of the cross, divine victories usually look like human defeats, just as human defeats miraculously turn into divine victories amid a sinful and fallen world.

Third, the Spirit's work of increasing human holiness in the Christian church concentrates on the forgiveness of sin. Christ's victory on the cross has dethroned but not destroyed human sin. Outside the church, it still reigns; inside the church, sin no longer reigns, but its all-pervasive persistence in the life of the redeemed is in need of daily forgiveness.

Luther helpfully clarifies that "apart from the Christian church" here really means "where the gospel is not." God's inbreaking reign is sacramentally centered in but not structurally limited to the divided and broken institutionalized churches that all call themselves "Christian." So Luther is not speaking ecclesiastically about institutional church membership as such. Rather, he is witnessing ecclesiologically to the impact of the gospel in the kingdom of Christ, whatever its hidden boundaries may be in the world. Hence Luther could also consistently affirm a non-Roman but nevertheless catholic view of the ecclesial dictum of Cyprian: "outside the church no salvation" (*extra ecclesiam nulla salus*).

> Further we believe that in this Christian church we have the forgiveness of sins, which takes place through the holy sacraments and absolution as well as through all the comforting words of the entire Gospel. . . . Meanwhile, because holiness has begun and is growing daily, we await the time when our flesh will be put to death, will be buried with all its uncleanness, and will come forth gloriously and arise to complete and perfect holiness in a new, eternal life. Now, however, we remain only halfway pure and holy. The Holy Spirit must always work in us through the Word.[64]

Luther is confident that this is the sanctifying "office and work" of the Holy Spirit: "to begin and daily increase holiness on earth through these two means, the Christian church and the forgiveness of sins. Then, when we pass from this life, in the blink of an eye [God] will perfect our holiness."[65] Based solidly on the witness of the Holy Scriptures, Luther interprets sanctification, or holiness, as a divine spiritual gift that continually works in and through us as ethical "fruit of faith."

Finally, it is important for our missional outreach to hear Luther's doctrinal witness to "the resurrection of the body and life everlasting." Christ's work of redemption is already an accomplished reality, but the Spirit's work of sanctification is not yet completed. Through the Word and by the Spirit, more persons are to be brought into the community of saints. Clearly it is the unique pneumatological mission of God (*missio Dei*) to speak and work through the church, to build it up, and to guide its mission throughout history into eternity. Luther writes:

> For creation is now behind us, and redemption has also taken place, but the Holy Spirit continues his work without ceasing until the Last Day, and for this purpose he has appointed a community on earth,

through which he speaks and does all his work. For he has not yet gathered together all of this Christian community, nor has he completed the granting of forgiveness. . . . Now we wait in faith for this to be accomplished through the Word.[66]

Of special significance for Christian theological ethics and a major part of the Holy Spirit's unceasing work is to empower the vocational sanctification of Christian believers. Since the Spirit's divine mission is "to glorify me, because he will take what is mine and declare it to you" (John 16:14), Christ's teaching in the Sermon on the Mount is of decisive importance for the Christian community. The Spirit's fusion of Christian faith and love serves to correlate our evangelical vocation (call) to eternal salvation and our daily occupations and avocations (callings) to service.

A series of sermons on Gospel lessons in Matthew preached in Wittenberg during the extended pastoral absence of his friend and collaborator, Johannes Bugenhagen, was the seminal origin of Luther's *Commentary on the Sermon on the Mount* (1532). Since the text's editors are unknown and therefore its reliability unverifiable, we will intentionally limit ourselves here to Luther's brief conclusion that is wholly consistent with our completed analysis of his lectures on Galatians. It illumines a major biblical insight into how we are to contextualize Christian love within our daily vocations for Luther's theological ethics. "'So whatever you wish that men would do to you, do so to them; for this is the Law and the Prophets' (Matt. 7:12). With these words He [Christ] completes what He has been giving in these three chapters, and wraps it all up in a neat package where it can all be found. . . . This is stated briefly and learned easily, if we only were diligent and serious in acting and living according to it."[67]

Luther believes that Christ's single "Golden Rule" ("Do unto others. . . .") is both a memorable "short sermon," but also "such a long sermon that it would be endless" if expanded by all that it implies. Central to Luther's theological ethic is the conviction that the new life in Christ is governed by the Spirit's singular gift of love as the evangelical alternative to any strict adherence to the rigid rules and regulations of a codified manual of moral conduct. Moral axioms are at best the regulative attempts of any given culture-conditioned group to try to obey the one normative command of love that the Lord God reveals to all historical ages and writes for every sinful human creature "in his own heart, in fact, in his whole life and activity."

> The book is laid in your own bosom, and it is so clear that you do not need glasses to understand Moses and the Law. Thus you are your own Bible, your own teacher, your own theologian, and your own preacher.
>
> If you are a manual laborer, you will find that the Bible has been put in your workshop, into your hand, into your heart. It teaches and

> preaches how you should treat your neighbor. Just look at your
> tools—at your needle or thimble, your beer barrel, your goods, your
> scales or yardstick or measure—and you will read this statement
> inscribed in them. Everywhere you look, it stares at you. . . . All this is
> continually crying out to you: "Friend, use me in your relations with
> your neighbor just as you want your neighbor to use his property in
> his relations with you."[68]

When Luther assures Christians against all moralistic clericalism that
"you are your own Bible," this is surely no license for immoral autonomy.
Rather, Christians are "entirely free with regard to everything" in finding
persons and places to love in the Spirit: "Do what you see fit to do, for God
is with you" (1 Sam. 10:7). The tools and instruments of our daily vocation
(*Beruf*) at once remind disciples in three ways "how to live and behave."

First, persons made in God's image "have no right to do business with
their property and manage it as they please, as though they themselves were
the lords of all."[69] Luther reminded believers earlier in his paradoxical
descriptions of *The Freedom of a Christian* (1520): "A Christian is a perfectly
free lord of all, subject to none. A Christian is a perfectly dutiful servant of
all, subject to all."[70] The gospel announces that God's baptized saints are
lords in faith on account of Christ and that they are also servants in love on
behalf of our neighbors. These are the two inseparable dimensions of our
reintegrated new life in the Spirit—the salvific and parenetic functions of
the gospel—that dare never be confused or separated.

Societally, Luther also cites here the benefits of the political function of
the law ("territorial and civil law") in constraining irresponsible and disobedient people to carry out their civic duties "in a proper and orderly way." It
is a violation of the Golden Rule by Christians and non-Christians alike, for
example, if we corrupt the common good by not "taking and offering only
good merchandise" and thereby practicing economic injustice.[71]

Second, Christ's command of reciprocal love "intends to appoint you as
our own witnesses to make us afraid of ourselves." "Love one another" can
also serve the law's theological function. It provides a built-in universal
standard for our consciences to use in making us "blush in shame" when
accusing us of lying to and stealing from our neighbors. God's law blames:

> "Look here, what are you doing? According to the usual fair-business
> practice, you ought to put such and such a price on this. But you are
> putting on a much higher price. Or the way you are debasing and mis-
> representing this merchandise, you would not want to have someone
> else sell you something like that." How it would annoy you if some-
> one charged you a *gulden* for something barely worth ten *groschen*![72]

Third, Luther concludes that the responsible and realistic application of
this Golden Rule to the challenges of the common life can provide the

Christian, inspired by "the mind of Christ," with "a daily sermon in your heart . . . from which to understand all the commandments and the whole Law, how to control and conduct yourself personally and socially."[73] We are called in obedient love to imitate not what Jesus did in his own unique calling as our Savior, but rather why and how he did what he did in our own temporal callings as responsible neighbors. In other words, the ethical choice is ours. The same primal command of love (*mandatum*) can be employed in the service of either the gospel insofar as one is already righteous, or the law insofar as one is still sinful. Moreover, it can also be employed both personally or socially, whether intimately as benevolence or corporately as justice, depending on how many neighbors are being served. Finally, it may even be employed by God to compel some degree of compliance by nonbelievers who are motivated solely by enlightened self-interest.

As Christians diligently carry out the practical, routine operations of daily life in concrete ethical decision-making (*Stuendelein*), Christ teaches us faithfully to pray, "Give us this day our daily bread" (Matt. 6:11). In response, we are graciously provided with our own working neighbors who also serve us as effective channels of God's preserving and caring love for humanity. This provision of God-pleasing societal justice and domestic well-being is normally (except for "heroic men," *viri heroici*, periodically sent from heaven) the temporal duty of civil authorities and responsible citizens. We act under God's twofold rule of Christians and non-Christians alike under the law of Caesar within God's mandates of preservation. Indeed, so important was vocational sanctification for Luther that he made it a distinguishing feature of Reformation faith. In the Preface to the Smalcald Articles (1537), written as his theological "last will and testament" for the postponed Council of Mantua/Trent (1545ff.), Luther could boldly cite "an understanding of the various walks of life [vocation, callings] and true works," as the ethical corollary of "the pure Word of God and the right use of the sacraments" in an evangelical summary of the heart of the Christian life.[74]

Priesthood of the Baptized

Luther's theology of sanctifying love in vocation was further reinforced by the ethical doctrine of the church's universal priesthood. This means that we are not our own priests but our neighbors' priests, for the biblical church is essentially a baptized priesthood that also has an ordained ministry. Hence, the laity's primary duty is not worship leadership but societal service, that is, not as cultic but as ethical priests. In conscious opposition to the clericalism of late medieval Rome, the Reformer stressed the holy calling (*vocatio*) of every baptized Christian to become her or his neighbors' priest, mediating to them the life-giving love of God. In doing so, however, Luther had first to counter centuries of developed tradition on the church's clericalized priesthood, as based on his own evangelical reading of the Holy Scriptures that is now briefly summarized here.

In the Old Testament, the word for "priest" means seer, truth-sayer, a mediator between God and humanity. The priest was first to receive the Word of God for believers and then to offer the sacrificial response from believers to God. Despite continual heathen corruptions of this ideal, the Old Testament priesthood was meant to incorporate its divinely ordained cultus within the covenant relationship that existed between Israel and its God (Exodus 24 and 25).

In early Israel, fathers and elder sons were often involved in leading the domestic worship of their households and local clans (cf. Judges 6:26; 13:19; 17:5). By the end of the period of the Judges, however, the Levites had established themselves as the recognized cultic specialists. In post-exilic times, an official Jewish priesthood gradually emerged; it was composed of the high priest, ordinary priests, and the Levites. Membership was limited to those descended from Aaron, one of the descendants of Levi, who in turn, was one of the twelve sons of Jacob (Exod. 29:4ff.).

With the rise of this professional clergy came also a division of labor. The proclaiming of the will of God was left to the prophets (and later codified into law by the scribes), while priests confined themselves to the cultic sacrificial system (cf. Leviticus, Numbers). Rites and ceremonies were greatly multiplied and elaborated, especially after the post-exilic temple at Jerusalem became accepted as the only proper place for sacrifices to be made. Here the high priest was given the greatest honor as the anointed successor of the pre-exilic kings of Israel. As the priesthood culminated in the high priest, the temple culminated in the sacred sanctuary of the Holy of Holies. Moreover, as Moses once ascended Mount Sinai to mediate between God and Israel, the high priest ascended annually into the Holy of Holies on the Day of Atonement to make intercession for Israel and to receive the blessings of God in the renewal of his covenant (Lev. 16:1ff.).

But delight in liturgical forms and practices for their own sake often degenerated into idolatry and ceremonial works-righteousness as the cultus became more and more separated from both the Word of God and the needs of the people. No lay persons were permitted inside the temple sanctuary; sacrifices were graded in the order of their value and sanctity; the ritual became mechanical and commercial. Whenever the priest encouraged such faithless perversion of divine worship, they were condemned by the prophets with the searing Word of God (for example, Amos 5:21-24).

The New Testament both radically corrects and fulfills the Old Testament in its witness to Jesus Christ as the true High Priest and to all baptized Christians as his royal priesthood. Although he, too, is a king, Christ has emptied himself of his royal glory and has voluntarily taken on the form of a humble servant (John 18:33-37; Phil. 2:5 ff.). As the "Word becomes flesh" (John 1:14), true God and true human, Christ reveals both God's saving action to humanity and its faithful response to God. Thus Hebrews declares Christ to be "the High Priest of the good things that have come," the God-sent "mediator of a new covenant" (Heb. 9:11,15).

The atonement on the cross of Calvary was accomplished because "God was in Christ reconciling the world to himself" (2 Cor. 5:19). No Jewish high priest was ever able to atone for sin (Heb. 10:4). But when the Son of God took upon himself the punishment for the sins of the world, he did so as the Holy One who had perfectly fulfilled the holy law of God (2 Cor. 5:21). Dying innocently on our behalf, therefore, Christ alone was able to atone for our sins. His saving righteousness can now be reckoned in grace to all those who truly believe that they have been redeemed "with the precious blood of Christ" (1 Pet. 1:18-19). Moreover, this "one mediator between God and humankind, Jesus Christ" continues to intercede for us as our eternal High Priest in heaven (1 Tim.2:5; Heb. 7:23-25).

Whereas the Jewish high priest had to reenter the Holy of Holies annually, the all-embracing self-sacrifice of Christ has taken place "once for all" (Heb. 9:12; 10:10). The very first result of Christ's victory on the cross, therefore, was that "the curtain of the temple was torn in two" (Matt. 27:51). This signifies that before God, no further meritorious sacrifices are either necessary or desired. In the New Covenant established by Christ, all baptized Christians are incorporated into "a chosen race, a royal priesthood, a holy nation, God's own people" (1 Pet. 2:9; cf. Exod. 19:5-6).

Conformed to the shape of their divine Head, all members of the body of Christ are likewise declared themselves to be "kings and priests" who are called to offer themselves as "living sacrifices" in obedient faith toward God and in loving service to other persons (Rev. 5:10; 12:1-20). For some, this service as ordained pastors will take the form of a public ministry of Word and Sacrament in the church. Most Christians, however, will continue to exercise their callings in domestic pursuits and temporal occupations. Wherever they are called, the once-for-all sacrifice of the true High Priest at Calvary permits and empowers all baptized Christian priests to redirect their sacrifices outward in loving service to needy neighbors.

Luther was convinced that late medieval Rome's "theology of glory" had completely distorted these teachings that he had rediscovered at the heart of the New Testament theology of the cross. On the one hand, Rome contended that the Jewish high priest in the Old Covenant was fulfilled in the New by St. Peter (and his successors) as the vicar of Christ to whom personally had been granted the keys of the kingdom of heaven. On the other hand, the priesthood of the Old Covenant has been fulfilled in the

New by the clergy of the Roman Catholic Church who, unlike the inferior laity, have received an "indelible character" in the sacrament of ordination that qualifies them to repeat the meritorious sacrifice of Calvary every time they offer the Eucharist in the celebration of the Mass.

The Reformer protested against both these false doctrines as injurious to the Christian faith. "Christ alone" (*solus Christus*) was his answer to the religious pretensions of the current Roman papacy. He denied that the papacy was anything more than a human administrative arrangement (*de jure humano*) since the "keys of the kingdom" had been given to the Christ-confessing Peter on behalf of the whole Christian community (Matt. 16:19; 18:18). Moreover, Scripture itself continually asserts that Christ—and Christ alone—is the sole Head of his body, the church, as the spiritual Lord of a spiritual kingdom (cf. Eph. 4:15ff.). The incarnate Son of God is declared to be the true High Priest of the new Israel as the heavenly fulfillment of the Old Testament prophecy: "Thou art a priest forever after the order of Melchizedek" (Ps. 110:4; Heb. 7:17).

With the once-and-for-all self-sacrifice of Christ restored to the center of the Christian message, Luther then attacked the late medieval Roman doctrine of the ordained priesthood as being incompatible with the biblical teaching on the "universal priesthood of baptized believers (1 Pet. 2:9)." Already in 1519, Luther's *Treatise on the Sacrament of Penance* argued that the ordained clergy have no exclusive monopoly on the declaration of absolution. God alone forgives sin, and in God's name "every Christian, even a woman or child," may privately (not publicly) declare the forgiveness of sin to a repentant brother or sister.[75] In the following year, his *Treatise on the New Testament* (1520) roundly condemned the medieval Roman notion of a meritorious sacramental sacrifice, declaring, "We do not offer Christ as a sacrifice, but Christ offers us." The only sacrifice Luther permits as legitimate for an evangelical Christian is the Spirit-worked response of "prayer, praise, thanksgiving, and of ourselves" in obedient gratitude for God's propitiatory act in Christ. "Therefore all Christians are priests. . . . Here there is no difference unless faith be unequal."[76]

The doctrine of the priesthood of all the baptized also comes to decisive expression in the three great Reformation treatises of 1520. In the *Babylonian Captivity of the Church,* Luther asserts vigorously that the Roman glorification of the clergy does violence to the true nature of the church as a communion of saints. "We are all priests, as many of us as are Christians. But the priests, as we call them, are ministers chosen from among us who do all that they do in our name."[77] In like fashion, the *Open Letter to the Christian Nobility* is addressed to the nobles of an officially Christian society as the leading lay priests of the German church. He insists that it is proper for them to help reform the church because the ordained ministry is one among many other offices of Christian priestly service. It is not, as claims medieval Rome, a superior order of men invested with an "indelible character" whose unique service is "spiritual" while that of the ordinary laity is merely "temporal." On the contrary, "Through Baptism all of us are consecrated to the priesthood . . . and there is no difference to all but that of office." Indeed, Luther asserts boldly, "A cobbler, a smith, a peasant—each has the work and office of his trade, and yet they are all alike consecrated priest and bishop."[78] In summary, as Luther put it in his powerful conclusion to *The Freedom of a Christian*, "I will give myself as a Christ to my neighbor, just as Christ offered himself to me. I will do nothing in this life except what I see is necessary, profitable, and salutary to my neighbor, since through faith I have an abundance of all good things in Christ."[79]

In his *Commentary on 1 Corinthians 7* (1523), Luther attempted to put Paul's theological ethic into vocational practice. His special interest is on the blessings of marriage and on the freedom of Christians to marry or not marry (some six years after his posting of the Ninety-five Theses and two years before his own 1525 marriage). It was intended as a kind of "wedding present" for a friend, Hans von Loeser, at whose marriage ceremony Luther had earlier officiated and who afterward was himself a sponsor at the baptism of one of Luther's sons, Paul. It is a song of praise to God for the human blessings of marriage and family life mandated by God (Gen. 1:28), against the unbiblical vows of obligatory celibacy in religious "orders."

Totally consistent in spirit but more thematically developed are Luther's comments on the Christian's priestly calling (vocation) in Paul's exhortation, "Only, let everyone lead the life in which the Lord has assigned to him, and in which God has called him. This is my rule in all the churches. . . . So, brethren, in whatever state each was called, there let him remain with God" (1 Cor. 7:17-24). This text provides the biblical point of departure for Luther's use of the term "vocation" (*klesis*). The theological ethical orientation is based on the fundamental affirmation of the goodness of God's preserved creation as the God-pleasing arena for Christian discipleship. "To a Christian, therefore, the entire world is holiness, purity, utility and piety. . . . Why is this? Because the pure, that is, the believers, can use (*uti*) all things in a holy and blessed way to sanctify and purify themselves. But the unholy and the unbelievers sin, profane, and pollute themselves incessantly in all things."[80]

Luther wishes to affirm Paul's insistence that "faith and the Christian life are so free in essence that they are bound to no particular order or estate in society."[81] Faith is to be practiced throughout all of life and one need not separate from society (for example, in monasteries or convents) in order to be saved. On the contrary, our mandated vocational sanctification takes

place in centers of responsibility within which our evangelical call to salvation may normally be proleptically actualized in obedient love. "Faith
alone justifies you, and it alone fulfills the commandment," without adding
on any other such nonessential works of the law regarding marriage, circumcision, and slavery.[82] "Briefly, all the laws in the book of Moses were
given until Christ should come; when He came, He was to teach and bring
faith and love. Where these are, there all the commandments are fulfilled
and annulled and set free, so that after the coming of Christ, no more commandments (*mandata*) are needed except those of faith and love."[83]

Luther's concrete pastoral application here of replacing the law of Moses
with the restored love command of Christ is that wives should remain obedient to their husbands, and serfs should remain subject to their masters, unless
they were "forced away from faith" or "compelled to associate with an evil
life." "In that case," counsels Luther, "it is time to leave him and run away."

We would rather personally argue in principled hindsight (as Luther
himself also does elsewhere) that there is a basic distinction to be respected
between theological and social ethics. Our present reaffirmation of one's
temporal calling as providing the societal context for living out Christian
faith in love and justice far transcends the culture-bound concrete applications of that position amidst the changing marital, economic, or political
conditions of the ancient or late medieval worlds of either Paul or Luther.
Today we sanctified Christians are still ethically bound to obey Christ's
universal and normative command of love within the Creator's mandates
of preservation, but surely not necessarily in the same specific and sin-
corrupted forms of regulative justice that were also then pastorally
endorsed, or at least unchallenged, in the compromised social ethics of our
doctrinal mentors in previous ages. Our evangelical call as Christians (*coram
Deo*) does not automatically endorse, and may at any given time even
prophetically challenge, the unjust secular standards set in the temporal
callings of civil righteousness by any given society (*coram hominibus*). Sin
presupposed, it is not fatalistically *to* a calling, but providentially *in* a calling,
that we are called by God the Spirit (*vocante Deo*) to live in holiness of life.

Nevertheless, Luther does conclude commendably with Paul's theological
ethical reaffirmation of Christian freedom regarding "outward things that are
optimal or free before God." It is a welcome invitation for the baptized
Christian priests' societal service and community participation: "In sum: We
owe nobody anything but to love (Rom. 13:8) and to serve our neighbor
through love. Where love is present, there it is accomplished that no eating,
drinking, clothing, or living in a particular way endangers the conscience or
is a sin before God, except where it is detrimental to one's neighbor. In such
things one cannot sin against God but only against one's neighbor."[84]

Luther is so intent on the Christian's societal responsibility, despite the
sins, compromises, and "lessers of evil" inevitably involved in traversing the

shoals of daily life, that he even risks another dangerous formulation that is ethically defensible only in opposing prissy, moralistic perfectionism. He asks rhetorically, "But what if the Gospel calls me in a state of sin, should I remain in that? Answer: If you have entered into faith and love, that is, if you are in the call of the Gospel, then sin as much as you please."[85] Taken out of context, Luther's statement is as subject to cavalier misinterpretation as the frustrated advice he once also gave to his "pussy footing" theological colleague, Philip Melanchthon: "Sin boldly, but believe and rejoice in Christ more boldly still" (*Pecca fortiter, sed fortius fide et gaude in Christo*). This counsel is grounded in Luther's firm conviction that "God saves no one but sinners, . . . not those who merely imagine themselves to be such but those who really . . . admit it."[86]

What Luther means to say here is that some sin is inevitable in a fallen world. Moreover, in any morally ambiguous situation, perfectionistic sins of omission may well be as bad as opportunistic sins of commission, and Christ's forgiving love will be needed to cover either in any case. On balance, Christians should remain responsibly and realistically in the service of needy neighbors through the least-worst of vocational sanctification available within the Creator's sin-conditioned mandates of societal preservation. Not to act may itself turn out to be an implicit action in support of a greater evil in an unjust status quo.

Indeed, the precarious character of all moral participation in a fallen and sinful world cannot be better exemplified than in Paul's concluding admonition here to the troubled Christians in first-century Corinth. It serves to substantiate our own earlier position that theological ethics (in principle) must be strongly distinguished from social ethics (in practice). Conscientious Christians today may well endorse the theological ethics of an apostle (Paul) or a reformer (Luther) in Christian righteousness, and yet also ethically reject or modify some of these leaders' own pastoral or political applications of such doctrinal foundations in civil righteousness amid current moral dilemmas (for example, appropriate forms of societal justice for Jews, slaves, women, children, racial minorities, gay and lesbian persons, revolutionaries, and so forth). What is finally governing is their own faithfully endorsed "mind of Christ" (Phil. 2:5) in forming and nurturing God's structured mandates in human community life.

For example, Paul's admonishing concession, "It is better to marry than to be aflame with passion" (1 Cor. 7:9), is hardly attuned to either Gen. 1:26-28 or Eph. 5: 31-32, and is surely at least partly conditioned by his mistaken anticipation of the imminent end of the world.

> I mean, brethren, the appointed time has grown very short; from now on, let those who have wives live as though they had none; and those who mourn as though they were not mourning, and those who rejoice as though they were not rejoicing, and those who buy as

though they had no goods, and those who deal with the world as
they had no dealings with it. For the form of this world is passing
away. (1 Cor. 7:29-31)

Fortunately, Luther does not dwell here on the ethical consequences of
the inaccurate chronology of the early Paul's radical apocalypticism.
Indeed, in a few years Luther would virtually repeat that same error himself in the midst of his own frantic despair and indefensible overreaction to
the societal chaos visited upon eastern Germany by the utopian-driven
leaders of the 1525 Peasants' Rebellion: "Let everyone who can, smite, play
and stab, secretly or openly, remembering that nothing can be more poi-
sonous, hurtful, or devilish than a rebel. It is just as when one must kill a
mad dog."[87] In the same class as Luther's *Against the Robbing and Murdering
Hordes of Peasants* (1525) was his similarly horrific anti-Judaic tirade, *On the
Jews and Their Lies* (1543), for which later twentieth-century Lutheran
churches have since abjectly apologized in official repudiation.

Instead, Luther concludes Paul's social ethical discussion with the pastoral principle that Christians "should rather behave like guests on earth,
using everything for a short time because of need and not for pleasure."[88]
This is the eschatological spirit of Luther's biblically based theological
ethic at its repentant best. Resounding with ultimate Christian hope,
despite inevitable persistent failures of imperfect application in need of
daily forgiveness and renewal, it is also perhaps best reflected in the
famous saying traditionally (but unverifiably) attributed to the ruthlessly
realistic Reformer, "If the world would come to an end tomorrow, I
would still plant an apple tree today!"

Gospel's Parenetic Function

Only the gospel's salvific function can provide the gracious foundation of
faith in the risen and indwelling Christ for the regenerated Christian's new
obedience. It goes without saying that the law's sin-related theological and
political functions also apply to imperfect Christians insofar as they still
remain sinful. However, insofar as they are already righteous, it is rather the
gospel's parenetic or ethical function, under the indwelling Holy Spirit's
governance, to empower and guide the joyful fulfillment of God's pre-fall
and perennial command of dominion-sharing love by God's renewed
Christian workers serving as responsible members of church and society.

For Luther as for Paul, "faith alone" is the way of salvation and "love
alone" is the way of service. Salvation is accomplished by God the Son's sacrificial work for us (*pro nobis*); service is enabled by the accompanying gifts
of God the Spirit also dynamically at work in and through us for the common good (*in nobis*). Therefore, in both the vertical and the horizontal
dimensions of our reintegrated new life in Christ, God's strange work
through the law has been graciously fulfilled by God's proper work through

the gospel. For Luther's theological ethics, our sinful and conditional works of the law are replaced by God's loving and unconditional fruit of the Spirit. In the history of salvation, God's interim law (post-fall and pre-Christ) intentionally bows to God's primal and permanent command, "You shall love your neighbor as yourself. . . . Love is the fulfilling of the law" (Rom. 13:9-10; cf. Gen. 1:26-28; Lev. 19:18; Matt. 19:19, 22, 39; Gal. 5:14; James 2:8).

Having firmly established God's eschatological command of love alone as *normative,* however, Luther can then (but only then!) also gratefully acknowledge the frequent attempts in Holy Scripture, preeminently in the Mosaic Decalogue, to practice and approximate God's love command more concretely in *regulative* standards of morality (Exod. 20:1-17). He asserts, "Now Paul shows beautifully on the basis of the Decalogue what it means to be a servant through love. . . . All the admonitions of the prophets in the Old Testament, as well as of Christ and the apostles in the New Testament, concerning a godly life, are excellent sermons on and expositions of the Ten Commandments."[89]

Following Paul, Luther rejects the law (*nomos, Gesetz*) only as a religious substitute for love but not in the ethical service of love (*mandatum, Gebot*). For Christians, natural law can still regulatively demonstrate what love alone normatively motivates. Love reveals "why and how" to be; law shows "what and what not" to do. Love generates piety and character ("fear, love and trust in God . . . and your neighbor as yourself"); law decrees morality and conduct in concrete life situations (blasphemy, disobedience, killing, adultery, stealing, perjury, and so forth). For fallen humankind, God's moral will is incomparably summarized in the (de-Judaized) Ten Commandments. Universally, they are to be "obeyed" according to the letter in the enlightened self-interest of civil righteousness (*iustitia civilis*). Only in faith and love, however, can they be "fulfilled" through the gracious assistance of the Holy Spirit in the piety of Christian righteousness (*iustitia Christiana*). All this illustrates Luther's foundational distinction between God's pre-fall "proper command" (*mandatum*) and post-fall "strange curse" (*nomos*) in shaping the content and context of the Mosaic, prophetic, Christic, and apostolic expansions and applications ("excellent sermons and expositions") of the Ten Commandments in the light of God's primal command of love (cf. chapter 3).

In the sixteenth century, Luther added his own post-biblical "admonitions on a godly life" by providing baptized Christians with a Christocentric rendering of the Mosaic Decalogue (as God's natural law summary) in three major works on Christian ethics, namely, his *Treatise on Good Works* (1520), *The Small Catechism* (1529), and *The Large Catechism* (1529).

In the earliest of these presentations, despite his accompanying polemics against late medieval Rome's alleged works-righteousness, Luther still turns freely to the Ten Commandments for universally shaping faith-activated love and justice in the ethical life of Christians. His Christocentric biblical rationale is asserted at the very onset:

> See for yourself what a difference there is between the fulfillment of the first commandment with outward works and its fulfillment with inner trust.
>
> The first thing to know is that there are no good works except those works God has commanded, just as there is no sin except that which God has forbidden. Therefore, whoever wants to know what good works are as well as doing them needs to know nothing more than God's commandments. Thus in Matt. 19:17 Christ says, "If you would enter life, keep the commandments." And when the young man in Matt. 19:16-22 asks what he should do to inherit eternal life, Christ sets before him nothing else but the Ten Commandments.[90]

In Luther's *Large Catechism,* the "Christian difference" is also dialectically demonstrated between the negative you-shall-nots of the Decalogue text as such and his own positive explications of the Ten Commandments for Spirit-empowered baptized Christians. Thereby baptized Christian catechumens, at once sinful and righteous, are both goaded by apodictic demands insofar as they are still sinful and guided by their evangelical explications insofar as they are already righteous.

That is, in the power of the indwelling Holy Spirit, sanctified Christians may find in the Decalogue's summary of God's natural law of love "the true fountain from which all good works must spring, the true channel through which all good works must flow." Following Paul's dialectic in Rom. 7:22-23 between the Christian's warring "two laws": (1) the persisting "old man" in Adam (*nomos*), and (2) the reborn "new man" in Christ (*mandatum*), Luther advocates his own post-Easter version of the psalmist's *Torah* piety. Insofar as one is regenerated with the sure confidence that "the Holy Spirit is present," a loving Christian may "occupy one's self with God's Word" as encountered throughout the Ten Commandments, the Apostles' Creed, and the Lord's Prayer (commands, precepts, promises, exhortations, and prayers) in the way that Ps. 1:2 calls those Old Testament saints "blessed" who delight in and "meditate on God's law day and night" (*dilectio legis Dei*). This climaxes Luther's view of theological ethics in sanctified fidelity to the law-free gospel of the church's final Adam in the New Testament's transformed "paradise regained."[91]

Likewise in the *Small Catechism,* inclusive of the Apostles' Creed and the Lord's Prayer, the repeated motivational refrain "We are to fear and love God, so . . ." always introduces a theological ethic of grace in Luther's explanations of each of the last nine Commandments of the Decalogue in total dependence on his governing first one: "We are to fear, love, and trust God above all things."[92]

In a fallen creation—seen fully only on this side of the cross—idolatry is our identity. So in the face of our infidelity, God is "jealous." The First Commandment says it all, and then goes on in nine other Commandments to illustrate it universally before God and throughout society: "You shall have no other gods" (Exod. 20:3). Luther explains in the *Large Catechism* (1529):

> A "god" is the term for that to which we are to look for all good and in which we are to find refuge in all need. Therefore, to have a god is nothing else than to trust and believe in that one with your whole heart. As I have often said, it is the trust and faith of the heart alone that make both God and an idol. If your faith and trust are right, then your God is the true one. Conversely, where your trust is false and wrong, there you do not have the true God. For these two belong together, faith and God. Anything on which your heart relies and depends I say, that is really your God. . . .
>
> This is exactly the meaning and right interpretation of the first and chief Commandment, from which all the others proceed. This word, "You shall have no other gods," means simply, "You shall fear, love, and trust me as your one true God." For where your heart has such an attitude toward God, you have fulfilled this Commandment and all the others.[93]

The theological problem then always arises: What is the role of the law for a Christian, insofar as that baptized saint in Christ is already righteous before God? More concretely, are the you-shall-nots of the Ten Commandments binding upon the Christian? Luther's startling response is typically dialectical: as Mosaic law—no, but as natural law—yes!

This profound view is developed most cogently in a decisive section of the work *Against the Heavenly Prophets* (1525). Luther has just concluded a defense of the freedom of evangelical Christians. They could either keep or destroy former Roman church images, depending on their state of faith and the state of local conditions. To answer Andrew Karlstadt's charge that such Christian freedom regarding images violates the letter of the Mosaic law, Luther replies vigorously that this does not concern him in the least! The reason: Christians who are under the dispensation of the New Testament gospel are not bound by the Old Testament dispensation of the Mosaic law. Christ has liberated us from the law—all of the law—from the minutest ceremonial nicety to the Decalogue itself. Says Luther, "For Moses is given to the Jewish people alone, and does not concern us Gentiles and Christians. We have our Gospel and the New Testament."[94]

Luther concludes that insofar as the Ten Commandments provide us with a concise statement of the Creator God's universal natural law governing all of sinful humankind ("to honor parents, not to kill, not to commit adultery, to serve God, etc."), they are to be obeyed absolutely. But insofar as they include special matters above and beyond the universal natural law that are historically peculiar to the Judaic theocracy ("legislation about images and the Sabbath, etc."), they may be regarded as time-bound statutes of the Jewish law code that are not binding upon Christians. Luther writes:

> It is as when an emperor or a king makes special laws and ordinances in his territory, as the law code of Saxony (*Sachsenspiegel*) and yet common natural laws such as to honor parents, not to kill, not to commit adultery, to serve God, etc., prevail and remain in all lands. Therefore one is to let Moses be the *Sachsenspiegel* of the Jews and not to confuse us Gentiles with it, just as the *Sachsenspiegel* is not observed in France, though the natural law there is in agreement with it.[95]

The church instructs its members in the Ten Commandments, therefore, because "the natural laws were never so orderly and well written as by Moses."[96] In no instance should this practice be used to justify the reintroduction of any Judaic legalism in Christian daily living. Insofar as a Christian still remains sinful, one is bound only by that part of the Decalogue that coincides with the natural law (civil righteousness). Consequently, insofar as they are already righteous, Christians will find it continually necessary "to make new Decalogues (*Imo novus Decalogue faciemus*) as did Christ, St. Peter, and St. Paul" in responding faithfully to the Holy Spirit of the living God.[97]

Luther himself models this Christian liberty "to make new Decalogues" by his pastoral provision in the Holy Spirit of ethical meanings of the Ten Commandments (*Gesetz*) in the spirit of God's "single command" of love (*Gebot*). Therefore, on the one hand, he intentionally does not include the historical prologue ("I am the LORD . . . who led you out of Egypt") within the First Commandment, and then he repeats the epilogue after both the First and Tenth Commandments, in order to proclaim a God whose holy and loving will both "[visits] the sins of the fathers upon the children" and "shows mercy" at once to those who hate and love their Lord (Exod. 20:2,5).

On the other hand, Luther takes the Ten Commandments for baptized Christians and freely normatizes the First ("fear, love, and trust God"), and in that obedience of faith freely offers parenetic guidance in the remaining nine commandments: that is, "not to curse or swear" along with "pray and praise" in the Second, "not to endanger or harm" but rather "help and befriend" in the Fifth, "not to rob but protect" in the Seventh, and so forth. In Christian freedom, he also treats the Sixth purely positively ("chaste and pure"), freely expands the Fourth ("parents and superiors") to include religious and civil leaders (*patres patriae*), and totally replaces the Third (Sunday for Sabbath worship).

Singularly illustrative of Luther's Christocentric freedom in subjugating Mosaic law to the Spirit's universal love is his ethical reinterpretation of the Third of the Ten Commandments, "You are to hallow the day of rest."[98] Sabbath observance on the last day of the week is deemed a distinctively Mosaic addition to the universal natural law of love that is regulatively embodied in the other nine Commandments. "Therefore, according to its outward meaning, this Commandment does not concern us Christians. It is an entirely external matter, like the other regulations of the Old Testament associated with particular customs, persons, times, and places, from all of which we are now set free through Christ."[99]

Luther then universalizes the root meaning of the Third Commandment in natural law for non-Jews (Gentiles) by shifting its obedience from observing the Sabbath to ceasing from labor on a day of rest. This side of Easter, teaches Luther, Christians can then also celebrate Christ's resurrection on the first day of the week by dedicating this universal rest time to worship God together and "to occupy ourselves daily with God's Word . . . and deal especially with the Ten Commandments, the Creed, and the Lord's Prayer, and thus regulate our entire life and being in accordance with God's word."[100]

It is clear how deftly Luther fulfills a double concern in his evangelical interpretation of the law of God: (1) he makes no religious compromises with Judaic law on the law-free gospel (*coram Deo*) while, simultaneously, (2) he makes common cause ethically with both Jews and all other human beings on whose hearts the essentials of God's natural law of love are still universally written, in however sin-corrupted a form (*coram hominibus*). It is the continuous reapplication of the Lord's primal command of love to ever new situations, and thereby righteously "making it new," that distinguishes Luther's contextual and non-legalistic approach to the natural law embedded in the Decalogue:

> All the commandments of the law are summed up in the law of love; that is, if they are not performed in love, they are against God and worthless. You must act accordingly. No matter what the work; your eyes should always remain centered on love. Laws may even be broken, if necessary, in order to alleviate a neighbor's troubles and suffering. For our deeds should exhibit the kind of love Christ assigns to our lives. . . . The love of the neighbor is like unto the first Commandment of the love of God.[101]

Luther's basic position, as we developed earlier in chapter 6, is that God's eschatological command of love is universally inscribed on the hearts of all human creatures made in God's image (Rom. 2:14-15). It is epitomized in the Golden Rule (Matt. 7:12) and likewise constitutes the "law of nature" (*lex naturae*), which is "the foundation of human law and all good works." With reason's corruption by original sin, however, it became necessary for the Mosaic Decalogue to clarify, summarize, and re-articulate essential dimensions of the natural law's witness to God's eschatological command of love within the human heart. As love provides law with its essential content, so law serves love with its societal forms.

Indeed, in his *Second Disputation against the Antinomians* (1538), Luther in later life reemphasizes that the Spirit-illumined Decalogue (as natural law summary) should continually be taught to remind Christians of the loving way of life that God intended for humans before the fall of Adam and still now intends for Christians after the cross of Christ (*ante lapsum Adae fuerimus et quid olim in Christo futuri sumus*).[102] What godly admonitions and exhortations still accuse sinful legalists and antinomians as law (*Gesetz*) can now also guide Christians in the Spirit as natural law expressions of God's eschatological command of love (*Gebot*). This is because the gospel transforms the hearts of justified Christians, and the Holy Spirit mollifies for them the various historical demands and threats of the law into mild expressions of friendly persuasion and winsome advice (*Lex est iam valde mitigata per justificationem*). Similarly, as Luther elsewhere commented on the decision of the Jerusalem Council not to impose the Jewish dietary laws on gentile Christians (Acts 15:28-29), "When a burden is no longer a burden, it is good to bear; and when a law is no longer law, it is good to keep, like the Ten Commandments."

> When Christ comes, the law ceases. The Ten Commandments also cease, not in the sense that they are no longer to be kept or fulfilled, but in the sense that the office of Moses in them ceases; it no longer increases sin (Rom. 5:20) by the Ten Commandments, and sin is no longer the sting of death (1 Cor. 15:56). For through Christ sin is forgiven, God is reconciled, and man's heart has begun to feel kindly toward the law.
>
> The church is God's holy people on earth, in whom Christ lives, works, and rules through the Holy Spirit (*per vivificationem et sanctificationem*), so that we do not remain in sin but are enabled and obliged to lead a new life, abounding in all kinds of good works, as the Ten Commandments or the two tables of Moses' law command, and not in old, evil works. That is St. Paul's teaching.[103]

For Christians, as righteous, there is also a "joyful delight" in God's law (*dilectio legis*), which in the Spirit is experienced no longer as threatening law (*Gesetz*), but is viewed rather as the applied renewal of God's primal command of love (*Gebot*). Luther testified that he himself learned God's will "as the Holy Spirit comes into my heart" during the study of God's Word.

It was in this sanctified sense that Christ made clear to his faith-liberated disciples that they were still to remain obedient not to Moses as such, but to God's eschatological command of love and to assume this "easy yoke" willingly (Matt. 11:30). Luther was convinced that this ethical message was also loyally transmitted by Paul as well, as the pastor preached on Paul's loving exhortations (1 Timothy 3–7) to his own congregation on March 17, 1525: "The law should not be brought in where it does not belong. For its proper use, you must clearly distinguish between the 'old man' and the 'new man,' as Paul did. The 'new man' should not be subjected to laws, while the 'old man' needs them continually. Then you have used the law rightly."[104]

So it is ultimately the law's salvific misuse, not its essential ethical or parenetic content, that is the enemy of the gospel of grace. Thus when Paul admonishes Christians in both Rome and Galatia that "the whole law is fulfilled in one word: 'You shall love your neighbor as yourself'" (Rom. 13:9; Gal. 5:14), he is witnessing to the God-pleasing inner coherence between the Spirit's gifts of faith and love, which no derivative human-made legislation (state or church) should be allowed to corrupt. Luther comments: "All this shows that love is much to be preferred to all laws and ceremonies. . . . Christ testifies to this when He says [of the Great Commandment] (Matt. 22:39): 'And a second is like it.'"[105]

Moreover, the "neighbor" whom we are called to love need not deserve it, any more than we deserved God's initiating love to us in Christ. Nor is "neighbor" limited to my fellow-Jew, as in post-exilic Judaic law. He or she (singular or plural) is "any human being, especially one who needs our help, as Christ interprets it in Luke 10:30-37."[106] Concretely, that "help needed" is most effectively provided in our vocational sanctification through "works performed by believers in any area of life. Thus someone who is a magistrate, a householder, a servant, a teacher, a pupil, etc. should remain in his calling and do his duty there, properly and faithfully, without concerning himself about what lies outside his own vocation. . . . Everyone should know that his work, regardless of the station of life in which he is, is a divine work, because it is the work of a divine calling and has the command of God."[107]

The Holy Spirit governs Christians being made holy and faithful by the gospel to become the cooperating "hands, tools and instruments" of God, the willing "vessels" or joyful "channels" of God's sanctifying love. With a "joyful heart" (*hilare corde*) they each receive God's love "from above" and pass it on "from below" to their neighbors in need. What is forced from unbelievers is freely transmitted by the faithful in the Spirit's "voluntary captivity." As Luther has tried to persuade Erasmus, persons in the Spirit who could never cooperate with God in Christ religiously for their once-for-all justification in heaven (*in coelo coram Deo*) are now empowered by their dominion-sharing God in the Spirit to cooperate ethically in their ongoing sanctification here on earth (*super terram coram hominibus*).

> When God operates without regard to the grace of the Spirit, He
> works all in all, even the ungodly, inasmuch as He alone moves, actu-
> ates, and carries along by the notion of His omnipotence of all things.
> . . . Then, when He acts by the Spirit of grace in those whom He has
> justified, that is, in His Kingdom, He actuates and moves them in a
> similar way, and they, inasmuch as they are His new creation, follow
> and cooperate, or rather, as Paul says, they are led (Rom. 8:14).[108]

Hence, while we often think anthropocentrically of persons apart from
God, Luther always depicts them theocentrically, as being either the
unwilling (sinful) or willing (righteous) human co-partners created in
God's image. God's twofold rule in law and gospel is exercised through
socially active women and men who are co-opted as "the workshops in
which God works." We are daily commanded to love even if it is "lost"
in the world through the continuous corruption of Satan (*verlorene Liebe*).
Since our creation is bi-dimensionally set in loving relation with both
God and neighbors, so is our sanctification. God serves us through others
and others through us, as the God-worked coworkers of God (*cooperatio,
synergia*).

> For God rules us in such a way that He does not want us to be idle.
> He gives us food and clothing, but in such a way that we should plow,
> sow, reap, and cook. In addition, he gives offspring, which is born and
> grows because of the blessing of God, and must nevertheless be cher-
> ished, cared for, brought up, and instructed for life by the parents. . . .
>   This is why God has given man reason, perception, and strength.
> Use these as means and gifts of God.[109]

While sin-corrupted reason universally governs all human morality, its
governance by renewing love and guiding natural law is the hallmark of
Luther's theological ethic for righteous Christians. It is Christ's law-free
gospel that inspires and empowers a lifestyle of spontaneous love in vocational service. This spontaneous love of others "bubbles over" (*quellende
Liebe*) as God's indwelling Holy Spirit encounters fewer inherent obsta-
cles while working on, through, and despite us. Insofar as Christians are
renewed by God's dominion-sharing Spirit—and that necessarily involves
lifelong growth in grace—they are continually blessed as new persons with
new life characterized by new obedience. And against such "fruit of the
Spirit," insists Luther following Paul, "there is no Law" (Gal. 5:24), for
"the Law was not laid down for the just" (1 Tim. 1:9).

> Thus a new creation is a work of the Holy Spirit, who implants a new
> intellect and will and confers the powers to curb the flesh and to flee
> the righteousness and wisdom of the world. This is not a sham or
> merely a new outward appearance, but something really happens.

> A new attitude and a new judgment, namely, a spiritual one, actu-
> ally comes into being, and they now detest what they once admired . . .
> a renewal of the mind by the Holy Spirit.
>
> For the just man loves as though he had need of no Law to admon-
> ish, urge, and constrain him; but spontaneously, without any legal con-
> straint, he does more than the Law requires. . . . It does not have the
> right to accuse them; for spontaneously they do what the Law
> requires, if not by means of perfectly holy works, then at least by
> means of the forgiveness of sins through faith.[110]

For Luther, then, love is the primal "single command" of God (*Gebot*)
that all persons are called to fulfill in the obedience of faith. Created,
redeemed, and sanctified in the image of a holy and loving God, we are
likewise pardoned and empowered to love one another realistically, whether
personally or socially, civilly or ecclesially, directly or indirectly, willingly or
unwillingly, within all of God's mandated sectors of human existence.
"Love your neighbor" takes on ethical form and concrete shape as the
Holy Spirit sanctifies God's baptized priests in the vocational service of
participating in the structures and institutions of everyday life. Ethically,
what God requires of us is simply what our neighbors need of us, no more
but no less. Grounded in the gospel of grace, gifts of the Spirit enable us
to progress in sanctification or, better, to allow the Spirit's sanctification to
progress in us. All this occurs as we serve others while carrying out our
daily duties, either justly in equity or if need be even sacrificially in suffering. So Christians are called and sent into God's world to co-participate
boldly in current struggles for peace, justice, and freedom by meeting the
varied needs of our interdependent neighbors within the Creator's mandates of societal preservation.

> In sum, believers are a new creature, a new tree. It is not that a new
> man is required to serve his neighbor, any more than a tree is required
> to bloom, or three plus seven are required to equal ten, or the sun
> required to shine. We may trust the children of God with liberty. The
> result will be service to others.
>
> Work, and let God give the fruits thereof! Rule, and let Him pros-
> per it! Battle and let Him give victory! Preach, and let Him make
> hearts devout! Marry, and let Him give you children! Eat and drink,
> and let Him give you health and strength! Then it will follow that
> whatever we do, He will effect everything through us; and to Him
> alone shall be the glory![111]

This completes our paradigmatic representation of Luther's theological
ethical analysis of God's dynamic and dialectical twofold rule of Christians within the world's two kingdoms. Just as the saving function of

God's gospel intersects the judging function of God's law for our justification in heaven (*coram Deo*), so too the parenetic function of God's gospel interpenetrates the political function of God's law for our vocational sanctification in daily life (*coram hominibus*). For Christ's sake and in Christ's name, Christians are called and empowered by the Holy Spirit to pray and work joyfully in critical cooperation with all persons of good will as God's coworkers in society.

Afterword

THIS VOLUME ADMITTEDLY PROPOSES a systematic construction in Luther's theological ethics that Luther never attempted himself. While all the quoted parts do come directly from Luther, he never joined them together in exactly this way. Indeed, neither Paul nor Luther ever wrote a textbook in Christian theological ethics for later followers. Instead, they boldly addressed God's living Word to actual pastoral situations, frequently to Christians needing urgent help in major moral conflict.

Although both the Apostle and the Reformer will always be remembered among the truly great theological minds of the Christian church, it must also be freely acknowledged that much of their prolific writings were occasional, polemical, paradoxical, and dense. Toward the end of his life, Luther publicly recognized that he, as Augustine, was one of those scholars who "have become proficient by writing and teaching," even as he had earlier poignantly reported that, "Not reading and speculation, but living, dying and being condemned make a real theologian."[1]

The resultant reform movement within the church catholic, with its multifaceted pockets of protest, took great charismatic leadership both to initiate and to unify. This dilemma was only exacerbated by Rome's official condemnations in the Council of Trent (1545–63), along with the prolonged illnesses prior to the death of Luther (1546). Moreover, Luther's younger comrade-in-arms, Philip Melanchthon, who was to live on until 1560, quickly proved both by temperament and by conviction that he was sorely incapable of becoming Luther's successor.

This precarious situation served only to fan the fires of intra-Lutheran and inter-Protestant strife, both in doctrine and in church life. With regard to theological ethics in particular, many of the important debates revolved around various aspects of Luther's central theological ethical paradigm of the two kingdoms and then later concentrated on the subsidiary issue of the alleged theological legitimacy of a "third use of the law" to guide the regenerate Christian's ethical growth in sanctification (*tertius usus normativus legis/usus didacticus/usus legis in renatis*). Through a summary of this book's conclusions, both of these controversial issues will now be joined in turn.

1. Addressing the first problem area, our introductory survey of theological ethical literature (chapter 1) has already commented at length on the most recent periods of scholarly debate surrounding conflicting interpretations of Luther's two kingdoms/two realms/twofold rule/dual reign/two regimes/two regiments. Benefiting from all the dedicated previous scholarship of many others, we have sought to take cognizance of the combination of Luther's (1) historically evolving views before and after the mid-1520s, (2) his paradoxical mind-set, and (3) his frequent disregard of terminological consistency in transposing highly nuanced biblical truth for a generation of theologically weak priests and laity (for example, using kingdom [*Reich*] and rule [*Regiment*] synonymously in an officially Christian land).

Hence, in terms of theological coherences, we have found it most faithful to the deepest doctrinal intentions of Luther to sharply distinguish the world's eschatological and dualistic two kingdoms of God and Satan and only subsequently God's historical and dialectical twofold rule against Satan with both right hand and left hand through Christ and Caesar. Moreover, these two sets of biblically revealed realities are not statically coextensive but dynamically interpenetrating, in congruent fidelity to Paul's (already/not yet) inaugurated eschatology.

We furthermore claim that the most profound cause for persisting difficulty in conceptualizing and accepting this complex paradigm rests finally within the Holy Scriptures themselves. There are a number of divergent models for relating eschatology and ethics within the Bible, and even Peter publicly confessed difficulty in always understanding Luther's chief mentor, Paul (2 Pet. 3:16). Additionally, theologians in general—and biblically governed theologians in particular—have always found the mystery of the diversified unity of God's eternal plan of salvation (*Heilsgeschichte*) virtually impossible to systematize in any totally comprehensive manner. After all, faithfully biblical authors of different centuries and cultures and audiences often reconfigured earlier or related testimonies of faith along with their own distinctive exposition and commentary. This traditioning process has taken place generation after generation both within and upon the Holy Scriptures, resulting in differently shaded meanings, sometimes expressed more broadly in generalizations, other times formulated more narrowly in differentiations.

In our own particular case, Luther-interpretation has been immeasurably complicated by Luther's own linguistic propensity to freely employ such key biblical categories as "world," "kingdom," "vocation," "flesh," "spirit," "gospel," "law," and "justification" in both an inclusive and an exclusive sense, depending on the particular context or the specific addressee of his writing (*aequivocationes vocabulorem*). Reflecting the richness of his scriptural sources, Luther's theological ethic is not necessarily confused and contradictory, but it certainly is contextually multivalent and paradoxical.

For example, *world* in a broad sense means the totality of God's good creation (chapter 3), but in a narrow sense—in contrast to the pre-fall "paradise"—it also refers to the corrupted realm of Satan-led rebellion against the Creator (chapter 4). Similarly, *kingdom* in a broad sense means the righteous reign of God in opposition to the sinful realm of Satan (chapter 4), but in a narrow sense when compared with the civil work of Caesar, it also refers to the salvific work of Christ (chapter 7).

Moreover, *vocation* in a broad sense means a Christian's calling to service in everyday life (chapter 8), but in a narrow sense it refers to one's call to salvation as a Christian in Baptism (chapter 7). Likewise, *flesh* in a broad sense means created human nature (chapter 3), but in a narrow sense—in opposition to *Spirit*—it refers to personal sin and enmity against God (chapter 4). Correspondingly, *gospel* in a broad sense means the entire doctrine of God that includes both grace and law (chapter 2), but in a narrow sense—in opposition to *law*—it refers solely to God's grace at work in Christ and the Spirit (chapters 7 and 8). Analogously, *law* in a broad sense (*Torah*) means the primordial will of God revealed for humanity's obedient conduct (chapters 3 and 8), while in a narrow sense (*nomos*)—as used preeminently by Paul in opposition to *gospel*—refers to the judging and regulating forms of God's wrath in opposing human sin after the fall (chapters 5 and 6). Perhaps most significantly for us, Luther (as Paul) can alternately use the term *justification* in both an exclusive and an inclusive sense. The exclusive (forensic) sense narrowly excludes *sanctification* (chapter 7), while the inclusive (parenetic) sense can broadly include sanctification (chapter 8).

On the one hand, narrowly and exclusively, justification points solely to the Christian's rebirth (regeneration) when God juridically declares believers to be righteous for Christ's sake (*propter Christum*). First hear the forensic Luther: "In short, the term 'to be justified' means that a man is reckoned or considered righteous."[2] On the other hand, broadly and inclusively, *justification* can also depict both the Christian's rebirth and inseparable growth in grace. It describes the lifelong process of events within which God the Father both forensically reckons to faith the shared grace of Christ's "alien" righteousness (Baptism) and also effectively sends us sanctifying gifts of love that begin to make us properly righteous in our own stead (renewal). Now hear the transforming and sanative Luther: "A believer's whole life consists paradoxically in waiting for the holiness he already has." Or elsewhere: "Everyone who believes in Christ is righteous, not yet fully in point of fact (*re*) but in hope (*spe*). For he has begun to be justified and healed, like the man who was half-dead (Luke 10:30)."[3]

Meanwhile, however, while he is being justified and healed, the sin that is left in his flesh is not imputed to him. In fact, precisely while debating the meaning of being "justified by faith apart from works prescribed in the law" (Rom. 3:28), Luther can freely assert the simultaneous interchange (*ineinander*) of both the forensic and effective dimensions of God's activity in forgiven sinners. "Paul embraces two parts in justification, according to Rom. 5:15–17, grace and the free gift. Accordingly, it is not only necessary for us to be justified, but also that a new obedience be begun in us."[4]

It is also a historical fact that in polemics, the early Luther (pre-1525) usually leaned more in the sanative direction against legalistic Christians, while in later years, more in the forensic direction against antinomian ones. Against the former, Luther developed justification and sanctification as two aspects of an ongoing dynamic process; against the latter, rather as two distinguishable phases of total Christian existence. It all depended on the adversary being opposed. In common is the abiding conviction that in the Christian life, there are always both new birth and new obedience, rebirth and renewal. However, the ever-essential "for Christ's sake" (*propter Christum*) demanded that the second always comes after the first, whether contextually presented as a sequence or as a consequence, in keeping with the ordered twofold command of love of God and neighbor.

Both views paradoxically and contextually coexist in tension with one another in Luther's variously directed writings. Indeed, as an active, practicing pastor himself, Luther freely acknowledged that his own contextually conditioned judgments and emphases had also changed along with changing times and addressees during his hectic career. Near his death he once reflected on different accents and emphases in his teaching on the law from "the early stage of this movement" in comparison with later developments,

> when the times now are very dissimilar from those under the pope. . . .
> Therefore, the Antinomians, who defend themselves with our example, deserve to be hated by all, even though it is manifest why in the beginning we taught as we did concerning the grace of God. . . . What else, then, could one do than encourage the disheartened people and hold out true solace to them? . . . One must speak differently to those who are sated, who are addicted to pleasure, and fat.[5]

In sum, to attempt to systemize the views of so creative, profound, and volcanic a thinker as Luther is to be tested sorely. Perhaps its final excuse lies only in its exasperating exhilaration. Wrestling with the proper distinctions between God's law and gospel (*discrimen inter legem et evangelium*) remains for him "the essential task of Christian doctrine" (*summa totus Christianae doctrinae*). Yet even Luther confessed, "There is no man living on earth who knows how to distinguish between the law and the gospel. We may think we understand it when we are listening to a sermon, but we're far from it. Only the Holy Spirit knows this."[6]

In any case, our study may help the serious theological student to appreciate more fully some of the dependent doctrinal treasures displayed in the related materials on "Justification," "New Obedience," "Free Will,"

"Faith and Good Works," and "The Power of the Bishops" as developed in Articles IV, VI, XVI, XX, and XXVIII of the Augsburg Confession and its Apology within the Lutheran church's confessionally authoritative *Book of Concord* (1580). Certainly its continuing ecumenical relevance has been most impressively demonstrated in the recent mutual approval of the Lutheran–Roman Catholic consensus document in the *Joint Declaration on the Doctrine of Justification* (1997).

2. The second controversial area in which our study has taken a determined stand is in rejecting any alleged third use of the law in Luther (*tertius usus normativus seu didacticus*), as a necessary guide for producing good works by regenerated Christians, insofar as they are already righteous. A rapid review will assist the reader to recall the historical setting and doctrinal issues that were later hotly debated in the second generation of the Reformation by various interpreters of the rich theological ethical heritage of Luther just completed in chapter 8.

A decade after Luther's death, Philip Melanchthon and his followers (Philippists) prevailed politically against their more Luther-oriented theological opponents (Gnesio-Lutherans) at the Eisenach Synod (1556). However, they were able to settle some of the intra-Lutheran doctrinal controversies regarding good works only by reverting to a pre-Reformation Scholastic understanding of God's law. While rightly rejecting the perfectionistic claims of the antinomians, the Philippists departed from the scriptural dialectics of both Paul and Luther (*nomos* versus gospel) by reverting to the Stoic-Aristotelian and Thomistic metaphysics of the Roman church's medieval Scholasticism. Departing from the biblical witness to the radical revisions in the revealed will of God before and after the fall of the first Adam and the rising of the last Adam, they reaffirmed an eternal law (*lex aeterna*) rather as the ontologically ideal and objectively just order of creation, to which both God and humanity were righteously bound.

Consequently, in addition to its continuing theological and political functions, a third or didactic use of the law for the regenerate (*in renati*) was now newly endorsed. However, the Philippists (Pfeffinger, Major, Menius, Strigel) never replaced the law's theological function with the third or didactic function as its principal and chief use (*praecipuus usus legis*), as was the case in John Calvin's moralistic contradiction of Luther's original 1535 formulation in his own contemporary *Institutes of the Christian Religion* (1536ff.). Melanchthon took rather an intermediary position between Luther and Calvin, which he first introduced publicly on Lutheran theological soil in the post-1525 editions of his own *Loci communes*. If not rightly interpreted, especially as so legally designated, it could easily endanger Luther's basic position on the freedom of reborn Christians from the curse of the law (*nomos*) insofar as they are already being renewed by the Holy Spirit.

In the approved dictum of the Eisenach Synod, the law's stated purpose was to guide the believer's good works, now likewise deemed necessary by God's immutable law for the reward of eternal salvation (*Bona opera sunt necessaria ad retinendam salutem in doctrina legis abstractive et de idea tolerari potest*). Here justification is deemed purely forensic, as the gospel serves the fulfillment of God's law, rather than biblically vice versa. Subsequently, two decades later (1577), reflecting the disciplinary penchant of Melanchthon and anticipating the neo-Scholastic hegemony of seventeenth-century Lutheran orthodoxy, the Philippists' supralapsarian (beyond the fall) view of God's law as an ontological and immutable moral absolute was destined to carry the day once again. By generically conflating in one "law" Luther's positive (*Gebot*) and negative (*Gesetz*) expressions of God's will, an alleged third use of the law was now also confusedly advocated for inclusion among other political and doctrinal accommodations made in Article VI of the Formula of Concord (1577), soon to become incorporated into the new Lutheran Church's normative *Book of Concord*:

> The law of God is used (1) to maintain external discipline and respectability against dissolute and disobedient people (2) and to bring such people to a recognition of their sins. (3) It is also used when those who have been born anew through God's Spirit, converted to the Lord, and had the veil of Moses removed from them live and walk in the law.
>
> Through it believers in Christ learn to serve God not according to their own ideas but according to His written law and Word, which is a certain rule and guiding principle for directing the godly life and behavior according to the eternal and unchanging will of God.[7]

In response to this "party position," the final text of Article VI vacillates on whether the law's third use is needed by the regenerate (*renati*) as already righteous (*iustus*) or as still sinful (*peccator*). At stake: Is sanctification in Christian theological ethics finally governed by the law or the Spirit of God?

The Philippists, while surely correct in repudiating antinomians such as John Agricola, thereby also opened wide their evangelical back door to later pietistic (as Calvinistic puritanical) legalism. They did so by introducing a progressive process of sanctification in completing one's personal order of salvation (*ordo salutis*) under a frequently casuistic and scrupulous guiding rule of law for the regenerate (*in renati*). This view strongly imperiled the evangelical coherence of Luther's law-gospel dialectic by seemingly replacing the Spirit with the Mosaic law (not as summarized natural law) to guide the regenerated Christian's ethical life, insofar as one is already righteous. Certainly Paul's alternative to moral license was not resorting to neo-legalism.

At least two things should be emphasized here. On the one hand, the Formula's Article VI on the "Third Function of the Law" is misleadingly governed by the late-medieval Scholastic (but non-Pauline) theological usage: "the word 'law' [*Gesetz, legis*] has one single meaning, namely, the unchanging will of God (*immutabilis voluntas Dei*), according to which human beings are to conduct themselves in this life."[8] This eternal law (*lex aeterna*) is the Thomistic designation for the timeless and objective order of holy righteousness that the Creator allegedly envisioned and established in the created world (chapter 6). Such a metaphysical description of law is organically unrelated to the biblical plan of salvation and the other related Pauline eschatological categories of love, command, sin, wrath, curse, gospel, and the Holy Spirit that we have carefully developed above in the Apostle's understanding of the uniquely biblical history and order of "command, law versus gospel, command" for salvation (chapter 3).

That is precisely why, in his *Preface to the New Testament* (1532), Luther evangelically insisted that "the little word 'law' you must here [in St. Paul] *not* fashion as a teaching about what works are to be done or not done."[9] Luther's case in brief: If you want Paul on justification, you must also take Paul on sanctification. How can God's one and the same law both spiritually always accuse (*lex semper accusat*) and yet simultaneously also morally instruct the regenerate as already righteous (*usus legis didacticus*)? Is this consistently Pauline? Along with their other humanistic and mediating concessions (for example, on conversion consent, predestination, free will, the Leipzig Interim, and Holy Communion), did Melanchthon and his followers agree here with Luther's Pauline heritage on God's law (*nomos*)? Luther's reminder:

> Paul is the only one to call the Law of God "elements of the world" or "weak and beggarly elements" or "the power of sin" or "the letter that kills." The other apostles do not speak this way about the Law. Therefore let every student of Christian theology carefully observe this way of speaking that Paul has, . . . [so that he] may faithfully lay the foundations of the doctrine of justification and set it down clearly.
>
> When Paul speaks of the Law, one should understand it according to the office (*Amt*) which it carries out, and not according to its nature (*Wesen*).[10]

On the other hand, to be both accurate and fair, the Formula of Concord's Article VI (however mislabeled) is surely faithful to both Paul and Luther in its clear repudiation of the twin ethical errors of legalistic activism and antinomian quietism.[11] It does so by rightly (but inconsistently?) teaching as well that the renewed Christian's deeds of faith-activated love "are not, properly speaking, works of the law but works and fruits of the Spirit, or, as St. Paul calls them, 'the law of the mind' and 'the law of Christ.'" Consequently, Christians are described as living "not under but in the law," as the Lutherans' intended equivalent for Paul's sharper alternative, "not under the law but under grace" (Rom. 6:14-15). Moreover, Article VI also rightly locates our central ethical dilemma: "In this life Christian believers are not fully renewed, and they are still torn between their flesh and the Spirit." However, all these recognizable teachings of Paul and Luther are then never really coherently related to the paradoxical nature of Christians as both righteous and sinful and, correspondingly, the paradoxical nature of God's will as at once both command of love and law of wrath in confronting human righteousness and unrighteousness.

As Luther feared already a decade before his own death in 1546, the proper use of the law "after our time will be obscured again and will be completely wiped out."[12] It was obscured but fortunately not completely wiped out in the later Formula of Concord, Article VI. In 1577, by way of mutual accommodation already achieved at Torgau (1576), the irenic views of Jacob Andreae's Six Sermons of 1548–1573 (in Article VI's paragraphs 1–14, 20–25) were editorially interpolated and balanced by the incisive views of Andreas Musculus (in paragraphs 15–19). Such a theological compromise could likely not have been negotiated during Luther's lifetime, on the specious basis of the non-Pauline supralapsarian view of God's *law* (rather than *command*) that is cited and developed here (paragraph 15) by Andreae from Eisenach (1556).

By way of summary contrast, the reader will readily recall that Luther's view of the law faithfully followed Paul's infralapsarian (beneath the fall) depiction of the Old Testament in which the law (*nomos, Gesetz*) functions very differently within the scriptural history of salvation. Luther's normative authority remained the Christocentric Word of God in Holy Scripture, but most especially as proclaimed by the Apostle to the Gentiles. In Gal. 3:19, Paul asks the rhetorical question, "Why then the law?" and in view of the cross of Christ immediately responds, "It was added because of the transgressions. . . . The law was our custodian until Christ came, that we may be justified by faith."

We recollect that in his 1535 *Commentary on Galatians* on this very verse, Luther obediently and explicitly develops his own evangelical position on a "double use of the Law" (*duplex usus legis*). It is inconsistent with the law's threefold use (*usus triplex*), whether as taught by Melanchthon, Calvin, or even in a student's editorially forged, alleged endorsement of Melanchthon's position by Luther himself at the conclusion of his *Second Disputation against the Antinomians* (1538).[13] Instead, the law's double use coherently corresponds to Luther's governing view of God's twofold rule of humanity against Satan within the two realms of creation and redemption.

> Here one must know that there is a double use of the Law. One is the civic use. God has ordained civic laws, indeed all laws, to restrain transgressions. . . . The other use of the Law is the theological or spiritual one, which serves to increase transgressions. This is the primary purpose of the Law of Moses. . . . Paul discusses this magnificently in Romans 7. Therefore the dual function and the chief and proper use of the Law is to reveal to man his sin. . . . And that is as far as the Law goes (*Da hort lex auff*).[14]

Therefore our own Pauline judgment remains that God's sin-predicated law (*nomos, Gesetz*) is no valid agent of ethical renewal for faithful Christians in Luther's theology. That is reserved exclusively for the Holy Spirit's gifts and exhortations (*parenesis*) that accompany the gospel.

Although holy in itself, the law addresses sinners who always encounter it as a "curse" (cf. Deut. 27:26; Gal. 3:12), in both its God-ordained functions this side of the fall. First, its theological function is to expose sin, for its impossible demands never provide persons under Satan with the transforming inspiration or sacrificial commitment to fulfill the loving will of God that it reveals (*impossibilitas legis in statu corruptionis*). Second, its political function is to promote justice, but its necessary alliance with sinful reason and armed force in an unregenerate world (*securi, praefecti, hypocritae, carnalis*) always finally corrupts it into one of the chief demonic powers that oppose God's loving will. At best, if consistently understood as the Pauline *nomos,* the law's "third use" in Article VI can rightly refer only to the legitimate application of these first two uses to the *persisting sin* ("like a stubborn, recalcitrant donkey") of imperfect Christians, as well as elsewhere to non-Christians. However, that is really not a new "third use" in kind, but solely a different area of the first two functions' implementation. Consequently, concluded Luther in *Galatians,* "that is as far as the Law goes." Why? Because then it is to be replaced by the Spirit's gifted fulfillment of God's restored primordial command of love (*mandatum*): "Hence a Christian is divided into two times: As far as he is flesh, he is under Law; as far as he is spirit, he is under gospel."[15]

Moreover, as if to document in his own theological "last will and testament" that this remained his definitive position, Luther's 1537 Smalcald Articles (Part III, Article II) repeated finally once again his own succinct earlier views on the two uses of the law for Rome's impending Council of Trent (1546), which was also incorporated still later into the Lutheran church's official *Book of Concord:*

> Here we maintain that the law was given by God, in the first place, to curb sin by means of the threat and terror of punishment. . . . The chief office or power of the law (*praecipuum autem officium*) is that it reveals inherited sin and its fruits. It shows human beings into what utter depths their nature has fallen and how completely corrupt it is.[16]

So this is the summary of summaries (*Summa Summarum*): There is
no law after the Spirit but there is a law after the flesh, because it does
not do what it should. However, the Spirit does. In this way you
should understand the giving of the law (I Tim. 1:8-11), and its
twofold use (*zween brauch des gesetzs*).[17]

As we have so extensively documented, Luther prefers the model of
Paul's loving admonitions and exhortations in the "imperatives of grace"
as recovered *Gebot* in Romans 12–16, Galatians 5–6, and elsewhere
throughout the New Testament. He turns from Christ's justifying work *for
us* to the Holy Spirit's sanctifying work *in* and *through* us, as the evangelical basis for the theological ethics of Christian renewal. It is the actual love
of God that the Holy Spirit pours into our hearts (Rom. 5:6). Hence, "If
you are led by the Spirit, you are not under law" (Gal. 6:11). Therefore it
is not by any alleged third use of the law (*tertius usus legis*), but through
what we have earlier proposed to call the second or parenetic use of the
gospel, that is, justifying faith active in sanctifying love and justice, that the
Holy Spirit calls and empowers us with new gifts to fulfill our new obedience to God's primal command of love (*mandatum*). Therefore the
mature Luther faithfully taught that this Christ-normed law of love (*lex
spiritus, caritatis Christi*) dialectically generates God's twofold rule of
humankind through interacting expressions of the law and gospel within
the world's two kingdoms.

Nevertheless, these persisting technical and linguistic discrepancies in
theological ethics (along with other such historically debated topics as the
Lord's Supper, Christology, and predestination) are now judged by the
Evangelical Lutheran Church in America (ELCA) and three Reformed
communities in America as being no longer church-divisive. They are
viewed rather "as diverse witnesses to the one gospel that we confess in
common. . . . The theological diversity within our common confession
provides both the complementarity needed for a full and adequate witness
to the gospel (*mutual affirmation*) and the corrective reminder that every
theological approach is a partial and incomplete witness to the gospel
(*mutual admonition*)."

With this dual commitment to reconciled diversity in a more charitable
and accommodating ecumenical age, both communities in a *Formula of
Agreement* (1997) have now officially declared themselves to be in "full
communion" with one another. This move is defensible in theological
ethics, considering both Luther's positive treatment of God's natural law of
justice within the realm of creation (chapter 6) and God's eschatological
law of love in the intersecting forces of redemption (chapter 8). In their
differently formulated but common rejections of the twin ethical errors of
casuistic legalism and situational license, Luther and Calvin, along with

Melanchthon and Martin Bucer, do all finally unite together in endorsing a biblical ethic of norms based on a theology of grace.

All this means that just as Lutherans in the ELCA have achieved a qualified or differentiated consensus with Roman Catholics on the relation of justification to sanctification, they have reached a formal agreement in mutual affirmation and admonition for relating love and law with the Reformed. Our common ecumenical challenge now is to implement this impressive extent of agreement in theological ethics through more critically coordinated expressions of Christian ethical service and protest within American society.

Notes

1. Survey: The Post-Nazi Recovery of Lutheran Public Responsibility

1. This chapter is an expanded and updated revision of the author's earlier theological ethical literature survey, "The Twentieth-Century Recovery of Lutheran Political Responsibility," in *The Ethic of Power: The Interplay of Religion, Philosophy, Politics,* ed. Harold D. Lasswell and Harlan Cleveland (New York: Harper, 1962), 119–39.

2. Roland H. Bainton, *The Reformation of the Sixteenth Century* (Boston: Beacon, 1952), 233–34.

3. Ernst Troeltsch, *The Social Teaching of the Christian Churches,* vol. 2, trans. Olive Wyon (Louisville: Westminster John Knox, 1992 [1911, 1931]), 568. See also his essays "Das Christliche Naturrecht" (Christian Natural Law) and "Das Stoische Christliche Naturrecht und das moderne profane Naturrecht" (Stoic-Christian Natural Law and Modern Secular Law) in *Gesammelte Schriften* (Collected Writings), ed. Hans Baron, 1925.

4. Helmut Thielicke, *Theological Ethics,* vol. 1, *Foundations,* ed and trans. William H. Lazareth (Philadelphia: Fortress, 1966), 365–66.

5. Arthur C. Cochrane, *The Church's Confession under Hitler* (Philadelphia: Westminster, 1962), 241.

6. The anachronistic correlation of the teachings of Luther with "these frightful aberrations of a particular manifestation" in later German Lutheranism is documented and criticized in Helmut Thielicke, *Theological Ethics,* vol. 1, 368–69.

7. Quoted in Stewart Herman, *The Rebirth of the German Church* (New York: Harper and Row, 1946), 140–41.

8. Rodney Hokenson, "The Awakening of Political Responsibility among German Protestants," *The Lutheran Quarterly* 8:4 (1956): 296.

9. Hanns Lilje, "Editorial," *Lutheran World* 1:1 (1954): 2–3.

10. Eivind Berggrav, Introduction to *Luther Speaks: Essays for the Fourth Centenary of Martin Luther's Death* (London and Redhill: Lutherworth, 1947), II:11. See also Berggrav's "Experiences in the Norwegian Church in the War," *The Lutheran World Review* 1:1 (1948), and *Man and State* (Philadelphia: Muhlenberg, 1951).

11. Anders Nygren, "Luther's Doctrine of the Two Kingdoms," *Ecumenical Review* 1:3 (1949): 301–2.

12. Reinhold Niebuhr, *The Nature and Destiny of Man,* vol. 2 (New York: Scribner's, 1941), 193.

13. Reinhold Niebuhr, "Love and Law in Protestantism and Catholicism" in *Christian Realism and Political Problems* (New York: Scribner's, 1953), 162–63. Italics mine.

14. Niebuhr, *Nature and Destiny,* 194ff.

15. Wilhelm Pauck, *Heritage of the Reformation* (Boston: Beacon, 1950), 12. Italics mine.

16. The texts of these social statements that were publicly debated and adopted at the Lutheran Church in America's churchwide biennial assemblies may be found in Christa R. Klein and Christian D. von Dehsen, *Politics and Policy: The Genesis and Theology of Social Statements in the Lutheran Church in America* (Minneapolis: Fortress, 1989), 179–290.

17. Richard John Neuhaus, *Christian Faith and Public Policy* (Minneapolis: Augsburg, 1977), 190.

18. Klein and von Dehsen, *Politics and Policy,* 173.

19. Robert Benne, *The Paradoxical Vision: A Public Theology for the Twenty-first Century* (Minneapolis: Fortress, 1995), 120.

2. Ethics: Captive to God's Word

1. Paul Althaus, *The Ethics of Martin Luther* (Philadelphia: Fortress, 1972), 43. It is this distinguished German theologian's laudable Luther research but deplorable Nazified politics that have prompted our own source analysis as a proposed model and corrective for a new generation of English-speaking scholars and pastors (cf. chapter 1).

2. American edition of *Luther's Works* (hereafter *LW*), ed. Jaroslav J. Pelikan and Helmut T. Lehmann (Philadelphia: Fortress and St. Louis: Concordia, 1955–86) 26:295 (1535). Translated primary sources (*LW*) cited in this chapter include *A Brief Instruction on What to Look for and Expect in the Gospels* (1521), *Prefaces to the New Testament* (1522), *Preface to the Epistle to the Romans* (1522), *Prefaces to the Old Testament* (1523), *Lectures on Genesis* (1535–45), *On Translating: An Open Letter* (1530), *Preface to the Psalter* (1528), *Defense of the Translation of the Psalms* (1531), and *Preface to the Prophets* (1532). Cf. *D. Martin Luthers Werke,* Kritische Gesamtausgabe (hereafter *WA* or *WATR* for the supplementary *Tischreden*), ed. J. F. K. Knaake, Karl Drescher, and Konrad Burdach (Weimar: Boehlau, 1883).

3. *WATR* 3:598 (1538).

4. *LW* 32:112 (1521).

5. *LW* 1:3 (1535).

6. *LW* 30:3 (1523).

7. Jaroslav J. Pelikan, *Luther the Expositor: Introduction to the Reformer's Exegetical Writings* (St. Louis: Concordia, 1959), 260.

8. Ibid., 48–70 *passim.*

9. *WA* 3:154 (1513); *LW* 1:7 (1535).

10. *LW* 33:146 (1525).

11. *LW* 52:205 (1522).

12. *WA* 10/1,2:48 (1522).

13. *LW* 13:35 (1521).

14. *LW* 30:321 (1527); 3:316 (1538–39); 12:255 (1533).

15. *LW* 14:46 (1530).

16. *LW* 39:217–18 (1521).

17. Pelikan, *Luther the Expositor,* 71–88 *passim.*

18. *LW* 35:396 (1522).

19. Ibid.

20. *LW* 31:75 (1518); 39:164 (1521).

21. *LW* 33:269 (1525).

22. *LW* 34:285 (1539).

23. *LW* 32:112 (1521).

24. *LW* 1:121 (1535).

25. *WA* 39/2:305 (1543); *LW* 41:83 (1539).

26. *LW* 40:55 (1524).

27. Pelikan, *Luther the Expositor,* 89–108 *passim.*

28. *LW* 1:104 (1535–36).

29. *LW* 1:19 (1535–36).

30. *LW* 9:7 (1525); 14:338 (1519).

31. *LW* 3:168 (1538-39); 40:174 (1525); 51:374 (1546); 37:177 (1528); 37:177 (1528).

32. *LW* 1:232 (1535–36).

33. *LW* 34:112 (1535); 10:7 (1513–16).

34. *LW* 25:405 (1516).

35. *LW* 9:25 (1525).

36. *LW* 25:4 (1516).

37. *LW* 3:37 (1538–39).

38. *LW* 1:252 (1535–36).

39. *LW* 4:344 (1539–40).

40. *LW* 1:255 (1535–36).

41. *LW* 4:65 (1539–40).

42. *LW* 2:54–55 (1535–36).

43. *LW* 2:197 (1535–36).

44. *LW* 4:322 (1539–40).

45. *LW* 4:71 (1539–40).

46. *LW* 2:101 (1535–36).

47. *LW* 1:105 (1535–36).

48. *LW* 6:186 (1542–45).

49. *LW* 1:248 (1535–36).

50. *LW* 5:247 (1541–42).

51. *LW* 2:228–29 *passim* (1535–36).

52. *LW* 2:233 (1535–36).

53. *LW* 30:19 (1523); 34:112 (1535).

54. *LW* 35:117–19 *passim* (1521).

55. *LW* 35:118–19 *passim* (1521).

56. *LW* 35:119 (1521).

57. *LW* 35:120 (1521).

58. Ibid.

59. *LW* 35:121 (1521).

60. *LW* 35:122 (1521).

61. *LW* 35:121–23 (1521).

62. *LW* 35:358 (1522).
63. *LW* 35:362 (1522).
64. *LW* 35:365 (1522).
65. *LW* 35:366,372 (1522).
66. *LW* 35:366–67 (1522).
67. *LW* 35:369 (1522).
68. *LW* 35:369–70 (1522).
69. *LW* 35:370–71 (1522).
70. *LW* 35:371 (1522).
71. *LW* 35:371–72 (1522).
72. *LW* 35:380 (1522).
73. *LW* 35:248 (1522).
74. *LW 35*:236 (1523).
75. *LW* 35:236–37 (1523).
76. *LW* 35:239 (1523).
77. *LW* 35:240 (1523).
78. *LW* 35:242 (1523).
79. Ibid.
80. *LW* 35:242–43 (1523).
81. *LW* 35:244 (1523).
82. *LW* 35:246 (1523).
83. *LW* 35:265 (1532).
84. *LW* 35:266 (1532).
85. *LW* 35:246–47 (1523).
86. *LW* 35:275 (1528).
87. *LW* 35:279–80 (1532).
88. *LW* 35:288–89 (1541).
89. *LW* 35:317 (1532).
90. *LW* 35:319 (1532).
91. *LW* 35:320 (1532).
92. *LW* 35:322 (1532).
93. *LW* 35:324 (1532).
94. *LW* 35:326 (1532).
95. *LW* 35:330 (1532).
96. *LW* 54:42 (1532).
97. *LW* 35:188–89 (1530).
98. *LW* 35:195 (1530).
99. *LW* 35:196–97 (1530).
100. *LW* 35:213 (1531).
101. *LW* 35:218–19 (1531).
102. *LW* 35:255–56 (1528).
103. *LW* 35:254 (1528).
104. *LW* 35:132 (1522); *WA* 8:287 (1545).
105. *WA* 35:236 (1523).
106. *WA* 48:31 (1541).

3. Adam and Eve: God's Command of Love

1. The textual dependability of Luther's *Lectures on Genesis* poses a historical problem. The material comes down to us without Luther's accompanying class notes (1535–1545), through students' transcripts that were only later collated and published by editors (for example, Veit Dietrich), who were also demonstrably influenced by Philip Melanchthon and the scholastic structures of the second generation of Lutheran orthodoxy. Nevertheless, as distinctively delivered during the last decade of Luther's life "with the help of St. Ambrose and St. Augustine" (American edition of *Luther's Works* [hereafter *LW*], ed. Jaroslav J. Pelikan and Helmut T. Lehmann [Philadelphia: Fortress and St. Louis: Concordia, 1955–86] 41:19 [1539]), the *Lectures* are critically judged to be "an indispensable source for our knowledge of Luther's thought" and, even as admittedly edited, "fundamentally reliable" (*LW* 1:xi,xiii,4). We shall therefore first sketch the lectures judiciously in order to document the biblical foundations of Luther's mature positions, and then corroborate the textual authenticity of his characteristic theological themes from the Reformer's earlier writings elsewhere, as here, in his groundbreaking *Lectures on Romans* (1515–16).

2. *LW* 12:311 (1538).

3. *LW* 1:3–7 (1535).

4. *LW* 1:9,12 (1535).

5. *LW* 1:10 (1535).

6. *LW* 1:11,15 (1535).

7. *LW* 1:16 (1535).

8. *LW* 1:17 (1535).

9. *LW* 1:47 (1535).

10. *LW* 1:39 (1535).

11. *LW* 1:56 (1535).

12. *LW* 1:57 (1535).

13. Ibid.

14. *LW* 1:60 (1535).

15. *LW* 1:61 (1535).

16. *LW* 1:113 (1535).

17. *LW* 1:61,63,65 (1535).

18. *LW* 1:62–65 (1535).

19. *LW* 1:62–63,113 (1535).

20. Ibid.

21. *LW* 1:65 (1535).

22. *LW* 1:66 (1535).

23. Ibid.

24. *LW* 1:64 (1535).

25. *LW* 1:64–65 (1535).

26. *LW* 1:75–76 (1535).

27. *LW* 1:84–85 (1535).

28. Dietrich Bonhoeffer, *Ethics,* ed. Eberhard Bethge, trans. Neville H. Smith (New York: Macmillan, 1955), 207.

29. *LW* 1:80 (1535).

30. *LW* 1:79,146 (1535).

31. *LW* 1:80–81 (1535).

32. *LW* 1:95 (1535).

33. *LW* 1:103–4 (1535).

34. *LW* 1:105 (1535).

35. *LW* 1:105–6 (1535).

36. *LW* 1:103 (1535).

37. *LW* 1:247 (1535).

38. *LW* 1:67,70,115 (1535).

39. *LW* 1:71 (1535).

40. *LW* 1:115 (1535).

41. *LW* 1:116 (1535).

42. *LW* 1:116–18,135 *passim* (1535).

43. The evangelical breakthrough of the Reformer's sexual and marital ethic was fully developed in my earlier *Luther on the Christian Home* (Philadelphia: Muhlenberg, 1960).

44. *LW* 1:134 (1535).

45. *LW* 82:103 (1535).

46. *LW* 1:104 (1535).

47. Ibid.

48. *LW* 1:105 (1535).

49. *LW* 1:107 (1535).

50. *LW* 1:107–8 (1535).

51. *LW* 1:109 (1535).

52. *LW* 1:109–10 *passim* (1535).

53. *LW* 1:138 (1535).

54. *LW* 25:433 (1516).

55. Ibid.

56. *LW* 25:434–35 (1535).

57. *LW* 25:257,336 (1516).

58. *LW* 25:435–36 (1516).

59. *LW* 25:436 (1516).

60. *LW* 25:437–38,444 (1516).

61. *LW* 25:441 (1516).

62. *LW* 25:442 (1516).

63. *LW* 25:444 (1516).

64. *LW* 25:461–62 (1516).

65. *LW* 25:474 (1516).

66. *LW* 25:475 (1516).

67. *LW* 25:475–76 (1516).

68. *LW* 25:477–78 (1516).

69. *LW* 37:364–65 (1528).

4. Satan: God's Foe, Human Woe

1. Translated primary sources cited in this chapter from the American edition of *Luther's Works* (hereafter *LW*), ed. Jaroslav J. Pelikan and Helmut T. Lehmann

(Philadelphia: Fortress and St. Louis: Concordia, 1955–86), include Luther's *Lectures on Genesis* (1535) and *Lectures on Romans* (1516). .

2. *LW* 3:49 (1538); 4:94 (1539); 33:227 (1525).

3. *LW* 1:141 (1535).

4. *LW* 1:142 (1535).

5. *LW* 1:143 (1535); *D. Martin Luthers Werke,* Kritische Gesamtausgabe, ed. J. F. K. Knaake, Karl Drescher, and Konrad Burdach (Weimar: Boehlau, 1883), 10/3:92 (1522).

6. *LW* 1:144 (1535).

7. *LW* 1:144–45 (1535).

8. *LW* 1:146–47 (1535).

9. *LW* 1:147–50,158,162 *passim* (1535).

10. *LW* 1:110,147,149,154,172 (1535).

11. *LW* 1:165 (1535).

12. *LW* 1:166,168 (1535).

13. *LW* 1:169–72 *passim* (1535).

14. *LW* 1:173–78 *passim* (1535).

15. *LW* 1:178–79 (1535).

16. *LW* 1:186 (1535).

17. *LW* 1:189 (1535).

18. Ibid.

19. *LW* 1:190 (1535).

20. *LW* 1:194,197 (1535).

21. *LW* 1:146 (1535).

22. *LW* 1:198 (1535).

23. *LW* 1:190,196 (1535).

24. *LW* 1:196 (1535).

25. *LW* 1:190 (1535).

26. *LW* 54:111 (1533); 1:197 (1535).

27. *LW* 25:28 (1516).

28. *LW* 25:310–11 (1516).

29. *LW* 25:135 (1516).

30. *LW* 25:152 (1516).

31. *LW* 25:159 (1516).

32. *LW* 25:168 (1516).

33. *LW* 25:19 (1516).

34. *LW* 25:174 (1516).

35. *LW* 25:273 (1516).

36. *LW* 25:274 (1516); 39:189 (1521).

37. *LW* 25:274–75 (1516).

38. *LW* 25:275–76 (1516).

39. *LW* 25:291 (1516).

40. *LW* 25:343 (1516).

41. *LW* 25:296–98 (1516).

42. *LW* 25:261 (1516).

43. *LW* 25:299–300 (1516).

44. *LW* 25:305 (1516).

45. Ibid.

46. *LW* 25:306 (1516).

47. St. Augustine, *City of God,* trans. Henry Bettenson (London: Penguin Classics, 1972), 430, 524, 842.

48. Ibid., 884.

49. Ibid., 429, 573.

50. Ibid., 571, 573, 593.

51. Ibid., 595, 877.

52. Ibid., 878.

53. Ibid., 842.

5. Cain and Abel: Law Judges before God

1. Translated primary sources cited in this chapter from the American edition of *Luther's Works* (hereafter *LW*), ed. Jaroslav J. Pelikan and Helmut T. Lehmann (Philadelphia: Fortress and St. Louis: Concordia, 1955–86), include Luther's *Lectures on Genesis* (1535), *Lectures on Romans* (1516), *Against Latomus* (1521), and *The Bondage of the Will* (1525).

2. *LW* 1:252 (1535).

3. *LW* 1:198 (1535).

4. *LW* 1:200 (1535).

5. *LW* 1:218–19,234 (1535).

6. *LW* 1:247 (1535).

7. *LW* 1:255 (1535).

8. *LW* 1:257 (1535).

9. *LW* 1:265,259 (1535).

10. *LW* 1:277–78 (1535).

11. *LW* 1:291 (1535).

12. *LW* 1:311 (1535).

13. *LW* 1:262 (1535).

14. *LW* 2:3–4 (1536).

15. *LW* 2:26–27 (1536).

16. *LW* 2:51 (1536).

17. *LW* 1:358 (1535).

18. *LW* 33:264 (1525).

19. *LW* 33:274–75 (1525).

20. *LW* 33:277–87 passim (1525).

21. *LW* 33:282 (1525).

22. *LW* 33:153 (1525).

23. *LW* 33:98–99 (1525).

24. *LW* 33:287 (1525); 13:194–95 (1534).

25. *LW* 25:30 (1525).

26. Ibid.

27. Ibid.

28. *LW* 25:235 (1525); 26:272 (1535).

29. *LW* 25:240 (1525).

30. *LW* 25:241 (1525).
31. *LW* 25:242–43 (1525).
32. *LW* 25:247 (1525).
33. *LW* 25:250–51 (1525).
34. *LW* 25:252 (1525).
35. *LW* 25:9 (1525).
36. *LW* 25:161 (1525).
37. *LW* 25:279 (1525).
38. *LW* 25:281 (1525).
39. *LW* 25:48–49 (1525).
40. *LW* 25:307 (1525).
41. *LW* 25:57 (1525).
42. *LW* 25:58 (1525).
43. *LW* 25:59–60 (1525).
44. *LW* 25:60 (1525).
45. *LW* 25:62 (1525).
46. *LW* 25:63–64 (1535).
47. *LW* 25:330 (1525).
48. *LW* 25:63 (1525).
49. *LW* 25:61 (1525).
50. *LW* 25:322 (1525).
51. Ibid.
52. *LW* 25:328–35 *passim* (1525).
53. *LW* 25:336 (1525); 32:213 (1521).
54. *LW* 32:xvi (1521).
55. *LW* 32:151 (1521).
56. *LW* 32:153 (1521).
57. *LW* 32:155–57 *passim* (1521).
58. *LW* 32:154 (1521).
59. *LW* 32:157 (1521).
60. *LW* 32:158 (1521).
61. *LW* 32:159 (1521).
62. Ibid.
63. *LW* 32:172 (1521).
64. Ibid.
65. *LW* 32:177 (1521).
66. Ibid.
67. *LW* 32:177–78 (1521).
68. *LW* 32:178 (1521).
69. *LW* 32:194 (1521).
70. *LW* 32:195–203 *passim* (1521).
71. *LW* 32:203–4 (1521).
72. *LW* 32:209 (1521).
73. *LW* 32:208 (1521).
74. *LW* 32:223–24 (1521).
75. *LW* 32:211–14,229 (1521).

76. *LW* 32:235 (1521).

77. *D. Martin Luthers Werke, Briefwechsel,* Kritische Gesamtausgabe, ed. J. F. K. Knaake, Karl Drescher, and Konrad Burdach (Weimar: Boehlau, 1883), 8:99 (1537).

78. *LW* 33:294 (1525).

79. *LW* 33:35 (1525).

80. *LW* 33:102–3 (1525).

81. *LW* 54:260 (1538).

82. *WA* 33:16 (1525).

83. *LW* 33:29 (1525).

84. *LW* 33:35 (1525).

85. *LW* 33:44 (1525).

86. *LW* 33:42 (1525).

87. *LW* 33:54 (1525).

88. *LW* 33:61 (1525).

89. *LW* 33:62 (1525).

90. Ibid.

91. *LW* 33:65–66 (1525).

92. *LW* 33:70 (1525).

93. *LW* 33:108 (1525).

94. *LW* 33:118–20 *passim* (1525).

95. *LW* 33:120 (1525).

96. *LW* 33:121 (1525).

97. Ibid.

98. *LW* 33:125 (1525).

99. *LW* 33:126 (1525).

100. *LW* 33:127 (1525).

101. *LW* 33:132 (1525).

102. *LW* 33:136–37 (1525).

103. *LW* 33:151 (1525).

104. *LW* 33:216 (1525).

105. *LW* 33:242 (1525).

106. *LW* 33:260,264 (1525).

107. *LW* 33:176 (1525).

6. Noah and Moses: Law Preserves in Society

1. American edition of *Luther's Works* (hereafter *LW*), ed. Jaroslav J. Pelikan and Helmut T. Lehmann (Philadelphia: Fortress and St. Louis: Concordia, 1955–86), 26:308–9 (1531). Translated primary sources (*LW*) cited in this chapter include Luther's *Lectures on Genesis* (1535), *How Christians Should Regard Moses* (1525), *Lectures on Romans* (1516), *Temporal Authority: To What Extent It Should Be Obeyed* (1523), *Sermons on Exodus* (1524–27), *The Bondage of the Will* (1525), and *Sermons on Exodus* (1524–27). Cf. *D. Martin Luthers Werke,* Kritische Gesamtausgabe (hereafter *WA* or *WATR* for the supplementary *Tischreden*), ed. J. F. K. Knaake, Karl Drescher, and Konrad Burdach (Weimar: Boehlau, 1883).

2. *LW* 26:313 (1535); *WA* 40/2:485 (1535).

3. *LW* 2:6 (1536).

4. *LW* 2:9 (1536).

5. *LW* 2:32 (1536).

6. *LW* 2:35–36 *passim* (1536).

7. *LW* 2:76 (1536).

8. *LW* 2:112 (1536).

9. *LW* 2:118 (1536).

10. *LW* 2:123–25 *passim* (1536).

11. *LW* 2:126 (1536).

12. *LW* 2:131 (1536).

13. Ibid.

14. *LW* 2:135 (1536).

15. *LW* 2:137 (1536).

16. *LW* 2:139 (1536).

17. *LW* 2:140 (1536).

18. *LW* 1:104 (1535).

19. *LW* 2:141 (1536).

20. *LW* 2:140 (1536).

21. *LW* 2:141–42 *passim* (1536).

22. *LW* 2:144 (1536).

23. *LW* 2:145 (1536).

24. *LW* 2:158 (1536).

25. *LW* 2:158–59 *passim* (1536).

26. *LW* 25:410 (1516).

27. *LW* 2:161 (1536); 13:161 (1534).

28. *LW* 2:234–36 *passim* (1536).

29. *LW* 25:19–20 (1516).

30. *LW* 25:187,377 (1516).

31. *LW* 25:187 (1516).

32. Ibid.

33. *LW* 25:109 (1516); 54:293 (1538).

34. *LW* 25:109 (1516); *WA* 39/2:81 (1539).

35. *LW* 25:110–11 (1516); 41:155 (1539)..

36. *LW* 25:111,135 (1516).

37. *LW* 25:471 (1516); 26:455 (1535).

38. *LW* 25:472 (1516); 13:195 (1534); 47:226 (1530); *WA* 28:24 (1528). Cf. Robert Kolb and Timothy J. Wengert, eds., *The Book of Concord* (Minneapolis: Fortress, 2000), 299 (1537). Hereafter *BC*.

39. *LW* 25:475 (1516).

40. *LW* 25:180 (1516); *WATR* 6:290 (n.d.); *WA* 17/2:92 (1525).

41. *LW* 25:477 (1516).

42. *LW* 25:477,480 (1516).

43. *LW* 25:344 (1516); 27:354–55 (1519).

44. *LW* 40:83 (1525); 33:155 (1525).

45. *LW* 33:90 (1525).

46. *LW* 33:20 (1525).

47. *LW* 33:21,24 (1525).

48. *LW* 33:28 (1525).

49. *LW* 33:91 (1525).

50. *LW* 33:99 (1525).

51. *LW* 35:162 (1525).

52. *LW* 35:164 (1525).

53. *LW* 35:165 (1525).

54. *LW* 35:167 (1525).

55. *LW* 35:168,173 (1525).

56. *LW* 35:168–69 (1525).

57. *LW* 35:169–74 *passim* (1525).

58. *LW* 35:173 (1525).

59. Adapted from an earlier, longer version of "Righteousness and Social Justice" in my *Luther on the Christian Home* (Philadelphia: Muhlenberg, 1960), 102–31.

60. *LW* 45:88–89 (1523).

61. *LW* 45:87 (1523).

62. *LW* 45:85–86 (1523).

63. *LW* 1:115 (1535).

64. *LW* 45:86–87 (1523).

65. *LW* 45:87 (1523).

66. *LW* 45:88-92 *passim* (1523).

67. *LW* 45:89 (1523).

68. *LW* 45:92 (1523); 21:3 (1532).

69. *LW* 26:376 (1523).

70. *LW* 26:94 (1523).

71. *LW* 45:95 (1523).

72. *LW* 45:96 (1523).

73. *LW* 45:90 (1523).

74. *LW* 45:91 (1523).

75. *WA* 25:410 (1516); 40/2:526 (1532).

76. *LW* 45:92 (1523).

77. *LW* 46:100 (1526).

78. *LW* 26:365 (1535).

79. *WA* 10/3:373 (1522).

80. *WA* 10/3:380 (1522).

81. *WA* 10/1,1:531 (1522).

82. *WA* 16:352 (1524).

83. Ibid.

84. *WA* 16:353 (1524).

85. *LW* 45:91–92 (1523).

86. *WA* 16:354 (1524).

87. *LW* 46:237 (1530).

88. *LW* 46:95 (1526).

89. *LW* 23:514 (1527); 13:197 (1543).

90. Kolb and Wengert, *BC*, 450 (1529).

7. Jesus Christ: Gospel Justifies before God

1. American edition of *Luther's Works* (hereafter *LW*), ed. Jaroslav J. Pelikan and Helmut T. Lehmann (Philadelphia: Fortress and St. Louis: Concordia, 1955–86), 2:245 (1535). Translated primary sources (*LW*) cited in this chapter include Luther's *Lectures on Genesis* (1536), *Lectures on Galatians* (1535), *Large Catechism* (1529), *Small Catechism* (1529), and *Sermons on the First Epistle of St. Peter* (1522).

2. *LW* 2:246–47 passim (1535).

3. *LW* 2:253–55 passim (1535).

4. *LW* 2:261 (1535).

5. *LW* 2:265 (1535).

6. *LW* 2:266–67 passim (1535).

7. *LW* 2:268 (1535).

8. *LW* 2:269–70 (1535).

9. *LW* 2:271–73 passim (1535).

10. *LW* 2:275 (1535).

11. *LW* 2:399 (1535).

12. *LW* 2:277 (1535).

13. *LW* 2:307 (1535).

14. *LW* 3:18–19 (1538).

15. *LW* 3:19 (1538).

16. *LW* 3:20 (1538).

17. *LW* 3:20,21 (1538).

18. *LW* 3:21–22 passim (1538).

19. *LW* 3:23 (1538).

20. *LW* 3:23,193 (1538).

21. *LW* 3:210 (1538).

22. *LW* 3:24–26 passim (1538).

23. *LW* 3:125 (1538).

24. *LW* 3:241–42 (1538). *D. Martin Luthers Werke,* Kritische Gesamtausgabe (hereafter *WA* or *WATR* for the supplementary *Tischreden*), ed. J. F. K. Knaake, Karl Drescher, and Konrad Burdach (Weimar: Boehlau, 1883), 36:9 (1532).

25. *LW* 26:iv (1535).

26. *LW* 26:4 (1535).

27. *LW* 26:5 (1535).

28. *LW* 26:6 (1535).

29. Ibid.

30. *LW* 26:7 (1535).

31. *LW* 26:8–9 (1535).

32. *LW* 26:10–12 passim (1535).

33. *LW* 26:15–16 (1535).

34. *LW* 26:21–22 (1535).

35. *LW* 26:25–28 passim (1535); *WATR* 2:439 (1532).

36. *LW* 26:30,172–79 (1535); 31:351 (1520).

37. *LW* 26:38 (1535); 2:45 (1535).

38. *LW* 26:42 (1535).

39. Ibid.
40. *LW* 26:54 (1535).
41. *LW* 26:72 (1535).
42. *LW* 26:85–89 *passim* (1535).
43. *LW* 26; 91:116 (1535).
44. *LW* 26:115 (1535).
45. *LW* 26:117 (1535).
46. *LW* 26:122–23 *passim* (1535).
47. *LW* 26:126–27 *passim* (1535).
48. *LW* 26:129–30 (1535).
49. *LW* 26:132–33 *passim*; 387–88 (1535); *WATR* 1:226 (1523).
50. *LW* 26:133–34,138 (1535).
51. *LW* 26:137,145 (1535).
52. *LW* 26:154–55 (1535); 34:111 (1535).
53. *LW* 26:267 (1535).
54. *WA* 21:264 (1531).
55. *LW* 26:276 (1535).
56. *LW* 26:277–78 *passim* (1535).
57. *LW* 26:279–80 *passim* (1535).
58. *LW* 26:282 (1535).
59. Ibid.
60. *LW* 26:282–83 *passim* (1535).
61. *LW* 26:284 (1535).
62. Ibid.
63. *LW* 26:284,285 (1535).
64. *LW* 26:287 (1535).
65. *LW* 26:288 (1535).
66. *LW* 26:290 (1535).
67. Robert Kolb and Timothy J. Wengert, eds., *The Book of Concord* (Minneapolis: Fortress, 2000), 440 (1529).
68. Ibid., 432.
69. Ibid., 434.
70. Ibid.
71. Ibid.
72. Ibid., 434–35.
73. Ibid., 355.
74. Ibid., 435.
75. *LW* 30:3 (1522).
76. Ibid.
77. Ibid.
78. *LW* 30:4 (1522).
79. *LW* 30:7 (1522).
80. *LW* 30:6 (1522).
81. *LW* 30:7 (1522).
82. Ibid.

83. *LW* 30:10,12 (1522).

84. *LW* 30:18–19 *passim* (1522).

85. *LW* 30:20 (1522).

86. *LW* 30:21 (1522).

87. *LW* 30:25 (1522).

88. *LW* 30:33–35 *passim* (1522).

89. *LW* 30:34 (1522).

90. *LW* 30:36–37 *passim* (1522).

91. *LW* 30:44 (1522).

92. *LW* 30:46 (1522).

8. Holy Spirit: Gospel Sanctifies in Society

1. Translated primary sources cited in this chapter from the American edition of *Luther's Works* (hereafter *LW*), ed. Jaroslav J. Pelikan and Helmut T. Lehmann (Philadelphia: Fortress and St. Louis: Concordia, 1955–86), include *Treatise on the Sacrament of Penance* (1579), *Treatise on the New Testament* (1520), *The Babylonian Captivity of the Church* (1520), *Open Letter to the Christian Nobility of the German Nation* (1520), *The Freedom of the Christian* (1520), *Treatise on Good Works* (1520), *Commentary on 1 Corinthians 7* (1523), *The Large Catechism* (1529), *The Small Catechism* (1529), *Commentary on the Sermon on the Mount* (1532), *Against the Heavenly Prophets* (1525), *On the Councils and the Church* (1539), and *Lectures on Galatians* (1535).

2. *LW* 26:280–81 (1535).

3. *LW* 26:283–84 *passim* (1535).

4. *LW* 26:287 (1535).

5. *LW* 26:331 (1535).

6. *LW* 26:333 (1535).

7. *LW* 26:334 (1535).

8. *LW* 26:342 (1535).

9. Ibid.

10. *LW* 26:343 (1535).

11. *LW* 26:348 (1535).

12. *LW* 26:349 (1535). *D. Martin Luthers Werke,* Kritische Gesamtausgabe (hereafter *WA* or *WATR* for the supplementary *Tischreden*), ed. J. F. K. Knaake, Karl Drescher, and Konrad Burdach (Weimar: Boehlau, 1883), *WA* 8:67 (1521).

13. *LW* 26:350–51 (1535).

14. *WA* 39/1:252 (1537); *LW* 32:24 (1521).

15. *LW* 26:354 (1535).

16. *LW* 26:357 (1535).

17. *LW* 26:375 (1535).

18. Ibid.

19. *LW* 26:375–76 (1535).

20. *LW* 26:367 (1535).

21. *LW* 26:376 (1535).

22. *LW* 46:29 (1525); 26:376 (1535).

23. *LW* 26:379 (1535).

24. *LW* 26:380 (1535).

25. *LW* 26:387 (1535).
26. *LW* 26:394 (1535).
27. *LW* 27:3–6 *passim* (1535).
28. *LW* 27:10–11 (1535).
29. *LW* 27:17 (1535).
30. *LW* 27:15 (1535).
31. *LW* 27:22 (1535).
32. *LW* 27:21 (1535).
33. *LW* 27:29–30 (1535).
34. *LW* 27:30 (1535).
35. Ibid.
36. *LW* 27:47 (1535); 33:150 (1525).
37. *LW* 27:48 (1535).
38. *LW* 27:30 (1535).
39. *LW* 27:49–50 (1535).
40. *LW* 27:59 (1535).
41. *LW* 27:62–63 (1535).
42. *LW* 27:65 (1535).
43. Ibid.
44. Ibid.
45. *LW* 27:68 (1535).
46. *LW* 27:66 (1535).
47. *LW* 27:73–74 (1535).
48. *LW* 27:81–82 (1535).
49. *LW* 27:82–83 (1535); 26:95 (1535); *WA* 31/1:436 (1532); 17/2:192 (1525).
50. *LW* 27:93 (1535).
51. *LW* 27:96 (1535).
52. *LW* 27:113 (1535).
53. *LW* 27:114 (1535); 2:340 (1535).
54. *LW* 27:119–20 (1535).
55. *LW* 41:114 (1539). Earlier versions of some material in the remainder of this synthetic chapter and the Afterword may be found in my "Priest and Priesthood" in Julius Bodensieck, ed., *The Encyclopedia of the Lutheran Church*, vol. 3 (Philadelphia: Fortress, 1965), 1964–966; "Love and Law in Christian Life" in Carter Lindberg, ed., *Piety, Politics and Ethics: Reformation Studies in Honor of George Wolfgang Forell* (Kirksville, Mo.: Sixteenth-Century Journal Pub., 1984), 103–17; and coauthored with Peri Rasolondraibe, *Lutheran Identity and Mission* (Minneapolis: Fortress, 1994), 43–48, 71–75.
56. *LW* 12:381 (1532). See also Robert Kolb and Timothy J Wengert, eds., *The Book of Concord* (Minneapolis: Fortress, 2000), 469 (1529), hereafter *BC*.
57. *LW* 41:148 (1539).
58. *LW* 41:148–66 *passim* (1539).
59. *LW* 41:165–66 (1539).
60. Kolb and Wengert, *BC*, 435–36 (1529).
61. Ibid., 436 (1529).
62. Ibid.

63. Ibid., 437–38 (1529).
64. Ibid., 438 (1529).
65. Ibid., 439 (1529).
66. Ibid.
67. *LW* 21:235 (1532).
68. *LW* 21:236–37 (1532).
69. *LW* 21:238 (1532).
70. *LW* 31:343 (1520).
71. *LW* 21:238 (1532).
72. Ibid.
73. *LW* 21:239 (1533); 27:60–61 (1535).
74. *LW* 13:154–55 (1534); Kolb and Wengert, *BC,* 299 (1537).
75. *LW* 35:12 (1519).
76. *LW* 35:99–101 *passim* (1520).
77. *LW* 36:113 (1520).
78. *LW* 44:127–30 *passim* (1520).
79. *LW* 31:367 (1520).
80. *LW* 28:35 (1523).
81. *LW* 28:39 (1523).
82. *LW* 28:41 (1523).
83. *LW* 28:42 (1523).
84. *LW* 28:46 (1523).
85. Ibid.
86. *LW* 48:282 (1521); 25:418–19 (1516).
87. *LW* 46:50 (1525).
88. *LW* 28:52 (1523).
89. *LW* 27:51 (1535).
90. *LW* 44:23,33 (1520).
91. Kolb and Wengert, *BC,* 381,386,390,428–29 (1529).
92. Ibid., 351–54 (1529).
93. Ibid., 386,429–30 (1529).
94. *LW* 40:92 (1525).
95. *LW* 40:98 (1525).
96. Ibid.
97. *WA* 39/1:47 (1535).
98. Kolb and Wengert, *BC,* 396–400 (1529).
99. Ibid., 397 (1529).
100. Ibid., 398 (1529).
101. *WA* 10/3:343–44 (1522).
102. *WA* 39/1:454 (1538); *LW* 22:144 (1537).
103. *LW* 41:75,144 (1539); 35:244 (1545); *WA* 39/1:485 (1538).
104. *WA* 17/1:122 (1525).
105. *LW* 27:51–55 *passim* (1535).
106. *LW* 27:58 (1535).

107. *LW* 27:119–20 (1535).

108. *LW* 33:242 (1525).

109. *LW* 8:94–95 (1545); *WA* 10/1,1:100 (1522).

110. *LW* 27:96,140 (1535).

111. *WATR* 6:153 (1536); *WA* 31/1:436–37 (1532).

Afterword

1. American edition of *Luther's Works* (hereafter *LW*), ed. Jaroslav J. Pelikan and Helmut T. Lehmann (Philadelphia: Fortress and St. Louis: Concordia, 1955–86), 34:388 (1545). Translated primary sources (*LW*) cited in this chapter include Luther's *Galatians 1–6* (1519), *Table Talk Recorded by John Schlaginhaufen* (1531–32), *Prefaces to the New Testament* (1546/1522), *Galatians 1–4* (1535), *The Disputation concerning Justification* (1536), *On the Councils and the Church* (1539), *Against the Antinomians* (1539), and *The Licentiate Examination of Heinrich Schmedenstede* (1542). *D. Martin Luthers Werke,* Kritische Gesamtausgabe (hereafter *WA*), ed. J. F. K. Knaake, Karl Drescher, and Konrad Burdach (Weimar: Boehlau, 1883), *WA* 5:163 (1519).

2. *LW* 34:167 (1536).

3. *LW* 27:277 (1519); *WA* 10/1,1:108 (1522).

4. *LW* 34:320 (1542); *WA* 39/1:83 (1536).

5. *LW* 40:50 (1539); 47:104 (1538).

6. *LW* 54:127 (1531).

7. Robert Kolb and Timothy J. Wengert, eds., *The Book of Concord* (Minneapolis: Fortress, 2000), 587 (1577); hereafter *BC*.

8. Ibid., 589.

9. *LW* 35:366 (1532); *WA* 20:244 (1526).

10. *LW* 26:366 (1535).

11. Kolb and Wengert, *BC,* 589–90 *passim* (1577).

12. *LW* 26:312 (1535).

13. Documented in Werner Elert, *Law and Gospel* (Philadelphia: Fortress, 1967) regarding *WA* 39/1:485 (1538).

14. *LW* 26:318–14 (1535); *WA* 39/1:485 (1538).

15. *LW* 26:342 (1535).

16. Kolb and Wengert, *BC,* 311–12 (1537).

17. *WA* 17/1:134 (2525).

Index of Names and Subjects

Index of Biblical References